P9-BZY-260

# The World the Cold War Made

# The World the Cold War Made

## ORDER, CHAOS, AND THE RETURN OF HISTORY

JAMES E. CRONIN

ROUTLEDGE
New York & London

Published in 1996 by
Routledge
29 West 35th Street
New York, NY 10001

Published in Great Britain by
Routledge
11 New Fetter Lane
London EC4P 4EE

Copyright © 1996 by Routledge

Printed in the United States of America on acid-free paper.

All rights reserved. No part of this book may be reprinted or reproduced or utilized in any form or by any electronic, mechanical or other means, now known or hereafter invented, including photocopying and recording, or in any information storage or retrieval system, without permission in writing from the publisher.

Library of Congress Cataloging-in-Publication Data

Cronin, James E.
    The world the Cold War made: order, chaos and the return of history / by James E. Cronin.
        p.     cm.
    Includes bibliographical references and index.
    ISBN 0-415-90820-5. — ISBN 0-415-90821-3 (pbk.)
    1. Cold War.  2. World politics—1945 –  I. Title.
D843.C688     1996
909.82—dc20                                                    96-1042
                                                                CIP

*To Mary*

# Contents

# Preface

The Cold War is over. What shall we make of it? The question must be posed with particular urgency at present, for it is essential to have at least a provisional understanding of the world that has recently ended if we are to make any sense at all of the more confusing and possibly more treacherous world bequeathed to us by the passing of the Cold War. Not only is it necessary to begin to summarize and interpret the era of the Cold War; it is now also possible to do so in a new way. So long as the Cold War lasted and engaged our passions and political identities, scholarship suffered. The problem was not a matter of bias so much as the way in which the ongoing character of the phenomenon prevented scholars from stepping back and viewing it broadly. So long as the arms race persisted and the United States and the USSR confronted one another in strategic locations around the world, it was inevitable that the Cold War would be understood primarily in terms of foreign policy, defense, and war-making, rather than as a world order composed of states whose internal structures were linked to their place in the geopolitical rivalry of the superpowers and in which were embedded rival social systems guided and described by contrasting ideologies. The ending of the Cold War, then, offers historians the possibility of studying the phenomenon anew, of constructing a narrative with a beginning and an end and many exciting moments in the middle, and, in the process, the opportunity to grasp its dynamics and consequences.

This book took shape gradually and indirectly. It began with a course that I taught during the late 1980s at Boston College with my colleague Peter Weiler. The course was called "A Historian's Guide to World Chaos," the title lifted from G. D. H. Cole's *A Guide Through World Chaos*, written during the Depression as a tract for the times. Initially, the focus was on various crises and zones of conflict: the arms race and the "Second Cold War," conflicts in the Middle East, South Africa, and Latin America. But as the Cold War world began to disintegrate in 1989, the focus of our course inevitably broadened to include the Cold War itself as the structure upon which postwar history had been founded and whose rise and fall now called out for renewed attention and analysis. That expanded task led to the present book. Ideally, it would have been researched and written jointly by Peter Weiler and me, and I am sure the outcome would have been more comprehensive and judicious and marred by fewer mistakes. But different timetables and prior commitments prevented that potential collaboration. The result is a book whose virtues, such as they are, are a shared responsibility but whose flaws are all mine.

No book stands entirely on its own, but few books are as dependent on others as this. Its scope required a wide reading in the secondary literature, supplemented in key places by further digging, and its interpretive framework came from an implicit dialogue with other scholars seeking in their own ways to understand the evolution of the postwar world. I began this book thinking that relatively little work of value had been done on contemporary history. I end it with great respect for what is in fact a growing body of highly sophisticated work on recent history and for its authors. This changed perspective stems in part from greater familiarity with the accumulated scholarship in diverse fields that had previously escaped my attention, but a good part comes from the tremendous outpouring of scholarship that seems to have been stimulated by the dramatic transformations of recent years. I cannot hope in this book to match the breadth displayed by Eric Hobsbawm in his *Age of Extremes* (1994), the reach of Paul Kennedy's *Preparing for the Twenty-First Century* (1993), or the narrative power of Martin Walker's *The Cold War* (1994), but the publication of these and numerous other titles has provided models to emulate, arguments with which to agree or disagree, and the inspiration to move ahead. This book has different purposes and makes a rather different argument than any of these others, but it could not have been written without them and would have looked very different if it had preceded, rather than followed, their impressive achievements.

It is impossible to distinguish clearly between the intellectual debts acknowledged formally in notes and the practical debts accumulated in writing a book of this sort. Part of the reason is that quite a few books and articles utilized here came to my attention in draft form, courtesy of authors willing to share their emerging thoughts and analyses. I am grateful in particular to Harold Perkin, Daniel Chirot, Moshe Lewin, John Stephens, and Robert Brenner for offering me early or easier access to work in progress, to Peter Bush for providing me with an advance copy of his translation of Juan Goytisolo's important article, and more generally to Peter Hall and George Ross, whose seminar at the Center for European Studies at Harvard has served for many years as a sounding board for much of the best work in political economy. I profited as well from discussions of the project with Eric Hobsbawm, Jürgen Kocka, Richard Price, Lou Ferleger, Jim Shoch, and Gary Cross, who arranged for me to present a summary of my ideas to a colloquium at Pennsylvania State University. I was fortunate also to be invited by the International Institute of Social History to lead a seminar in Moscow during the summer of 1995 and thus given the opportunity to view up close the debris left behind by the collapse of Soviet socialism. Particular thanks for this are due to Marcel van der Linden and to Irina Novicenko, head of the Moscow program.

Closer to home I greatly appreciate the supportive environment created by friends and colleagues, mainly but not solely at Boston College. Paul Breines was full of ideas and suggestions; Ali Banuazizi provided important references on Islam and the Middle East; Ray McNally offered suggestions on Russian and Soviet history; Carol Petillo, John Rosser, and Paul Spagnoli shared administrative burdens that, unshared, would have delayed this book several years, and Lois Bilsky kept everything in order during repeated distractions; Kevin O'Neill and Alan Rogers shared burdens and were great companions as well. Robin Fleming and Larry Wolff have inspired by example and have helped me to understand that research projects are not complete, and arguments never fully worked out, until they come together on the printed page. Four valued critics—Lou Ferleger, Bob Moeller, Peter Weiler, and Larry Wolff—read and commented on the entire manuscript. Their suggestions were immensely valuable and helped me to clarify and improve the text at many points.

The other examples that have guided me in this project have been offered by my family. Rebecca and Johanna have made it clear to me what is truly important and what is not, while reminding me of the need to bring one's knowledge up-to-date if one aspires to even a modest audience. Mary Cronin provided critical encouragement, urging me to write a broad book about the recent transformations through which we have all lived and showing by her example that it was possible to venture into new territory and make a success of it. This book is dedicated to her, with love and admiration.

# Introduction

## THE COLD WAR AS
## STRUCTURE AND HISTORY

Virtually no one dared to predict the end of the Cold War before it actually happened; and when the Cold War did end, quite a few refused to believe it. Until the Cold War was no longer there, nobody who knew or studied Eastern Europe or the Soviet Union dared to imagine that "actually existing socialism" would effectively evaporate in that enormous region before the end of the twentieth century.[1] The Cold War appeared to be a permanent fixture of the world in which most of us came to intellectual maturity, and it was the central feature dominating the intellectual maps we constructed in order to orient ourselves to that world. The Cold War—and the ideological and geopolitical rivalry that were at its center—was the primary legacy bequeathed by the generation that fought and defeated fascism, and if we are to make sense of the disorder left behind by the Cold War's abrupt ending, we must come to a fuller understanding of the world order the Cold War created.[2]

2

The starting point of this book is the assumption that the Cold War world order was extraordinary and is still very much in need of study and analysis. It was first and foremost a postwar settlement, not unlike the settlements that attended the endings of the Napoleonic Wars and the First World War, but more far-reaching and effective.[3] It was more global than earlier settlements, for the alliances to which it gave rise came ultimately to embrace most of the world and to enlist most nations, old and new alike, on one side or the other of the great struggle between the forces of capitalism and those arrayed against it.[4] It was an economic as well as a political and military order. The leaders who crafted the postwar world could not and did not distinguish between politics and economics, and their competing visions were composed of models that integrated political and economic regimes.

The Cold War world order was even more unusual in the congruence it achieved between internal and external settlements. The socialist bloc purported to be an alliance of similar social systems, and its constituents shared a great deal, particularly in the way political power was distributed and exercised. Within the alliance of developed capitalist states, political power and social relations also came increasingly to converge around a norm not terribly far removed from that displayed by the United States. It was on the periphery of the two systems that internal and external settlements were more likely to diverge. Thus, the Western nations and Japan enrolled in the anticommunist alliance states that maintained almost feudal social structures and made no pretense of political democracy, and the socialist states welcomed to their camp regimes and rulers of societies that in critical respects failed to conform to the Soviet or any other model of socialism. Nevertheless, the Cold War world order was marked to a much greater extent than previous international systems by a symmetry between internal and external developments.

These traits imparted to the Cold War world order an unusual strength and resilience. Precisely because internal and external relations reinforced each other, both sets of arrangements remained firmly anchored. Choices within the two blocs were severely limited in foreign policy and domestic affairs, and were only slightly less restricted on the margins of the superpowers' spheres of influence. The peoples of Eastern Europe felt the force of such constraints most brutally, but constraints operated powerfully throughout the two blocs. The rules governing the world economy were especially hard to contravene, for they were embedded in a set of institutional arrangements and strengthened by the increasingly free flow of trade and capital; they tended to enforce norms and models that sharply circumscribed the authority and limited the discretion previously accorded sovereign states.

The fault lines of the Cold War accordingly determined not only the foreign policies and strategic alliances of states, but also their economic systems, political institutions and cultures, and patterns of social life. The world order to which the Cold War gave rise was thus unusually coherent and comprehensive. As a postwar settlement, it was a remarkable construction, even if those who oversaw its creation were disappointed by the compromises it entailed and by the Cold War's birthmarks of hostility, confrontation, the competitive development of nuclear weapons, and outright war in Korea. The settlement required a vast mobilization of resources and sustained political will. The post–Cold War unwillingness of Western nations—their citizens, politicians, and economic elites—to put themselves out for a new Marshall Plan for Eastern Europe and the states of the former Soviet Union, or to accept responsibility for maintaining civility and political stability in regions where these are threatened, such as Rwanda, Somalia, and Bosnia, make the achievements of the early Cold War clearer and more impressive. What compelled leaders on both sides to bear the costs of constructing and then maintaining the Cold War world order?

The costs of the endeavor were both economic and political. For the United States, the economic costs alone were enormous. There was, first of all, the price of relief and occupation in the defeated nations and the resulting strong temptation to skimp on these tasks and, by implication, to work toward a rapid normalization of political and economic life among the former enemies. But the war had been fought and prosecuted as a political and ideological crusade against fascism as a social order, a crusade that precluded the simple restoration of old institutions, purged only at the top, in either Germany or Japan. Occupation thus led to a much more serious and protracted effort to democratize the institutions, cultures, and key personnel of the formerly authoritarian foes. Of course, the onset of what might be called the "high Cold War" foreshortened the endeavor and made it less thorough than originally envisioned. Still, it was an unusually intrusive reshaping of the domestic political and social arrangements of two major powers, and it succeeded in implanting political institutions that, however imperfect, would evolve over time into stable and relatively responsive democratic polities.

The United States also oversaw the economic revival and political rebirth of Western Europe more generally. The cost, first in relief and temporary loans, then in the more substantial Marshall Plan, and later in continued military aid, was again considerable. Among U.S. allies, only Great

Britain paid a reasonable share of this burden. It can certainly be argued that the U.S. got much in return for its investment. Its hegemonic position in the world economy and in the balance of world power undoubtedly brought rewards for its domestic industries. So, too, did the long economic boom set off by the creation of a new world economic order and the funding of this order by U.S. dollars. But making the initial investment entailed considerable political difficulties as well: it meant keeping taxes high and diverting expenditure away from social programs; it meant continuing to recruit and train armed forces at a level unprecedented in peacetime; and it meant organizing political support for an effort that approximated mobilization for war but that promised to drag on indefinitely.

If the Cold War's most visible economic burdens fell upon the U.S., the costs were more indirect and more political for its erstwhile allies. The countries of Western Europe, for example, were told in effect that the price of aid was a partial ceding of political and/or military authority to international institutions dominated by the U.S. This in itself was a genuine threat to political stability, for it challenged the sense of national identity so central to the political cultures of the European states. In practical terms, it provoked the breakup of the center-left coalitions that, emerging from the war and the resistance with considerable popular appeal, had assumed power in 1945 and had given communist parties a prized share of government in France and Italy. The price seems to have been acceptable, and it might well have been the only way the European states could retain or recover control of matters of local concern.[5] Nevertheless, it was by no means trivial.

The cost of adapting to the realities of the Cold War was at least as great, if not greater, for the Soviet Union. There can be no doubt that Soviet leaders wanted to prolong the wartime alliance. They hoped in particular to secure Western aid for rebuilding their nation's economy; they hoped also to channel their own resources toward reconstruction and for that reason undertook a rapid and extensive demobilization in 1945–1946. The Soviet Union also had a definition of its own security that involved the creation of friendly, if not totally dependent, regimes along its western border, and it sought more influence in places like Turkey, Greece, and Iran. It seems that Soviet leaders did not fully comprehend how thoroughly these goals violated the U.S. vision of the postwar world, for they were genuinely shocked at the reactions of the United States to their moves in Eastern Europe, the eastern Mediterranean, and the Middle East. Not unreasonably, they concluded that U.S. principles had been firmed up by sole possession of the atomic bomb and, again not unreasonably, the

Soviets redoubled their efforts to acquire their own nuclear capability and at the same time halted, or at least slowed, demobilization. In those early years of the Cold War the strange and asymmetrical balance of military power—the U.S. the only atomic power; the Red Army vastly bigger, battle-tested, and highly mobile—was peculiarly destabilizing because each side was emboldened by its unique capabilities but terrified as well by the other's, and hence determined to match them.

For the Soviet Union, the costs of meeting the U.S. threat on its own were extremely high. Resources had to be stolen from the domestic economy and poured into the military. Equally important, the opportunity for liberalizing the regime was lost; Stalin and his allies reverted to rule by terror, military-style economic mobilization, and the imposition of a rigid ideological conformity. A wave of purges ensued and a new Five-Year Plan, with all the familiar misplaced priorities and unrealistic expectations fully in place, was proclaimed. In a clear signal that a new orthodoxy would be imposed, Stalin's protégé Andrei Zhdanov took charge of cultural policy and launched an immediate criticism of the intellectuals. A simultaneous purge of "national deviationists" was carried out in Eastern Europe and the new regimes were forced to adopt the Soviet model and path of economic development. This renewed Stalinism, at home and abroad, lasted until the death of Stalin in 1953.

The economic, political, and human costs of waging the Cold War were extraordinary for both sides, but each was willing to undertake the task. Four considerations were critical. First, the costs were great but not so great as to be unimaginable or unbearable. The U.S. and the USSR had, after all, just concluded immense military, organizational, and production feats in the war, and their leaders knew how to mobilize populations who had recently demonstrated remarkable tenacity and fortitude. Second, the recent horrors had convinced both sides that preparation for war was worth the price. Third, leaders of the capitalist nations were to a man committed to rebuilding the world economic order as well as to creating a stable political environment; from this grew their willingness to erect a framework for economic development that supported and was in turn reinforced by the emerging framework for defense and security.

What turned these considerations into the commitment actually to wage the Cold War was the belief that the conflict was ultimately a battle between rival and incompatible social systems. This belief was partly ideological, a way of thinking about capitalism and communism, but it was also based on the recognition that the United States and the Soviet Union were in fact at odds. Their antagonisms were rooted in contrasting economic orders and political regimes that aspired to universal applicability, and each state possessed the military means to project its competing vision far beyond its borders. The systemic and ideological dimensions of the Cold War have not always been central to those who have written about the era, and historical arguments about its meaning have seldom portrayed it as the systemic contest between capitalism and communism that it was. It is almost as if the professed aims and objectives of those who fought the Cold War cannot be credited as having serious significance; that they must mask more substantial economic interests or reasons of state; and that they should be regarded as rhetoric, propaganda, and mere ideology. This seems to be mistaken both as method and as a matter of fact. It is surely reasonable to try to penetrate rhetoric, to probe and interrogate discourse, but it is wrong to ignore it. It is peculiarly myopic to discount the conflict of systems, values, and worldviews in arriving at an understanding of the Cold War, for it was a time when geopolitical alignments entailed a clear choice between social systems and ideologies. The Cold War was a uniquely ideological phenomenon, and although it can be argued that all societies and political arrangments can and will be defended by reference to the values and virtues they embody, never before was ideology so transparently important, so essential to the structure of the international system.

Despite its contemporary salience and visibility, however, there has been a reluctance to credit fully the significance of the systemic confrontation between capitalism and communism and its accompanying ideological polarization in the postwar settlement and in the subsequent functioning and evolution of the Cold War world order. Instead, scholars have chosen to portray the confrontation of the U.S. and the USSR as an instance of great-power rivalry, admittedly played out in a highly unusual context characterized by a grotesque disparity between the power of the two predominant nations and that of all other contenders and by an enormous political and social vacuum left by the defeated Germans and Japanese. This perspective is by no means without purchase in telling the story of the geopolitics of the 1940s and early 1950s. It seems rather inadequate, however, as a way of explaining the intensity of the rivalry between the United States and the Soviet Union at the onset of the Cold War and its persistence in the decades that followed.

To emphasize the systemic and ideological dimensions of the Cold War does not mean accepting the terms within which the architects and tribunes of the confrontation defined the competing social systems and values or deploying without demur the discourse through which they denounced the behavior and aims of their opponents. The demonizing rhetoric of the early Cold War obscured far more than it illuminated and is seriously misleading as historical description. It ascribed base motives to people acting out of honest belief, turned disagreement into disloyalty, and demanded a conformity that was intellectually debilitating and politically stifling. But just because ideology distorted reality and politicians utilized ideology cynically and because the mass media reacted hysterically in the West, especially in the United States, and slavishly in the East, does not mean that ideological commitment was ignoble or irrational, or that beneath the rhetorical excesses there were not fundamental choices and conflicts at issue.

Taking ideology and the contest of social systems seriously therefore means recognizing difference and choice without acceding to the definitions proffered by partisans. It means granting, at least provisionally, that partisans did indeed have a point and that neither anticommunism in the West nor the extreme fear of capitalist hostility expressed in the East was without some minimal basis in fact and in the behavior of the antagonists. And it implies that there was at least a limit to the ability of the rivals to come to terms and live in "peaceful coexistence." Discussions of the Cold War often seem to proceed on the assumption that, however understandable its origins and however distasteful the outcome of the postwar division of the world, the antipathies aroused at the time ought to have faded sooner than they did. The logic of the position is that because both sides appeared by the early 1950s to have accepted the broad outlines of the postwar settlement, it should have been possible to engineer a "thaw" in superpower relations and to replace confrontation and "brinkmanship" with détente. That this did not happen, or that it took so long to happen, is taken as evidence of the irrationality of the rivalry and as evidence that leaders were blinded by ideology, too set in their rhetorical posturing to abandon it, too cynical to give up a useful tool for the manipulation of domestic opinion, or compromised by their commitment to the arms race and those who profited from it.

It seems to make at least as much sense to suggest that what doomed successive détentes to failure was that the two systems and their ideological orientations were genuinely in opposition. It is necessary only to list the crises of the era, from the Berlin crisis of 1948 to the outbreak of détente in the early 1970s, to demonstrate that what kept superpower tensions high was not mere ill will or misunderstanding but real antagonisms: the Chinese Revolution; the competitive creation of NATO and the Warsaw Pact; the explosion of the Soviet atomic bomb and the U.S. decision to build the "super" or hydrogen bomb; war in Korea; Dien Bien Phu; the suppression of the Hungarian uprising; Sputnik and the U.S. determination to match, if not surpass, Soviet efforts in space; the U-2 incident; the Cuban Revolution; the building of the Berlin Wall; the Cuban missile crisis; and, of course, the revival of conflict in Indochina. None of these issues sufficed to provoke all-out war or a nuclear exchange, but they were neither trivial nor imaginary. Together, they point irrefutably to the conclusion that the two blocs were in deadly serious competition for influence across the globe.

Giving proper attention to the incompatibility of social orders and the conflict of ideology thus helps to account for the persistence of the Cold War long after the initial occasions for superpower confrontation had been settled and long after it had become clear that neither side seriously entertained the possibility of a direct attack upon the other. It also makes more understandable the coming of the "Second Cold War" in the late 1970s. The waning of hostilities in the early 1970s may be regarded as triumph of common sense over ideology, a recognition that nuclear war would destroy both sides, and a new realism about the likelihood of altering the established framework of states, alliances, and domestic political accords. Still, it was not unrealistic for Soviet leaders to see the new realism of the United States as weakness, and Leonid Brezhnev did claim détente as victory. Nor was it entirely wrong for U.S. leaders to see that recent Soviet successes in foreign policy and defense, the victory in Indochina, and a rough nuclear parity with the United States had changed the overall balance. The heritage of Cold War thinking almost guaranteed that these geopolitical shifts would be interpreted ideologically as the advance or retreat of those social systems whose competition virtually defined the Cold War. What was played out in the 1940s and 1950s as tragedy would be reenacted in the 1980s as farce, with a retired actor appropriately appearing in the lead role. By the 1980s, there were few true believers on either side: few in the United states who truly feared the advance of communism or believed the Soviet Union would risk nuclear war to further its global position; and not many in the Soviet Union who kept faith with the regime's rhetoric. But even as ideology lost its meaning, it continued to signify real differences in social systems, it still set the boundaries of political discourse, and, in framing debate, it defined the range of possibilities for policy.

Ideology thus mattered profoundly throughout the Cold War. It took shape as description and defense of competing social and economic systems; offered ideal versions of their respective strengths, weaknesses, and likely trajectories; and by elaborating visions of the past, present, and future of both capitalism and communism, it contributed to their actual development. The ideologies with which the Cold War was fought were, moreover, far more nuanced and complex than is often recognized. The United States, for example, did not undertake its global mission armed with a crude defense of laissez-faire or with a Manichean anticommunism of the sort associated with demogogues like Senator Joe McCarthy. Rather, the U.S. took to promoting the American way of life with a much more attractive patchwork of ideas that might best be labeled anticommunist liberalism. The anticommunist thrust was central, but it was an anticommunism whose critique of the Soviet Union and regimes of the Soviet type took its main themes from the effective wartime denunciation of fascism: it centered more upon communism's threat to civil liberties than to property rights, and emphasized communism's disdain for democratic rights and procedures, its intolerance of dissent, and its suppression of the institutions of civil society—the press, churches, trade unions, and opposition parties and movements. Anticommunist liberalism was a critique, in short, of totalitarianism.[6] By implication, the United States was distinguished by its commitment not merely to free markets but to an open society, and, drawing heavily upon the New Deal inheritance, to controlling capitalism in order to secure citizens' social and economic rights. The legacy of New Deal reform and wartime planning, and its success in generating good jobs and decent wages, meant also that anticommunist liberalism could present itself as a politics of growth, as the political philsophy justifying and underpinning Keynesian policymaking, the mixed economy, and the welfare state. By the late 1940s, moreover, the liberal consensus that prevailed among Democrats, and whose broad outlines would come to be incorporated in Republican views as well, included opposition to racism and colonialism. The sincerity of these positions would be sorely tested over the next two decades, and to a great extent found to be wanting, but the commitment was there in theory at least at the beginning of Cold War ideological mobilization.

It took longer for the Soviet Union to develop an ideology with which to compete with modern capitalism. The reason is obvious: Stalin's personal authority denied the Soviets the flexibility to develop a credible response to the challenge. The task fell to Nikita Khrushchev, who managed over his relatively brief and troubled tenure atop the political order to redefine it, give it a new set of operating principles, and provide its citizens and its rulers with a model of a more civilized and prosperous society. His innovations inspired three generations of socialist reformers in the Soviet Union and Eastern Europe: his own generation, whose prime concern was de-Stalinization and "normalcy"; a generation of Eastern

European socialists who emerged in the early 1960s eager to implement Khrushchev's reforms in what was mistakenly thought to be the more hospitable context prevailing in that more culturally and industrially developed region; and the generation of Mikhail Gorbachev. Khrushchev articulated in his inarticulate manner a vision of socialism that would in the first instance be free of terror, of intimidation, of the crudest forms of repression. Khrushchev also envisioned a more productive socialism. He echoed the longtime critics of Stalinist planning in acknowledging the overemphasis on heavy industry, the failures of collectivized agriculture and the inefficiencies of central planning. He offered instead a model of balanced growth that would allow the Soviet Union ultimately to overtake the capitalist world in the creation of material wealth. Ironically, Soviet leaders chose to espouse a politics of growth at precisely the same moment as did the champions of democratic capitalism in the West.

Khrushchev's project of reformed communism was, of course, even more distant from reality than the liberal vision of reformed capitalism. More important, it was destined not to produce its intended results, for the relaxation of Stalinist terror neither unleashed pent-up energies within the economy nor liberated Soviet society; rather, it removed the final barrier to the consolidation of the power of the party and of the state bureaucracy. As the authority of party elites and state officials became more secure, the possibility of reforming the system became more remote. Reform would jeopardize the perquisites and privileges of the entire class of *nomenklatura* and so could not be tolerated. Khrushchev would have to go. But the unintended consequences of his departure—the paradoxical way in which it further entrenched interests that would resist change— were by no means obvious during his tenure as general secretary, and more than a few Western leaders worried that the Soviet leader's boasts about the superiority of the socialist model of development might well be prophetic. Hence the model of reformed socialism, once announced, exercised considerable attraction within and outside the socialist bloc.

Neither of these rival ideological formulations could have been conceived without the confrontation of social systems of the Cold War. The image of reformed capitalism was crafted in part to adapt to the socialist critique of capitalism's prior failures. The imagined path to a reformed communism, adumbrated in Khrushchev's thinking and intitiatives, was likewise offered to overcome historic defects in existing socialism that were made more obvious and became more of a liability in the contest with the U.S. and its allies. There were, of course, domestic sources and stimuli behind these emerging perspectives. Absent the external challenge, however, it is doubtful whether the internal evolution of Soviet or U.S. society or the debates through which internal development proceeded in the two nations would have produced ideologies that were so symmetrical and so transparently competitive. For that, the Cold War rivalry was essential.

Both anticommunist liberalism and Khrushchev's amalgam of "ghoulash" communism and "soft authoritarianism" were effective not only in justifying the realities to which they referred but also in creating discourses within which to plan the development of the two societies. Indeed, it might be argued that subsequent political life in both was in essential respects dominated by the sustained efforts, at times by leaders but more often by reformers, to make the societies conform more closely to the models conjured up by the languages of the Cold War. The United States was far less open and pluralistic in the 1940s and 1950s than Cold War rhetoric implied, but much of the politics of the 1960s and 1970s had to do with an attempt to make it so. Likewise, reform communism was more aspiration than coherent program, but belief in the possibility of reform came to occupy an increasingly prominent place in the ideological orientation of the Soviet Union and its defenders. The gradual relaxation of repression, dissident Andrei Amalrik argued in 1969, had "given rise to yet another ideology in our society, possibly the most widespread one; it can be called the 'ideology of reformism.' It is based on the view that a certain 'humanization of socialism' will take place and that the inert and oppressive system will be replaced by a dynamic and liberal one."[7] This vision filled a desperate need for hope and inspired efforts to restructure the system until its dissolution. Perhaps of equal importance was that the writ of these rival ideological discourses to a considerable extent provided the models for social and political development within the two blocs. They did not uniformly prevail, of course. Capitalism took shape with a quite different mix of institutions and with distinct cultural legacies and practices in Germany and Japan, and with ever-greater divergence in the newly industrialized countries in East Asia. Similarly, within the socialist camp there were sharp divergences from the Soviet approach to development. The Chinese were for a time the most vocal and effective, but however bright the luster of Mao Zedong Thought, the Soviet Union continued to provide the paradigm for socialist development worldwide.

So long as the Cold War lasted, then, it had profound effects upon the politics and economies of the states at the center of the conflict and their allies, satellites, and sometime rivals. Its effects were felt, too, in the less developed regions and even in states that proclaimed themselves "nonaligned," as the globalization of the Cold War in the early 1950s saw its protagonists projecting themselves into the affairs of far-flung states. The effects were frequently contradictory and unintended, but never unimportant. The United States and the Soviet Union had been deeply involved in international affairs prior to the Second World War, as had Great Britain and France, two of the most important U.S. allies in Europe and major colonial powers before and after the war. But the spectacular increase in world trade since the war and the multiplying linkages between the developed and the less developed regions meant that how the superpowers conducted their relations with the rest of the world now became much more significant. In this context, it mattered tremendously that the framework governing relations with the "global South" was erected on Cold War foundations. The Cold War shaped and bridged the period between the period of European domination and the more globalized present. It served as prologue to an entirely new era.

The Cold War simultaneously prolonged Western (or northern) domination and allowed non-Western states to begin to assert their autonomy. The clearest cases of Western domination, or "neocolonialism," occurred where movements of national liberation or social reform were deemed threatening to the global balance, and the Western powers, the U.S. primarily, propped up preferred local establishments. Elsewhere, the constraints were powerful but less overt; states were locked into alliances or relations of economic dependency that severely circumscribed local choice. Perhaps less obvious was the way the Cold War affected the politics of less developed nations even when the proximate impact was to empower local elites or states. In many cases, political leaders were able to rely on aid from one or the other superpower in building up the military or police forces that were often used against a state's own people. In this way local strongmen used external support to obviate the need to come to terms with their own citizens. The effect was to hinder the processes of political mobilization and bargaining through which democratic polities might have come into being. In other cases, there was little or no incentive for states or political movements to negotiate settlements with neighbors or rivals because they could count on outside support. It seems, for example, that the prospect of peace and compromise between Israel and the Palestinians was for a long time diminished by the ability of the antagonists to invoke the support of the U.S. or the USSR. Just how to assess the impact of the Cold War outside the blocs is not yet completely clear, but what is obvious is that the presence of the superpowers could not be ignored.

Eventually, the Cold War world order came to an end. The U.S. lost its position as capitalist hegemon; the USSR was overcome by its economic problems; and the U.S. and Soviet models, reformed or unreformed, ceased to inspire respect, fear, or emulation. The Cold War system of states and military alliances became increasingly irrelevant and lost its capacity to order international relations. When that happened, the framework within which relations between East and West, and North and South, were managed collapsed, opening up a great range of possibilities. Among the possibilities were disturbing scenarios in which the absence of international coordination would unleash local hatreds and free up irresponsible powers and "rogue states" to make trouble within regions too far removed or too lacking in strategic importance to force the great powers or the international community to get involved.[8] On balance, however, the new geopolitical freedom seemed more likely to provide greater opportunity for peoples to control their own destinies and a strong incentive to create stable and responsible political systems.

The end of the Cold War not only marked the passing of a particularly effective geopolitical settlement but also definitively concluded the competition between the liberal and socialist models of the good society. To this extent, the argument about "the end of history" makes sense.[9] All history has not ended, but the central historical drama of the past half-century has drawn to a close and there is no mistaking the outcome. Because the Cold War was much more than a new version of great-power rivalry, because it was a conflict between social systems and ideologies, its resolution has significance far beyond its impact on the foreign relations of its leading actors. The Cold War defined a unique era of world history during which the direction of social and economic development was the subject of a great debate, and in which bold, if often misguided and mismanaged, experiments were undertaken. The debate was decided in favor of capitalism. The outcome has liberated millions in Eastern Europe and the former Soviet Union from "tyrannies of certitude" and distinctly unhappy economic fates, but it has also narrowed the range of types of societies, economies, and political systems possible in the years to come.[10]

Future states and economies will be built under conditions that are becoming more and more difficult. A defining characteristic of the Cold War world order was its integration of politics and economics. Among capitalist states, international economic institutions provided a framework for economic development and gave to the major states, especially the United States, a considerable measure of control over economic life. Control was even more effective in the socialist states, even if its effects were ultimately counterproductive. But the world economy has long since outgrown the institutions that once nurtured and shaped it, and thereby escaped their control. By the late 1980s and 1990s, production and distribution were globalized as never before, competition was more intense than at any time in the past, and the mechanisms of macroeconomic regulation were increasingly ineffective. The collapse of socialism thus occured at a particularly unfavorable conjuncture, which has compelled the formerly socialist countries to seek entry into the world market and to begin the transition to capitalism with little aid, with little or no practical experience, and with few resources. It is, of course, the same hostile climate faced by the less developed nations, but that only makes the struggle for growth harder. And without economic growth, the creation of stable political systems is nearly impossible.

The task of this book is not to assess the prospects for economic growth or political stability but to recount and reassess the origins, development, and demise of the Cold War order. Doing so requires questioning the sense of closure and historical inevitability that pervades the emerging conventional wisdom on the Cold War and the history of socialism. It is essential, in other words, to recall the obvious fact that the Cold War was carried out by people who cared deeply and who really did disagree, who had no way of predicting the eventual triumph of liberal capitalism, and who had to make choices in a context of highly imperfect knowledge. The implication of this interpretive strategy is not that the choices were wrong or that the issue should be reopened. The hope, instead, is that in retracing the path we shall come to a better understanding of the circumstances that gave birth to the world in which we now live and to the conditions that will shape the future.

# The Legacy of
# 1 Depression and War

Perhaps the crucial decision taken by the Allies during the Second World War was to seek the unconditional surrender of Germany and Japan. There would be no compromise with fascism. Its defeat would be complete and its authoritarian regimes, wherever imposed, would be replaced. The effect was a political vacuum in most of the European continent, Japan, China, and many of the former European colonies in Asia. Change was also in store for significant portions of the Middle East, and the question of the future of Africa loomed. These new, or newly open, political spaces would be filled relatively quickly, but in 1945 the shape and complexion of the successor regimes could not easily be predicted or controlled. Nor could it be foreseen how they would relate to one another and to the rest of the world. Stalin, Churchill, and Roosevelt began early on to try to plan for the postwar period, but because their interests were at odds, little was agreed upon before the end of hostilities—and even that was often reversed in practice.

That the Allies had very different visions of a postwar order was almost inevitable. Histories and interests diverged sharply; more uneven still was the distribution of resources with which each power could make its will prevail.[1] The structure of the new United Nations endowed five governments—the United States, Britain, the Soviet Union, France, and China—with the status of great powers by providing them with permanent seats on its Security Council. The decision represented more a geopolitical wish than a recognition of actual clout. Charles de Gaulle may have dominated the parade celebrating the liberation of Paris on August 26, 1944, but the French had contributed little to the defeat of Hitler.[2] The Chinese government under Chiang Kai-shek was equally ineffective during the war and even more beleaguered afterward. Chiang could never decide who was his real enemy, the Japanese or the Communists, and the result was that much of the resistance was done by the Communists and the credit went largely to them. The hope was, of course, that France would reemerge as a major power in Europe to balance the defeated, but still much feared, Germans, and that a stable China would help stabilize Asia.

A more realistic assessment of political and economic power would also have undermined Britain's claim to the status of world power.[3] Churchill's bluster could not disguise the fact that the British war effort, heroic as it was, was utterly dependent on the United States. What made the claim at least credible in 1945 was the British Empire, but relationships within the empire had shifted dramatically. The Commonwealth countries were essentially autonomous; India had been promised independence; British authority was already beginning to recede in the Middle East; and imperial control still had to be reasserted in parts of Asia. But again, there was the hope that a strong Britain linked in some form to its former and remaining imperial possessions could provide a bulwark against anarchy in various potentially unstable areas. This alone seemed to justify the pretense of great-power status.

Only two powers truly merited great-power status: the United States and the Soviet Union. Both had enormous military strength. The Soviets had borne the brunt of the battle with the Nazis and had won decisively. At war's end, the Red Army was the world's biggest, and it was well supplied. The cost of victory had been staggering: 20 to 25 million dead, much of the best land laid waste, and industry destroyed. The United States, by contrast, emerged from the war with greatly augmented material strength and few scars. Its losses were real but proportionally much less than those of the Soviets, and the U.S. economy was far stronger than it had been in 1939. The nation had the second-largest armed force and by far the best equipped. U.S. industry had shown itself capable of prodigious wartime feats, and the U.S. arsenal included atomic bombs. Very few such bombs were on hand in 1945, and it would have been hard to justify their use, but their very existence colored international relations nonetheless.

There were, then, no great powers in the nineteenth-century sense but two (or perhaps one and a half) superpowers who, in concert or competition, would decisively influence the emerging postwar system of states. Both, moreover, brought to the task of rebuilding not merely the usual set of geopolitical considerations but ambitious and antithetical conceptions of how other nations should organize themselves. Neither was entirely blinded by ideology: the United States was committed to democratic capitalism but would put up with less than perfect approximations; the Soviets were committed to world revolution but were not averse to putting off its "inevitable" triumph in particular places, for example, in China. And to some extent, the universalist pretensions of U.S. and Soviet policies were but rationalizations of more traditional geopolitical aims. The Soviets were resolved to provide a buffer between themselves and the Germans whatever political and social system prevailed in the countries between; the United States had interests in Latin America and in the Pacific that preceded and transcended immediate political preferences. Still, the ideological competition between the U.S. and the USSR was genuine, and it greatly complicated the coming into being of a stable postwar order.

Ideological differences merged imperceptibly with, and were reinforced by, history, or more precisely, by disparate readings of the recent past. The war was the most proximate experience whose lessons had to be absorbed, but its meaning was filtered through an understanding of the conditions that had produced it. Soviet leaders had little difficulty explaining the war. They had long expected an attack from the West, and fascism, the latest and most degenerate phase of capitalism, had from the beginning been directed at the Bolshevik threat.[4] The fascists were merely continuing what had been started by the capitalist democracies. The Soviet Union had been conceived and taken life in the midst of war. The First World War had brought the collapse of tsarist rule in February 1917, and the continuation of Russia's participation had critically weakened the Provisional Government of Alexander Kerensky. Compelled to accept a humiliating peace settlement with the Germans in early 1918, the Bolsheviks had hoped to regain lost territory in the aftermath of Germany's surrender in November, but the Allies had intervened in the civil war on the side of the Whites and encouraged the grandiose designs of the new Polish state. By the early 1920s the emerging Soviet state had beaten back the Poles and won the civil war, though at tremendous cost. The experience taught the leaders of the new state to expect nothing but hostility from the West. Throughout the interwar years, Soviet foreign policy was dominated by fears of "capitalist encirclement" and nothing that happened prior to 1939 allayed those fears. With the triumph of fascism in Germany in 1933, the Soviets shifted their stance and instead began to argue for collective security and sought desperately to ally with France or Britain against the German threat. Their efforts were in vain, and in several key confrontations the Western powers chose not to resist Hitler's demands. With some justice, Soviet leaders concluded that the capitalist democracies preferred appeasement to an alliance with the USSR and that many in the West believed a war in the East that would destroy fascism and communism alike would be the best outcome.

By 1939 the Soviets were desperate. To their west was a militant Nazism whose armaments were growing by the day. To their east was a militant Japan, allied with Germany in the Anti-Comintern Pact, that had successfully occupied Manchuria and now threatened to move north. There were recurring border clashes during 1938 and 1939 along the tense frontier shared by Soviet and Japanese troops and more serious confrontations at Lake Khasan and Khalkin-Gol (Nomonhan).[5] The Soviets won important victories in these remote engagements but were nonetheless convinced to make deals with both the Germans and the Japanese. The Nazi-Soviet pact was signed in August 1939; a neutrality pact with Japan, in April 1941. The bargain struck with the Nazis particularly dismayed the Soviets' sympathizers in the West, but the Soviets showed little hesitation in using the pact to regain control of the Baltic nations and to gobble up the eastern portions of Poland.

For the Soviets, then, the historical memory of prewar diplomacy was dominated by a deep distrust. The war did little to overcome this legacy. The alliance between the Soviet Union and the Western powers was forged by Hitler when in the spring of 1941 he postponed an invasion of Britain in favor of an eastern offensive. By then neither Britain nor France could offer genuine aid to the USSR, and the United States had yet to enter the war. The Soviets were left virtually alone to face the Nazi assault.[6] The Americans began to ship supplies to the embattled Soviet forces in 1942, but few had arrived by the time of the Battle of Stalingrad (November 1942–February 1943), regarded as the turning point in the war. It took a very long while, moreover, for the Allies to open a second front against the Germans, which meant that the Soviets continued to bear the brunt of the fighting until at least the summer of 1944. Allied landings in North

Africa diverted few German troops from the eastern front, and the slow Allied progress through Italy took away only a few more. Not until the landings at Normandy in June 1944 did the Allies make what Stalin considered a serious military contribution. By that time the Red Army had largely succeeded in pushing the Germans back across Eastern Europe.

It was not likely, in the circumstances, that the Soviets would retreat voluntarily from the lands that they saw themselves as having liberated. The Soviet Union had suffered terrible losses at the hands of the Nazis.[7] The countries of Eastern Europe, by contrast, had offered little resistance to Hitler's advance, and some had actually assisted it. A not insignificant number of Eastern Europeans had also been tempted by ancient and not so ancient hatreds and resentments into collaborating with the Nazis in the extermination of Jews and other racial, political, or religious enemies. The war, then, had not diminished Soviet fears, and as the U.S. diplomat W. Averell Harriman explained in January 1945, "The overriding consideration in Soviet foreign policy is the preoccupation with 'security,' as Moscow sees it."[8] As the war drew to a close, Soviet and Western leaders met at Yalta, Teheran, and Potsdam, where they proclaimed a desire to work together to shape the new world. Not far beneath the facade of cooperation, however, was a store of resentment and suspicion that quickly surfaced.[9]

U.S. leaders shared the general Western hostility to the Soviet Union, but it was far from being their central preoccupation. The United States had joined with Britain and France just after the First World War in the ill-fated effort to bring down the new Bolshevik regime, but had done so halfheartedly. U.S. attention was subsequently focused elsewhere and on other issues, especially the question of naval supremacy vis-à-vis Britain and Japan. The United States had had little to do with the diplomatic maneuverings provoked by the resurgence of German power under the Nazis, and during the war its opinion makers were firmly behind the alliance with the Soviets. In 1945 most Americans supported continued cooperation, but their main concern was the nation's economic prospects.[10] The depression of the 1930s had shattered cherished beliefs about U.S. economic prowess; had wrought the most dramatic realignment in politics since the Civil War; and had initiated a thorough transformation in the relationship between state and society and in the philosophy of government.[11] Its impacts ensured that policy makers would carry into the deliberations about the postwar order a desire to avoid a recurrence of the slump.

Prescriptions for the future inevitably grew from diagnoses of past errors. To most U.S. leaders it seemed obvious that governments had failed to respond properly to the Great Depression, and that failure had prolonged and deepened the crisis. They were particularly critical of the retreat into autarchy and neomercantilism undertaken by almost all governments in the early 1930s. British decisions—first to go off gold in 1931 and then to construct a wall of tariffs and preferences around the empire (the Ottawa Accords of 1932)—were seen as especially shortsighted, for they served mainly to reduce the scope of world trade and thus worsen the prospects of recovery. Similar moves by the French, the Germans, the Japanese, and even the United States had, in this view, threatened to replace the open world market with a set of relatively closed trading blocs—sterling, gold, dollar, and yen blocs, and the system of managed bilateral trade erected by Germany and its neighbors in eastern and central Europe.[12] Overall, it has been argued, "the actions…by individual countries to protect their economies and to defend their shares of international trade had the inevitable effect of shrinking the total quantity of international trade."[13]

The retreat into economic nationalism also affected international relations. As U.S. Secretary of State Cordell Hull put it, "Unhampered trade dovetailed with peace; high tariffs, trade barriers, and unfair competition with war."[14] More practically, Americans came to believe that the U.S. economy was too large to function in anything but a global, or nearly global, environment. No regional or even hemispheric bloc could provide the "grand area" supposedly required for prosperity.[15] U.S. policy makers thus concluded from the experience of the depression and from the all-too-easy slide from the depression into war that the key to prosperity *and* peace was an open system of world trade. Their commitment to what scholars have rather inelegantly called "liberal multilateralism" would be the overriding objective of U.S. policy in the negotiations that began with the signing of the Atlantic Charter in August 1941 and continued through the Bretton Woods Agreement in 1944, the creation of the International Monetary Fund and the World Bank, the British loan in 1946, the Marshall Plan, and the bargaining over trade that issued ultimately in the General Agreement on Tariffs and Trade (GATT). It was a simplistic vision of what it would take to rebuild the international economy, but it provided clear guidance to politicians and planners as they designed the institutional framework of the postwar world economy.

The U.S. vision was not the only vision offered, nor was it uncontested. The British held rather different views, and there was also disagreement among policy makers, economists, and officials within the U.S. government. The major alternatives to the projected program of growth through trade all derived in some measure from the same source. In *The General Theory* (1936), John Maynard Keynes had persuasively argued for the view that demand left to its devices will not always match supply and that the market economy can reach equilibrium at less than full employment.[16] Keynes had for some time advocated government measures to increase demand; he now presented what seemed an irrefutable defense of such action. Keynesian thinking seemed also to be confirmed by practice. The stimuli applied by Roosevelt during the early years of the New Deal appeared by 1935–1936 to have had a positive impact on employment; so, too, did Swedish public spending programs. The rearmament undertaken by Hitler also served to reduce unemployment in Germany, although not many outsiders took comfort from that apparent success. But spending on armaments also began to work its magic in Britain and the United States: unemployment virtually disappeared during the war. Many concluded from this that public spending did in fact create jobs, and that if it was prudently done, inflation would not inevitably result.

Keynesian theory, particularly when combined with the full employment created by war mobilization, offered an alternative model of postwar economic policy that placed less emphasis upon trade than did the vision of many U.S. officials. The Keynesians did not oppose trade but tended to doubt its ability to generate the level of employment that Western publics were likely to insist upon after the war. Efforts to open up world markets, therefore, would have to be coupled with policies that allowed leaders to stimulate demand domestically by utilizing the fiscal and monetary tools at the disposal of national governments. In addition, Keynes and those who thought as he did believed that the disruptions caused by the war and by the legacies of prewar policies would mean that re-creating an open world market would take some time. Keynes had, after all, made his reputation by criticizing the unrealistic expectations of world leaders on precisely this issue after the First World War.[17] As Alvin Hansen explained in 1945, policy makers had sought after the First World War to "reconstitute as rapidly as possible the automatic forces in economic life. The drive all around was a return, in the broad essentials, to laissez-faire."[18] The eagerness of politicians and officials to bring about an idealized version of the pre-1914 world economic order, Keynes postulated, had caused them to overlook or minimize the enormous cost in lost output and employment that would have to be paid. He worried openly during the 1940s that U.S. plans for an open world economy were likewise unrealistic and would lead to renewed suffering.

Before 1939 Keynes's influence among policy makers had been marginal.[19] His eminence among economists had had little effect upon those who set economic policy in Britain or elsewhere. With the coming of war, however, his views received a retrospective vindication and he was brought into the Treasury to advise the Churchill government on war finance and, more important, postwar planning. From that position Keynes sought to shape the institutional and policy framework of the postwar world: he participated in most of the principal discussions on international finance and trade with U.S. representatives, and he took the lead in negotiating the U.S. loan essential to Britain's transition from a wartime to a peacetime economy. Ironically, Keynes had more impact outside Britain than within. The coalition government under Churchill was reluctant to commit itself wholeheartedly to the employment goals advocated by Keynes, and the Treasury was not eager to adopt the new policies and carry out the associated responsibilities. By contrast, British foreign economic policy at the end of the war was esssentially Keynesian. Keynes's belief that employment should not be sacrificed to a wistful pursuit of balanced budgets, a favorable balance of payments, and the confidence of international bankers would have appalled earlier generations of policy makers. By 1945, however, even the most traditional British bankers and Treasury officials had accepted that Britain could not compete with the United States in a truly open world economy and that the nation's interests would not be well served by slavish devotion to orthodoxy. The British input into postwar planning was hence largely Keynesian.

The Keynesian vision also had adherents in the United States. An early proponent was Marriner Eccles, chief of the Federal Reserve, whose talented band of young economists was eager to apply Keynes's ideas to problems facing the United States and the world. Before the war Keynesians had gained influence in the Treasury, the Budget Bureau, and the Commerce Department; during the war, they held important positions in the Office of Price Administration and the National Resources Planning Board.[20] The State Department, however, remained relatively unaffected by the new economic thinking and instead continued to put its faith in the workings of a restored and more open international economy. That was Hull's view, and it was shared by key officials and advisers like Dean Acheson and William Clayton. Acheson, for example, saw the postwar economic situation as "a problem of markets. You don't have a problem of production. The United States has unlimited creative energy. The important thing is markets.... You must look to foreign markets." In Clayton's slightly more precise calculation, "We have got to export three times as much as we exported just before the war if we want to keep our industry running at somewhere near capacity."[21] Because the State Department was central to postwar planning, the internationalist vision prevailing there would largely predominate. But because its influence was often countered by that of officials from other departments, and because the key U.S. ally in shaping the postwar world held to somewhat different views, the outcome was a mix: a compromise between the U.S. (specifically the State Department) commitment to an open international economy and various hesitations, qualifications, and concessions that were first forced on U.S. planners by the British and later reinforced by the emerging realities of postwar politics.[22] The system would be liberal and multilateralist in its framework, but embedded within it would be a variety of institutions and policies that would allow individual national governments the flexibility to pursue policies designed to create full employment and to bring about social reform.[23]

The political realities that would gradually force themselves upon the consciousness of U.S. and British leaders were visible at least in outline in 1945.[24] Most obvious was the political vacuum in much of the world as German and Japanese occupation ended. Equally apparent was the enhanced military power of the Soviets. These two realities suggested to British and U.S. leaders the great likelihood that regimes hostile to the West would be established in areas only recently dominated by Germany and Japan. So, too, did the fact that within those areas the politics of occupation, collaboration, and resistance had by and large weakened the traditional forces of order and strengthened the left. This occurred equally in occupied Europe and in Asia, though for rather different reasons.

The key to the outcome in Asia was that the Japanese had displaced not legitimate and indigenous regimes but imperial bureaucracies with troubled and uncertain ties to those they ruled. The Japanese conquest could thus be portrayed as a "holy war" for Asian liberation whose goal— creation of a "Greater East Asia Co-Prosperity Sphere"—was to provide the framework for a broader material prosperity. From the early 1930s Japan had conceived of its economic future in continental or "Pan-Asian" terms, and its recovery from the Great Depression had come through devaluation and greatly increased exports. Only further expansion could provide continued growth. Grafted onto this essentially economic vision was a sense of cultural mission: Japan would lead the resurgence of Asia against the West and its corrupting values. This sense of mission was hardly egalitarian: "To view those who are in essence unequal as if they were equal is in itself inequitable. To treat those who are unequal

**24**

unequally is to realize equality."[25] The "new order" would be a "racial community" in which the Japanese, the "Yamato" race, would lead and others would follow and, where appropriate, obey. The Japanese staked their claim to Asian domination in terms that clearly echoed the views of their Nazi allies: "We, the Yamato race, are presently spilling our 'blood' to realize our mission in world history of establishing a Greater East Asia Co-Prosperity Sphere. In order to liberate the billion people of Asia, and also to maintain our position of leadership over the Greater East Asia Co-Prosperity Sphere forever, we must plant the 'blood' of the Yamato race in this 'soil'."[26]

Inevitably, Japanese efforts to institute this new order produced complicated results.[27] Japan's swift defeat of the British at Singapore and of the Dutch in Indonesia provided a vindication of its claims, as did the unseemly haste with which the French in Indochina came to terms with Japan. The collapse of colonial authority discredited the Western powers and in many cases encouraged the aspirations of local nationalists. An exception was the Philippines, which had become quasi-independent in 1934 and where the Japanese met sullen resistance. In general, though, the Japanese relied on more or less willing collaborators to administer and to organize political life. Unlike in Europe, where collaboration ultimately meant disgrace and occasionally death, in Asia many collaborators went on to important roles in postwar politics. Sukarno, the Indonesian nationalist, is perhaps the best example; the "thirty comrades" in Burma, another. In some countries, of course, resistance proved the surer path to political legitimacy. Before the war, for instance, Ho Chi Minh had been the leader of the very small Indochinese Communist Party. During the war, however, he put together the Viet Minh as an anti-Japanese, anticolonial coalition and by 1945 he had become a symbol of national resistance. Even more dramatic and significant was the emergence of the Chinese Communists as the leaders of the national resistance. By the same logic, the nationalists under Chiang Kai-shek lost considerable popular support because of their inability or unwillingness to mount an effective resistance.

By the end of the war several of the old regimes in Asia had been overthrown and their claims to rule undermined; local forces of radically nationalist and distinctly anticolonial orientation were typically much stronger. Insurgent movements of nationalist and/or communist complexion greeted the liberation from Burma to the Philippines. Even in countries not occupied by Japan, imperial rule was threatened. In India, for example, the Raj had proved surprisingly capable of mobilizing society for war, despite the passive resistance of the Indian National Congress, but by war's end the British faced a Congress whose support among Hindus was undiminished and whose resolve to become independent had become more insistent. They also faced a better organized and more popular Muslim League committed to an independent Pakistan. Decolonization would prove immensely complicated but was nonetheless inevitable.

The position of European colonial powers in Africa and the Middle East was less dramatically affected by the war. There was no political vacuum to be filled by rival powers or anticolonial revolutionaries. Still, there were changes that suggested a dimming of the prospects for long-term domination. In Egypt and in Iraq, for example, the British had intervened to force changes of government upon weak and reluctant monarchs, who, in consequence, became still weaker in the eyes of their subjects. Iran was effectively occupied by foreigners—British, American, and Soviet nationals—and not happy about it. The situation in Palestine was explosive: the steady arrival of Jewish settlers threatened the land and the rights of Arabs, and the outlook for an end to the British mandate made any peaceful compromise unlikely. In Africa, the colonial regimes appeared more secure, but the war had stimulated economic development that brought social changes whose political impact would be felt sooner or later. The fledgling nationalist movements that had appeared during the prewar depression were not yet strong enough to threaten colonial rule, but were becoming sufficiently visible to force the imperial powers to adopt a new rhetoric of progress and eventual self-government. At the same time, the mobilization for war had allowed white settlers in places like Kenya and southern Africa to prosper and gain control of local administration, greatly complicating the path to self-government.

The Second World War thus dealt a sharp blow to European colonialism, even if the impact was not everywhere visible. But the war also made it difficult for the Western powers to envision an alternative. U.S. policy was particularly ambivalent. The United States had long conceived of itself as anti-imperial, even if its practice—particularly in Latin America—often belied that self-image. Its leaders harbored a special and historic resentment against the British Empire but were no more favorably disposed to the imperial pretensions of the French or the Dutch. Roosevelt spoke for many when he quipped that "anything must be better than to live under French colonial rule."[28] These long-standing predispositions were reinforced by the peculiarly American reading of the causes of the Great Depression. At the onset of the war, therefore, U.S. negotiators had forced the British to agree to open up the empire as a condition of Lend-Lease arrangements. American thinking about the postwar world was similarly

26

marked by a distaste for continued imperial rule. As the war drew to a close, however, and the Allies saw postwar prospects more clearly, the attractions of imperial rule came to the fore, and the British, French, and Dutch were naturally eager to restore their control over lost possessions. What proved decisive, however, was the gradual transformation of U.S. views. Faced with the possibility of instability or, worse, the coming to power of regimes friendly to the Soviet Union and hostile to Western imperialism, the United States reluctantly changed its mind. The reorientation did not happen immediately—it would not be fully accomplished until after the victory of the Chinese Communists in 1949 and the outbreak of the Korean War in 1950—but the first step was acquiescence in the British, French, and Dutch reoccupation of the territories in Asia from which they had been ousted.

The altered political balance in the East and in colonial lands generally was more than matched by the changed landscape of domestic politics in Europe. Again, the key was the way foreign occupation interacted with prior political arrangements. In much of central and eastern Europe the Nazis did not displace democratic regimes but authoritarian governments. Just after the First World War democratic governments had been set up in virtually all of the successor states to the Habsburg, Hohenzollern, and Romanov empires, but few survived the Great Depression with democratic institutions intact. One after another they succumbed to authoritarian rule (by the late 1930s the only genuine democracy left was in Czechoslovakia, which Hitler quickly eliminated). In Austria, a "clerical fascist" regime took power in 1934; in Hungary, Admiral Miklós Horthy presided over a truncated democracy; in Romania, the king dispensed with democracy early in the 1930s and encouraged the outrages of the fascist "Iron Guard" movement late in the decade; in Poland, no one could confuse the "colonels'" regime with a functioning democracy; and in the Baltic states, Greece, and Yugoslavia, democracy was a thing of the past.

The Nazis encountered little resistance when they rolled into or over these countries on their way east, and they often found willing collaborators. When the Nazis were pushed back by the Red Army, the local rulers were swept away as well. And because these local rulers had done their best to suppress liberals and social democrats before the war, there were very few moderate democratic forces in place to take over from the dictators, generals, and collaborators. The most successful resistance movements, in Yugoslavia and Greece, had been led by the left; only in Poland had there been a significant anti-Nazi and anticommunist movement, the Polish Home Army. Who, then, could put together a credible alternative to a Soviet-dominated regime after the war? It was difficult for the Allies to locate anyone for the task; hence, the sense of agony, impotence, and anger among U.S. and British leaders as the prospects of a democratic eastern and central Europe, freed from Soviet domination and open to the West, faded rapidly.[29]

Allied leaders did not feel much better when they shifted their gaze to the West. In France the impact of the war was to discredit politicians and parties of the center and the right and to boost enormously the prestige of the left. The bulk of the French establishment—including most bureaucrats, military officers, judges, policemen, and party leaders—had come to terms with the Nazis. De Gaulle himself had been a mere colonel in 1940 whose exalted wartime position as leader of the "Free French" was due to the fact that virtually all of the more senior officers chose silence or collaboration. And despite a grand style, de Gaulle did not command many more divisions than did the pope, and he lacked the latter's moral authority.[30] The resistance on the ground, morever, which was never as strong as postwar mythology would have us believe, was led largely by Communists. By liberation, then, the left was by far the strongest organized force, and there were few representatives of the right and center who were sufficiently untainted by the past as to remain credible and viable candidates for political power.[31] The situation was comparable in Italy. More than twenty years of fascist rule had decimated or fatally compromised Mussolini's political opponents of the center and the right. Only the left, beaten down but nonetheless active in the resistance, survived with a reasonable level of organization and with political respect. The Italian Communist Party had emerged from the war as the largest party, and it remained strong for many years thereafter.[32]

The political balance within Western Europe had thus shifted noticeably to the left, and British and U.S. policy makers were forced to take note. But even in the United States and Britain public opinion had moved to the left in the course of the war. Part of the change had to do with the image of the Soviets, who went from being prewar villains to wartime heroes and comrades in arms. This shift was, of course, greatly aided by Allied propaganda. Of more lasting import were changes in the power of organized labor. In Britain, for example, the Conservative government that went to war in 1939 left office in disgrace less than a year later, replaced by a coalition government led by Churchill but dominated, in terms of cabinet ministries dealing with domestic affairs, by Labour. Trade union leader Ernest Bevin became minister of labour and from that position oversaw the mobilization of the nation's resources for war. He and

28

other Labour party leaders were able to alter government policy significantly, making it easier for unions to organize; forcing employer concessions to organized and unorganized workers alike; insisting on progressive tax policies to finance the war; and, most important, pushing the wartime coalition into planning for postwar social and economic reform.[33] The centerpiece of that planning was the 1942 Beveridge Report, which held out to ordinary citizens the promise of state support to deal with unemployment, ill health, and poverty.[34] Its author, William Beveridge, went on to issue a more radical and contentious plan for full employment that helped to push the government into a commitment to aggressive measures to maintain employment after the war. The discourse out of which these commitments came helped to ensure that just before war's end, the Labour party handed Churchill and the Tories a decisive electoral defeat. Britain entered the postwar world with a government dedicated to using the powers of the state to bring about social justice and full employment.[35]

U.S. politics did not witness such a decisive move to the left but in subtle ways traced a similar path.[36] The major political transformation had begun with the triumph of Franklin Roosevelt's New Deal, but it would require the exigencies of war to create a political culture that took for granted its virtues and accomplishments. By some measures, the reformist impulse appeared to end with the war. The Congress elected in 1940 was very uncooperative, and the president's historic legislative achievements were behind him. But this is only part of the story. As late as 1937 Roosevelt had resisted Keynesian arguments for deficit spending and instead heeded the warnings of advisers committed to fiscal rectitude when he decided to cut spending dramatically. The economy slipped into a recession the next year. Only with the aid of military spending did it manage to climb out, but the experience convinced an entire generation of the wisdom of Keynes and the narrow-mindedness of his critics. By the early 1940s Democratic leaders were pursuing a much more activist program of state intervention in the economy.

Mobilization for war brought into the growing bureaucracy economic and social reformers who sought to turn their notions of responsible government into a reality. The federal government became involved not only in war production but in labor relations and civil rights, and, as in Britain, in the elaboration of a vision of the postwar world that was grand enough to inspire Americans and their allies to the effort needed to achieve victory. A prime consequence was the strengthening of the labor movement. Organizers made effective use of the high demand for workers and of institutions like the National War Labor Board to force recognition and contracts upon employers. By 1945 most of heavy industry was unionized.[37] The war also occasioned one of the first and most important federal initiatives in civil rights: the 1941 executive order mandating fair employment practices in war industries. And Roosevelt in 1944 went so far as to propose an "Economic Bill of Rights" that would include the "right to a useful and remunerative job," the right of every farmer to "a return which will give him and his family a decent living," the right to "a decent home," "to adequate medical care," and "to a good education." These domestic war aims were crucial. As Roosevelt put it, "After this war is won, we must be prepared to move forward, in the implementation of these rights, to new goals of human happiness and well-being."[38] Practice would undoubtedly fall far short of this agenda, but its very proclamation indicates the transformation of political discourse. By 1945 the political culture had shifted to the left and the tenets of the New Deal, so contentious and embattled as recently as 1940, had come to embody consensus.

The new discourse would place limits upon what U.S. leaders could do to influence the international postwar order. Even if Americans did not pay much attention to foreign policy, they were nevertheless unlikely to support a policy that promised merely a return to open markets and to the mean and cramped political philosophy of the 1930s. On the contrary, many Americans would seek to export the best features of the New Deal and the democratic capitalism it had produced. This was particularly evident in proposals for breaking up monopolies—the German cartels and the Japanese *zaibatsu*—and for policies aimed at land reform and at fostering labor organization. U.S. planners believed such structural reforms would enhance the prospects of political democracy in Germany and Japan and that the resulting redistribution of wealth and dispersal of economic power would expand their domestic markets, stimulating internal demand and diminishing the frenzied pursuit of foreign markets that—especially in the case of Japan—had been at the root of earlier policies of expansion.[39] This populist political economy was quite different from the "corporate liberalism" that Americans are often said to have imposed, or to have sought to impose, on the postwar world. It was a much more democratic vision that, if naive in crucial respects, was not much less idealistic than the belief of other Americans in the nearly magical power of free trade. Neither view, of course, would prevail in undiluted fashion, and both would contribute significantly to the extremely mixed and unanticipated outcome of reconstruction.

The world leaders responsible for the making of the postwar order saw tremendous possibilities and were armed with ambitious plans and grand designs. But they saw severe constraints as well. What in one view consti-tuted a tempting opportunity in another was a dire threat. What to one side was a favorable balance to the other was a major problem. Nowhere was this bifurcation more obvious than in regard to Germany and Japan, where the viability of any postwar order would be decisively tested. In those two nations the Allies could thoroughly refashion political institu-tions and values and, in the process, advance their visions. But, of course, the visions of the Soviet Union and the Allies were quite opposed, and there were disagreements as well among the Allies and even within the U.S. and British political establishments. U.S. policy makers, for example, vacillated between plans to punish and rehabilitate Germany. Treasury secretary Henry Morgenthau proposed to "repastoralize" Germany; the State Department tended to the view that a revived German economy was critical to a revived and stable Europe. Roosevelt never made a clear choice, and Truman proceeded with a policy that was in fact quite punitive and that involved extensive denazification, at least for a time.[40] There was less ambivalence in Soviet policy. In the Soviet zone denazification was pursued more ruthlessly and the economy pillaged under the guise of repa-rations.[41] Because the Soviets were effectively excluded from the formu-lation of occupation policy for Japan, the only important disagreements in that instance were among U.S. policy makers. Overall, however, there was consensus as to the remaking of Japanese society and purging from it the elements held responsible for the war. The occupation would be a com-pletely American affair; Japan would be, in General Douglas MacArthur's words, the "world's great laboratory for an experiment in the liberation of a people from totalitarian military rule and for the liberalization of gov-ernment from within."[42]

Whether Germany or Japan would be receptive to the remaking of their societies, cultures, and political institutions was a complicated matter. It has been common in Germany to refer to the moment of defeat in 1945 as *Stunde Null* (zero hour), as if the nation's history simply began again then. It is a self-interested conception, for it avoids the need for a serious reck-oning with the Nazi past and implicitly minimizes the extent to which the Nazi experience not only reflected but itself helped to shape the national identity, the political culture, and even the legal framework within which the new Germany would be created.[43] On the other hand, the Nazis were a destructive force within the society. Although they had been aided in their rise to power by the old elites that were so heavily represented in the bureaucracy, the judiciary, and the military, and although many of these traditional conservatives had collaborated with the Nazis for some time after 1933, Hitler in the end turned on even these erstwhile allies. The Nazi policy of *Gleichschaltung* aimed to bring the entire society and its political values and practices in line with Nazi ideology, and over time it worked. Ironically, by 1945 many of the elites who had resisted for so long and so effectively the genuine democratization of Germany had themselves been eliminated. Those who would seek to refashion German politics confronted, therefore, a complicated legacy of institutions, interests, and outlooks.

A complicated legacy awaited as well those who would direct the reshaping of Japan. The structures of the society were really quite opaque to the Americans who oversaw the occupation and reconstruction, and there was a long Japanese history of selectively absorbing what was useful and necessary from the West and assimilating it to distinctively Japanese ends. The United States, of course, possessed great leverage over Japan and exhibited a genuine resolve to rid it of the forces and values that had prompted aggression. But Japan's American rulers would find their options limited after the war by their own ignorance and inexperience, drawbacks that dictated the U.S. decision to administer Japan indirectly, through the established, if suitably purged, government. The Americans were also hindered by the resilience of Japanese culture, by the need to rebuild the world economy, and, ultimately, by the vagaries of the Cold War.[44]

The shaping of the postwar world order was a daunting enterprise and the contours of its institutions and of constituent states remained unclear for some time. Eventually, a relatively stable system of states, alliances between states, and international institutions was put in place and functioned well enough to persist in outline form until the late 1980s. A viable economic order emerged as well, even if it worked much better for some than for others. The nature of this postwar settlement, however, differed in critical ways from the visions held so dear by the leaders of the great powers. It instead reflected the confrontation of those visions with the extremely complex legacy from the turbulent era that was just drawing to a close. The war and the depression became memories, but their consequences affected the entire trajectory of the postwar world.

# Nations, Boundaries,

# 2 and Cold War Realities

   History is ordinarily told as the history of nations, as
the working out over time of national identities, goals,
and political projects. As such, it often slights the local,
the personal, and the interpersonal, and it approaches the
international order either as the sum of national developments or in terms of relations between stable, clearly delineated
states. The omissions that follow from this practice of ground-
ing history in "the national experience" are many and serious, but
the most debilitating effect of this bias is that it keeps hidden the
traumatic and highly consequential processes by which nations
themselves come into being, are held together, and are sometimes
torn apart.[1] Unlike the Versailles settlement, the reshaping and
regrouping of states that occurred after the Second World War
was not conceived of in particularly national terms. People
spoke, instead, of world orders or of confrontations
between rival ideologies and social systems, and national
boundaries were less often explicitly debated than had
been the case after the First World War. Nevertheless,

what the post–Second World War settlement did was to reconstitute nations, national identities, and national political systems within a new set of international constraints. To speak, then, of a postwar world order, or international system, without attending to the transformations of national realities, is to miss what was really at stake in the turbulent politics of the early Cold War era.

The political vacuum created by the collapse of German and Japanese power, together with the changed balance of political forces in countries less directly and dramatically affected, meant that for much of the globe the nature of political systems was quite undecided as of 1945. By the early 1950s, the issue was no longer in doubt in most places. In the interim the two superpowers and their allies had put into place a framework of economic relations and of military alliances within which states and nations would be formed and forced to operate. The framework was not designed and imposed according to a rational and preconceived plan but, rather, emerged from the evolving confrontation between the two dominant powers—a confrontation that had proceeded through successive crises whose resolution led ultimately to a divided and militarized world. It was a world whose structure would frustrate the aspirations of numerous peoples to independent nationhood, democracy, and social justice. While the history of this era of reconstruction is often told as primarily a succession of crises—over Poland, Iran, Greece, Malaya, Berlin, China, and Korea—it is essential to see their combined impact on the emerging system of states and on the fates of peoples with and without states of their own.

The antagonism between the United States and the Soviet Union colored nearly all local contexts and tended to overshadow local or regional considerations in determining political outcomes. The roots of that antipathy went back as far as 1917; subsequent events, especially the diplomacy of the 1930s and the conduct of the war, had nurtured its growth. The unsettled character of so much of the world in 1945, however, provided unusually fertile ground for its further growth and ensured that this heightened antagonism would dominate the shaping of the postwar order. The full logic of a world organized on Cold War principles—and its implications for domestic politics—would not be manifest for some time, but its force would be felt immediately in the parallel efforts to erect an institutional framework for the world economy and for international relations.[2]

## FROM BRETTON WOODS TO THE MARSHALL PLAN

Certain basic features of the international economic regime had already been agreed upon by 1945. Representatives of forty-four countries met at

Bretton Woods in July 1944 and approved plans for the creation of the International Monetary Fund (IMF), which, functioning in coordination with a new international bank, would oversee the establishment of an open international economy. The agreement was the outcome of protracted discussions between British and U.S. representatives and embodied a compromise between their rather distinct visions of what would be required to get the world economy going again. Basically, the Americans wanted an international economic order that would impose strict limits upon the discretion and profligacy of national governments and move rapidly toward complete currency convertibility and freer trade. The British were more cautious, less ideological, and more realistic. Keynes, for example, wanted the IMF to make larger sums available in order to give countries more time to get their accounts into surplus and to pressure successful exporters, whose current accounts were already in surplus, to import more and thereby spread their momentary good fortune around. The British were also reluctant to accept U.S. demands that tariffs, quotas, and other trade preferences be eliminated immediately. The Bretton Woods agreement more closely approximated American than British ideals: the guidelines for the IMF would be far less generous and more orthodox than Keynes had proposed; in return, the United States accepted that exchange controls could be maintained during the transition from war to peace and that progress toward free trade could be gradual. Even so, the Americans thought that the arrangements in place in 1945 were too loose and afforded too much scope for government intervention and the protection of vested interests. After the war they sought to circumscribe further the workings of the new institutions and to insist even more forcefully upon fiscal orthodoxy and trade liberalization.

The gap between these rather ideological American goals and postwar realities was exposed repeatedly after 1946. A critical instance involved the British loan negotiated at the end of 1945. To Keynes's great disappointment the United States had insisted that the loan, considered essential to Britain's ability to pay for needed imports in the two years after the war, be tied to an agreement to adopt virtually uncontrolled currency convertibility by the middle of 1947. As might have been predicted, the plan failed: a drastic run on the pound forced Britain to suspend convertibility indefinitely in August 1947. The fiasco was a major embarrassment to the Labour government but an even more serious setback for American plans to use the wealth of the United States to push other countries—first Britain, then Europe, then the rest of the world—toward a more open global economy. If the closest and most prosperous U.S. ally could not live

36

up to the ideal, others would be even less likely to be able to do so. Eventually, but not happily, the United States saw the need to compromise and provided through the Marshall Plan more generous assistance that would amount by the end of 1952 to more than $13 billion.[3] That decision, however, was prompted as much by a sense of political crisis as by a rethinking of economic goals.

The Marshall Plan would prove to be the central and most creative policy initiative of the postwar period. Behind it lay the recognition, on the part of American strategic planners, that U.S. hopes for the postwar world were threatened by the ongoing economic crisis facing Western Europe and its political ramifications. Recovery from war was much slower than anticipated across most of Europe and clearly called for more financial support than the United States had first thought necessary. Earlier, two years of support for relief, organized through the United Nations (UNRAA), and loans to Britain, France, and Italy had been deemed sufficient; by 1947 it was clear that they were not. The British, for example, were using up their loan much faster than anticipated, and its likely exhaustion threatened further imports of both food and the raw materials essential to industrial recovery. Other countries also faced payment problems: they desperately required dollar imports, but their export industries were unable to compete in either the American or other markets.

The adjustment from war to peace was everywhere troubled, and in no country had conditions returned to anything like normal by 1947. Output had begun to revive in most countries during 1946 but faltered in 1947. Partly, this was due to the fuel crisis in the harsh winter of 1946–1947. Partly, to social unrest and political instability. Whatever the cause, living standards were threatened in France, Belgium, and Italy, and dire conditions persisted in Germany. In Italy, for example, inflation ran far ahead of wages, and the government's response—the austerity measures introduced in June 1947—sharply reduced employment. Wages lagged behind prices in France and Belgium as well; according to one authority, "In 1947 the rise in retail prices was almost twice as great as that in wages and salaries both in Paris and the provinces."[4] Food consumption remained well below prewar levels in Germany, Austria, and Italy. Overall, conditions were bleak. When combined with the threat to continued recovery posed by the mounting and widespread balance-of-payments problem, the economic indicators strongly suggested a major modification of, or initiative in, prevailing economic policy on the part of the United States.

Economic agonies provided merely the background within which the Marshall Plan emerged. What truly moved U.S. policy makers was the

Cold War. Between 1945 and 1947 relations between the superpowers had worsened drastically. Initial disagreements over Eastern Europe had been followed by diplomatic confrontations relating to Iran, Turkey, and Greece. As early as February 1946, Stalin had spoken of the danger of war with the capitalist West; on March 5, Churchill delivered his famous "Iron Curtain" speech. Soon the United States and the Soviet Union were at odds over German reparations and control of atomic weapons. Early in 1947 the British made it plain that they were financially unable to provide further aid to Greece and Turkey. Secretary of State George Marshall understood immediately what this meant: "It was tantamount to British abdication from the Middle East with obvious implications as to their successor."[5] It was now President Truman's turn to pronounce upon the consequences of these disputes for the pattern of international relations. The "Truman doctrine" was presented to Congress on March 12, 1947. The president's speech described a worldwide contest "between alternative ways of life" and summoned Americans to assist "free peoples" in resisting "totalitarian regimes." The proposal was, as a prominent Senator remarked, "almost like a Presidential request for a declaration of war." And he got it.[6]

The Truman administration also elicited from Congress support for a major package of financial aid for European reconstruction. The Marshall Plan, outlined by the secretary of state in a major speech at Harvard on June 5, 1947, was addressed to specifically economic problems, but its aim was essentially political. The emerging Cold War cast things in a new light. In particular, Europe's lingering—and by some accounts deteriorating—economic travail was reinterpreted in terms of its likely effect on politics. Americans worried that distress would translate into support for communism, a fear seemingly confirmed by the drift of events in France and Italy, where the left scored electoral victories and mounted effective direct industrial actions. To the list of woes must surely be added the growing impasse over Germany. The destruction of its cities and industries had been much more extensive than had been thought in May 1945, and in the immediate postwar era conditions were extremely worrisome. The division of responsibility over Germany among the four occupying powers proved an impediment to relief and reconstruction alike. The nation's economic infrastructure had been badly damaged and required a major diversion of scarce resources without which revival would be impossible. Inflation was out of control and shortages plagued the system of distribution. For their part, the Soviets insisted on stripping German assets in their sector and demanding reparations. The French were also determined that the Germans should be made to pay for what they had wrought during the war. U.S. and British authorities became increasingly frustrated by what they perceived as Soviet and French obstructionism and chafed at the mounting cost of the occupation. They were concerned, too, that continuing distress might turn Germans against the West and also retard the restoration of economic viability across Europe. U.S. leaders, in short, were faced with a serious challenge to their efforts to create a workable postwar system of states linked to a prosperous world economy.[7] Their response was to offer aid that, they hoped, would revive the economy, stabilize politics, and in the process tie Europe firmly to the United States.

The Marshall Plan was brilliantly successful, both economically and politically.[8] Economically, it provided the liquidity and stimulus to allow a genuine recovery to begin. The political consequences were at least as important. The process of seeking and getting Marshall aid set in motion far-reaching political changes. A nation's request for aid entailed submission of its national economic plans and priorities for approval by the United States. In consequence, the Soviet Union and East European nations made no requests—an outcome anticipated by U.S. planners—and prompted the communist parties in the West to oppose participation. That was a major mistake, for it placed the parties in opposition to a program likely to benefit their own societies and exposed their subordination to Moscow. From that moment, parties of the left were at a great disadvantage; and they lost considerable support in the late 1940s.

The administration of the Marshall Plan aid had its own effects. U.S. officials believed that European prosperity depended in the long term on the creation of a larger internal market. These "customs-union" notions, sometimes elaborated into more ambitious schemes for European unity, led officials to insist that nations seeking aid work toward a more integrated and open European economy. The obstacles to unity remained immense: Britain was quite unwilling to give up its treasured status as a world power to stand together with other Europeans in a queue for U.S. largesse, and French fears of Germany were intense. Nonetheless, the United States succeeded in nudging most of Europe toward greater cooperation and managed to secure French acquiescence in plans that would ultimately result in a revived German economy.

The pressure for economic coordination had as well the curious effect of encouraging a measure of economic planning on regimes that were otherwise opposed to state intervention in economic life. Each government had to inventory its needs and explain to Marshall Plan administrators how it planned to get from its present parlous condition to one in which further aid would be unnecessary. That did not always entail collectivist solutions but did require a degree of planning and compelled governments to submit their macroeconomic policies to U.S. review. There was inevitable grumbling at this affront to national sovereignty and specific fears that U.S. representatives would use their authority to impose a more conservative and laissez-faire vision upon governments that were more collectivist in orientation. In practice, Marshall Plan administrators were reluctant to veto the plans of democratically elected governments, although the threat may well have made those plans more timid. In several cases, moreover, American advice seems to have pushed governments—in Italy, Belgium, and the emerging West German state, for example—slightly to the left. The main effect of the particularly American administration of Marshall Plan aid was probably registered in the way it constrained national governments, restricting choices to the spectrum of policies that would be acceptable to the United States. That foreclosed the sort of options advocated by local communist parties, and it probably ruled out as well more-right-wing alternatives. In so narrowing the scope of debate and disagreement, however, the plan undoubtedly smoothed the path toward domestic political stability.

Even after the Marshall Plan came into existence and began to ease immediate economic burdens, U.S. leaders continued to press European governments to move toward the U.S. vision of an open world economy unfettered by narrowly national interests. Still, they met resistance. The plan for an International Trade Organization, for example, had been central to the hopes of the "multilateralists" since the signing of the Atlantic Charter, but had foundered on British demands that the United States respond to concessions by Britain on imperial preference with a more wholehearted commitment to full employment. The British had finally agreed as a condition of the 1946 loan to begin talks on trade, but the negotiations ground to a halt in 1947. Despite the lure and lubrication of Marshall Plan funds, no further progress was made and the plan was formally abandoned in 1950. Rather than a permanent organization with rules and policies, there was an agreement to work over time toward the reduction of trade barriers: the General Agreement on Tariffs and Trade (GATT).

U.S. efforts to encourage European economic cooperation also produced surprisingly little, for the British refused to cast their lot with the Continent and persisted in linking their economic fate with the sterling area. The European Payments Union was set up in 1950, but its impact was initially quite limited. Progress toward a more open and prosperous world economy thus seemed stalled in 1949–1950, as even the U.S. economy slipped into a sharp recession. What ultimately overcame these difficulties was more American money, this time in the form of spending extracted from taxpayers for the purpose of rearmament in response to the outbreak of war in Korea. The organization for the Marshall Plan, the Economic Cooperation Administration, was replaced by a Mutual Security Administration, and economic assistance was continued as an essentially military affair.

By the early 1950s the system of international economic relations arising from the interaction between U.S. plans and other people's problems bore only a family resemblance to the arrangements supposedly agreed upon at Bretton Woods. The new regime was a distinct hybrid: undoubtedly more open and multilateral than America's competitors would by themselves have constructed; less open, multilateral, and fiscally orthodox than U.S. planners had advocated. Thus the IMF was operating under a quite restrictive code, but its policies were counteracted in detail and overwhelmed in the aggregate by the economic stimuli occasioned by the Marshall Plan and rearmament. Trade between nations was far from free and open, although the course had been set toward gradual tariff reductions that would over time open up ever-larger sections of the world economy to genuine competition. Tentative steps toward European economic integration had also been taken with creation of the European Payments Union and, later, by acceptance of the Schuman Plan, which led to establishment of the European Coal and Steel Community. Exchange rates were fixed, though full currency convertibility had to wait until 1958. What really made the system work, it seems, was abnormally large defense spending by the United States. This "military Keynesianism" was not what anyone had foreseen or argued for in 1945. No one had planned it, and no one could have imagined how it would operate in practice. It was in fact a novelty, though it might well be considered the wholly apposite economic base for a new world order structured not upon the principles enshrined in the rhetoric of the United Nations but upon the harsher politics of the Cold War. It was by no means a rational or natural economic order, and although it generatd a high level of aggregate demand and thus stimulated the world economy, it also distorted priorities, patterns of trade, finance, and consumption. The imbalances it produced came eventually to haunt the process of continued growth and to exacerbate relations between the developed and less developed nations. Still, it worked for some time and produced the most sustained period of expansion in the history of the world economy.

## THE COLD WAR INTERNATIONAL ORDER

Both the promise and the problems in the new world economic order were yet to come, and in the years when it was being bargained into existence people were largely preoccupied with questions of war and peace. The celebrations that greeted the end of the Second World War had quickly given way to bitter antagonism between the United States and the Soviet Union. In short order the plans for a postwar order of cooperation between the superpowers were replaced by strategies designed to further the interests of one against the other. These new strategies resulted in an international order organized around the polarity between the two powers. Most nations were trapped in the field of force of either the Soviets or the Americans, and the processes by which nations came to be were similarly transformed by the new structure of international relations.

The logic of a bipolar world was to some extent irresistible in the context of 1945, when the two mightily armed, historically antipathetic victors—equipped with rival ideological commitments—faced off across an enormous power vacuum. It was a situation that would tempt even the most passive and pacific nation to impose its will upon a largely shapeless world. But there was nothing inevitable about the details of the evolving confrontation, nor about the precise lineaments of the emerging world order, which was far more ideological, militarized, and extensive than it might otherwise have been. There was bound to be conflict over the fate of Eastern Europe. The Soviets, after all, were unable or unwilling to contemplate a hostile or even neutral array of states along their western border, and the United States could not bring itself to acknowledge the more or less permanent establishment of Soviet hegemony in Eastern Europe. Churchill, of course, had come close to accepting it—the so-called percentages agreement of October 1944 seemed to sanction Soviet predominance in most of Eastern Europe in exchange for Stalin's acquiescence to British power elsewhere. But U.S. leaders had less reason to compromise, particularly after explosion of the atomic bomb in August 1945. Even so, conservative critics would charge repeatedly that U.S. and British leaders had "sold out" East Europe at the famous meeting at Yalta in February 1945.

The bomb, in fact, changed everything by disturbing the strategic calculations of both superpowers. Prior to August 1945, U.S. leaders were deeply worried by the losses they might incur in a full-scale invasion of Japan, and hence were eager for Soviet assistance in the East. U.S. leaders also understood the limits upon their power in Europe: the Red Army had liberated most of Eastern Europe and would not easily be dislodged.

Both considerations led to a muting of U.S. criticisms of Soviet intentions in Eastern Europe. Exclusive possession of the bomb, however, produced a climate in which such criticisms would more easily surface and ultimately become the dominant theme in U.S.–Soviet relations. U.S. attitudes toward the Soviets stiffened in the summer of 1945, and truly hard bargaining had replaced wartime cooperation by fall. President Truman considered the bomb to be "the greatest thing in history" and was emboldened by the fact that the United States had it and the Soviets did not. He and his advisers believed that with "this weapon rather ostentatiously on our hip," as Secretary of War Henry Stimson put it, it was no longer necessary to coddle Stalin or to acquiesce in Soviet hegemony in Eastern Europe or to accept Soviet advances in the Middle East or Asia.[9]

The Soviets undoubtedly had great respect for the destructive power of atomic weapons and intensified their own efforts to acquire the new technology, but they were not so impressed as to give up their wartime gains. Over the years Soviet strategists had evolved a view of warfare that downplayed the impact of new weapons in favor of what Stalin called the "permanently operating factors" that determined victory or defeat. These were essentially social and economic factors and were typically interpreted to give the decisive advantage to the Soviet Union, with its huge land mass, its wealth of natural resources, and its tremendous reserves of manpower. Supposed U.S. plans to use the threat of atomic weapons to extract geopolitical concessions from the Soviet Union were explicitly derided: "These venturous schemes," argued the marshal of aviation, "are…based on the calculation that the peoples of the USSR and the People's Democracies [of Eastern Europe] will be intimidated by the so-called 'atomic' or 'push-button' war. These ideas emanate from the completely distorted view that the outcome of a war can be settled by one kind of weapon alone. History has proved the reverse more than once."[10] The Soviet response to the U.S. monopoly, accordingly, was largely the opposite of what Americans might have wished. Rather than retreating from the lands they had so recently liberated, Soviet leaders interpreted the newly aggressive rhetoric of the West as a sign of the need to consolidate their control of Eastern Europe and its resources in anticipation of a long siege against U.S. imperialism. The asymmetry of military and geopolitical resources made both superpowers genuinely fearful of war from roughly 1947 to the end of the conflict in Korea.

The addition of nuclear weapons to the arsenals of the United States and, from 1949, of the Soviet Union thus did not bring peace but instability and a uniquely expensive arms race. Its rival's obvious superiority in atomic weapons led the Soviet Union not only to develop nuclear weapons of its own but also to adopt strategies that made good use of its superiority in conventional forces and armaments. That meant, among others things, a tightened grip on Eastern Europe. The United States, on the other hand, came to understand the practical limits on the use of nuclear weapons and to feel a need to match, or at least counter, Soviet strength in conventional weaponry. So the Soviet Union began a quest for nuclear parity and the United States a quest for parity in traditional military might. The two parallel but mutually reinforcing patterns of military competition took hold in the 1940s and characterized the strategic interaction of the United States and the Soviet Union for decades. Both superpowers, for example, undertook rapid demobilization after 1945; both halted the process in the mid- to late 1940s and left in place garrisons far larger than normal for peacetime defense. Both also undertook costly programs to develop nuclear weapons and delivery systems. When the Soviets gained the ability to explode an atom bomb in 1949, the United States proceeded to develop the hydrogen bomb and the Soviets, of course, quickly followed suit. By the early 1950s the military of both had substantial arsenals of nuclear weapons *and* unprecedented conventional forces, despite the fact that they were at peace with each other and faced no other remotely credible threat.

The two superpowers also started in the late 1940s to recruit allies and surrogates and to secure military outposts from which to threaten or defend against each other. The most effective alliance was the North Atlantic Treaty Organization (NATO), founded in 1949 and understood by many as the military accompaniment to the Marshall Plan. The Soviets responded to the Marshall Plan with the Molotov Plan in July 1947, which initiated a series of trade agreements with Eastern Europe and formally proclaimed an economic sphere with the establishment in 1949 of the Council for Mutual Economic Aid (Comecon). This was followed by a military alliance, the Warsaw Pact—signed in 1955 but in practical existence much earlier. During the 1950s the search for allies was extended to the Third World, with special efforts directed at nations just emerging from imperial rule. Even before that, the locus of competition had shifted to Asia. With the triumph of the communist insurgents in China in 1949, the United States and its allies began to fear a broader spread of communist, particularly Soviet, influence. Despite evidence of considerable antipathy between the communists in Moscow and in Beijing, U.S. politicians regarded the "loss of China" as a terrible defeat for the West and a victory for the Soviets. Fear of further losses led the United States to send troops to Korea and begin a huge rearmament in 1950.[11]

The U.S.–Soviet encounter was becoming progressively wider and more hostile, and brought into being military forces of increasingly destructive power. The encounter also became more ideological. Anticommunism had a long history in the United States, but it had been somewhat muted during the war. After the war, politicians and journalists spared no effort to "scare hell" out of the American people, as an influential senator urged, and let loose a flood of anticommunist hysteria. Popular anticommunism was echoed among the literate and respectable. A critical role was played by liberal intellectuals such as Reinhold Niebuhr, Arthur Schlesinger, Jr., and George Kennan, whose famous 1946 dispatch from Moscow sounded the alarm on the Soviet threat and who in 1947, as Mr. X, outlined the strategy of containment with which Americans should respond.[12] This anticommunist liberalism would ultimately become the guiding principle of domestic and international politics. The key moment was the adoption by Truman of the famous National Security Council document NSC 68, which committed the United States to rearmament and resistance to communism around the world. The document was presented to the president in April 1950 and approved in September, during the early stages of the war in Korea. It offered a scary description of a new world marked by "the polarization of power which inescapably confronts the slave society with the free." The Soviet Union, it argued, "is animated by a new fanatic faith, antithetical to our own, and seeks to impose its absolute authority" throughout the world. Soviet goals required "the dynamic extension of their authority and the ultimate elimination of any effective opposition to their authority…. To that end Soviet efforts are now directed toward the domination of the Eurasian land mass." To counter this strategy, the United States must continue to develop both its nuclear and conventional forces. It must also for the moment abandon the hope of a negotiated settlement with the USSR and refuse to renounce the first use of nuclear weapons; it must create a strong alliance system anchored by U.S. power and mobilize an anticommunist consensus at home.[13]

The turn to a more embattled and ideological stance was even more obvious in the Soviet Union. The more open and favorable wartime view of the West had given way by 1947 to an extremely orthodox one. The new rigidity was proclaimed most forcefully by Andrei Zhdanov, who served as Stalin's spokesman in the campaign of moral and ideological rearmament with which the Soviet Union would fight the Cold War.

In response to the Marshall Plan, the Soviets set up the Communist Information Bureau (Cominform), a latter-day version of the once fearsome Comintern. At its founding meeting, Zhdanov declared that the world was divided into "two camps" and called for renewed resistance to Western imperialism. Within the Soviet Union there was a notable intensification of ideological thinking as well. At the end of the war many in the Soviet Union had dared to hope for a more relaxed, "normal" path to socialism, and some had begun to argue for a more moderate view of the West and for a less spartan approach to economic development. By 1947–1948, there were few such hopes or voices. Instead, Stalin and his advisers clamped down on dissent and instituted a ruthless program of economic reconstruction that imposed steep burdens on peasants and workers and sacrificed consumption to heavy industry. Fewer were purged than before the war, but there were still some. Millions more toiled and often died in labor camps. There were, moreover, eerie echoes of the past—with, however, a novel anti-Semitic inflection—in the late-1940s campaign against "cosmopolitanism" and subsequently in the "doctors' plot."[14] Whatever opportunity the victory over fascism might have offered for an easing of Soviet rule or a nonauthoritarian path to socialism was thus quickly foreclosed in the late 1940s. Nor would such a path be left open for the peoples of Eastern Europe.

The logic of Cold War and superpower antagonism was the organizing framework for international relations and for the world economy by the late 1940s and early 1950s. The Cold War simultaneously structured the political settlements that defined the borders and the internal arrangements of states. The political crises through which the Cold War developed were typically occasioned by choices and initiatives that had the effect of coloring in the blank spaces on the world map of 1945. With each local settlement, the Cold War became more institutionalized; and as these local outcomes became clear, so, too, did the shape of the postwar system of states and the set of interests and identities it would recognize, embody, and reflect. The settlements were everywhere and by definition unequal: some nations and ethnic groups got states, others did not; different class balances were reflected and served by various national political systems as well. On balance, the settlements reached in areas dominated by the Soviets would do the greatest violence in national, ethnic, and social terms, but the societies and polities that made up or were dominated by the capitalist West were often less than perfect exemplars of the ideals proclaimed by Western leaders.

## NATIONS AND CLASSES, WINNERS AND LOSERS

46 Wars have often become religious and cultural crusades. This has been particularly true of the twentieth century, for the need for total mobilization has required the elaboration and propagation of a compelling rationale for the enormous sacrifices and disruptions. The war against fascism was no exception, and antifascism came during the war to embody more than just resistance to German, Japanese, and Italian aggression. The critique of fascism developed for that reason into a criticism of its components and corollaries as well: of its elitism and authoritarianism, its racism and anti-Semitism, its antimodernism, and the various other noxious and undemocratic cultural trends with which it was associated. (Its misogyny, it must be admitted, was less marked and scarcely repudiated.) Antifascists came to oppose not only fascism, then, but also kindred outlooks and policies. In the United States, for example, political forces that defined themselves as antifascist had, almost of necessity, to involve themselves in efforts to combat racism. Antifascist discourse also created opportunities for oppressed groups to press their claims. The U.S. example is again appropriate: black activists were able to use the occasion of war against a racist and reactionary enemy to demand elimination of racist hiring policies, which began to be dismantled by the Fair Employment Practices Commission set up in response to a threatened march on Washington. In Britain, the rhetorical opposition between fascism and democracy was likewise transferred to the debate over the future of the empire. Elsewhere, the struggle against German and Japanese occupation gave rise to demands for freedom and democracy, principles whose application could not later easily be restricted. The criticism of fascism as a reactionary and elitist social system was even more subversive, for it served to couple efforts to create democratic political systems with efforts aimed at bringing about social and economic democracy.

Almost as a matter of definition, then, the victory over fascism represented a victory for democracy and its values, for the rights of oppressed races and nationalities, and for social justice. It was assumed that the postwar order would enhance the cause of nations and classes whose rights and claims had previously been ignored or trampled. The logic was clearly understood by, among others, Josip Broz Tito, leader of the Yugoslav partisans:

> Our national-liberation struggle would not be...so successful if the peoples of Yugoslavia did not see in this struggle, today, not only the victory over fascism, but...the victory over those who oppressed and aim to continue oppressing the

peoples of Yugoslavia. The term "national-liberation struggle" would be only a phrase, moreover a deception, if it did not have—in addition to its general Yugoslav sense—a national sense for each separate people, that is, if—in addition to the liberation of Yugoslavia—it did not also mean the liberation of Croats, Slovenes, Serbs, Macedonians, Albanians, Muslims, etc., if the national-liberation struggle did not have the content of liberty, equality, and fraternity for all the peoples of Yugoslavia.[15]

However ironic such an argument may appear in the aftermath of Yugoslavia's bloody collapse, it was believed and acted upon in the 1940s. The war against fascism had a social as well as a national meaning. Wartime political mobilization led almost everywhere to an emboldened working-class presence at the same time that it produced an increased patriotism and consciousness of national identities and interests. The peculiarities of the fascist enemy—as a foe that threatened national and class interests simultaneously—in fact allowed class and national awareness to grow together and in some cases to feed off one another. For the duration of the war, of course, the pursuit of national unity might well take precedence over the redress of social and economic grievances, but the net effect was to infuse the national with the social, ensuring that class issues would emerge with full force soon after the war. Hence, postwar planning typically and rapidly moved from questions of politics to matters of social and economic reform.

Those most active in the resistance against fascism regularly imagined a future marked not only by political freedom but also by social justice. Predictably, the Allied powers envisioned a package of reforms that would make the world more like them, but they were not utterly complacent. Reconstruction, it was understood, would also affect the Allies themselves and move them toward a more expanded definition of the rights of citizenship. The Soviets, for their part, had a somewhat less grand vision; they were more preoccupied with security and with punishing the fascist foe than with fostering revolution. Parties aligned with the Soviets were in fact encouraged during the war, and into 1947, to downplay their interest in social and economic transformation. The aim was to preserve the wartime alliance and the antifascist front and thereby relieve pressure on the Soviet Union. Too much insistence on reform and reconstruction, it was feared, would frighten the "bourgeois" parties and lessen the desire for postwar cooperation between the superpowers. Despite this tactical decision to submerge class beneath national interests, however, the impulse toward social and economic reform was nevertheless greatly strengthened by the politics of war.

Hopes for social reconstruction were bound to be disappointed, for even where the will remained undiminished, inherited structures proved resilient and the resources for building new structures were often not available. Most often, of course, the political consensus on the need for political and social reform broke down as its implications became clearer and as other issues crowded reform from the agenda of high politics. More specifically, it was the Cold War and its complications that transformed postwar politics and distorted local outcomes. In consequence, the postwar settlement would not only fail to satisfy the full variety of national aspirations aroused during the war but also fall far short of the ambitious plans for social restructuring offered in 1945.

The violence done to national aspirations was greatest in Eastern Europe, although its dimensions would not be visible for a very long time. Part of the reason was that the replaced regimes had themselves been largely discredited. Part had to do with the similarity between the map of Eastern Europe drawn at Versailles and the borders imposed in 1945. If the Yugoslav state restored in 1945 was an unworkable amalgam, it was no more so than the prewar Yugoslavia. Indeed, the resistance under Tito could make at least some claim to having bridged the divisions separating the major ethnic groups. Similarly, if Polish nationalists had cause to complain about Soviet encroachments in the East, they were quite happy with the extension of the border to the west into formerly German territory. The postwar transfer of populations and the overwhelming numbers of refugees were, of course, traumatic, but no less so than the forced relocations of wartime—and there was now at least the hope that peoples would be settled in places where ethnic and national grievances would be minimized.

The imposition of Soviet-sponsored rulers in Eastern Europe was also facilitated by the lack of viable alternatives. The prewar regimes of Admiral Miklós Horthy or King Zog or Tsar Boris hardly provided models for postwar democratic rule. Aside from Czechoslovakia, none of the governments holding power in Eastern Europe before the war could credibly be labeled democracies, and the ease with which they fell to, or fell in line with, the Nazis confirmed their obsolescent and undemocratic character. The experience of Nazi occupation and war further undermined established interests and parties, and convinced many Eastern Europeans of the need for a democratic order built upon social-structural reform—upon land reform and the diminution of the power of old elites, a more activist state, and a much enhanced role for labor. Thus the Czech leader Edvard Beneš argued for a genuine "social and economic democracy," and the Hungarian Oscar Jaszi explained that "in Hungary the road is open to really constructive experiments in socialization, since there are very few people there who would shed tears for that hybrid form of capitalism which amassed profits by the ruthless exploitation of monopolistic positions."[16] The fulcrum on which political alignments rested had shifted toward the left: centrist politicians and parties had come to accept the inevitability of structural transformation, the right had been marginalized, and the left now had the backing of the Red Army.

In the rush to reorganize political life, moreover, the left had a considerable advantage. Its participation in the resistance against fascism had allowed, or forced, a higher level of organization; and where resistance forces had been weak, as in Germany, it had the assistance of the Soviets. Walter Ulbricht, the future East German leader, had spent much of the war in Moscow and was flown to Berlin immediately after the war to rebuild the party organization. Parties allied with the Soviets everywhere profited from the connection, and hence came to dominate the coalitions that took power throughout Eastern Europe in 1945.

The domination began subtly enough. The Communists continued to follow the "popular front" program in place since 1935 and reinforced by the coalition politics of wartime. The priority was not socialism but, rather, destruction of the roots and remnants of fascism. The parties themselves were usually led by men—such as Anton Ackerman in Germany, Imry Nagy and László Rajk in Hungary, Wladyslaw Gomulka in Poland, and Rudolf Slánskí in Czechoslovakia, who could be best characterized as "national Communists." What made them "national," and what allowed them later to be vilified as "nationalist" by their Stalinist rivals, was that they had little or no desire to impose the Soviet model upon their own peoples. As Gomulka argued, "Our democracy is not similar to Soviet democracy, just as our society's structure is not the same as the Soviet structure." Instead, they favored cooperation with nonsocialist parties and truly believed in the "popular-front" policies espoused by the Soviets. Nonetheless, they served to secure more or less exclusive political control for the parties tied to the Soviets. The "bourgeois" parties were eliminated from the governing coalitions across Eastern Europe between 1946 and 1948, and others on the left were pressured into merging with the Communists or into new parties, such as the Socialist Unity Party in East Germany (SED), dominated by the Communists. Almost as soon as the Communist monopoly on power was secured, the "national Communists" came under attack within the Cominform. They were soon replaced with a new crop of leaders more supinely loyal to the Soviets and ready to subject their own parties and peoples to "Stalinization." Ulbricht, Boleslaw Bierut, Klement Gottwald, and Mátyás Rakosi all came to power in this way and oversaw a sustained effort to recast their societies in the mold of the Soviet Union. The process—which involved ruthless collectivization along Soviet lines, economic plans that favored heavy industry over consumption, and stern political repression—ended only with Stalin's death in 1953, by which time the new regimes had been thoroughly compromised. Whatever space might have existed within which to chart a path to socialism independent of the Soviet Union and more sensitive to local needs and traditions had long since disappeared. The regimes thus forfeited whatever slight legitimacy they might have retained in the 1940s, and they would never regain it.[17]

The imposition of essentially alien governments and social systems upon the peoples of Eastern Europe meant that, quite irrespective of political boundaries, aspirations for national independence were frustrated. Nor was the postwar settlement in Eastern Europe a model of social justice. Land reform had been followed quickly by brutal collectivization; workers' immediate interests had been sacrificed to the development of heavy industry; and Soviet economic exactions had further deprived these nations of physical resources vital for national development. The middle classes and professionals, decimated by the experience of war, remained politically suspect and under pressure, and their places in the bureaucracy and in management were routinely taken over by party members. The party would become what Milovan Djilas later called "the new class," and the new states and societies would be run by what would subsequently be labeled the *nomenklatura*. The new regimes would suffer repeated setbacks and repudiations from those they sought to rule, but genuine reform would prove impossible. In this sense and in this area the postwar settlement never took, never established itself firmly, and would prove incapable of reproducing itself.

Questions of national identity, legitimacy, and power were even more at issue in lands still, or recently, under the control of Western imperialism. The Cold War, however, would have a distorting effect on the process by which nations gained national independence. Accordingly, progress was more rapid prior to 1950, by which time the growing antagonisms of the Cold War had crystallized into a bipolar and highly-militarized international system. At the end of the war many observers had foreseen the end of empire. The logic of antifascism, when applied to relations between colonizer and colonized, led clearly to the conclusion that imperialism was unjust. The United States traditionally defined itself as an essentially anti-imperial power; likewise, ever since Lenin's denunciations of the imperialist aims of the West during and after the First World War, the Soviet Union was committed to independence for colonial peoples. The influence of both nations, together with the shift in thinking about imperial rule, seemed likely to produce a rapid withdrawal from empire. The efforts of local nationalists tended in the same direction, and where they were well organized and/or well armed or where imperial authority had been displaced, independence became a very real and enticing prospect.

The imperial powers themselves came reluctantly to accept that metropolitan rule could not be maintained everywhere and in its prewar form. The British, for example, had conceded during the war the eventual independence of India and Burma and the end of the mandate in Palestine. The coming to power of a Labour government in 1945 meant that these promises would be kept, even if the development after that of ethnic/religious/national antagonisms vastly complicated the process. In India, it was the growing antipathy between Hindus and Muslims, itself partly a reaction to the divisive policies of the colonial regime, that overwhelmed the plans for a smooth transition to a independent and unitary state and led to the partition of the subcontinent into India and Pakistan. The breakdown of political unity in Burma stemmed from antipathies between urban and rural populations, between Christians and Buddhists, and between different ethnic groups. Exacerbating the situation, again, was the legacy of hatred and jealousy stemming from the British practice of using Christianized ethnic groups (like the Karens in Burma) to staff the colonial state. In Palestine, of course, it was the contest between Jews and Arabs over who ultimately could lay claim to the land of Israel (or Palestine) that made the actual granting of independence so traumatic. Nevertheless, the anti-imperial thrust generated by the war against fascism ensured that political fragmentation in the colonies and even the prospect of violent disorder did not prevent, or much delay, the end of imperial control. The process would leave a legacy of bitterness and instability, but it is by no means obvious that a more prolonged transition would have produced better results.

France and Holland proved less willing to free their colonies. No doubt some of their reluctance stemmed from the wounds inflicted on national pride by Nazi conquest and occupation. De Gaulle, for instance, was keen to restore the glory of the French nation and unwilling to give up control in either Indochina or Syria/Lebanon. Faced with the British decision to get out of Palestine, the French had to relinquish their foothold in the Middle East. But in Indochina they held firm and waged a bitter war against the Viet Minh. The Dutch were also determined to restore imperial control over the independent republic proclaimed under Japanese auspices and launched "police actions" to that effect in 1947 and 1948. They sought as well to weaken the nationalists, led by Sukarno, by setting up a federal system across the archipelago and by encouraging localist and separatist allegiances. At the Round Table Conference of 1949, however, the Dutch came to terms with the insurgents and granted independence. Within a year, the federal system had been replaced by a unitary state, though the underlying antagonisms between groups and regions persisted.

Between the ending of Dutch authority in Indonesia and 1954, when the French and Vietnamese joined the great powers for negotiations at Geneva, the Cold War had become much more thoroughly institutionalized. The Communist victory in China and the subsequent Korean conflict, moreover, had guaranteed that the process of decolonization would henceforth be closely bound up with Cold War rivalries. The compromise over Indochina embodied in the Geneva Accords was therefore far less satisfactory: it divided the nation into North and South, and allowed Ho Chi Minh's opponents the opportunity to regroup in the South in a new state receiving extensive support from the United States. The creation of rival and antagonistic states made further war nearly inevitable. Moreover, the bitterness with which the French left Indochina made them reluctant to grant independence elsewhere. The subsequent struggle over Algeria became very nasty and produced a constitutional crisis within France itself.

After 1950, in fact, decolonization tended to become more unpleasant and controversial everywhere. Nations that had failed to gain independence in the immediate aftermath of the Second World War would find doing so very difficult. Assertions of independence from the west would be interpreted in Washington or London as a victory for the Soviets; while Soviet support for liberation movements invariably meant that they would not be welcomed. African nations, where nationalist movements had made less progress during the war and where European rule was less damaged by the war, saw genuine independence delayed for at least a decade. By the 1950s the United States could no longer be considered an anti-imperial power.[18] It was by no means converted to the virtues of empire but had set itself firmly against the national liberation struggles that sought to end imperial domination. The United States had also come to oppose more forcefully than ever before the movements and politicians in Latin America who resented domination by U.S.-based corporations and who therefore opted for nationalist and populist programs of land reform and state-sponsored economic development.

The postwar international system thus did not constitute a very fertile terrain for the formation of independent national states and for the growth and consolidation of national identities in the so-called Third World. Half a century or more of Western imperialism had created political entities whose boundaries seldom coincided with ethnic, religious, or linguistic divisions. Imperial rule had, moreover, regularly proceeded by privileging one native community over others and by accentuating local differences. And the cultural challenge posed by Western imperialism had provoked a revitalization, in some instances indeed the creation, of religious, ethnic, and linguistic identities whose strengthening would later threaten the ability of postindependence states to construct stable national political cultures and viable political orders. The emergence of a world system organized around the antinomies of the Cold War made decolonization more difficult and more violent. Throughout the less developed world, then, political regimes emerged and stayed in power despite major problems of legitimacy. Such states were prone to corruption, frequent coups, and periods of military rule, and could do little to address social and economic needs. Neither national aspirations nor the most elementary requirements of social justice would be met for a very long time.

A quite different array of national and social issues confronted the capitalist democracies of Western Europe and North America. On balance, these were less serious and for the most part better handled. Still, the contests they engendered were not without drama or consequence. In the United States, for example, the war had produced a surge of patriotism and pride in the nation's ability to outproduce and outfight the fascist powers and hence in the superiority of its social and political institutions.[19] This sense of confidence, which was not without a certain justification, underpinned the U.S. pretension to world leadership. But Americans differed among themselves on what it was that made their way of life a model and on the extent to which their politics and society were in need of reform. Mobilization for war had allowed the New Deal innovations to be consolidated and a new institutional framework for the representation of interests and the relationship between state and society to take root. But absent the pressures of war, the normal pattern of partisan struggle resumed and opponents of the New Deal gained control of both houses of Congress in 1946. At precisely the moment when the critical decisions about the shape of the postwar order were being made, government was gripped by intensified political conflict. The new balance guaranteed that the key initiatives in foreign policy would have to be essentially bipartisan. More specifically, aid to rebuild the world economy would have to be sold to Congress not on its own terms, not as part of the creation of a multilateral trading system—which was, in fact, opposed by many interests in the United States—but as part of the struggle against communism. Increasingly, then, the basis of unity between contending forces in U.S. politics was anticommunism.

Anticommunism would become, in fact, the fundamental premise of the nation's political culture. It would inform discourses as varied as those of pedagogy, gender and sexuality, popular film and literature, and social science.[20] In the process, anticommunism itself would be transformed. Before 1940 it had been a narrowly sectarian creed, espoused by the most conservative elements and intermingled with racism, anti-Semitism, and fierce antipathy to the New Deal and the labor movement. The late 1940s, by contrast, saw the emergence of a liberal anticommunism or, perhaps more appropriately, anticommunist liberalism. It was a perspective that criticized the Soviet Union for its totalitarianism and that mixed resistance to socialism with support for the policies and philosophy of the New Deal.

President Truman himself defined and embodied the new, hybrid outlook.[21] Throughout 1947, in fact, he had been groping toward a successful politics by moving simultaneously to the right and to the left. The Truman Doctrine and the loyalty program had signaled a turn to the right; the Marshall Plan, unveiled shortly after, displayed a nobler vision more in keeping with the spirit of the New Deal. In November 1947, Clark Clifford, Truman's strategist and confidante, sized up the president's election prospects and urged continued emphasis upon anticommunism; he foresaw "considerable political advantage to the Administration in its battle with the Kremlin." Antipathy to communism was not a sufficient political program, however. To rally the diverse constituencies necessary for victory, Truman required a more popular appeal and a more positive message. Both could be achieved by proposing reformist initiatives—on housing, taxes, health care, and civil rights—that the Republican Congress could be counted on to reject. The effect would be to reemphasize Truman's links with Roosevelt's legacy and to garner support for his own "Fair Deal," the program upon which the president fought the election of 1948.[22]

Probably the key to Truman's surprise victory in 1948 was the support of labor. Unions had come out of the war far stronger than before, and in the 1940s organized labor was an essential element of the Democratic coalition. The unions were unwilling to allow business to reestablish the managerial perquisites that had been routine before the war. Rights wrested from management so very recently were not going to be given up without a fight. The result was a series of bitter strikes, the most famous of which was the hundred-day confrontation between General Motors and the United Auto Workers in 1946. Most such conflicts in 1946–1947 were negotiated, and the deals struck were unusually favorable for labor. Employers made concessions for the short term, however, and sought redress over the long term by turning against the Democrats and waging a campaign to overturn the New Deal labor legislation, which they believed ceded too much ground to the unions.

Two critical battles were fought in Capitol Hill in 1946–1947. One was over a full employment bill passed by the Senate in 1945 but greatly watered down before being approved as the Employment Act by the full Congress in 1946. The second was over the Taft-Hartley bill, which substantially narrowed union rights and which became law over Truman's veto.[23] The offensive of business made the unions eager for a more formal alliance with the Democrats and for Truman's reelection.[24] The effort at coalition building was greatly facilitated by the purging of Communists from the trade unions, a process begun just after the war and effectively completed by 1949.[25] Truman's adoption of a more populist program helped as well, so that in the 1948 election—fought largely on class issues—working-class support for the president overcame the ordinarily decisive preference of middle-class voters for the Republicans and provided the margin of victory for the Democrats.

Truman's win ensured that there would be no "return to normalcy" akin to what had happened in the 1920s and that in the postwar settlement labor would have a much more prominent place than it had before the war.[26] It meant, too, that the gains made by organized workers during the New Deal and the war would be retained and that unions, though relatively tame by European standards, would be allowed to bargain for a reasonable share of whatever wealth the postwar economic order could generate. But the augmentation of union strength did not imply a corresponding diminution of employer clout, for U.S. business was bigger, more profitable, and more politically sophisticated than ever. It was also better organized and had succeeded in forging alliances with agricultural interests, the Republican Party, and southern Democrats against efforts to use the federal government as an instrument of social and economic reform.[27]

The new balance of organized interests effectively set the boundaries for political discourse and policy innovation in the postwar period. It produced a systemic bias toward compromise and stasis, reflected in the peculiarly noninterventionist brand of Keynesianism that came to be practiced in the United States and in the failure of efforts to create a welfare state.

The system has attracted the labels "corporate liberalism" or simply "corporatism" because of its privileging of organized interests and of business. It was in this respect a more business-oriented arrangement than the "social-democratic" or "social Keynesian" settlements that are said to have characterized European politics after the war. Probably none of these labels does justice to the nuances that distinguished the political outcomes across Western Europe and North America, but they constitute not unreasonable approximations.

The outlines of the U.S. postwar settlement were clear by late 1948, but it would take until the early 1950s for the arrangements to become firmly fixed. The reconciliation of the interests that faced off against one another so bitterly in the 1940s was greatly facilitated by the Korean War. The postwar boom had peaked in November 1948 and the economy faltered in 1949. Unemployment remained uncomfortably high well into 1950. The Korean War changed that, however, and instead stimulated a prosperity that ameliorated the tense relations between workers and employers and postponed indefinitely a potentially very divisive battle over planning, deficit spending, or other actions that the government might have turned to in an effort to create jobs. Rearmament eventuated in a level of military spending that gave a sustained boost to aggregate demand in the United States and elsewhere.[28] The war also provided an opportunity to reshape the institutions of government. The highly militarized "National Security" state that emerged was well organized for developing and producing weapons but far less adept at guiding the economy or delivering social services. Most important, it permitted numerous lucrative arrangements between the public and private sectors and became not so much a pork barrel as a collection of protected niches and fiefdoms, each part of which simultaneously linked key interests and constituencies with government largesse and tied them to the government's overall strategic orientation.[29]

The Korean War would also put an end to uncertainties about the shape of postwar politics in Europe, and again the main outlines were clear by 1948–1949. The compromises struck in Britain, France, and Italy were not wholly dissimilar to that reached in the United States.[30] The main complicating factor was the tremendous variation in the sense of national identity with which these countries emerged from the war. In Britain, where national identity had escaped challenge and had even been strengthened, politics was less troubled and thus more stable, a better environment for working out social and economic conflicts. In France and Italy, where defeat and occupation left a legacy of recrimination and where pre-

56

war interests and parties were fatally compromised by association with a discredited past, politics was far less stable, and the settlement bargained out in the late 1940s would be less effective in resolving social questions. To take the most obvious example, reconstruction was undertaken in Britain by the Labour Party, elected in 1945, whose participation in the wartime coalition gave it a large share in the victory over fascism. For the first time, therefore, Labour could pose legitimately as a national party. Inevitably, Labour's understanding of the "national interest" differed considerably from the Tories'. Labour was deeply committed to a program of reform designed to guarantee workers and their families effective social and economic citizenship and therby create a genuinely national community. The Conservatives envisioned a community held together by a combination of patriotism and deference made slightly more tolerable by measures of paternalistic social reform. Labour's view of the world was also more democratic than the Tories'. It viewed the empire, naively perhaps, as a vehicle for shared progress and was much more willing to contemplate real political independence for at least some colonial peoples.

Precisely because the war had not damaged the British sense of "national identity," it was possible for Labour to undertake both an extensive program of social reform and the first, critical steps toward decolonization without provoking a major challenge to the legitimacy or stability of the state.[31] The radicalism of the Labour government should not, of course, be exaggerated: its domestic innovations were all adumbrated in the debate on reform and reconstruction that flourished during the war, and in foreign policy it pursued a vision of the national interest that was quite traditional. Foreign Secretary Ernest Bevin, who shared the basic assumptions of the Foreign Office mandarins whose work he directed, was an early convert to the Cold War, and served as an architect of both the Marshall Plan and NATO.[32] Nevertheless, the outcome of the postwar settlement in Britain was an extremely stable political order in which the major organized interests, business and labor especially, had a stake and a voice. In retrospect, scholars and politicians would look back on the postwar settlement and say that it gave too much clout to organized interests, that it was too "corporatist," and that it overburdened the state with commitments it could not fulfill. But the system held for nearly a quarter century, ensured social peace, and allowed, if it did not positively foster, sustained economic growth and rising living standards.

The outcomes were less happy elsewhere in Europe. Technically, France came out of the war victorious and Italy vanquished, but in each country the recent past weighed heavily on postwar politics and effectively foreclosed options that in an ideal world might have served national and class interests better. French politics, for example, would have been less troubled through the 1950s and early 1960s had there been a clear break from the imperial past. Italy was not allowed the choice of whether to keep its imperial possessions, so at least that issue was removed from political contention. In Italy, however, the taint of fascism precluded rational and centrally coordinated state planning for economic growth and produced, instead, not a genuinely laissez-faire political economy but a system of regional party fiefdoms characterized by corruption and clientelism.

What most distinguished the French and Italian settlements was the marginalization of the working class. Communist leadership of the resistance had left the local parties strong in both countries; under Moscow's guidance, the PCI and the PCF had renounced social revolution at the liberation and chosen to maintain the "popular front" of wartime and to participate in the coalition governments set up just after the war. As Cold War tensions increased, such arrangements became anomalous. In particular, the Communists were unwilling to acquiesce in the austerity policies that came to be seen as essential to economic stabilization. Nor were they eager to embrace the alternative, which was continued reliance upon U.S. aid and hence policies more acceptable to the United States. The break came in the spring of 1947, when the Communists were forced out of the governing coalitions in both nations. This was followed quickly by the Communists' public opposition to the Marshall Plan, which further isolated the two parties and sealed their oppositional status. The elections of 1948 in Italy and of 1951 in France confirmed the rough balance of party strength: the Communists remained the dominant working-class parties but were unable to attract support among other social groups. The "bourgeois" parties were left to cobble together a series of coalition governments, none of which was terribly strong, effective, or long-lived.

Beneath the apparent instability of politics were coherent and consistent patterns of influence and policy making. In Italy, this derived from the political preponderance of Christian Democracy. In France, the analogous party—the Mouvement républicain populaire (MRP)—played an stabilizing, important role just after the war but was soon overtaken by the Gaullists.[33] Absent a dominant party, the institutions of the state undertook direction of public policy in France. In the two nations, hence, there developed a visible disjuncture between political institutions, parties, interests, and policies. In particular, working-class interests were seriously unrepresented and workers' needs were not addressed. Unions, for example, were kept at a distance by management and throughout the early postwar era social inequality was undiminished. The ensuing French and Italian "economic miracles" would be sustained by demand generated elsewhere, not domestically. Questions of welfare remained hidden in the underdeveloped countryside or were addressed by the state's paternalistic social policies or outright patronage. The forms of politics in both countries were thoroughly democratic, but politics lacked substance and social meaning. Again, the Cold War was critical, for it was the bipolar international system that froze in place systems of representation that served French and Italian society so poorly.

The Cold War had an even more decisive impact on Germany and Japan. At war's end it seemed that whatever the precise character of the postwar order, German and Japanese national identities would be challenged and transformed. The Allies agreed that the political cultures of Germany and Japan had been premised on definitions of national character and self-interest that could not be permitted to persist. There was consensus, too, that these political cultures were socially rooted, which made imperative fundamental reforms in the structure of industry, agriculture, and the organs of the state. This shared opinion did not survive the onset of the Cold War. The reason was simple: genuine social and political transformation in either nation would be economically disruptive. It would be easy enough to dislodge the old elites in business and agriculture and to remove them from the bureaucracy or judiciary, but replacing them would delay economic revival and require time and money. The United States was the only source of funds for relief and reconstruction in 1945 and the demands upon its largesse were considerable. Very quickly, policy makers in Washington became convinced that relief should be tied to policies designed to revive the world economy and return most nations to self-sufficiency, a conviction intensified by fear of, and antipathy, toward the Soviet Union. Continued distress, U.S. leaders came to believe, would permit the spread of communist influence, especially in Western Europe. The result was a decision not only to provide aid for economic recovery in the form of the Marshall Plan but to scale back efforts to transform Germany and Japan in favor of policies designed to allow their industries to recover.

This reversal of policy was effected during 1947–1948.[34] Highly controversial, it prevailed because the absence of superpower cooperation made the alternatives unworkable. Several aspects merit comment. First, the denazification and reeducation policies pursued during the early postwar years did make a difference. The authoritarian, fascist, and militarist elements in German and Japanese political life were truly discredited. Even if many individuals with tainted pasts continued to hold office or power within industry or regained such positions after a brief retirement, they did so on different terms and within a vastly different context. Fascism as an ideology and political program had been defeated and would not reemerge, and the political cultures of postwar Germany and Japan were marked by a profound distrust of militarism. Structural change, too, had made real progress before the "reverse course" was adopted. The landed classes had lost control over agriculture and over those who worked the land. Less effective were efforts to break up industrial monopolies, for in industry the argument for revival and efficiency was more pressing. The right of workers to organize and bargain with employers was nevertheless quite firmly established. Unions, in consequence, were far better organized and more regularly consulted in Germany and Japan than in France or Italy.

The fact that the political systems set up in Germany and Japan were so closely locked into the very structure of Cold War alignments meant that they were unusually stable. The most steady, if not immobile, arrangements were established in what became the German Democratic Republic. Soviet domination would be effectively unchallenged until the Soviet Union itself decided to loosen its grip some forty years later. In West Germany and Japan, democratic forms coexisted with stable, one-party governments. The Christian Democrats in Germany and the Liberals in Japan quickly became identified as bearers of the national interest. The two parties were sufficiently antifascist to be credible to the outside world, but both were very "safe." During the late 1940s the Christian Democrats shed whatever residue of concern for social welfare they may have inherited from the interwar years and became the party of the "social market economy." The Liberals did not even require such a conversion. Neither party was, in fact, fully committed to the laissez-faire vision so dear to American ideologues and proponents of the market, but their rhetorical commitments made them acceptable to the United States. The two center-right parties were thus better positioned than any of their opponents, most of whom had deeper commitments to social reform, to deal with the United States and its Western allies in the effort to bring the defeated countries back into the "community of nations." Even so, national sovereignty would be compromised to the extent that the reintegration would be mediated. Both nations would be firmly tied into an alliance dominated by the United States, and both would be encouraged to develop as regionally dominant economic powers. Aspirations to hegemony would be replaced, then, by sincere if transparently self-interested efforts at regional coordination.

It is commonplace to argue that Germany and Japan, defeated in war, nevertheless emerged victorious in the peace. The assertion is at least partially true. Neither nation was forced to suffer as their victims had. Both were brought back into the international economy quickly and on relatively favorable terms. Germany was, of course, divided, and Japan stripped of its overseas possessions, but both West Germany and Japan were readmitted into the international system as close allies of the United States and were able to profit from its "military Keynesianism" while avoiding the cost of their own defense. East Germany inevitably did not fare as well in its attachment to a far less developed and prosperous bloc, and its interests were regularly subordinated to those of the bloc and to its dominant power.

The structural reforms aimed at making the German and Japanese societies democratic, though never fully implemented, may also be counted a plus, for they forced the development of institutions that were more suited to modern industrial society and that provided relative social peace and political stability. The institutional frameworks evolved in postwar West Germany and Japan seem to have been particularly helpful in generating economic growth. East Germany, by contrast, was roughly treated under the Soviet occupation, and the system imposed on it would prove far less adaptable and far less productive.[35] Still, East Germany was and remained to the end the most prosperous and developed country in the Soviet bloc.

The political and social arrangements worked out after the war were, then, extremely varied. What was common was that in almost every country domestic politics was closely linked to international politics or, to be more precise, to where each nation fit in the bipolar Cold War system of states. Bipolarity was never absolute or complete, local contexts and histories never without impact on political outcomes. But the rivalry and antipathy between the superpowers had been projected onto a world scale by the early 1950s and all national regimes were thenceforth located within the field of force—which was simultaneously ideological, economic, and military—created by the confrontation. The system was not static: the intensity of antagonism between the superpowers would vary; some states would move from one camp to another, although such movement was not easy; with the revival of Europe and Japan and the spread of decolonization there was at least the potential for the emergence of one or another "third force" or "nonaligned" grouping; and there were clear limits to the writ of the superpowers, as the United States found in Vietnam and the Soviets learned in Afghanistan. All in all, however, the system proved remarkably stable and retained its shape and force for forty years.

# American Power, 3 American Dreams

The contours of the postwar settlement were firmly and visibly set by the early 1950s. But contemporaries had as yet little basis for believing that the Cold War international order would function or persist. Few would have dared predict that it would produce not war but a prolonged era of *relative* peace between the superpowers and their major allies. Nor was there any reason to imagine that the capitalist democracies stood at the beginning of an era of unprecedented economic growth. And only the most naive could be confident that the political bargains and systems of representation worked out in the East and the West would come to be recognized as legitimate and thus endure. Indeed, peace between the superpowers and the resumption of growth proved easier to achieve than political stability. The domestic arrangements in Eastern Europe, for example, persisted for four decades but never acquired genuine legitimacy; and throughout the less developed world, political transformation was the norm rather than the exception. Only in the prosperous West did legitimate political systems take root, and there were notable exceptions even there.

Nevertheless, the world order established in the shadow of the Cold War did last. Central to that achievement was the United States, which played a predominant role in shaping the postwar settlement. The settlement itself accorded that nation a hegemonic position. That status was contested, and locally checked, by the Soviet Union, but the Soviet Union never came close to wielding the clout of its superpower rival. As anchor to the world order, the United States ensured its stability and its routine workings. The United States could not have done that, however, without prosperity and political stability. Nor could the international order have functioned effectively if the antagonisms of the Cold War had produced major armed confrontation between the two powers. Somehow, then, Americans had to engineer economic growth, rework the intense and highly ideological politics of the late 1940s and early 1950s into a more inclusive and less fractured political culture, and manage the international tensions of the Cold War. There were grounds for worrying about each of these issues in the early 1950s and no blueprint for resolving them. The three challenges were nevertheless met, and the United States kept the postwar settlement intact and prosperous for nearly a quarter of a century.

## FROM STAGNATION TO AFFLUENCE

When Keynes and his fellow economists debated the causes of the interwar slump, they argued about equilibrium, stability, and the full, or less than full, utilization of labor and capital. The term "growth" was not typically a part of their vocabulary or their conceptual framework. Growth would result implicitly from the fuller utilization of resources, but the notion that steady growth could become the norm in capitalist economies was foreign to the thinking of the generation of economists and policy makers who came to maturity when the world economy was trapped in a prolonged crisis. Not surprisingly, the prescriptions for economic management that emerged from the economists' arguments focused not upon growth but upon overcoming business cycles and maintaining a high and stable level of employment. The experience of the 1930s, when unemployment averaged more than 18 percent, made American economists particularly worried about the apparent long-term tendency for the nation's economy to stagnate. Only gradually, as economic growth erased fears of a sustained slump, did they turn their attention from cycles to growth and build into their assumptions the premise of continued advance.[1]

Coexisting with the fretful view of the professional economists was a more optimistic popular political economy of abundance. Americans were justly proud of their prodigious wartime feats of production and of the nation's obvious leadership in technology and business organization of the United States. To many, this record suggested a postwar era of progress and plenty. Even cynical European commentators were swept up in admiration of the U.S. economy: "There never was a country more fabulous than America," declared a British observer in the late 1940s. "She sits bestride the world like a Colossus.... Half of the wealth of the world, more than half of productivity, nearly two-thirds of the world machines are concentrated in American hands; the rest of the world lies in the shadow of American industry."[2] Rhetorical assertions about a dawning "American century" were based upon the same perceptions. It was widely assumed in the 1940s and early 1950s that U.S. industry was more productive and efficient than industry elsewhere. Under the Marshall Plan, for example, delegations of businessmen and trade unionists from around the world were brought to American manufacturing centers to learn the secrets of mass production.[3]

It was perhaps naive to think that the conditions that facilitated development in the United States could be simply and rapidly recreated on foreign soil. What was not naive, but in fact quite accurate, was the intuitive understanding on which such claims and programs were founded. The popular intuition was correct in recognizing that several distinctive features of the society had come together to create a uniquely favorable environment for growth in the third quarter of the twentieth century. The "American model," if not universally applicable, nevertheless worked extremely well in its native habitat and was not incorrectly seen as a system—a set of social and economic structures, cultural traits, technological capabilities, and public policies—capable of generating sustained economic progress.

What were the features of this system? How did it work? Why did it prove to be so much more productive than the professional economists had anticipated? Surely, the most obvious characteristic of the economy was high wages. The United States was historically a high-wage country: labor shortages in the early stages of industrialization set the pattern, which continued even after mass migrations from southern and eastern Europe began in the late nineteenth century. Higher wages meant more capital per worker and hence higher productivity. The result was a higher standard of living and the earlier development of mass consumption. But the interwar slump put a brake on the growth of consumption and prevented the full emergence of a new "structure of demand" appropriate for mass-produced consumer goods until after 1945.[4] Between 1939 and 1950, however, wages increased dramatically and allowed labor's share of national income to grow significantly. During the war progressive taxation effected a further redistribution of income away from the rich and toward the lower and middle classes. Thus, the share of income going to the top 20 percent of American families declined from nearly 52 percent in 1935–1936 to under 45 percent in 1951, and the portion going to the middle 60 percent went from 44 percent to just over half.[5] The consequence was that by the early 1950s ordinary people—manual workers and those more often considered members of the lower middle class—were in a position to consume far more of the goods and services produced by industry than ever before. They also spent on a different mix than before: less on textiles and clothing, utilities, rent, and basic foodstuffs; more on processed foods, appliances, medical care, recreation, and automobiles. Much of what they bought was not of the highest quality but inexpensive and mass-produced. Still, workers' standard of living was better than it had ever been.

The high wages that gave the postwar economy a permanently higher level of internal demand continued to rise with increases in productivity throughout the 1950s. Unions were critical in this process. They had come out of the war stronger than at any time in their history. Labor in all of the major mass-production industries was now well organized and unions began to make headway in the service sector as well, especially among public employees, and even in the South. The unions also pressed an agenda of far-reaching social reform that, if implemented, would have created something like a Beveridge-style welfare state. They met with indifferent success in the late 1940s. The effort to organize the South, "Operation Dixie," failed utterly. The Republican Congress elected in 1946 proved unresponsive to all schemes of reform and was eager instead to tame the unions through the Taft-Hartley bill. But labor did hold onto the organizational gains it had made under the New Deal and during wartime, and managed to win through collective bargaining much of what it could not win from the state. The great symbolic breakthrough was the bargain struck between General Motors and the United Auto Workers (UAW). In 1948 the automaker offered an agreement containing a cost-of-living adjustment (COLA) and an "annual improvement factor" of 2 percent. Initially skeptical, the union accepted the deal and improved it substantially two years later. The 1950 "Treaty of Detroit," as it was called, was a five-year agreement that provided more generous allowances for cost-of-living, better annual increments, and modest pensions.[6]

The gains secured by auto workers were replicated by workers in other unionized industries. The advances, some have argued, were made at the cost of loss of control over the work process, deterioration in working conditions, and—because these losses would surely have been resisted by an active and enfranchised rank and file—the "bureaucratization" of the unions themselves.[7] The evidence seems to suggest, however, that whatever the fate of union democracy, always a fragile plant, workers represented by strong unions obtained not only higher wages but also greater protection of shop-floor rights and at least some mechanisms and prospects for redressing workplace grievances. What made these genuine advances possible was the unique, if ultimately impermanent, advantages enjoyed by American companies in the world market. Even before 1939 business in the United States had pioneered in mass-production techniques in the newer, consumer-goods industries such as cars, electrical goods, home appliances, and processed foods. The worldwide depression of the 1930s had deprived these industries of markets and limited their growth,[8] but by the late 1940s a new structure of demand allowed for a more sustained expansion. Companies like General Motors, which already had in place both the latest technologies and the organizational capacity to tap into the expanded market, could sell just about everything they produced. They faced little or no competition from abroad and were left virtually alone to exploit the burgeoning consuming potential. All this made it possible for business and labor to mute their historic antagonisms and share in the productivity of the expanding economy. Even if the shares were unequal, workers took to the prospect of secure jobs and steadily rising incomes with enthusiasm. For unionized workers, the 1950s were a period of unprecedented material consumption.

The unusual convergence of the interests of organized workers and big business was, then, a defining characteristic of the postwar political economy of the United States. It was specific, of course, to a particular moment of technological development. It would not have been possible in an earlier period, when profits had depended upon the use of a mass of unskilled and underpaid labor to produce cheap, inferior products intended largely for export—which is one way of describing the British economy of the nineteenth century. Nor would it have worked in an era like the present, when the market for mass-produced goods is relatively sated and growth centers instead on high-quality products produced by highly skilled and flexible workers and aimed at highly differentiated markets populated by sophisticated consumers. The capital-labor postwar compromise was thus predicated upon the triumph of what has been called the Fordist model of mass production.[9] The Fordist model was marked by a high level of demand for goods of medium quality that could be produced by semi-skilled workers whose efforts would be coordinated according to the logic of the assembly line and harnessed by extremely large companies whose power in the marketplace accorded them substantial control over the shape of consumer demand. The relatively high wages paid to workers in these industries in fact directly fed into the demand for the products of Fordist mass production.[10] It was a virtuous circle of production and consumption that fueled economic growth for a quarter of a century: from 1947 to 1972, the U.S. economy grew at an average annual rate of 3.7 percent; real per capita income grew by 2.3 percent annually; and consumer spending climbed to new heights every single year.[11]

There were, of course, limits to the success of the Fordist model, but they were easy to overlook in the prosperity that suffused American life in the 1950s and 1960s. The most important exception was the large number of workers who did not work for big firms and were not organized. Precisely because unionized workers did earn high wages, were provided with reasonably good health and retirement benefits, and enjoyed the right to bargain, employers were often reluctant to hire new workers. Instead, they increasingly resorted to subcontracting, farming out important portions of the production process to firms where workers were less well paid and less well organized. Other employers moved to nonunion locales in the South and the West. Gradually the U.S. economy came to be divided into firms and industries that offered good jobs with high wages, extensive benefits, and union protection, and firms and industries that did not. Workers in the former category experienced the postwar era as a time of growing affluence; workers outside these protected niches—in what has been dubbed the secondary labor market—saw little improvement and far less to praise in the growth record of the new system. Often, these distinct labor markets were populated by different kinds of workers: white males largely in the protected sector; women, blacks, and Hispanics disproportionately in the less favored jobs.[12]

Racial and sexual inequality were in this sense virtually built into the structure of the economy, or at least the labor market. Still, the line that separated good from bad jobs was not fixed. It moved with the changing frontier of unionization to include or exclude various groups. Indeed, the bulk of the workers who after the war benefited from the bargaining power and job protection of the unions had themselves been quite unprotected before 1935 and the heroic wave of organization that followed the Wagner Act (National Labor Relations Act). They were the immigrants and children of immigrants of an earlier era who, prior to unionization, occupied the lowest positions in the labor market.[13] But they managed to use the favorable political and legal environment of the New Deal and war mobilization to create the United Auto Workers, the Steel Workers, the United Mine Workers, and other industrial unions and thereby wrest from management the wages and benefits, as well as the seniority and procedural rights, that so greatly improved their conditions. The bulk of mass-production workers in the United States had been enrolled in unions by 1945. Organizing slowed markedly after the war, partly because of the changed political climate but largely due to the inhospitable terrain on which further gains had to be won. It proved especially difficult for workers in smaller firms, less advanced industries, and the service sector to build comparably powerful unions. Because a defining feature of their jobs was impermanence and irregularity, they often lacked the resources and security needed for stable organization. The fact that so many of these workers were women and minorities made it still harder to achieve the status and recognition previously won by the mostly white and predominantly male workers who were organized in the major industrial unions.

The mix of jobs on offer in the postwar economy was thus less than ideal, and it appears that as the economy grew, more bad jobs were added than good ones. As a result, few of the most recent entrants into the urban labor force got the jobs they wanted. Genuine opportunities for upward mobility, especially from unskilled to semiskilled or skilled jobs or from blue-collar to white-collar jobs, were often limited as well. The blacks who moved from the rural South to the industrial North—a million and a half during the 1940s, slightly more in the following decade—were particularly affected.[14] Employment prospects for women also grew less than the growth of the economy might have implied. The number of clerical and sales positions increased dramatically, of course, and these were largely filled by women, but openings were fewer in the better-paid manufacturing industries and fewer still in professional occupations other than the traditional ones such as nursing, teaching, and social work. The gap between the expansion of the economy overall and the lack of progress for minorities and women would eventually give rise to protests and demands for redress. In the early postwar era, however, it was the phenomenon of growth, not its limitations, that dominated public discourse on the nation's economic life.

Despite the obvious strength of the forces promoting steady economic growth, what some have called the underlying "social structure of accumulation," the economists who worried over the likelihood of a postwar slump had not been entirely misguided. Throughout the late 1940s and 1950s growth was strong enough but fitful and uneven. Private investment was too weak to sustain a consistently high level of employment and regularly had to be supplemented by government spending in order to maintain the upward curve of production. After 1951, when the Federal Reserve secured its independence from the executive, monetary policy was restrictive and the Eisenhower administration was reluctant to use the Keynesian tools of demand management to stimulate the economy.[15] In this context, the unprecedentedly high levels of peacetime military spending proved essential. The recession of 1948–1949 was overcome by rearmament and defense spending connected with the Korean War; the ending of the Korean War coincided with another downturn in late 1953 and early 1954, followed by a rather anemic recovery that was aided significantly by another increase in military spending during 1957–1958. According to at least one authority, the economic record through 1957 indicated that military demand had been "the major and almost exclusive dynamic growth factor in recent years."[16] The recovery that began in mid-1958 failed to restore investment to its 1957 level and left unemployment above 5 percent in mid-1960.

More rapid growth came in the 1960s. The election of John F. Kennedy put in office a party and advisers more committed to using government to stimulate the economy. Tax cuts were implemented by Kennedy and his successor, Lyndon Johnson, in 1962 and 1964, as was a special investment tax credit, and an important new round of trade negotiations was begun. The Kennedy and Johnson administrations also pushed up military spending by 15 percent between 1960 and 1962 and raised expenditures on the space program from $400 million in 1960 to $5 billion in 1965. Military spending continued upward during the mid-1960s because of the Vietnam War. The net effect of these stimuli was spectacular growth. Kennedy and Johnson presided over the longest sustained expansion in U.S. economic history, 1961 through 1969, lifting the rate of investment by close to a third.

Defense was only part of total government spending, and the spending itself constituted only one aspect of the government impact on the economy. As a share of GNP, government expenditures rose from 18.8 percent in 1939–1940 to more than 25 percent throughout the 1950s. Transfer payments were about a third higher than they had been in the 1930s.[17] Of at least equal economic importance was the government's role in encouraging infrastructural investment. The mechanisms were often indirect, but it sponsored a variety of programs that stimulated or underwrote the building of highways, housing, schools, and hospitals. The GI Bill, for example, pumped $14.5 billion into the economy in the first postwar decade; three Federal Highways Acts (1944, 1956, 1968) created both the Interstate Highway System and the lesser roads that allowed for ongoing suburbanization; and the Federal Housing Administration, established in 1934, greatly expanded its lending after the war.[18] Much of this activity did not involve significant cash outlays. Instead, the government set up institutions such as the self-financing Highway Trust Fund or used its credit to guarantee low-cost mortgages. At little cost to the taxpayer, then, the government facilitated investment of such amplitude that it helped to transform the physical environment and context in which Americans lived and did business.

The government's contribution to growth thus far exceeded its direct fiscal impact. Nonmilitary spending in fact remained modest until the 1960s, when both transfer payments and infrastructural investments went up. Indirectly, however, public policy helped to put in place precisely the conditions most compatible with the Fordist model of growth. The combination of highway building and support for new, suburban housing constituted an outsize subsidy to the automobile industry. The results were spectacular: just under 26 million cars were registered in 1945, nearly 62 million in 1961; and one-sixth of American businesses were integrally linked with the motor industry by the mid-1960s. The manufacture of cars was in this sense not merely the prototypically Fordist industry but the dominant sector in a dynamic economy. The automobile and the suburb, moreover, served to create a lifestyle, and hence a market, ideally suited to absorbing the mass-produced consumer durables of the new industries. Relatively cheap furniture and appliances, television sets, and processed foods defined the consumer culture of the 1950s and early 1960s. The more or less homogeneous markets called into existence by a pattern of development that gradually eroded local contexts, traditions, and tastes could not be satisfied by small businesses selling their wares in the old ways. The markets needed and got the big company, the huge department store, and all the accoutrements of mass marketing. The fit between demand, production, and distribution was unusually close, the interaction more than ordinarily productive and reinforcing.

The society was not merely more prosperous but looked and felt very different. The move to the suburbs, the growth of motorized transportation, the ubiquitous advertising, the building of vast numbers of single-family homes, and the steady accumulation of material goods by people of rather humble origin combined to remake the nation's physiognomy, social structure, and popular culture. The transformation was widely noted and debated; indeed, intellectuals reckoning with the new society criticized its crude "consumerism." It was almost inevitable that the tastes in evidence would be rather common. The new consumers and their parents had long lived without many things; they were happy enough to buy a Ford or Chevrolet and frankly could not afford much better. Likewise, the new, essentially lower-middle-class consumer seldom had more than a high school education and often not that, and so a relatively unsophisticated cultural fare sufficed. TV programs were not especially challenging or uplifting, but there was no disputing their popularity. Cultural critics faulted the values attached to, or embodied in, mass consumption and bemoaned the shallow conformism increasingly said to characterize popular culture. Sociologists wrote of the triumph of "the lonely crowd" or "the organization man," in implicit and often explicit contrast to the more autonomous and robust personalities supposedly the norm in earlier eras. The condescension of such critiques is, in retrospect, transparent; less so perhaps is their lack of historical sensibility. The novelty of the postwar prosperity guaranteed that older patterns of consumption, which had served as markers of class identity and social distance, would be disturbed and that social distance would need to be reasserted as matters of style and aesthetics. The discourse in which the dramatic social and economic changes produced by the postwar economic boom was registered and discussed could not avoid being affected.[19]

Contributing to the dissatisfaction with the culture of the "consumer society" was a sense that in their personal lives Americans were making quite conservative, traditional decisions. Many, it seemed, could think of no better use for their newfound prosperity than to get married, buy a house, and start a family.[20] The postwar baby boom was indeed phenomenal: it broke the steady decline in fertility that had marked the previous two centuries. However "exceptional" its political history may have been, the United States had been at one with other advanced nations in experiencing a dramatic "demographic transition" in the modern era: high birth and death rates had been replaced by low birth and death rates, small families, and relatively stable levels of population.[21] The "baby boom" not only halted, but actually reversed, the path of the transition. The upturn in births began in 1942 and peaked in 1957, with elevated rates persisting into the early 1960s.[22] Greater fertility was accompanied by a rise in number of marriages; a lowering of age at marriage and age at time of first birth; a clustering of births in the early years of marriage; and a brief pause in the otherwise steady increase in divorce. A few telling statistics: between 1932 and 1946, the marriage rate more the doubled; in 1940, the percentage of women married at age 24 was only 42 percent, by the late 1950s, 70 percent; from 1940 to 1957, the fertility rate jumped by half; from 1940 to the late 1950s, divorce rates remained virtually stable, halting a consistent pattern of roughly 3 percent growth per decade since the mid-nineteenth century.[23]

The baby boom was accompanied by a rhetorical insistence upon the value of families and the virtues of parenting. In 1944, for example, the *Ladies Home Journal* suggested that the experience of paid work was unsatisfying for women and predicted that "increasing numbers of women, disillusioned with their present roles or with what the workaday world can offer, will turn toward motherhood as the happiest road to fulfillment."[24] Work, it was regularly asserted, could not provide the level of meaning ordinary people craved; only family could do that. "The employee of a large, bureaucratic-type organization [finds that a job] offers little in the way of meaningful personal relationships.... In this mushrooming of size and anonymity, the family stands out as a haven of intimacy.... Children are seen as providing security." Thus both men and women, argued *McCall's* in 1954, could find their "deepest satisfaction" in "marrying at an earlier age, rearing larger families" and, presumably, moving to the suburbs to enjoy the fruits of the postwar prosperity as a family unit.[25] Even politicians felt competent enough to weigh in on behalf of traditional families. Adlai Stevenson in 1955 lectured women at Smith College on their duty to the nation: they were to "influence us, man and boy" and in this way "restore valid, meaningful purpose to life in your home." A year later J. Edgar Hoover lauded women who had chosen a career as "homemaker and mother," for in that role they could effectively combat "the twin enemies of freedom—crime and communism." And not long after, Richard Nixon achieved perhaps his greatest moment in the national media by posing as the defender of the American kitchen. In a famous debate with Nikita Khrushchev in Moscow in 1959, Nixon pointed to the array of consumer goods available to the average worker as decisive confirmation of the superiority of the American way of life.[26]

It is unlikely that the baby boom was caused by the discourse on the family. It seems, rather, to have been a rational response to the greatly enhanced economic opportunities suddenly made available to people still in the midst of the "demographic transition."[27] The Great Depression had reduced not only fertility but also marriage rates to unnaturally low levels. Marriage was simply not a viable option for young people without jobs or the prospect of homes of their own. This changed with the war. Just prior to the war four in ten men in their early twenties earned no money at all; by the late 1940s fewer than 10 percent were without incomes. Their postwar incomes were also relatively higher—a product no doubt of successful union organizing and bargaining and of the type of jobs on offer—and they continued to improve during the 1950s. Expectations rose as well, of course, but less so. Hence, by the late 1950s, the economic prospects of young couples were much improved. Those same years witnessed the peak of the baby boom.

The fashion for marriage, families, and babies cut across lines of class. By some accounts, the baby boom began with a rash of very public pregnancies during the war among movie stars: Lana Turner, Maureen O'Hara, Rosalind Russell, Loretta Young, Dorothy Lamour, and even Joan Crawford.[28] After the war, it affected highly educated women of the middle and upper classes as well as those of more modest means. In the 1950s two-thirds of women students dropped out before finishing college, most because of marriage.[29] Still, the contribution of middle- and upper-class women to the baby boom is easily exaggerated; they were a distinct minority. Far more important were the changes in the reproductive behavior of the millions of ordinary people whose fortunes were lifted by the coming of prosperity. The effects of prosperity were accentuated by differences in class, ethnicity, and religion. The working class, which had been so adversely affected during the depression, was made up largely of descendants of the immigrants who had come to the United States between 1890 and 1924 and who were disproportionately Catholic. In the long run Catholics were not immune to the forces that had produced "the demographic transition," but they did resist in the short term and so the drop in fertility for Catholic couples came later than for Protestants, especially middle-class Protestants. It is thus highly likely that the low birth rates that nonetheless prevailed even among these groups during the 1930s were due primarily to the lack of economic opportunity. But it was precisely these people who benefited most from the full employment and higher wages of the postwar Fordist boom, which in effect commenced with the declaration of war in late 1941, and it was they whose decisions about marriage and childbearing did the most to create the baby boom.[30]

Whatever the mix of factors that produced the demographic explosion of the postwar period, the effects were clear. Rising population added further impetus to housebuilding and moving to the suburbs. It also helped to ensure a steadily increasing demand for just the sort of goods that industries organized on Fordist principles were best equipped to provide. The baby boom thus reinforced the myriad factors that kept the economy moving along, expanding production and distribution, and generating a consistently high rate of profit to the companies meeting consumer demand.

## THE POLITICS OF PROSPERITY

The unusual prosperity of the quarter century after the war created a uniquely favorable environment within which Americans conducted the debates and contests that made up the nation's political life. Uninterrupted growth smoothed the edges of argument, muting depression-era class antagonisms. The combination of genuine economic progress and Keynesian thinking about the economy replaced the "zero-sum" premise of prewar politics with a sense that the gains secured by one or another interest would come not at the expense of others but from the proceeds of economic development.[31] This novel reasoning did not automatically translate into increased government expenditures: the Eisenhower administration was prudent with the taxpayers' money and resisted Keynesian remedies for economic problems. But the new assumptions informing political discourse did ensure that rival visions of public policy would not produce an intense and highly polarized politics. Prosperity served as well to sustain the newly expanded U.S. role in world politics without placing too great a strain upon either the loyalties or the resources of citizens. A buoyant economy allowed military outlays to remain at extremely high levels for peacetime without recourse to heavy taxation or cuts in social services. The relative ease with which the United States discharged its burden as leader of the anticommunist coalition in the Cold War accordingly removed yet another possible source of political disagreement. Foreign policy could be conducted on a largely "bipartisan" basis. Without a flourishing economy, none of this would have been possible.

The underlying conditions making for stability were very powerful, enough so as to prevail over the ideologically charged rhetoric that had marked the politics of the immediate postwar era. The political battles that accompanied the working out of the postwar settlement in the United States were ugly, with Democrats and Republicans vying over who was more committed to the battle against communism. Anticommunism became uglier still in the frenzied rantings of Senator Joseph McCarthy, who would not have mattered had his attacks not been useful to the Republican Party in its bid to oust the Democrats from the White House. But McCarthy proved an embarrassment rather than a help to the new Republican administration, and he fell quickly from favor. The passing of McCarthyism, as it was called, produced a sort of truce that allowed the parties to resume their normal and effective functions, aggregating and articulating the needs of their quite distinct and diverse constituencies and thereby affording at least some influence and input to the largest, best-organized, and most self-conscious interests.

In retrospect, it is perhaps difficult to see the politics of the 1950s and the early 1960s as a system of representation that effectively connected ordinary citizens to the exercise of national power. From a distance of a quarter century the range of opinions expressed in the 1950s seems so very narrow, the voices expressing them so few, so similar, so polite and tame. The contrast with the urgent, engaged, and contentious politics of the 1960s is particularly sharp. So, too, the difference between the dominant participants: the middle-aged white men in dark suits in the earlier decades and the activists of the late 1960s, who were typically younger, less well dressed (and purposely so), occasionally black or Hispanic or even female, and who faced off with genuine antipathy. Even more startling is the expanded definition of what it was possible to think and to speak openly about in the later time. The contrasts are real, if often exaggerated, but they ought not to so overwhelm the received picture of political life during the two decades after 1945 as to obscure the quite complicated reality. Political discourse was undoubtedly circumscribed by the taboos of the Cold War, but it was broad and lively enough to offer viable alternatives to Americans with quite diverse interests. And the political balance of the period was such as to convince most Americans that it was better to participate in political debate than not. This is what made the system work; and in contrast to earlier and later eras, and other nations, it worked well. The two major parties managed between them to give voice to most Americans; few in consequence chose to exit or to oppose the system. The outcome was loyalty to what might well have been a flawed but was nevertheless a workable set of arrangements.

The key to the effectiveness of American politics after the war was the way the major parties were connected with the interests and constituencies that could be said to constitute civil society. The Republicans, for example, gave voice to business, both large and small; to the middle classes, who dominated small-town and suburban life; to white Protestants of a more traditional orientation on social and cultural issues; to at least some farmers; and to the more ideologically committed and sophisticated conservatives. The Democrats were the party of labor, of the ethnic, working-class communities of the big cities in the North and the Midwest, and of the more liberal and progressive middle classes and professionals. The Democrats also received some support from farmers loyal to the programs of the New Deal, particularly in poorer agricultural regions. They had as well a legacy of support in the South. That support was jeopardized by the growing numbers of black voters lining up behind the Democrats. The movement of blacks to the Democrats began with the election of Roosevelt and continued through the war. It was reinforced by the commitment of Truman to the cause of civil rights in 1948. From 1948, white support for the Democrats began to weaken. Strom Thurmond of South Carolina led a revolt of southern Democrats—"Dixiecrats," they were called—in 1948 and the hemorrhage of white voters continued through the 1950s, accelerating further in the 1960s. Nevertheless, the Democrats could still win elections in the South, and Republican growth and organization there was surprisingly weak until the late 1960s. The parties thus effectively spanned major regions and provided most major constituencies and interest groups with at least the prospect of genuine representation.

Parties were not, of course, the only access to influence. Politics was highly fragmented; the federal structure of the state created competing and overlapping authorities whose very existence elicited mobilization and pressure, as did the separation of executive and legislative powers. Economic interests that were able to create stable relationships linking bureacracies within the executive branch with congressional committees responsible for their funding and supervision could virtually guarantee favorable political outcomes. These so-called iron triangles could not easily be broken or bypassed, for they routinely involved representatives of both major parties. Professional organizations, industrial interests, and trade unions all sought to colonize the agencies supposedly invented to regulate them. The effect was a proliferation of such groups and development of at least the infrastructure for "corporatism." But "corporatist" bargaining never became as dominant in the United States as it did elsewhere in the postwar era; the very multiplicity of interests and points of access precluded the stable and centralized bargaining essential to "corporatism." It did not therefore provide a viable alternative to more formal types of political activity, and hence never threatened to make parties or elections superfluous or irrelevant.

The system of representation in place in the postwar era worked not only for the well-organized or otherwise privileged but for those still seeking a voice in the nation's affairs and whose right to a voice was still contested. Thus labor, blacks, and women all oriented their activities so as to gain entry to or increase their role within the existing array of parties and political institutions. By choosing to demand greater voice within the system rather than to exit from it, these groups offered indirect testimony to the legitimacy with which most Americans regarded the political system.

That sentiment was registered more directly in a variety of polls and surveys taken in the late 1950s and early 1960s. In the famous "civic culture" study, for example, Americans expressed much higher levels of satisfaction with the country's political institutions and customs than did those of any other developed society.[32] Party allegiance and identification were also extremely high; and despite the oft-repeated assertion that the Democrats and Republicans offered voters few real choices, support for the two parties continued to increase through the election of 1964.[33]

However restricted the choices offered by the two parties, they kept the interest of most voters. Of course, the role played by the Democrats was quite different from that of the Republicans. The former served as the vehicle through which the relatively less privileged, and in some cases literally disenfranchised, gained entry to the political system and with that, it was hoped, some modest influence; for the most part, the latter gave voice to established interests. Integrating elites and privilege groups into democratic arrangements is of no minor importance, as the experience of many countries attests, and the Republican achievement in this area merits genuine recognition. Nevertheless, much more interesting and complicated questions attended the efforts of the Democrats to represent the interests of the disadvantaged. Neither party, however, could effectively play its assigned role in the postwar political order without first adjusting its outlook to the tasks and conditions it confronted after 1945 and, in particular, after the Cold War settlement.

For the GOP, the problem was somehow to come to terms with the changes in the balance of domestic interests and in the relations between state and society wrought by two decades of Democratic rule and with the new role of United States as "leader of the free world." The Republicans had long been suspicious of big government and hostile to redistributive social programs, and their antipathy to labor unions was deep and undisguised. By the late 1940s, however, the interventionist state created by the New Deal could not be dislodged and unions had to be bargained with. Republicans had worked hard to secure passage of the Taft-Hartley Act in 1947 and it did serve to make life more difficult for unions. Further union organization would be much more difficult to achieve, but there would not be a rollback in union power. When Dewey lost the 1948 election to Truman, moreover, it became clear that the legacy of the New Deal was secure for the foreseeable future and that unions would continue their major role in industry and in politics.

The Republicans carried with them as well a tradition of isolationism. They were not eager for "foreign entanglements," and generally unwilling to pay for them. The standard-bearer for this tradition in the postwar period was Senator Robert Taft, who elaborated a strong critique of the emerging "national security state" and its pretensions to world leadership. Had he captured the nomination for the presidency in 1952 and gone on to win the election, he would have brought to the White House a quite different vision of the U.S. role in world affairs. But he lost to the war hero Dwight Eisenhower, who may have been as socially conservative as most Republicans but who was committed to the fundamental structure of the Cold War settlement and to the U.S. role within it.[34] With his election, the prospect of a radically different stance was ended, and the political and economic compromises in place since the late 1940s were confirmed.[35] The federal government did not expand or engage in either social experiments or Keynesian policy making during the Eisenhower years, but the existing array of policies and programs remained, as did the newly enhanced role of the defense establishment and the fiscal policies needed to sustain it. "Modern Republicanism" became, in consequence, tamer and more internationalist in outlook, even if isolationist or nativist sentiments continued to predominate in some quarters.[36]

The ideological challenge confronting Democrats was more daunting and unpleasant. During the New Deal, the Democrats had been the party of "the people"—that is, the poor and otherwise less privileged—and also the party of "progress" and of the Left. The trade unions, for example, typically supported the party. The Democrats also cemented their ties to the ethnically rooted urban political machines, which benefited greatly as distributors of federal money. The Jewish community was also an important element in the New Deal coalition. During the 1930s, moreover, blacks began to abandon the party of Lincoln and rally around the Democrats. These attachments were reinforced after the war, particularly during the contentious election of 1948. The Democrats were always, of course, a coalition of rather diverse interests held together by the vaguest of ideological commitments to a sort of reforming, populist progressivism. The onset of the Cold War threatened to disrupt the coalition by forcing political rhetoric to become much more ideological.

There was a genuine irony in the Democrats' dilemma, for they were themselves largely responsible for the foreign policy choices that had brought about the Cold War era. But the rhetoric with which they rationalized their actions inevitably escaped their control, and its logic led to loyalty oaths, efforts to purge unions, schools, and public bureaucracies of Communists and their "sympathizers," and ultimately to McCarthy's crude red-baiting. In crafting a response to the escalating and polarizing discourse, Democrats had somehow to recognize its vast appeal to groups within the New Deal coalition—urban Catholics, for example—and to accommodate as well the "progressive" sentiments of the party's more liberal supporters and activists. The result was the elaboration of a liberal anticommunism, or "Cold War liberalism," that sought to maintain the Democrats' commitments to reform and social justice while distinguishing the party from the ideological left. It was not an especially original or inspiring creed, but it proved quite serviceable.

Cold War liberalism denounced the Soviet Union less for its economic inefficiencies than its lack of freedom both at home and abroad. Following on that critique, liberals staunchly defended the forms of democratic rule and the essentially "bourgeois rights" to freedom of speech, religion, and political participation. In addition, they made a particularly strong case for free trade unions, thus distinguishing themselves from communists abroad and conservatives at home. They sought as well to preserve a vision and program of social reform, arguing for progressive taxation, generous social policies, equal access to education, and, most important, full employment. It was not a socialist or even social-democratic vision, however, and it was held together by faith not in Marx but in Keynes. The political function of Keynesian economics was not so much to guide specific government interventions in the economy but, rather, to make the case for reform by asserting that social justice and economic growth were compatible and that both could be achieved without major structural change. As the liberal critic Richard Chase put it in 1958, "A revolutionary politics or economics makes no sense in contemporary America. What does make sense is the liberal virtues: moderation, compromise, countervailing forces, the vital center, the mixed economy."[37] Just what made "the mixed economy" into a virtue rather than a mere sociological fact is not clear. What is clear was the profound desire of American liberals to maintain a commitment to progress and reform while repudiating the politics of structural transformation.

The coherence and integrity of this refashioned liberalism has seldom been recognized, largely because of the inauspicious circumstances of its birth.[38] It was cobbled together in the opening years of the Cold War and was almost inevitably complicit in the illiberalism of that era, most specifically in the frequent infringement of civil liberties. The struggle over the role of Communists in the unions, for example, was conducted with considerable bitterness and without regard for procedural niceties; likewise, both the American Civil Liberties Union (ACLU) and the Americans for Democratic Action (ADA) failed to repudiate McCarthyism at crucial moments. The theoretical foundations of Cold War liberalism, moreover, were neither intellectually impressive nor emotionally alluring. Niebuhr was no Marx or John Stuart Mill; Leon Keyserling was no Keynes; and there were no American equivalents of British thinkers like William Beveridge or T. H. Marshall. In consequence, the agenda of liberalism remained constricted and unimaginative; its most articulate spokesmen purveyors of a political philosophy marked by realism, modesty, and prudence.[39]

The Cold War liberalism that came to define the ideology of the Democratic Party was nevertheless different enough from the prevailing outlook of the Republicans to convince most Americans that politics did matter and did offer real choices. Through the early 1960s voter turnout stayed high. Most significant, however, was the political behavior of the groups not well represented within the political system. Labor, blacks, and women all had reasons to doubt the efficacy of political participation, and the temptation to exit the arena and engage in more direct action was considerable. In fact, labor unions and civil rights organizations and advocates of equality for women all did mobilize their constituents outside the parties. But they did not eschew party politics and were drawn inexorably toward the Democrats in the two-party competition. Gradually, labor was to merge its interests almost wholly with the Democrats and come to constitute its mass base of activists. The civil rights movement had a more troubled relationship with both the unions and the Democrats, but there was never any genuine prospect of long-term political abstention or of an alliance with the Republicans. Women's groups likewise saw progress as more likely within rather than outside the Democratic Party.

The record seems to validate these strategic choices. The trade unions, for example, continued to grow into the mid-1960s. Membership did not increase quite as fast as employment, of course, and because so many of the newer jobs were in industries or regions where unions were historically weak, the share of the work force belonging to unions declined slightly. Still, the steady expansion of union strength was impressive, as were the decisive breakthroughs in the public sector and among health care workers and professionals. In 1955 a mere 400,000 government workers were in unions; less than two decades later more than 4 million were union members. Unions also struck impressively good bargains with employers. Having concluded that the prospects of creating a European-style welfare state were rather dim, unions such as the auto workers began to construct welfare systems specific to particular industries and firms. The United Mine Workers (UMW) secured medical insurance in 1947; the steelworkers gained pension rights in 1949; and the auto workers got both during 1949–1950. In 1949 the Supreme Court accepted that such fringe benefits were appropriate to collective bargaining. Thereafter, lesser unions secured similar gains, and the stronger unions expanded coverage and increased the value of existing provisions. Undoubtedly, the greatest success was that of the UAW, which managed in 1955 to win supplemental unemployment benefits (SUB) to provide workers with something akin to a guaranteed annual wage despite the long and recurring layoffs so characteristic of the auto industry.

Unions simultaneously increased their political clout. The merger of the American Federation of Labor and the Congress of Industrial Organizations in 1955 meant combining political activities as well; through its Committee for Political Education (COPE), the newly created AFL-CIO would wield increased influence within the Democratic Party both locally and nationally. As one of labor's opponents declared at the time, the "skill and potency of this machine" has "given organized labor its position as the most politically powerful economic bloc in America."[40] Union support would prove critical to the election of John F. Kennedy in 1960, and the trade unions were repaid with the appointment of Arthur Goldberg, legal counsel to the steelworkers and the CIO, as secretary of labor and with Kennedy's executive order of January 1962 encouraging the unionization of federal workers. The unions were even more favorably placed to influence policy after Lyndon Johnson's landslide victory in 1964, and the result was the passage of a long list of union-supported legislation. Labor did very well during the interlude of Democratic rule: membership grew by more than 3 million between 1960 and 1968, and wages and incomes continued upward until near the end of the decade.

The great majority of African-Americans were workers and so shared in the gains wrested from employers by the trade unions. As Martin Luther King, Jr., told the 1961 AFL-CIO convention, "Negroes are almost entirely a working people. There are pitifully few Negro millionaires and few employers. Our needs are identical with labor's needs.... The two most dynamic and cohesive forces in the country are the labor movement and the Negro freedom movement."[41] Surely, one of the main reasons for the increased incomes of blacks during the 1960s and the diminished inequality in earnings was the growing integration of blacks into trade unions. Nonetheless, the relationship between the unions, the civil rights movement, and the Democrats was complex and often tense. There was a bitter debate, for example, about the status of all-white union locals at the time of the AFL-CIO merger. The new organization asserted that minorities must "share in the full benefits of trade union organization" but did not immediately outlaw segregated locals and other discriminatory practices. It failed, too, to support several early civil rights efforts. By 1958 the labor secretary of the National Association for the Advancement of Colored People (NAACP) was moved to issue a sharp critique of racism within the trade union movement. A major confrontation over the question of racial barriers within unions occurred at the 1959 AFL-CIO convention, and in 1960 the Negro American Labor Council was founded to give the crusade for racial equality within the labor movement a more organized voice.

The mostly white leadership of the unions did not sympathize spontaneously with the grievances of black workers or the demands of civil rights leaders. They were themselves often the children of immigrants who had achieved their slim measure of prosperity only recently, and they were reluctant to acknowledge the far more serious problems affecting African-Americans. More concretely, it had taken a truly heroic effort to impose seniority provisions upon employers. Seniority rules protected workers from arbitrary layoffs, but inevitably they protected those with jobs, who were typically white, and did little or nothing for those who did not have jobs or who, as the last hired, would be the first fired—and these were more often blacks or Hispanics. White trade unionists therefore resisted blacks' efforts to secure more representation within the labor movement and a greater commitment to racial equality. But not for long. Even in the 1950s unions had supported civil rights politically: the CIO had filed a brief in support of school desegregation; both the AFL and CIO had welcomed the decision in *Brown v. Board of Education* (1954); and labor had lobbied hard for passage of the admittedly very modest Civil Rights Acts of 1957 and 1960. After 1960, moreover, unions began to elect or appoint black officials, segregated unions were barred, and the unions became more fully committed to an agenda of civil rights. The AFL-CIO supported the civil rights march of August 1963, and strongly backed the Civil Rights Act of 1964 and the Voting Rights Act of 1965.

The difficult relations between unions and African-Americans had their counterpart within the Democratic Party. The party's deep roots in the segregated South meant that as the civil rights movement took aim at Jim Crow, it inevitably ran into conflict with southern Democrats holding state and local offices. Even in the North, the demands of black workers were often seen to be at odds with the interests of key elements within the New Deal coalition. Indeed, that coalition was often anchored at the local level by urban political machines that drew their support from white ethnic groups who dominated local labor markets, especially in construction and in police and fire departments. Those were, of course, jobs that many blacks would have eagerly accepted. But they were not on offer, and black demands for equity within urban polities and labor markets were often viewed as a major threat to urban political machines and their constituencies.

In the South and in the North, then, the civil rights movement challenged the Democrats. There were innumerable local conflicts, but despite some awkward hesitations, the party as a whole maintained its long-standing commitment to civil rights. Submission of new civil rights legislation in June 1963 meant that the Democratic administration became even more firmly identified with the cause of black progress.[42] With passage of the Civil Rights and Economic Opportunity Acts in 1964, establishment of the Equal Employment Opportunities Commission that same year, and subsequent enactment of the Voting Rights Act of 1965, the Democrats demonstrated the wisdom of the civil rights movement's strategic orientation toward the party.[43] Events over the next few years suggested that many doubted that judgment, but the long-term attachment of black voters to the party indicates that ordinary African-Americans appreciated the advantages that came with loyalty to the Democratic coalition.

The gravitational pull that the Democrats exerted upon labor and African-Americans also affected women. Women's organizations had been badly split during the 1930s and 1940s between advocates of the Equal Rights Amendment and those who opposed it for fear of jeopardizing protective legislation for women. Support grew slowly, therefore, but by 1940 the Republican Party had endorsed the amendment and the Democrats did so in 1945; and for the next several years a major effort was undertaken to gain passage. The movement nonetheless failed, and by 1953 it was effectively abandoned. The effect was to encourage activists to pursue other agendas: expansion of women's employment; increased access to education and the professions; elimination of inequalities in pay; and political representation. Progress was minimal until the Democrats recaptured the White House in 1960.

In 1961 Kennedy set up the Presidential Commission on the Status of Women; in 1963 Congress passed the Equal Pay Act; and in 1964 the Civil Rights Act was passed with a provision prohibiting sex discrimination in employment. The Commission proved catalytic. It called for the creation of state commissions and thereby conjured up a national network of activists. The commission reported in 1963 and recommended twenty-four areas in which to work against sex discrimination.[44] Frustrated at the lack of progress in the area of employment discrimination, representatives from the state commissions met in Washington in 1966 to found the

National Organization for Women (NOW) to pursue the battle against sex discrimination more forcefully. The Democratic connection was instrumental in getting women's rights onto the national political agenda and eliciting the mobilization and organization necessary to make those rights a practical reality.[45]

Through the mid-1960s the Democratic Party demonstrated an impressive flexibility and responsiveness. It managed to offer enough to the core constituencies in the New Deal coalition to keep their loyalty while simultaneously forging tighter bonds with labor unions and African-Americans and beginning at least to position itself as the natural ally of women. The effect was to make the political system as a whole more inclusive and, on those grounds alone, more legitimate; the most vocal and best-organized interests and constituencies all had representation within either the Democratic or Republican coalitions. They would inevitably compete for dominance within the two parties and the conflicts would occasionally be bitter, but the overall impact was to reinforce rather than to undermine the vitality of the parties and the system of representation within which they were located.

Within a very short time, however, that system was severely challenged. By 1970 many citizens felt utterly disenfranchised by, and alienated from, the structures of politics. Voter loyalty decayed rapidly, leaving both major parties without firm bases of support. The Democrats were the more adversely affected. President Johnson experienced precipitous declines in approval ratings and was forced to withdraw from the 1968 presidential race by rebellion within his party. In 1968 and then again in 1972, large sections of the Democratic coalition deserted, abstaining or voting Republican. The drift prompted speculation about an "emerging Republican majority," but it was more a matter of dealignment—voters turning against both parties—than of realignment from the Democrats to the Republicans. Americans were disillusioned with the political system as a whole, not merely with one or the other party.

The crisis in politics in the late 1960s had numerous causes, but the essential problem was that the balancing act that held the New Deal coalition together had failed to work. The underlying tensions between blacks and whites became far more salient as ghetto rebellions swept the large cities and as affirmative action and busing came to dominate the civil rights agenda. The cultural radicalism that had arisen on university campuses had a similar effect: the student movement served up a range of social issues concerning authority, lifestyle, and gender that widened the gap between the younger generation of the professional classes and many working people, especially older workers previously loyal to the Democrats. Most important, however, were the political antagonisms generated by the administration's futile prosecution of the war in Vietnam. If anticommunist liberalism served well enough as domestic politics, it served very poorly as foreign policy and disastrously as a guide to relations between the United States and the Third World. Ultimately, it proved the undoing of the New Deal coalition, for it led so logically to the war in Vietnam.

Vietnam exposed the very foundations of postwar politics to intense and effective criticism; it undermined support for the Cold War assumptions that had united the major parties; it destroyed the latent but utterly necessary sympathy between liberal intellectuals and the labor movement, whose leaders loyally supported the war; and it weakened critically the historical attachment of both labor and liberals to the Democratic Party. The effect was to fracture the Democratic coalition at a critically important moment and to deprive it of intellectual support, coherence, and self-confidence, leaving a wide array of established and emerging interests without effective representation and thereby discrediting the entire system of representation. The tragedy is that it was not inevitable: U.S. politics before 1965 had worked reasonably well; the crisis that followed was not structurally determined and in no sense inevitable. But the crisis became structural and had a serious and long-term impact on political life.

# Economic Miracles,
# 4 East and West

At the end of the Second World War Germany and Japan were devastated. Large portions of their cities had been leveled, their populations were decimated and demoralized, their infrastructures were fractured, and their industrial resources were largely spent. Such destruction, of course, was the fair wages of defeat. So, too, the accompanying political impotence. But the extent of German and Japanese weakness made reconstruction, inevitably taken on by the victorious powers, that much more daunting. To restore the two nations to economic health, restructure their polities along more or less democratic lines, and reintegrate them into the system of international relations would constitute, in fact, the most difficult challenge facing the leaders of the victorious allies. Meeting the challenge would be the severest but also the most trustworthy test of the viability of the Cold War world order that they would work so hard to construct.

The tasks, which would in all likelihood be accomplished together or not at all, were perceived by contemporaries to be in conflict. It was feared, for example, that to establish regimes democratic enough to reflect the wishes of the nations' citizens might well result in states not fully committed to international peace. A thorough process of rooting out undemocratic elements, however, came to be seen as likely to cause social revolution rather than bring about political stability. Most important, the reform of political and social structure came quickly to be defined as inimical to economic recovery and self-sufficiency. The reestablishment of political order and the rebuilding of the German and Japanese economies would require, Western leaders reluctantly concluded, the active participation of many of the old elites and institutions. The leaders of the occupying powers came to believe that although it might be possible and desirable to purge those in the political and military establishment guilty of the worst wartime abuses, it was nevertheless dangerous to push such a policy too far. More specifically, if the process cut too deeply into the leadership of industry and finance, the economic consequences would be dire. Such calculations led the occupying forces gradually to modify policies. Beginning with ambitious plans and reformist goals in 1945, by late in the decade they had tempered their hopes and put in place structures and leaders far less threatening to established, albeit not long before defeated and disgraced, interests.

The institutions and policies in place by the early 1950s represented a compromise between the desire to reform and restructure the authoritarian regimes and regressive social systems of Germany and Japan and the exigencies of Cold War politics. But would they work? Would the imposed constitutions and parties gain legitimacy within the German and Japanese polities; would the bureaucracies and policies implemented under duress function effectively; would the two economies grow, and would they do so within the new geopolitical boundaries of the postwar world order? Neither growth nor stability was assured, and there was reason to fear that the new world order would founder on the question of Germany's and/or Japan's role within it. Remarkably, however, both nations embarked on an era of prolonged economic growth and domestic political stability. Neither assumed a leading role within the international order but played lesser parts with skill and effectiveness. Over time economic success and political stability reinforced each other, becoming to some extent self-sustaining and enhancing the stature of the two countries in world politics. But just what brought about prosperity and domestic tranquility initially and ensured their persistence through the 1950s and early 1960s remains very much in need of explanation.

Perhaps the key factor allowing the Germans and Japanese to avoid political conflict and to get on with the business of making money was the set of external constraints and assumptions that limited the scope of political discourse and decision making with the two societies. Both nations, for example, were forced to operate under constitutions that were not of their own devising, and neither was allowed to chart its own path in international relations. In consequence, potentially divisive issues were simply not on the agenda. This meant, of course, that German and Japanese political identities remained for some time "inauthentic" and that popular support for diminished roles in the postwar world order was to that extent superficial and untested. But the earlier quest for a world order compatible with the quite popular and authentic national identities of Germany and Japan had produced a world war and cost the lives of millions. Few Germans, fewer Japanese, and virtually none of their victims would tolerate a resurrection of that no longer viable aspiration. Both Germany and Japan were indeed forced to cede what was ordinarily an essential aspect of national sovereignty—autonomy in foreign affairs—as the very condition of national survival after 1945.

It is commonly assumed that an agreed definition of the nation is the precondition for its political stability. As one eminent student of politics put it, "Until a political culture includes a stable and secure sense of national identity all other problems will be subordinated."[1] The postwar experience of West Germany and Japan seems to suggest otherwise.[2] Indeed, despite the fact that the question of national identity was largely off the agenda of high politics, in neither West Germany nor Japan did the effective loss of sovereignty become a matter of serious contention. Thus, although the recovery of at least the semblance of national sovereignty was an overriding goal of West Germany's dominant political figure, Konrad Adenauer, it was to a considerable degree a largely symbolic sovereignty he craved. At best, it would operate only within the geopolitical constraints established by the superpowers and it would be cloaked in a rhetoric of "Europe." Almost immediately after their defeat in war, in fact, prominent Germans realized that rehabilitation ran only through Europe. A prominent executive at Krupp, for example, told Isaac Deutscher that "now...everything depends on whether we are in a position to find the right, great solutions on a European scale. Only a European scale, gentlemen, isn't that so?"[3] Soon such private thoughts and hopes entered public and official discourse.

Beginning with the preamble to the Basic Law that established the West German state in 1949, Germans formally sought to identify their national interest with that of Europe: "The German people," read the founding document, "...animated by the resolve to preserve their national and political unity and to serve the peace of the world as an equal partner in a united Europe...have enacted...this Basic Law."[4] National identity, then, dared not speak its name in post-Nazi West Germany; and "the recovery of sovereignty"—a "leitmotif of the history of the Federal Republic," according to a recent analysis—could be achieved only in the name of western Europe and only after the Germans had yielded to broader "European" institutions "some of the traditional authority and powers of a nation-state."[5] In Japan, the limitations on sovereignty were even more constraining but also more convenient. As one analyst has written perceptively: "Japan's first important post-war Prime Minister, Yoshida Shigeru, made the notable political discovery that Japan need not exert itself for national security in the traditional sense, since the USA was ready to take care of it. It was subsequently realised that all other activities by which a state is externally known and recognised could similarly be carried out by US proxy."[6]

As if to compensate for this lack of national sovereignty in the sphere of international politics, both Germany and Japan were offered the option of playing a major role in the world economy. The trade-off was surprisingly explicit. U.S. planners early on decided that the two economies should be rebuilt by encouraging exports. Increased exports would, in particular, lessen dependence on U.S. aid and provide the basis for sustained growth. The Marshall Plan was thus crafted and administered so as to increase trade within Europe. Nations receiving aid were required to liberalize controls over imports and exports, and the United States used the leverage of aid to encourage creation of a European Payments Union designed to facilitate intra-European trade. Germany was specifically encouraged to throw in its lot with Europe and to become its dominant producer and exporter.[7] The occupation authorities in Japan thought along much the same lines. In late 1948 President Truman signed on to a plan calling for adoption of "whatever measures may be required...to achieve fiscal, monetary, price and wage stability in Japan and *to maximize production for export*" (italics added). Officials on the scene in Tokyo developed the more concrete Program for a Self-supporting Japanese Economy, urging the "most rapid possible re-entrance of Japan into world markets, particularly in the Far East."[8] The two defeated nations were thus invited to resume their quest for a greater role in the world economy but were required to do so peacefully, without military conquest, under the aegis of the United States and the Western alliance, and as part of efforts to promote regional integration rather than German or Japanese domination.

Nationalists in Southeast Asia and patriots in France had some understandable difficulty in distinguishing this latest effort to project German
and Japanese economic power from the recent, bloodier attempts to do
so. Nevertheless, the context had changed decisively, and with the United
States as sponsor and guarantor of the new international order, the reintegration of Germany and Japan into the world economy largely worked.

Part of the reason that reintegration worked was that both Germany
and Japan were forced to shift the geographical focus of their foreign economic relations. With the effective withdrawal of Eastern Europe from
the world economy, Germany turned away from the East and from world
export markets in general and toward Europe. It was able to benefit simultaneously from protected markets within the European Community and
from its historic ties to European countries outside the Six. Over the years,
the West German economy would become the most European of all
economies.[9] Japan was likewise prevented by the geopolitics of the Cold
War from resuming its economic relations in northeast Asia, and sheer
underdevelopment kept Southeast Asia from becoming a major destina-
tion for Japanese exports. The lack of local markets was solved, however,
by a series of military procurement programs, beginning with the Korean
War and continuing into the Vietnam conflict, by which the United States
poured roughly $10 billion into Japan. By 1970 the Japanese were able
to compete effectively in Western markets, and Asian markets were growing as well, enabling Japan to emerge as a major force in world trade.

The emergence of Germany and Japan as exemplars of export-led economic growth depended on two additional factors: attainment of domestic political stability and development of a framework of institutions and
policies that could make growth a reality. In the early postwar era political stability was ensured to a large extent by the fact that critical decisions
were taken out of German and Japanese hands; effective political choice
was restricted first by the occupation authorities and then by the imperatives derived from the near-universal desire to regain a measure of sovereignty. Only gradually, then, did the achievement of political order come
to depend primarily on the exertions of domestic political actors.

Economic growth, by contrast, did require that Germany and Japan
develop institutions and policies that would allow the two nations to cope
with the problems of reconstruction and then of generating real economic
growth. They did so in different ways, but the outcomes were less dissimilar than the divergent mechanisms might suggest. Both nations evolved
what came at the time to be labeled "mixed economies," but the institutional framework within which the German economy operated was dom-

inated largely by the market, with the state playing a relatively modest and indirect role. In Japan the state's influence was more marked. The Germans, in effect, broke more decisively with their economic past than did the Japanese. In neither country, however, was the economic past totally obliterated, nor was its institutional legacy thoroughly replaced.[10]

Economic policy within Germany was dominated by Ludwig Erhard, who ran the Bizonal Economic Council from 1948 and served as economics minister in the Bonn government from 1949 through 1963, and was later chancellor from October 1963 to December 1966. Erhard was firmly committed to a strategy of export-led growth: "Foreign trade," he said in 1953, "is quite simply the core and premise of our economic and social order."[11] That order was conceived of as a *soziale Marktwirtschaft*, or social market economy. The social market economy was itself based on the principles of "ordoliberalism," which derived from the theoretical and historical analyses of the Freiburg school of economic thought. Between the wars the Freiburg school had elaborated a sharp critique of German economic and political development that discerned the roots of the Nazi elevation of role of the state in the transformation, beginning with Bismarck's turn to protection in 1879, of "the laissez-faire economy…into a corporatist sytem" that worked by granting privileges to sectional interests and thereby eroding the distinction between state and market, public and private.[12] Such views gained added purchase after the war, when the economy built by the Nazi state lay in shambles and ordinary Germans were struggling for daily survival.

Erhard and supporters such as Alfred Müller-Armack prescribed a distinctly limited role for the state: it should provide monetary stability and a social and political "order" compatible with free enterprise. The focus was not on policy but on *Ordnungspolitik*. As one of its most articulate spokesmen, Wilhelm Röpke, explained, their program consisted "of measures and institutions which impart to competition the framework, rules and machinery of impartial supervision which a competitive system needs…if it is not to degenerate into a vulgar brawl."[13] Part of the necessary framework of order was a modest level of social provision. In consequence, the neoliberals did not challenge the inherited legacy of social policy, which guaranteed a substantial measure of social security for most Germans, but did resolve to keep spending down and government budgets balanced. Throughout the 1950s the only serious social policy initiative was the long-overdue reform of pensions in 1957. Even with that, however, from 1950 through the mid-1960s public expenditures grew no faster than the economy as a whole and consumed a stable portion of the GNP.[14]

The program pursued by Erhard was facilitated by the choices made by the occupation authorities and the constitutional settlement they did so much to shape. The currency reform of 1948, for example, went a long way toward creating the monetary stability deemed essential by the Freiburg school. The federal constitution adopted in the following year created a relatively weak central government and endowed the states (*Länder*) with responsibility for key areas of public policy and with the taxing power to carry them out. A very large proportion of tax revenues and public expenditures have thus been channeled through the state governments.[15] The federal government has had correspondingly limited powers of taxation and has been forced to operate within a requirement to balance the budget for current spending (excluding investments). The new state would have a central bank—called the Bank Deutscher Länder until 1957, when it was restructured into the present-day Bundesbank—but it was modeled on the Federal Reserve and is largely independent of direct political influence.

This framework placed sharp limits on the state's involvement in the economy. In practice, of course, the state did intervene to some extent. Informal connections still linked various ministries, even the fiscally conservative Ministry of Finance, to particular firms and industries and helped to ensure that favored firms would get privileged access to credit and government contracts.[16] More significant still were the tax incentives. The occupation authorities had imposed a progressive tax system upon Germany that was modified slightly with the currency reform of 1948. The new government deliberately set out to reverse this pattern through reforms adopted in 1950, 1953, and 1955. Top rates were reduced from 80 percent in 1948 to 55 percent and the extent of progression lessened.[17] Despite the gradual lowering of the top rates, personal taxes remained relatively high throughout the 1950s, and there were significant corporate taxes in place as well. This situation provided considerable scope for tax reductions aimed at capital formation. The government adopted both selective and nonselective policies relative to lowering taxes: deductions were granted for investments in specific industries, such as coal mining and shipbuilding, and extremely rapid and generous depreciation allowances were implemented more broadly. In addition, the Economics Ministry made use of Marshall Plan funds to target investments in specific industries through the Kreditanstalt für Wiederaufbau. An even more drastic intervention was the so-called Investment Aid Law (Investitionshilfe-Gesetz) passed in December 1951, which levied a tax of 3.5 percent on industry profits in order to create a fund for investment in key industries such as energy, railways, coal, iron, and steel, where bottlenecks were believed to be hindering recovery.[18]

Erhard, ideologically committed to an unfettered free market, resisted many of these interventions, which were in any case temporary and most of which had lapsed or become economically insignificant by the mid-1950s. But in the first years of the new regime, which witnessed both rising prices and intolerably high levels of unemployment, Erhard's capitalist orthodoxy faced intense domestic criticism. For a time, too, it incurred in addition the displeasure of the Americans, particularly those involved in administration of the Marshall Plan. In early 1950 Marshall Plan Mission Chief Robert Hanes complained that German economic policy reflected a "laissez-faire and defeatist attitude" and called instead for a "careful expansionist monetary and fiscal policy." The persistent German failure to "develop and put into operation a program for industrial expansion" actually convinced U.S. High Commissioner, John McCloy, to return $35 million to the Treasury in May 1950.[19]

The details of the complaints against Erhard and German economic policy would inevitably change with the altered circumstances produced by the Korean War. The upsurge in world demand led to rapidly rising import prices, a balance-of-payments crisis, and hence to calls for controls on prices and on the allocation of scarce raw materials. Again, Erhard and his supporters resisted in the name of a free market. The upshot was another round of criticism from the Americans. In March 1951, for example, McCloy wrote to Adenauer demanding "a significant modification of the free market economy" over which he and Erhard were presiding. Adenauer acquiesced, agreeing that the government would work informally with business to bring about the "factor allocation and investment planning" demanded by the Americans and by the immediate economic crisis. In practice, central control was not exercised directly by the state but instead was delegated to the Federation of German Industry (BDI).[20] Very quickly, however, the balance-of-payments crisis passed and prices reverted to a more normal level, allowing such efforts at coordination to become less important and less stringent. The occasion for this corporatist expedient in economic management was brief, but the experience of coping with the consequences of the Korean War boom were sufficient to demonstrate the enduring power of "organized business" in the German political economy and to legitimize its continuing operation.[21] The government might continue to preach the doctrine of laissez-faire, but the reality was rather different.

Laissez-faire was also qualified in practice by the fact that the historically close relationships that had existed between private banks and firms persisted into the postwar era, facilitating business borrowing and at the same time imposing a degree of long-term planning upon capital. Allied plans for "decartelization" and "deconcentration" had initially threatened to disrupt such linkages, as did Erhard's personal zeal for competition. But the U.S. enthusiasm for breaking up cartels and large firms quickly waned and was replaced by a sense that recovery required the reassertion of property rights. The right to property was incorporated into the Basic Law of 1949, and subsequent legislation on cartels, adopted in 1957, was characteristically anemic. The connections between industry and finance were thus preserved, and the nation's three gigantic commercial banks—Deutsche Bank, Dresdner Bank, and Commerzbank—continued to dominate banking after the war and to control the bulk of the capital invested in industry. They formed a powerful bloc in favor of policies aimed at economic growth, including the maintenance for at least two decades of an exchange rate that undervalued the D-mark and that served as a subsidy to exports and a tax on imports.[22]

On balance, the "ordoliberal" constraints on government intervention in the economy were resonably strict and precluded many overt efforts by the state to manage the direction and pace of economic development in postwar Germany. Planning and control instead operated indirectly, through linkages between industry and the big banks and through informal networks and formal organizations collaborating subtly with government or more openly with other economic actors. The state itself therefore did basically play the *ordnungspolitische* role prescribed by the teachings of the Freiburg school and so contributed to economic growth primarily by creating and maintaining an environment conducive to capital accumulation.

A critical feature of that context, of course, was a flexible and facilitating labor market.[23] Labor was skilled and plentiful in postwar Germany, relatively cheap and pliant as well; and it would remain that way throughout the 1950s. The accommodating labor market was not primarily the product of government. The German labor movement had a lengthy and honorable tradition as one of the few indigenous institutions firmly committed to democracy, but at the end of the war it suffered from serious organizational weakness. Labor leaders sought desperately to overcome this legacy by establishing a united movement outside the Soviet zone. The Deutsche Gewerkschaftsbund (DGB), established in October 1949, was a federation of sixteen previously separate unions that could claim to speak for 85 percent of organized labor. The federation undertook to refashion local unions on the same principle, encouraging all workers to be covered by the same union in each industry and within each firm. This more rationalized structure left the unions well equipped to engage in "corporatist" bargaining with the state and employers. Under Adenauer and Erhard, however, the state was not much interested and unions were left to make the best deals they could with employers.

The unions' task did not prove easy, for employers had the advantage of an extremely elastic supply of labor during the early postwar era. With the currency reform of mid-1948, unemployment grew from just 3.2 percent to 10.3 percent in late 1949. It remained high throughout the early 1950s: by the end of 1952 production was better than one-and-a-half times the level of 1936 (and roughly three times the level of the first half of 1948), but unemployment still stood at more than 10 percent.[24] The supply of labor was swelled by two distinct sources: refugees from the East and, a bit later, an influx of rural labor into industry.[25] Together, these two streams meant that unions were largely on the defensive from the conception of the Bonn Republic through at least the first decade of its existence.

The labor leaders knew that their ability to push up wages was limited. What they sought instead was representation within firms. They aimed to create a "fundamental new order" by implementing a system of worker participation, or "codetermination" (*Mitbestimmung*). There had been legal provision for codetermination during Weimar and, with the defeat of the Nazis, workers had taken de facto control of many factories. Union power was particularly well entrenched in the coal and steel industries of the Rhine-Ruhr region, but the Allies, especially the United States, asserted that codetermination constituted a security risk and moved to restrict its application. The unions fought hard to make it both permanent and widespread and achieved a modest victory with the *Montanmitbestimmung* law of 1951, which institutionalized arrangements within coal and steel. Labor and management were granted parity on boards of directors, with one neutral member jointly chosen, and the unions were given the right to appoint a labor director to oversee personnel and safety issues. In addition, works councils were set up within factories to deal with local grievances. The law establishing codetermination was bitterly contested, and passage had required extensive mobilization by the unions. The following year witnessed a further struggle over the extension of *Mitbestimmung* to the rest of industry. The *Betriebsverfassungsgesetz* (Works Constitution Act) of 1952 was, however, much weaker than the earlier legislation. The unions got at best a third of the slots on boards of directors, and works councils had a much restricted mandate.

Labor, then, was poorly positioned in the early years of the republic. Lacking effective control over the market for labor and with but a weak voice within industry, the unions were unable to make significant progress toward their proclaimed goal of economic democracy. Ironically, the weakness of labor undoubtedly aided economic recovery and, in the long run, may have been of more benefit to workers than greater representation or higher wages granted in the context of a less rapidly growing economy. The *Wirtschaftswunder* was a classic instance of export-led growth: the rate of growth of exports (13.5 percent) far outpaced that of the economy (8.9 percent) and of private consumption (7.8 percent) in the 1950s.[26] The pattern continued, enabling the German share of world exports to grow from 3.7 percent in 1950 to 10 percent in 1970.[27] Part result and part cause of this process, productivity rose faster than wages and unit labor costs went down steadily. Stable or declining costs were an ongoing spur to exports and led to further growth.

Economic growth ultimately led to rising real incomes and increased consumption, but with a considerable lag. The economic miracle was in this crucial respect built upon the willingness, coerced or freely granted, of workers to postpone improvements in the standard of living. Even so, the success of the miracle was not guaranteed by the labor market or by the institutional framework of the "social market economy." It rested as well on two further foundations. First, growth resumed in the early 1950s due largely to the boom in world trade sparked by the Korean War. Second, Germany was better able to take advantage of the boom because of the enormous spare capacity of industry. A good portion of the capital stock was a product of the Nazis' incredibly successful buildup of the war economy. As of 1950, manufacturing industry was utilizing only three-quarters of its capacity and was therefore capable of rapid expansion. Expansion was also made possible by a more than ample supply of skilled and trained labor at what amounted to a bargain price.[28] There has been some reluctance to acknowledge the contribution of U.S. military spending to German economic revival and even more resistance to the notion that Nazi investment policies laid the basis for the *Wirtschaftswunder*. Erhard himself, for example, argued strongly that the Korean War hurt rather than helped the economy, and that it was the institutional framework of free enterprise, not the de facto Keynesian stimulus of the Korean War that was responsible for long-term growth.[29] Such ideological reasoning obscures the reality, which was that a political economy constructed largely on laissez-faire principles profitably interacted with a world economy dominated by the Americans, who were willing to spend billions in prosecution of the Cold War.

Japan's response to the opportunities proffered by the United States and by the world economy differed in form from that of Germany, but its substance and its effects were broadly comparable. The challenge confronting Japan was in two respects greater than that faced by the Germans. First, wartime destruction of the economy was more extensive, and war mobilization had been less effective. As Edwin Reischauer has argued, "The war left Japan a thoroughly devastated and demoralized land. Probably none of the other major participants suffered proportionately such heavy damage, and no other industrialized country was so slow in starting to show signs of recovery."[30] More specifically, Japan did not have the spare industrial capacity enjoyed by the Germans and the corresponding ability to respond quickly and efficiently to a surge in export demand. Second, the occupation authorities imposed a harsher regime on the Japanese than they did on the Germans. The Americans approached the reform of both nations with similar diagnoses and remedies but applied them far more rigorously in the East.

Under U.S. direction, the structures of landholding, business organization, and labor relations were transformed. The land reform of October 1946 was extremely radical and transferred ownership of more than 80 percent of land worked by tenants to those tenants, in effect virtually eliminating absentee landowners as a class. Former tenants achieved a new level of prosperity and dignity, and the share of the labor force working in agriculture actually increased (from 44 percent in 1940 to 48 percent in 1950).[31] Within industry, older leaders who had cooperated with the government were purged and a new generation, albeit nurtured within the same system, acceded to positions of responsibility. At the same time, the great concentrations of business power wielded through the *zaibatsu* were broken up by the Antitrust Law of 1947.[32] On the labor side a series of laws passed between 1945 and 1947 gave workers the right to organize, constructed fair labor standards, and established a framework of negotiation for the conduct of industrial relations. Unions multiplied and membership increased dramatically in the immediate aftermath of the new legislation; a wave of strikes ensued and there was a corresponding, if brief, upsurge in support for the Socialists. Soon the occupation authorities reacted to the spread of worker unrest, banning a general strike planned for 1947, and by late 1950 they had undertaken a "red purge" designed to rid the labor movement of troublesome left-wing militants.[33] Japanese unions evolved into enterprise unions enjoying relatively cooperative and docile relationships with management, but it took well over a decade for this to occur.

The effect of the reforms upon the Japanese economy has been much debated. At the time, they were widely seen as inimical to economic growth. Thus, when the occupation authorities decided to encourage Japan's economic revival, they began to reverse or ease up on reform implementation. On the other hand, some of the reforms definitely "took" and became basic parts of the institutional framework of postwar society. The predominance of small farmers within agriculture, for example, has persisted; and organized labor, though tamed, remains a key feature of the industrial landscape. There is also reason to believe that the breakup of the *zaibatsu* helped to open up business, increase competition, and unleash entrepreneurial effort.

The effort to deconcentrate industry was nonetheless short-lived and easily reversed. Destroying the old holding companies actually increased the power of the "economic bureaucrats" scattered throughout government and made government intervention more effective; it also provided the space within which the four powerful business federations— Keidanren, Nikkeiren (formed to deal with labor issues), the Chamber of Commerce (representing small business), and Keizai Doyukai—were formed. Most important, it did not prevent the emergence during the 1950s of a new constellation of *gurupu* or *keiretsu*, slightly less formal but no less effective corporate groupings centered around the banks that provided the key sources of business financing to constituent firms. Beyond this, by the early 1950s the Ministry of International Trade and Industry (MITI) had secured authority to sponsor or approve the formation of old-fashioned cartels in particular industries.[34]

Whatever the precise contribution of restructuring to long-term Japanese economic development, revival after the war was not easily achieved and would in the end require more drastic measures by government as well as the largely fortuitous outbreak of the Korean War. Sustained growth throughout the 1950s, moreover, would to a considerable extent be engineered by the state. Indeed, perhaps the most distinctive feature of the economic revival was how hard political leaders worked at making it happen. The Economic Stabilization Board was established as early as August 1946 to oversee economic reconstruction, and by June 1947 it had announced the Emergency Economic Policy. This was quickly following by the White Paper "A Report on Actual Conditions in the Economy," drafted by economist and planner Tsuru Shigeto, which explained the rationale of the government's policy. The White Paper established a pattern by which the state took it upon itself not merely to describe economic conditions but also to set economic goals and appeal for public support for their realization.[35] In 1948, therefore, the government issued an "economic rehabilitation plan" that would guide policy through the early years of recovery.

The Japanese government had at its disposal a variety of instruments to make its goals happen. Many were legacies from the prewar and wartime regimes. The "priority production system," for example, by which scarce resources were directed first into coal and steel and then into other heavy industries, contained within it strong echoes of the Material Mobilization Plan adopted after the outbreak of war in 1937. The very organization of the state itself was well suited to exerting leverage over the economy.[36] The Ministry of Finance inherited a controlling influence over finance through the Bank of Japan, and MITI moved quickly after its establishment in 1949 to develop very strong ties with industry.[37] The departments of Post and Telecommunications, Health, Transport, and Agriculture also had large sums to spend and strong connections with interests in their respective spheres. Another wartime carryover was a system for controlling and, in many cases, subsidizing imports. Because imports of raw material and capital goods were prerequisites to a successful response to export demand and hence to postwar growth overall, government control proved decisive in determining which industries would be allowed to grow. Of course, government also set taxes and did so with an eye toward growth, instituting large tax breaks for export earnings and for investments, and in the process creating a "capital accumulation tax system."[38] Most important, however, was its role in allocating financial resources.[39] Through the Bank of Japan—aided by such state-sponsored institutions as the Reconstruction Finance Bank (later the Industrial Bank of Japan), the Japan Development Bank, the Fiscal Investment and Loan Program, the Export-Import Bank, the Smaller Business Finance Corporation, the Housing Loan Corporation, and the Agricultural, Forestry, and Fishery Finance Corporation and facilitated by the central bank's formal and informal ties to private banking—the state was critical in deciding who got funds for investment.

Though the state had at its disposal an impressive array of tools for directing the economy, the domestic and international economic environments remained distinctly unhelpful through the late 1940s. The government's early efforts, directed by the Finance Minister Tanzan Ishibashi, were expansionary and aimed at getting production going, relying on increased production to lower prices over time. The occupation authorities disagreed, and Ishibashi was removed.[40] Despite this, the Japanese government continued to encourage production over monetary stability and by 1948–1949 inflation was worse than it had been just after war's end. Late in 1948, therefore, the Americans appointed the banker Joseph Dodge to impose a more financially orthodox policy. A new exchange rate was set and what was dubbed the "Dodge Line," a mandate to balance the budget and eliminate subsidies, was promulgated in May 1949. The two measures quickly brought inflation under control but did not stimulate growth, which had slowed appreciably by late 1949 and gave little sign of resuming during the first half of 1950. In June 1950 fortune intervened: the Korean War broke out, stimulating an enormous increase in demand. The United States instituted a military procurement program that the governor of the Bank of Japan appropriately, if a bit hyperbolically, labeled "Divine Aid."[41]

What made the Korean boom "divine" for Japan was that it simultaneously facilitated the nation's rapid reintegration into the system of international relations and gave an absolutely vital boost to an economy still suffering from the effects of "Dodge-Line" austerity. The United States was desperate to shore up its support in Asia and to enlist Japan on the proper side of the Cold War grown suddenly very hot. This obvious geopolitical consideration lay behind the San Francisco Treaty of 1951 and also explains the procurement program through which Japanese goods were purchased even though they were not necessarily the best value for the money. Indeed, as late as 1952 the U.S. government reported that critical Japanese products were 30 to 40 percent more expensive than those of competitors. The reasons were the high cost of the raw material imports needed by Japanese producers and the undercapitalization of industry, but despite these liabilities, the Americans bought and Japanese exports tripled between 1949 and 1952.

Japanese business and government used the somewhat artificial stimulus to launch a major modernization of capital equipment, adumbrated officially in the First Rationalization Plan of 1950–1951 and effectively fostered by the institutional framework so carefully crafted to aid capital accumulation. During the 1950s investment would rise to 10 percent of national product. Coal and steel were selected for special attention, and over the brief period 1951–1955 the latter doubled its capacity. Other industries, such as chemicals, shipbuilding, and synthetic fibers, were quickly targeted for development as well. By 1955, they were exporting at world market prices; by 1960 they could beat rivals on price; soon after they began to win on quality as well.[42]

In 1956 the government's Economic White Paper declared that "it is no longer postwar" and outlined a plan for further "growth and modernization." Policy was largely unchanged, though it was now possible to contemplate much more ambitious goals. Despite a severe contraction in 1957–1958, provoked by a balance-of-payments crisis and enforced by government monetary policy, the economy continued to grow by close to 10 percent annually. By 1958 policy makers were discussing plans to double the national income. The National Income-Doubling Plan was introduced by the cabinet of Ikeda Hayato in 1960 amid considerable political turmoil. The plan envisioned an annual rate of growth for the coming decade of more than 7 percent (actual growth approached 11 percent). From the mid-1950s onwards government plans and efforts continued the policies of the early 1950s, with aid targeted at industries with the potential to generate substantial exports. In the late 1950s, however, the plans began to reflect a perception that Japan was entering a stage of industrial maturity that would require a different society and industrial structure.

Japanese leaders understood that recovery had been achieved despite structural backwardness. There was, for example, little evidence in the 1950s that Japan was about to become a center of advanced industry and high technology: in 1955 better than two-fifths of the labor force worked in agriculture and 65 percent of industry was devoted to textiles and food processing.[43] The nation's "semideveloped" occupational structure had its advantages, of course, for the economy benefited greatly from a steady migration of agricultural labor into industry throughout the 1950s and 1960s. As in Germany during the same period, the elastic supply of labor allowed industry to respond with great effectiveness to demand upsurges generated by a buoyant world market. So, too, did the price of labor. Japanese industrial relations were in consequence troubled throughout the 1950s, for wages lagged considerably behind productivity. Unit costs fell steadily, especially with the rapid replacement of old equipment, and workers understood that they were not reaping their full share of the benefits of growth. Employers were not moved, however, and instead were convinced by the memory of the labor militancy of the early postwar years to try to break the power of the unions. Bitterly fought strikes occured at Nissan in 1953, in the steel industry in 1954, at a major paper company in 1958, and at the Miike coal mines in 1960. The result of such confrontations was typically not only the defeat of the union, but its replacement by a company-based "second union" dominated by white-collar workers or those with considerable seniority and committed to a cooperative relationship with management.[44]

The taming of the unions was, in turn, one of two critical preconditions for the spread throughout industry of what has come to be seen as the uniquely Japanese system of lifetime employment, seniority wages, and loyalty to the firm. Previously, such favorable terms of employment were limited to a small number of firms and workers, but the bargains struck by a cowed labor movement were sufficiently favorable to employers as to encourage its more widespread adoption. The other precondition was the full employment and labor shortages that began to affect the economy in the 1960s. Throughout the 1950s a plentiful supply of underemployed rural labor had fed industry's enormous appetite for expansion. Much of the resultant growth of the labor force, however, had been accomplished by the extensive use of subcontracting through the networks of small firms clustered around and dependent upon the industrial giants. The effect was a sort of dual economy: workers in the core firms enjoyed better wages and more security; those outside the core firms earned less and did so less reliably. After 1960 employers were forced to recruit lifetime workers from the ranks of those previously left out of the system. During the early 1960s the ratio of job offers to applicants rose dramatically, wage differentials between large and small firms narrowed noticeably, and wages overall began to rise more rapidly.[45] The dual economy began to disappear.

These structural adjustments were not only foreseen but actually encouraged by Japanese planners. In discussions that preceded adoption of the National Income-Doubling Plan, for example, questions of welfare were addressed explicitly, and in 1959 plans for the National Health Scheme and National Superannuation Programmes were announced. In the Income-Doubling Plan itself were commitments to investments in infrastructure and "social overhead capital"; education and training; and elimination of the dual economy through equalization of wages between firms, sectors, and regions. Although the plan was later criticized for neglecting the social and environmental costs of growth, and although subsequent plans—specifically the Medium-term Economic Plan of 1965 and the Economic and Social Development Plan of 1967—gave even greater prominence to the quality of life and "social development," at least rhetorically, it is obvious that from the late 1950s Japanese leaders envisioned a transformed economy and society.

Japan's economic success seems, therefore, to have owed more to conscious guidance than did Germany's success, but there was more in common than not. In neither country did the market reign supreme; each government molded an institutional framework uniquely favorable to capital accumulation. Industries that had been decartelized or deconcentrated during the occupation were allowed to regroup, and critical ties that linked industry and finance were allowed to stand, while in Japan the government itself became directly involved in the allocation of investment. Foreign trade was essential to both nations and actively pursued by the two governments. Under pressure from the United States, the Japanese undertook trade liberalization in connection with the income-doubling plan, but many key imports remained controlled and "infant industries" stayed well protected. The Germans became the strongest advocates of European unity, which meant that they could effectively maintain a theoretical commitment to widening trade while enjoying the protections of the Common Market.

Probably the greatest contribution both states made to growth lay in the nature of the social compacts they devised and implemented.[46] A cheap and easily expanded labor supply not only facilitated growth, it virtually defined it. The two defeated nations emerged after 1960 as technologically advanced winners that could afford to pay high wages to a skilled work force, but they had reached that point by restraining wages and maintaining a highly elastic labor market—and that was made possible only because of relative internal social peace. Labor was highly organized in both Germany and Japan, but weak in the overall labor market and at the level of the firm, and even more marginalized in terms of public policy at the national level. Welfare measures to provide income security were kept very modest through the early postwar years and resources were successfully diverted to investment. The quiescence of the domestic populations was essential to this outcome, and governments did what they could to engineer that circumstance. Eventually, of course, the tranquility began to erode, and it is surely no coincidence that by the late 1960s the discourse of public policy had become focused on equity, welfare, and quality of life. But by that time both nations' economies were prosperous enough to begin to redress shortcomings and resilient enough to weather the economic storms just ahead. The political systems of Germany and Japan had been in place for roughly twenty years and had provided peace and prosperity for longer than any regime in their troubled twentieth-century histories. The systems of representation in the two countries were not beyond criticism—in Japan especially the parties were poor vehicles for the translation of popular sentiment into effective public policy choices—but they were sturdy and flexible enough to allow the forceful expression of grievance and genuine debate about the course of social and economic policy. Such debate, in turn, helped to advance the still incomplete process by which a healthy democratic politics would emerge in both nations.

Progress toward democracy was protracted. It had commenced with constitutional settlements to which neither country, left to its own devices, would have agreed. In Japan what came to be known as the "peace constitution" was drafted by Japanese leaders but important passages had been written first in English and then hastily and clumsily translated into Japanese. It was adopted in 1947. Key features were its insistence on civilian authority—as against that of the emperor, who "shall not have powers related to government," and/or the military; its specification of the legislature, or Diet, "as the highest organ of state power"; its stress upon individual liberties; and Article 9, which renounced war as a "sovereign right of the nation."[47] The constitution has occupied a central, if contested, position in the political culture. Its foreign origin and its renunciation of rights routinely claimed by sovereign states have provoked resentment on the right and the left and led to repeated calls for its revision. On the other hand, its most controversial features have considerable support among elites and the general public. There is a very strong commitment, for example, to the no-war clause and to formal political democracy.[48] Accordingly, when at various times conservatives have proposed to revise the constitution, their efforts have been countered not only by the organized political left but also the general public, who continue to suspect the right of seeking a return to an authoritarian and militarist past. Indeed, the body appointed to consider the issue, the Commission on the Constitution, concluded its seven years of deliberations in 1964 without recommending any specific amendments, thereby conferring a quasi-legitimacy upon the alien document.[49]

Genuine political legitimacy, of course, ordinarily depends less on support for the constitution than on the effectiveness of parties in aggregating, articulating, and representing interests. On this score the postwar Japanese political system performed rather poorly. By the early 1950s the proliferation of parties and sects had given way to an electoral system dominated by three major parties: the Liberals; the Democrats, or Progressives; and the Socialists, each of which had strong prewar roots. The Liberals, for example, were the lineal descendants of the *Seiyukai*, and the Progressives, of the *Minseito*, groupings of the 1920s and 1930s. The two nonsocialist parties were less parties united by program or ideology than coalitions of locally and sectorally rooted factions. The central question for the shape of postwar politics was whether the Democrats (Progressives), who had a legacy of concern for social welfare and a more centrist orientation than the more right-wing Liberals, would ally with the left or the right.

The election of 1947 produced a Socialist plurality and led to the formation of two coalition governments of the center/left, the first led by

Katayama Tetsu, a Socialist, and the second by Ashida Hitoshi, a Democrat. The coalition failed dramatically, partly due to its internal divisions but largely due to the coinciding of a period of leftist and reformist government in Japan with a turn to the right by the occupation authorities that was provoked by a worsening of the Cold War.[50] The fall of the second coalition cabinet in October 1948 marked the beginning of a reorientation of the centrist Democrats (Progressives) toward a semipermanent alliance with the Liberals and hence the start of a prolonged conservative rule.

Conservative hegemony was aided by the impotence of the opposition. The Socialist Party had been cobbled together in 1945 but lost support rapidly after 1948. It split over opposition to the San Francisco Treaty in 1951, reunited in 1955, and broke up again in 1960. Its thinking has been rigidly orthodox at least until the mid-1980s, its attention fixated on questions of security and foreign policy that virtually ensured its electoral isolation.[51] Though the party, united or in parts, could for a very long time count on securing roughly a third of the votes in national elections, it could not get beyond that and so remained an opposition.

Even with an ideologically crippled rival, conservative dominance was not untroubled. The fragmented and factional character of the two conservative parties left the competition for political funds too visible and the pattern of corruption too transparent and led to widespread public cynicism and gains for the left during the early 1950s. In response, the two parties merged in 1955 into the Liberal Democratic Party. At the same time Keidanren, the nation's leading business federation, helped found the Economic Reconstruction Round Table, which devised a new method "to channel money directly to the parties' headquarters, thereby obviating the factionalism and unseemly individual scrambles and helping to unify the 'conservatives.'"[52] Business funding was routinely supplemented by infusions of cash from the U.S. Central Intelligence Agency.[53] Together, they helped insure that conservatives would have the resources to wage successful political campaigns. And the strong ties between the Liberal Democrats and the agricultural cooperatives, mediated and manipulated by the Agriculture Ministry and Nokyo, the national federation of cooperatives, produced support in rural districts.[54] The net effect was a string of decisive victories.

The Liberal Democrats' strong links to organized business and to organized agricultural interests did not produce strong and stable voter allegiances, however, and the tenuous ties between the party and ordinary citizens was demonstrated with exceptional clarity in the crisis of May–June

1960 over ratification of the security treaty with the United States. The first U.S.–Japan treaty had been negotiated in 1951, as part of the ending of the occupation, and took effect in 1952.[55] In the late 1950s, Japanese politicians were unanimous in support of its revision. In fact, government negotiators wrested major concessions from the Americans, who accepted the need to secure agreement before using bases for military action or before introducing nuclear weapons. Nevertheless, the treaty represented a decision to continue the alliance with the United States and, by implication, to prolong and perhaps increase involvement on the U.S. side of the Cold War. Inevitably, Socialists—many of whom agreed with the Chinese Communists' contention that U.S. imperialism was the "main enemy" of the people of Japan and of China—disapproved. So, too, did many others who saw the treaty and the alliance as a threat to peace; in fact, the connection did seem to entail a revival of militarism, at least to some extent. It was, after all, General Douglas MacArthur who had initiated creation of the National Police Reserve in 1952, and it was in response to continued U.S. prodding that the force had been expanded and transformed in 1955 into the so-called Self-Defense Force. By the time of the treaty-renewal crisis, roughly 200,000 troops were under arms.

There was considerable popular opposition to a Japanese military and there were repeated, though unsuccessful, legal challenges to its constitutionality. The security treaty did not itself call for an expansion of the force but certainly betokened a continued role for Japan in the alliance against communism. Unfortunately for the government of Kishi Nobusuke, the debate over the treaty coincided with a worsening of relations between the United States and the Soviet Union. The Japanese had been heartened by the apparent lessening of Cold War tensions in the late 1950s and had themselves reestablished relations with the Soviets in 1956. The decision on the revised treaty, however, would be made in a context that ensured ratification would be seen as an aggressive and partisan move. The treaty had been signed in January 1960 and submitted in early February to the lower house for ratification. Debate dragged on throughout the spring. The government decided to push the treaty through in May, with the object of having it take effect upon the planned visit of President Eisenhower in June. But on May 2, the Soviets shot down a U.S. U-2 spy plane, an embarrassing incident for the United States. In the ensuing diplomatic posturing the upcoming U.S.–Soviet summit was canceled.

Opposition to the treaty had been serious but not widespread before the U-2 affair, whereupon it took on new dimensions. It could now be argued that Japan was being further implicated in a Cold War that was heating up and over which it had no control. Despite public concern, the government pushed ahead and forced a vote on May 19. The Socialists refused to go along and staged a sit-down in the Diet. They were removed by force and the resolution was approved, but the "May 19 incident" provoked a great outcry not only from the Socialists but also the press and even some within the government camp who had not been consulted beforehand. Very quickly opposition to the treaty was transformed into a "movement to defend democracy," led now by student activists and labor leaders and joined by thousands of citizens. There were frequent demonstrations, including one on June 10 in which the car carrying Eisenhower's press secretary was surrounded and jostled, forcing the American to be lifted to Tokyo by helicopter. Demonstrations continued into mid-June and led in one instance to real violence when a right-wing extremist drove a truck into a crowd of protesters near the Diet. On June 19, the day before the treaty was to become law, 300,000 demonstrated outside the Diet. The treaty came into effect at midnight on June 20, and three days later Prime Minister Kishi resigned.

The treaty crisis put into sharp relief the peculiar character of the postwar Japanese political system. The ruling Liberal Democratic Party did not lose power. Another faction of the same party simply took office and presided over a mix of policies not especially different. Nor was the alliance with the United States altered. Nor did the Socialists, whose opposition to the treaty brought down the government, profit from the crisis. On the contrary, they split once again and remained unable to capitalize at the polls on their recent extraparliamentary success. The dominant features of the system, in other words, were structural and thus extremely resilient. But the crisis had demonstrated that the structure of representation and of rule had not sunk deep roots into the political culture. The elite consensus on what role Japan should play in the Cold War world order was just not shared by the public, and whenever issues of national identity and of foreign and defense policy arose, they elicited deep concern and provoked bitter political divisions.

In consequence, Japanese leaders chose to focus political attention on economic growth.[56] The response to the crisis of May–June 1960 was Ikeda's National Income-Doubling plan, and governments throughout the 1960s regularly renewed their commitment to the politics of growth by issuing new, revised, and ever-more-attractive plans promising not only continued economic progress but growth designed to increase the welfare and living standards of ordinary citizens. Meanwhile, they eschewed controversial issues that might rekindle the passions of 1960. Even so, questions of defense and foreign policy periodically intruded upon the nation's otherwise rather stable political consciousness: there was agitation over continued U.S. control of Okinawa and violent student demonstrations over Japan's complicity in the U.S. war in Vietnam. The government was forced to acknowledge that, as its foreign minister conceded, "Japan is not neutral in the Vietnam War," but it sought to keep such matters off the agenda of high politics.[57] The effort to separate the economy from political questions, to the neglect of the latter, worked reasonably well throughout the 1960s. The artificial dichotomy began to break down in the 1970s when Japan was forced to deal first with the two "Nixon shocks" of 1971—his decisions to let the dollar float and to visit China— and then with the oil crisis of 1973–1974. Both crises represented the unwanted and unanticipated intrusions of foreign policy into the nation's economic fate and required confronting the lingering, unresolved questions of Japan's status in international relations. By the 1970s, however, Japan's leaders were readier to deal with these questions than they had been in earlier decades, as evidenced by their quick moves to regularize relations with China in 1972 and their effective public-policy response to the energy crisis.

Japan's postwar political evolution demonstrated that not all issues needed to be faced head-on immediately and that certain controversial matters were better postponed than addressed. The postwar political history of West Germany seems to demonstrate a similar beneficial prudence, although there issues of foreign policy and defense were not so much avoided as recast in terms of the Cold War and Europe. The effect was a polity more tolerant of debate and dissent and, it appears, more capable of reaching decisions on key issues. Nevertheless, as in Japan, political stability owed as much to a shared desire for economic growth as to genuine consensus on deeper and more contentious questions affecting national identity.

In West Germany, too, the quest for a viable political order began with a constitution, though as in Japan the origins of the Basic Law of 1949 lay at least partly with the occupation authorities. Although the Basic Law was conceived of as a temporary document that would be revised later, its features soon took on a permanent look and feel. The constitution was created under the influence of the occupation and also with an eye toward the failed Weimar democracy—indeed, Carl Schmitt labeled it the "Anti-Constitution" because it was so obviously designed to avoid the fate of Weimar. The *Grundgesetz* set up a parliamentary republic with a weak president and a strong chancellor, a form of proportional representation that institutionalized the role of parties, a large share of sovereign rights reserved to the states, explicit commitments to individual rights (including women's rights), and a powerful constitutional court.[58] Unlike the Japanese constitution, it was amended frequently but nevertheless achieved near universal acceptance as the foundation of politics in West Germany. It would even survive reunification four decades later.

From 1949 to 1966, West German political life was dominated by the Christian Democrats (CDU/CSU).[59] The party had strong Catholic and regional roots in the western and southern states and began its existence proclaiming its commitment to social justice. Its "Christian social" origins prompted the new, nonconfessional party to speak in its Ahlen Program of 1947 of the need for a new economic order based upon "economic democracy" and socialization of key industries. Rather quickly, however, the party turned to the right and embraced Erhard's plan for a *Sozialmarktswirtschaft*, leaving behind its reformist enthusiasms. Nonetheless, its social vision remained reasonably broad and its commitment to the market was tempered by a tradition of collective provision. In the elections of 1949 the Christian Democrats emerged as the largest party, but not by much. The revived Social Democrats (SPD) had run a close second; the liberal Free Democrats (FPD) attracted a substantial minority of voters and thus parliamentary representation; and there were several minor parties as well. Because no party commanded a majority, the immediate questions confronting the new regime were what sort of coalition could be put together and whether it could govern effectively. Though there was speculation and discussion about a possible "grand coalition" of the two largest parties, the government was actually formed by a coalition of Christian Democrats and Free Democrats, led by the former mayor of Cologne, Konrad Adenauer, and Economics Minister Erhard. The coalition ruled for almost two decades.

The plan for a "grand coalition" had not come into being in 1949 because the two parties, though sharing a commitment to the new regime, differed sharply on key issues concerning the economy and foreign policy. The Social Democrats, for example, retained their historic attachment to democratic socialism as well as their equally venerable support for economic democracy. Hence the intense debate over "codetermination." More important was the SPD's opposition to the government's foreign policy. The Socialists were unfailing in their support for German unification, and they believed strongly that integration into the western alliance, especially into a militarized and heavily armed alliance, would prolong the division of Germany. The CDU/CSU, by contrast, made participation in the Western alliance and integration into Europe the centerpiece of its foreign policy as the only realistic path to achievement of greater international legitimacy for the new state and for the nation it sought to represent in world affairs.

The differences between the two main parties in what has been called the West German "party state" were great enough to give voters a genuine choice between alternative definitions of the national interest and rival visions of the nation's future.[60] But the differences were not so wide as to prevent compromise and occasional cooperation. In fact, the apparent divergence on policy questions to some extent masked shared views on fundamentals. Surely, the most important was the anticommunism that characterized all three major parties. The SPD, and its trade union backers, had clashed bitterly with the Communists during the struggle over the division of Germany, and it was the Socialist Ernst Reuter who led the resistance of Berliners to the 1948 blockade. It would again fall to a Socialist mayor, Willy Brandt, to rally West Berliners after the building of the wall. Indeed, one reason the SPD adduced for not acquiescing in the division of Germany was that the acceptance of two Germanys would consign millions of Germans in the East to permanent domination by a bleak and oppressive regime.

The Christian Democrats were no less anticommunist and throughout the 1950s never tired of contrasting the freedoms enjoyed in the West with the oppressions common in the East. They also, of course, declared support for a united Germany. It was their decision to promulgate in 1955 the so-called Hallstein doctrine, by which West Germany severed relations with any government that recognized the German Democratic Republic (GDR). The Christian Democrats, however, believed it was better to build a free and powerful Germany attached to the West that might serve as a magnet for the East. Perhaps they were able to contemplate such a protracted strategy because, with their roots in western and southern Germany, they did not feel so deeply the loss of the eastern, formerly Prussian, portion of the country. The Adenauer government therefore did not hesitate long before rejecting Stalin's offer in 1952 of reunification in exchange for a neutral status in the Cold War.[61] The CDU opted instead to join up with the Western allies through NATO and the West European Union and successfully negotiated membership in the alliance with the Paris treaties of 1954. The treaties took effect on May 5, 1955, the "day of sovereignty" to West Germans. Having chosen the West over the East and over the prospect of becoming the neutral power at the center of Europe, the government immediately proceeded to normalize relations with the Soviet Union. Adenauer actually visited Moscow in September that year and, in addition to reestablishing diplomatic relations, secured the release of roughly ten thousand prisoners of war.

The approach of the two parties to foreign and defense policy therefore differed, but not enough to prevent the new state from functioning. Equally important, the two parties grew closer in their views over time. The most obvious transformation occurred on the part of the Social Democrats and the unions supporting them, who were moved to reform their appeals after successive electoral defeats in 1953 and 1957. In September 1959 the unions voted to reconsider the left-wing program they had adopted in 1949; shortly after, the SPD congress at Bad Godesberg adopted a more centrist program in which the party accepted the "mixed economy"; proposed the formula "as much competition as possible—as much planning as necessary" as a guide to social and economic policy; and moved away from its opposition to rearmament. The following June party spokesman on foreign policy Herbert Wehner uttered the SPD's fundamental assent to the Western alliance and formally proposed a bipartisan foreign policy.[62] Even before erection of the Berlin Wall, the two main parties had reached de facto consensus on the essentials of West Germany's position in the international alignments of the Cold War era.

The subsequent evolution of West German politics confirmed the growing convergence underlying party politics. With the replacement of Adenauer by Erhard in 1963, for example, West Germany undertook to expand trade relations with various eastern bloc countries despite the constraints of the Hallstein doctrine. When the "grand coalition" took office in 1966, the government continued its policy of maintaining its firm position within Europe and NATO while pursuing openings with the East. The Hallstein doctrine was formally abandoned when diplomatic relations were established with Yugoslavia and Rumania. When the Bundestag elections of September 1969 registered further gains for the Social Democrats, the SPD switched coalition partners and formed a new government with the Free Democrats as junior partner and itself as the dominant party. Willy Brandt became chancellor and began to pursue a more forceful and explicit *Ostpolitik*, seeking to normalize relations with the eastern bloc and the Soviet Union. Treaties were signed with Moscow and Warsaw in 1970 and talks begun with the GDR. A four-power agreement on the status of Berlin was worked out in September 1971. After a contentious debate, the treaties were approved by the Bundestag in May 1972. The government went to the polls in November that year and received a strong endorsement. In December the newly strengthened Brandt government signed the "Basic Treaty" with the East German government, the two states agreeing to recognize each other's legitimacy and borders and renouncing the use of force between them.

The speed and decisiveness with which Brandt advanced his *Ostpolitik* undoubtedly upset the Christian Democrats, now in opposition. They were reluctant to be seen as approving deals that granted international status to their eastern rivals or that conceded either the territorial settlement in the East or the continued Soviet role in the region. Still, they did not use their control of the upper house to block any of the treaties and in the end accepted all of them. When the Christian Democrats returned to power years later, they carried *Ostpolitik* even further than Brandt and his colleagues had envisioned. By the early 1970s, in other words, the major parties had come to share adherence to the shape of the recast German polity and its location in the Cold War world order.

Perhaps inevitably, there was less consensus on economic and social policy. During the 1950s and early 1960s the socialists had remained at odds with the direction of public policy but could do little about it. Meanwhile, their supporters began to enjoy the fruits of prosperity and evinced little taste for industrial confrontation. For their part, SPD and union leaders encouraged—both by what workers did and by what they neglected to say and do—workers' adherence to the implicit social compact that underpinned the postwar growth regime. The Christian Democrats, on the other hand, reaped the benefits of a growing international economy and the strongly progrowth institutional framework they had put in place during the early postwar years. More precisely, the government was able to oversee a prolonged period of growth without having to exert itself greatly on matters of economic policy. Meanwhile, the state and the central bank implemented extremely orthodox fiscal and monetary policies aimed at controlling inflation, policies that occasionally slowed growth but never blocked it for long. Ultimately, the contradiction between encouraging growth and holding down inflation eventuated in the economic crisis that brought down the Erhard government in 1966 and led to its replacement by the "grand coalition." The CDU-dominated government had taken a number of actions to stimulate the economy in the run-up to the 1965 elections—including a large cut in the income tax and several major spending programs—whose effects combined with an international revival to create an enormous boom in 1965–1966. The boom brought rising prices and a severe balance-of-payments deficit. In response, the Bundesbank raised interest rates sharply and the government adopted a series of austerity measures; the combined effects were a sharp contraction in investment and a rapid rise in unemployment. The result was the political crisis of October 1966 and the first genuine change in government since establishment of the Bonn Republic.

The most significant departure from past policy was the appointment as economics minister of Dr. Karl Schiller, who had emerged as West Germany's "most famous Keynesian" and who had used his position on the Council of Experts (*Sachverständigenrat*), set up in 1963, to provide economic advice to the government.[63] Schiller and fellow Social Democrats undertook to refashion the institutional framework of social and economic policy inherited from the early postwar era. The Growth and Stability Law of 1967 imposed upon the state a broad mandate for economic management and seemed to presage a fundamental conversion to Keynesian policy making. After changing coalition partners in 1969, the SPD-dominated government sought to alter the balance of power within industry through two key pieces of legislation: the Work Promotion Law of 1969 and the Works Constitution Law of 1972. These innovations had relatively modest effects, however. Employers and the CDU/CSU continued to resist the extension of codetermination, and the conversion to Keynesian policies proved short-lived.

The entry of the Social Democrats into government nevertheless provided the opportunity for a basic renegotiation of the social compact that had for so long governed class relations in postwar West Germany. Chastened by their fear of unemployment (provoked by the brief economic crisis of 1966–1967) the unions heeded the advice of the Social Democrats in government and put forward only moderate wage demands in the bargaining rounds of 1966 through 1968, instead focusing on greater employment security. With the resumption of growth in the late 1960s, however, expectations expanded and rank-and-file workers pressed for more substantial increases in wages. An explosion of strikes in the steel and coal industries in September 1969 marked the beginning of a labor militancy that lasted through 1973 and resulted in a major advance in wages and working-class living standards. Though industry resisted, the long era of growth ensured that it could afford to pay higher wages. Germany had long since ceased relying upon infusions of cheap labor to fuel growth and since the 1960s had relied more upon technological leadership to compete in export markets. The renegotiation of the postwar social contract confirmed this transition to a high-wage, high-consumption economy. It did so, moreover, in a manner that further enhanced the legitimacy of the postwar political order. By the 1970s virtually all indicators pointed to a major increase in popular support for and faith in the political system.[64]

West German democracy may have been far from perfect, but it had sunk deep roots in the nation's political culture in the quarter century since the defeat of fascism.

The growing acceptance of democratic norms and practices in Germany and Japan owed much to the fact that democracy was in both nations accompanied by unprecedented material prosperity; without economic growth, politics would surely have looked very different. It also owed a great deal to the fact that the prevailing political culture of authoritarianism had been so thoroughly defeated in the war. In 1945 Germany "resembled a desert strewn with the relinquishments of war...", and part of what had been lost was popular faith in the inherited wisdom and culture of the nation.[65] Japanese culture, especially political culture, was similarly discredited. The absence of intact political traditions that could be deemed legitimate in the eyes of both occupiers and the occupied dictated that the restoration of politics would occur first through the setting up of effective administration, then through the drafting of constitutions and the supervised reestablishment of parties and elections. The growth of a democratic political culture and civil society would come much more slowly. The success of the democratic project thus depended on rendering prior political connections and traditions passive and penetrable.

The defeat that deprived German and Japanese political culture and institutions of their viability served in practice to make the entire cultures vulnerable to replacement, or penetration, by foreign imports. The result was a flood of American cultural products that accompanied the occupation, the permanent integration of West Germany and Japan into military alliances dominated by the U.S., and the mass consumption of American goods.[66] With the inevitable Americanization of taste and popular culture came, of course, resentment and efforts to discover the unique features of German and Japanese culture and to reassert these allegedly more authentic traditions.[67] But the privatized culture of consumption fit exceptionally well into societies committed to forgetting unpleasant aspects of the past. The net effects were in any case difficult to assess: German and Japanese habits, beliefs, and lifestyles did become more similar to those prevalent in the United States, but local cultures nevertheless proved remarkably resilient. Those who so avidly consumed U.S. products displayed considerable ability to use them for their own purposes, to imbue them with distinct and unintended meanings, and to assimilate them to older, or to recently invented, customs and traditions.

Whatever the cultural consequences, then, both West Germany and Japan have to be counted as success stories in the period 1945–1970. The achievment there of economic growth and political stability and the relatively painless reintegration of these formerly rogue states into the system of international relations must, more specifically, be counted as victories for the U.S., or Western, or capitalist side in the continuing rivalry of the Cold War. This did not yet mean that the West would prevail in the Cold War. Indeed, as of the early 1970s there was every reason to believe that the communist challenge would continue to be formidable for a long time to come. Still, the rehabilitation and revival of the two nations constituted a notable addition to the resources with which the United States and its allies confronted the challenge of socialism.

# The Cold War and the
# 5 "Socialist Project"

"We will bury you" was the way Nikita Khrushchev's famous outburst was translated into English. Uttered in November 1956, it produced an understandable flurry of outrage in the West and repeated Soviet efforts to explain it away. A more literal rendering of the phrase is "We will conduct your funeral," hardly less threatening but a bit different. Not long after, Khrushchev himself tried his hand at clarification. "I can prophesy that your grandchildren will live under Communism," he suggested, but he went on to reassure Americans about how this would come about: "We believe that our socialist system will be victorious, but that does not mean under any conditions that we want to impose that system on anyone." With memories of the imposition of Soviet control on Eastern Europe still quite vivid—and recently reinforced by the bloody suppression of dissent in Hungary—it is unlikely that Khrushchev's words had the calming effect he intended. It is likely as well that his recent announcement of the policy of "peaceful coexistence" failed fully to convince West-

ern leaders of his nation's pacific intentions.[1] Khrushchev's pronouncements, after all, had come in the same year that news of his "secret speech"
to the 20th Party Congress reached the West, and it was understandable
that the primary impact of this acknowledgment of Stalin's crimes was to
confirm the worst fears and charges concerning the nature of the Soviet
Union.[2]

The confusions and contradictions surrounding Khrushchev's potentially threatening but essentially enigmatic statements were typical.
Understanding the Soviet Union was never simple. Still, there is one message conveyed in Khrushchev's words that seems incontrovertible: he
believed in the system over which he presided. "This admirable rough diamond," as he has recently been described, "a believer in reform and peaceful coexistence, who incidentally emptied Stalin's concentration camps,
dominated the international scene" during the late 1950s and early 1960s.[3]
He was surely no naive idealist, having risen to prominence under Stalin,
proved his ruthlessness in the Ukraine, and cleverly but decisively outma-
neuvered his rivals for leadership in the years just after the dictator's death.
Nor, given his plebeian background and modest intellectual training, could
he be considered an ideologue. But he nevertheless believed deeply in the
socialist project and its future. And he would continue to believe right up
to the moment when his reform efforts collapsed and he himself was driven from power in 1964. Not only did Krushchev keep faith with the creed
he inherited, he also updated and revitalized it. His halting and ultimately
ineffective reforms helped to create a new vision of socialism applicable
to the postrevolutionary and post-Stalinist phase of Soviet development, a
vision of steadily advancing material production accompanied by a gradual liberalization of the system of political authority. His efforts suggested
that socialism did not require terror for its survival, and that the Soviet
Union might evolve in a fashion that could allow it to compete with
Western capitalism as an alternative model of modern society.

Khrushchev was not alone in his zeal. He had many allies in the Soviet
Union who shared his vision of socialism. His attempts to overcome the
legacy of Stalin and to reform the Soviet system elicited genuine hope both
from ordinary citizens and from many among the Soviet intelligentsia.
From his reign, in fact, date the first stirrings of the dissident movement.
Khrushchev's enthusiasm for socialism, moreover, was mirrored beyond
the borders of the first socialist state in the beliefs of the impressive generation of revolutionary leaders that included Mao Zedong, Ho Chi Minh,
and Tito. Enormous differences of style and disagreements over strategy
divided these diverse leaders, but none lacked for commitment to socialism

or faith in its ultimate victory. Their sentiments, of course, were echoed by millions of followers in their respective countries, where variations on the original socialist theme were played out. However deep the issues that divided the Chinese Communists from their Soviet comrades, however bitter the denunciations and recriminations that marked relations between the Soviets and the Yugoslavs, the sense that they labored toward a common goal of a revolutionary socialist world order was almost tangible. This shared framework was surely one reason that their quarrels were so nasty. U.S. policy makers may have been willfully obtuse in refusing to credit reports of the developing Sino-Soviet split and to modify their strategic calculations accordingly, but in so doing they were only taking seriously the rhetoric and ideology that the Communists themselves set forth as the basis of their actions.

It was perhaps harder to locate such true believers in the Eastern European nations where the sole base for the triumph of socialism had been the Red Army. Even so, the regimes there gave strong indications of becoming permanent. Other indicators of the real power and solid achievements of what would come to be called "actually existing socialism" told the same story. During the 1950s and 1960s, and well into the 1970s, the various movements and states committed to socialism seemed on the whole to be advancing: their political reach was becoming broader, their military might more formidable; their economies appeared to be growing; and everywhere it seemed that communist regimes, once established, became progressively more institutionalized. From a geopolitical perspective, the dominant facts of the era seemed to be the consolidation of communist power all along the line of demarcation between the two camps and the growing acceptance of this division of the world by the United States and its allies. There was no "rollback" in Eastern Europe and no credible response from the West when Soviet military might was ruthlessly deployed to put down local protest in East Germany in 1953, in Hungary three years later, and in Czechoslovakia in 1968, or when regimes loyal to the Soviets took action against their own populations, as happened most spectacularly with the erection of the Berlin Wall in 1961. The boundary in Asia was equally firm: the two halves of Korea settled into a prolonged confrontation behind positions from which neither side seemed likely to be dislodged; the Chinese Revolution developed in its peculiar fashion behind secure borders; and in Vietnam the strength of the communist regime in the North was not to be doubted.

The overall balance in the reach of the two camps changed little during the first quarter century of the Cold War. The most notable advance for the

Soviet bloc was in Cuba; the United States had to content itself with having encouraged and exacerbated somewhat the fissiparous tendencies within the Soviet bloc. By the 1950s Yugoslavia had been effectively detached from the bloc; by 1969 China and the Soviet Union were engaged in border clashes with each other; and by 1972 the United States had inserted itself between the dominant communist powers. Still, no country had defected from the cause, at least not officially, and neither China nor the Soviet Union had renounced the goal of ultimately creating a revolutionary world order. Most important, by the early 1970s all of the non-communist countries had come around to accepting the broad outlines of the Cold War world order. The accord over Berlin in 1972 effectively settled the question of Eastern Europe; the nearly simultaneous rapprochements, first between the United States and the People's Republic of China, and then between the PRC and Japan, conferred legitimacy and relative permanence on the division of east and northeast Asia; and the signing of the Strategic Arms Limitation Talks (SALT) agreement and the anti-ABM treaty at about the same time betokened not only a détente between the United States and the Soviet Union but a mutual acceptance by the super-powers of their claims to hegemonic status within their respective spheres of influence.

Underpinning communism's diplomatic advances was steady progress in the building up of military power. The forces of world communism had fought the United States and its allies to a standstill in Korea and were en route to beating them thrice over in Vietnam—the 1954 defeat of the French at Dien Bien Phu; a victory symbolized by the Tet offensive of January 1968; and the 1975 fall of Saigon. At least equally significant was the emerging superpower parity in nuclear weapons. The Soviet Union had embarked upon the Cold War seriously deficient in such weaponry but made frantic efforts to overcome its inferiority throughout the 1950s and 1960s. The Soviets stunned U.S. military leaders with the rapidity with which they developed the atomic bomb and then, not long after the U.S. breakthrough, their own hydrogen bomb.[4] The Soviets nevertheless lagged considerably in weapons production and in delivery systems. With the launching of Sputnik, however, they appeared to leapfrog ahead, skipping over the stage of bombers and moving directly to the creation and installation of long-range missiles. In fact, Soviet missile technology was vastly overrated and the capacity of the Soviet military to deliver missiles remained weak. With the prospective placement of missiles in Cuba in 1962, it appeared briefly that Soviet inferiority in this aspect of the arms race would at last be overcome, but that ploy failed. In response, the Soviet leadership began a heroic effort at building bombs, bombers, and missiles. In 1962 the Soviets had one launcher for every eight possessed by the United States; by 1971, they possessed an equal number and in the next year went beyond. The United States retained its clear lead in warheads and, as American military commanders regularly asserted, was far ahead technologically. Nonetheless, by the early 1970s the Soviet Union could plausibly boast that it now was the rough equal of its rival. And it was in this context and this frame of mind that both sides undertook the series of diplomatic initiatives that came to be known as détente.[5]

The progress of socialism was also registered economically. From the late 1940s through the early 1970s the Soviet Union posted higher growth rates than any capitalist nation. Growth was equally notable, if more uneven, in China. Eastern Europe got off to a slower start, largely because of Soviet efforts to exact reparations in kind from nations held to have been complicitous in Nazi aggression, but by the 1950s growth was visible there as well. Doubtless official statistics exaggerated economic achievement, but even after a rigorous deflation the data show real advances. Anecdotal evidence confirms that these nations managed substantial recovery from wartime dislocation and began to put in place the rudiments of modern economies. In the Soviet Union, for example, the economy actually outperformed Stalin's boastful plans outlined in 1946, at least down through 1960.[6] Much of the growth of the communist economies stemmed, of course, from the restoration of order and domestic stability. Much flowed, too, from the extraordinary mobilization of labor and its diversion from agriculture to industry, and from the crude exploitation of natural resources. The Soviet Union was a sort of frontier country, where growth resulted from the mere extension of economic activity into previously uncultivated territories and the founding of new industries, not from the more efficient utilization of resources. The Chinese and Eastern European economies were also able to reap the benefits of backwardness.

Despite brutal policies toward both workers and peasants the socialist economies moved forward through at least the early 1970s. Of course, they were extremely wasteful. The command economies not only failed to satisfy consumer desires but aimed not to. Soviet agriculture, though treated better than under Stalin, was nevertheless everywhere subjected to impossible demands and denied the resources and flexibility that might have allowed it to prosper. Industry was similarly overplanned, overmanned and distorted. The sector that worked best, as even the system's advocates readily conceded, was defense. The Soviets and their allies thrived best when given a military purpose and mobilized in military fashion. Still, the system appeared to work moderately well through the first two-and-a-half decades of the Cold War. Growth in the East may not have matched growth in the West, but it was sufficient to demonstrate at least the temporary viability of the system and strong enough to inspire a few, like Khrushchev, to believe that in the long run it would surpass capitalism as an engine of material prosperity.

The linked political, military, and economic achievements of the communist bloc not only served to give it the appearance of permanence and viability but allowed communism to be seen as a possible model for economic and social development in the so-called Third World. From a geopolitical standpoint, the most important postwar development was decolonization. All of the European empires began to be dismantled, and one nation after another achieved formal, political independence. This profound transition provided opportunities for the Soviets and the United States to recruit or, far worse, to lose allies in the great, "zero-sum" game of Cold War politics. The Soviet Union had for years placed itself on the side of colonial peoples struggling for independence. Indeed, its own founding myth interpreted the triumph of socialism in the Soviet Union as a break in what Stalin declared to be the weakest link in the "imperialist" chain. As early as the 1920s, Lenin and then Stalin had oriented Soviet foreign policy to take advantage of colonial discontent, and over the years the Soviets had furthered Lenin's revisions of Marx and elaborated a full-blown strategy of national liberation leading ultimately to socialism. The theory remained largely abstract until the victory of the Chinese Communists in 1949, but from that moment it became a serious force in the politics of Third World liberation.

The attractions of socialism within the less developed regions of the world were twofold. It was, first of all, a strategy for conducting the struggle for independence, a strategy with muscle, for movements following such a path could count on support from the Soviet Union either in the form of weapons or, at the very least, diplomatic leverage. Even if Soviet support was inconsistent and niggardly, it was nevertheless a key resource. Socialism was also a strategy for economic development. Resistance to Western imperialism inevitably carried over into a critique of capitalism; more precisely, into a determination on the part of newly liberated countries and their leaders not to accept the dependent roles apparently assigned to them by capitalism and the international division of labor worked out in the capitalist metropoles. So even where nationalist leaders had come to power without following the socialist strategy of national liberation, the lure of socialism as a model of autonomous national economic development was considerable. The Soviet Union, it appeared, had by its own efforts and in isolation from the world market transformed itself from peasant backwardness to superpower status through a strategy of socialist economic development, and the Chinese appeared to be doing the same thing. Why then, Third World leaders reasoned, not adopt a similar approach? In the competition for allies and possible clients among the developing countries, then, the Soviet Union had some real advantages. Add this strategic asset to the achievements of the socialist bloc in terms of the consolidation of political power at home, the gradual recognition afforded these nations by the international community, and growing military strength, and it is clear that the "communist challenge," at least through the early and mid-1970s, was formidable.

It was certainly serious and threatening enough to explain the persistence of the Cold War. There were many moments when the Cold War seemed ready to die down and settle into a traditional great-power contest, and when moderates on both sides seemed likely to prevail over more bellicose and ideologically aggressive partisans. But moderation, stability, and détente proved elusive, for just as conflict abated in one place, it flared up in another. Even before tensions lessened over the postwar division of Eastern Europe, for example, the Chinese Revolution and the explosion of the first Soviet atomic bomb put Western leaders in panic. Before these shocks could be fully assimilated, the Korean War broke out. That conflict had wound down by 1953, but the same year witnessed the suppression of the rebellion in East Germany. The next year saw the Viet Minh victory at Dien Bien Phu. After a brief hiatus in 1955, Khrushchev announced the policy of peaceful coexistence in 1956. In that year, too, his "secret speech" confirmed the worst claims of the critics of the Soviet Union, and the crushing of the Hungarian Revolution suggested that the Stalinist past was far from dead. Sputnik followed quickly, serving notice that the Soviet Union was firmly committed to overcoming its strategic inferiority vis-à-vis the West. A brief thaw was followed by the Cuban Revolution, the U-2 incident, the building of the Berlin Wall, and the Cuban missile crisis, which together brought the superpowers extremely close to a nuclear exchange.

The test ban treaty of 1963 betokened another lessening of tension, but it was not long before the war in Vietnam brought the superpowers back into at least indirect confrontation. The seemingly unstoppable communist advance in Southeast Asia had a contradictory effect on the Cold War. Vietnam demonstrated to the United States and its allies the limits of their

124

strategic reach and hence the need for a more realistic assessment of threats, possibilities, and accommodation with the Soviets and/or with the Soviets' antagonists, the Chinese Communists. At the same time, the advance showed the potential of indigenous liberation movements and inspired emulation by insurgents elsewhere in the Third World. The outcome was a series of agreements that could easily be interpreted as implicit ratification of the improved fortunes of socialism. The 1972 agreement over Berlin, the Paris peace process, the SALT agreement, and ABM treaty, moreover, were bargained out at precisely the moment when the nuclear balance ceased to favor so completely the United States and its allies. In the context, détente represented not merely a relaxation of the Cold War but the mutual recognition of a new balance of forces decidedly more favorable to the Soviets and the socialist bloc. It was an unstable arrangement that would once again dissolve into intense rivalry and superpower antagonism labeled by some the "Second Cold War."[7]

The prolongation of the Cold War for at least a quarter century after the initial dispute over who would prevail in Eastern Europe was far from irrational. Irrationality there was, and lots of it. Leaders on both sides encouraged and manipulated irrational fears of communist aggression, capitalist encirclement, and imperialist warmongering. There were economic interests, too, as well as convenient coalitions between these interests and military establishments, that did their best to sustain the irrationalities that flourished in the atmosphere of the Cold War. But it was not unreasonable to regard socialism as a dynamic force through the mid-1970s. Nor was it unreasonable to hold that the rivalry between the Soviet Union and its allies and the United States and its allies was real; that it represented the clash of alternative and fundamentally incompatible social systems, each of which took the entire world for its sphere of operations and each of which harbored truly global and universal pretensions; that ideology mattered to both sides and was therefore more than incidental or instrumental to the conflict; and that for all these reasons, the Cold War was something much more than a modern variation of traditonal great-power rivalries.[8] This uniquely ideological and systemic antagonism defined the essence of the postwar contest of superpowers and ensured that the confrontation was conducted at too many sites for any truce to become permanent. Despite repeated efforts to moderate the conflict and recurring proclamations of peaceful intent and ongoing—and at times even sincere—attempts at arms control, the Cold War endured and continued to structure the postwar system of international relations, the structure of politics within its constituent states, and alliances between states.

With hindsight, it is easy enough to see that the apparent gains of socialism were largely illusory and offset by lingering problems. But the retrospective gaze can blind as well as illuminate. It would be ahistorical to
ignore the facts that convinced at least a generation of leaders, scholars,
and ordinary citizens—East and West—that in the global contest of social
systems the outcome was very much in doubt. Surely no account of the
progress of socialism in the early postwar years can afford to neglect the
decisive evidence provided by its ultimate collapse in Eastern Europe and
the Soviet Union, but neither should it read back into the earlier period
failures that were yet to happen. What is required is a balance sheet that
credits communism with an almost uncanny ability to engineer the consent
and acquiescence of its subjects; with the ability to bring a measure of
prosperity out of economic chaos and to command a primitive effort at
economic modernization; and with a demonstrated capacity to build, sustain, and deploy military might. But an accounting must simultaneously
recognize the underside of these achievements as well. Such a balance sheet
is needed for all of the areas in which communism made its mark during
the 1950s and 1960s: the Soviet Union, Eastern Europe, and China.

## THE SOVIET UNION AFTER STALIN

It was perhaps in the Soviet Union that the record of socialism was most
evenly and precariously balanced. The central question in postwar Soviet
history is Stalin. Unfortunately for its citizens, the USSR undertook reconstruction with Stalin more firmly entrenched than ever—flushed with the
confidence derived from the victory over fascism but, according to most
accounts, at least as paranoid as ever before. Despite widespread hopes
for "normalcy," it did not happen. Instead, Stalin reimposed his version
of Leninist orthodoxy, associated at the time with the rise of Andrei
Zhdanov, and promoted recovery through promulgation in 1946 of the
Fourth Five-Year Plan, which contained economic policies redolent of the
1930s. The highly centralized planning mechanism was maintained, as
were the primacy attached to heavy industry and military production, the
neglect of production for consumption, and, most important, the exploitation of the peasantry.

As if to underline the futility of hopes for reform, Stalin in 1949 purged
roughly two hundred party members previously associated with Zhdanov,
who had been murdered in 1948. The "Leningrad Affair," as it was called,
witnessed the executions of Nikolai Voznesensky, who had largely run the
Soviet economy during the war and who, as head of the state planning
agency (*Gosplan*) had advocated a series of policies more favorable to the

peasants, and of the first secretary of the Leningrad party organization, another wartime hero.[9] It appeared to some that Stalin was about to engineer yet another major purge when he used the occasion of the 19th Party Congress in 1952 to restructure the Central Committee and the Politburo. These fears were confirmed and amplified with the announcement in early 1953 of the discovery of the so-called Doctors' Plot, which purported to implicate a number of (mostly Jewish) doctors in the murder of Zhdanov. Fortunately, Stalin died on March 5. Almost immediately the restructuring of the party leadership was reversed and the Doctors' Plot was found to be a mistake.[10]

Stalin was gone, but his memory cast a long shadow and his institutional legacy was even more powerful and enduring. The Soviet leaders were determined to avoid another Stalin and the terror characteristic of the Stalin era; but their very positions were part of Stalin's legacy. The great contradiction of Soviet politics after Stalin, then, was that the leaders strove mightily to escape from his legacy of terror while maintaining the broad outlines of the Stalinist system. Their ability to resolve this dilemma would constitute the test of socialism's viability as an economic and political system. Could they make socialism "normal"? Could the system survive when stripped of the means of coercion perfected by Stalin? Were the horrors of Stalinism a perversion of the system, an aberration, or its logical consequence? These questions were asked by analysts both in the West and in the Soviet Union. For the latter, however, it was a matter of life and death, of personal freedom and political survival.

What neither Soviet nor Western analysts could discern with any certainty in the early 1950s was the distinction, if one existed, between policies imposed by Stalin the dictator and policies that flowed from the system he ruled. Because so much of what passed for policy under Stalin was personal whim and thus utterly arbitrary, it was impossible to know what was structural, systemic, or sociological in origin. The confusion led Soviet leaders (and many others) to believe that anything was possible after Stalin, and it tempted his successors into a decade of reform and experimentation, most of it associated with the efforts of Nikita Khrushchev. During those years the system visibly softened and the worst excesses of the Stalinist regime were reversed. But it turned out that much could not be changed, or to be more precise, that fundamental alterations in the political and economic system were not acceptable to those who occupied its higher reaches. Under Khrushchev, then, the system became a functioning and routinized social formation capable of reproducing itself but also revealing itself through what it permitted and what it did not. The system was thus defined through, and in opposition to, Khrushchev's efforts to transform it.[11] His failures in particular may be used to trace the lineaments of the system as it had evolved by the early 1960s.

Failures and successes both abounded in the Khrushchev era, for the man was a whirlwind of activity and innovation. His treasured province of expertise was agriculture, where his impact was initially very favorable. Stalin's legacy in the countryside was disastrous, as Khrushchev and other Soviet leaders were well aware.[12] The forced collectivization of the late 1920s and early 1930s had left the agricultural population sullen and embittered and the rural economy virtually lifeless.[13] By the postwar period a relatively small amount of land was worked as state farms; the bulk of the land and the bulk of the population were organized into collective farms, or *kolkhozes*. The livelihood of peasants depended on the fertility of the soil and the weather—the normal risks attached to farming—but also, and less explicably, on state policies in three areas: the level of mandatory deliveries to the government and the prices paid for them; the costs of inputs available through the state; and the relative freedom accorded peasants in their holding and use of private plots. Government policy was nasty and regressive in each area. Procurement levels were high and prices paid extremely low; the inputs, delivered largely through the Machine Tractor Stations (MTSs) by which the regime sought to direct peasant life, were expensive and involved unwarranted interference in the routine activities of the *kolkhozes*; and private plots were subject to policies that vacillated between encouraging and penalizing private production for market and that drastically diminished the contribution such production could make to total agricultural output. In Stalin's last years, there had been no relaxation in his long-standing antipathy toward the peasants but, rather, an intensification of their exploitation, designed to facilitate industrial reconstruction. Mandatory deliveries were kept high and prices low, there was a drive to reduce the number and thereby increase the size of collective farms, and severe taxation was imposed upon income from private plots. Thus while industry made rapid progress between 1946 and 1952 and the wages of urban workers increased significantly, agriculture stagnated, peasants struggled to survive, and livestock numbers sagged. Georgii Malenkov ridiculously boasted at the 1952 Party Congress that the grain problem had been solved; while the reality was not merely otherwise but troublingly so, for agricultural failure threatened to hold back the entire economy.

It took two years before the question of Stalin's successor was definitively settled. But even before Khrushchev's emergence and Malenkov's fall, Soviet leaders concluded that the economic problems bequeathed by Stalin required quick action. None was more urgent than "the depressed state of the villages and of agriculture."[14] Procurement levels were cut and prices paid for grain raised more than sevenfold. Overall, peasants got two-and-a-half times more for their produce in 1956 than they did in 1952. Payments for transport and for the work of the MTSs were reduced; the production and availability of tractors and fertilizer were increased; peasants were finally given access to electricity; the tax on private plots was drastically reduced; and private farming went from being ideologically suspect to being encouraged by the state. Together, these measures added up to a fundamentally new deal for the peasants. The impact on production was more ambiguous. Between 1953 and 1958 total agricultural production grew by half, production of grain by slightly more. However, more than the entire increase in grain production came from the expansion of cultivation due to Khrushchev's "virgin land" program which brought more than 35 million hectares into productive use. The real increase in peasant productivity came in milk, meat, and livestock, and much of the growth took place not on the collective farms but through more effective use of private plots. Overall, the improvement in the lot of the peasants took the form either of better living standards for the agricultural population itself or an expansion of what they did on their private plots. Very few gains were registered within the sphere of collective farming.

Krushchev's second wave of innovation was aimed more directly at the collective-farming sector. In March 1955 the government had decreed an administrative reform allegedly giving more autonomy and discretion to the *kolkhozes*. Two years later Khrushchev launched a campaign to encourage the transformation of collective farms into state farms and the amalgamation of small *kolkhozes* into larger ones. In 1958 Machine Tractor Stations were abolished, their equipment sold to the *kolkhozes*, and their functions devolved upon the *kolkhozes* as well. The aim was to reduce unnecessary friction and allow more efficient decision making. Unfortunately, the effort was accompanied by renewed pressure on private plots and livestock. Taxes were again pushed up and various restrictions were imposed. It seemed impossible to engineer simultaneously greater production from both the state and/or collective-farm sector and from peasants' private efforts.

Reforms were equally dramatic in industry and in the status of urban workers. In 1953–1954, under Malenkov, wages were increased, food prices reduced, and a major housing program begun, even as the prices paid to peasants were raised. The economics behind these politically understandable decisions was not sound, and there were political liabilities as well. Industries privileged under Stalin, together with their allies in the military, objected, and Malenkov did not have a base of support sufficient to fend off their criticisms. When he was forced to resign from leadership in February 1955, he was accused of neglecting heavy industry and producers' goods in favor of consumption. But Khrushchev, his successor, followed similar policies, although rather more cautiously and with more attention to the need for political support from the powerful military establishment. (Indeed, when Khrushchev's own preeminence came under attack in the so-called antiparty conspiracy of 1957, he survived only because of the timely assistance of Marshall Georgii Zhukov and the Ministry of Defense.)

Production of a wide range of consumer goods, from textiles to wristwatches, was increased beginning in 1954, and plans for further increases were included in the Sixth Five-Year Plan. Still more important were changes in wages, working conditions, and social services. A committee to overhaul the wage structure was established in 1955. Improved rates were set and slowly applied across the economy; wage differentials were thereby lessened and in 1956 a minimum wage was adopted. Hours of work were shortened; paid vacations instituted; maternity leave extended; absenteeism and unapproved leaves were decriminalized; taxes on low incomes were decreased; fees for secondary and higher education abolished; and major improvements in pensions and disability pay were implemented. A huge program of housebuilding was also undertaken. Improvements in the quality of life were made possible by continued industrial growth.

The Sixth Five-Year Plan had to be abandoned almost as soon as it was adopted, but officials quickly began working on a Seven-Year Plan to cover 1959–1965. It aimed at major growth in producer and consumer goods, and came close to achieving its objectives. Its most distinctive feature was its focus on exploiting the mineral resources of the East, oil and gas in particular, and on building up newer industries, such as electricity and especially chemicals. The plan had a distinctly modern flair, and coming as it did on top of the party's recent commitment to adopting new technologies—as reflected in the establishment in 1955 of the State Committee on New Technique (*Gostekhnika*) and demonstrated spectacularly with the launching of Sputnik in 1957—and its long-standing interest in education, it represented the peak of optimism about economic planning and the potential of the Soviet system.

The plans' architects understood, however, that modernizing the Soviet economy would require a restructuring of the apparatus of control through which economic life was directed. Khrushchev and his advisers perceived that the existing system was rigidly unresponsive and that a great deal of the recorded growth in production was due to the application of enormous amounts of human and capital resources, with only modest returns, and from the crude exploitation of new lands and the country's bountiful natural resources. Increases in productivity within existing industries remained elusive, and improvements in quality and efficiency were rarer still. Khrushchev's ambitious plans were thus accompanied by equally bold ideas about restructuring the state machine. The various moves in the late 1950s aimed at strengthening *kolkhoz* autonomy were one manifestation of this; others included efforts to give greater independence and flexibility to industrial managers and to reshape the planning bureaucracy.

Khrushchev's most dramatic intitiatives concerned the central planning mechanism itself. As early as 1953 *Gosplan* was strengthened and the various economic ministries were amalgamated, given more autonomy, and placed under the control of senior party leaders. These reforms were somewhat contradictory and so largely canceled one another out, and in the process they produced a lack of coordination that led to further changes during 1955–1957. In 1955 *Gosplan* was divided: one part dealt with the long term; the other was supposedly charged with the implementation of current plans. The reorganization was followed by a critique of the recently upgraded industrial ministries for having hindered coordination across the economy. In 1957 Khrushchev announced a plan to replace most or all of the economic ministries with more than one hundred *Sovnarkhozy*, regional authorities whose work would be coordinated by *Gosplan*. The predictable result was greater disorganization, which led in turn to a series of more or less *ad hoc* measures to compensate for the lack of central direction. With the ministries emasculated, a variety of committees were established to provide the missing coordination. Between 1960 and 1962 the *Gosplan* apparatus was reorganized three more times.[15]

By the early 1960s it had become obvious to the more perceptive Soviet leaders, and especially to Khrushchev, that existing planning methods worked very poorly and that previous efforts to "perfect" the planning mechanism had been too modest and too simple.[16] Prompted mainly by frustration over the fate of successive efforts at administrative and economic reform, Khrushchev launched a second stage of de-Stalinization in 1961. The first had begun in 1956 but had not gone very far. Ideological conformity continued to be enforced, and the regime's self-confidence—reinforced now by the Soviet Union's economic and technological achievements—combined with Khrushchev's desire to revitalize the party actually intensified the drive for ideological hegemony. In the early 1960s, however, Khrushchev reversed course and decided to allow a further liberalization, which produced a notable "thaw" in the intellectual climate. Writers like Yevgeny Yevtushenko were encouraged, or allowed, to come forward, and Khrushchev himself approved publication of Aleksandr Solzhenitsyn's *One Day in the Life of Ivan Denisovich* in the literary journal *Novy Mir*. A similar tolerance was extended to discussions of economic policy, and there was considerable interest in the writings of the liberal economist Yevsei Liberman. The publication in *Pravda* in 1962 of his article "Plan, Profit, Premium" signaled interest in reform at the very top of the party and the beginnings of genuine debate about the nation's underlying economic problems.

Khrushchev was apparently also willing to contemplate changes in the nation's governing apparatus. He made particularly effective use of the Party Congress of 1961 publicly to denounce Stalin and his crimes and then proceeded to propose a series of reforms in the very structure of the party. Over the period of Khrushchev's domination, party membership had increased from less than seven to nearly twelve million, and its composition had shifted slightly toward workers and peasants. Now it was proposed to limit the terms of office of party officials, a reform that would have allowed many of these new recruits to rise to the top of the hierarchy. The party was also to be deployed more effectively so as to utilize the loyalties generated by party membership to counterbalance and offset the defects in economic organization. In 1962 Khrushchev went so far as to split the party in two, half responsible for agriculture and the other for industry. This was a truly courageous but also risky move, for it weakened the structure of the party while making its component parts responsible for economic performance.

Just where Khrushchev's reforms would have led is impossible to say, for they were not given the chance to work. Khrushchev was removed from office in 1963 and replaced by a collective leadership dominated by Leonid Brezhnev and Aleksei Kosygin. His fall was the product of many mistakes. He was held responsible, for example, for the international embarrassment suffered by the Soviet Union over the placement of missiles in Cuba and for the growing rift with China. He was hurt, too, by the fact that his success in raising agricultural production began to fade and that the Soviet Union was forced in 1963 to import grain from the

West. But what probably sealed his fate was the fear he spread within the state and party apparatus and the sense of disorganization and upset that his numerous and not always well thought out reforms occasioned. As a leading scholar of Soviet politics has written, "The elites, who under him [Khrushchev] attained security of life, were yearning by the end of his rule for security of office."[17] But now it was Khrushchev himself who stood in the way. His efforts to breathe new life into the party and into the command economy threatened to disrupt the job security of party officials and industrial bureaucrats.

Sociologically, the Soviet system had evolved in the post-Stalin period from one in which the party was predominant but itself terrorized, to one in which the party elite ruled as a new sort of bureaucratic caste. As yet another authority has explained, "The chief benefactor of the emancipation from Stalin's rule was the bureaucracy for whom the road to full domination of the state, previously blocked by Stalin's power, was now open." That road led to a new phenomenon, a "Soviet bureaucratic absolutism," over which ruled a new elite of professional bureaucrats.[18] Whether this new elite should be seen as a new class, as Milovan Djilas argued, or as a novel sort of mandarinate or *nomenklatura* matters less than the fact that as a group it was unwilling to countenance the kind of thoroughgoing reform envisioned by Khrushchev.[19] As if to prove this point, among the first acts of the new leadership were its proclamation of the principle of "stability of cadres" and its decision to reunite the party into a single, hierarchically structured, entity. The outcome suggests that there were indeed structural limits to reform, limits that were perhaps unseen and no doubt poorly understood but that nonetheless constrained a leader as dynamic and strong willed as Khrushchev.[20]

The new leadership not only reversed Khrushchev's innovations on the role and structure of the party but dispatched his liberal cultural policies and, under the influence of party theoretician Mikhail Suslov, moved to reinstitute rigorous ideological control. The turn to orthodoxy was manifest in the arrest in 1965 of two writers, Andrei Siniavskii and Yuri Daniel, and their subsequent trial and exile. Dissidence continued, of course, and by the late 1960s the ranks of the party's critics had expanded to include Andrei Sakharov and the historian Roy Medvedev.[21] But repression, if less draconian than under Stalin, persisted as well. The space within which critics could safely operate was sharply constricted after 1968 as Soviet authorities sought to immunize the Soviet system from the threat represented by the "Prague Spring." To cite a particularly obvious example, in 1969 Aleksandr Tvardovsky, the editor of *Novy Mir* who had published so many symbolically important articles, was replaced by an editor willing to follow the party line more closely. That same year Solzhenitsyn was formally expelled from the Writers' Union.[22]

These reversals in the spheres of politics and ideology were serious and deeply disappointing to reformers inside and outside the Soviet Union, but they did not signal a wholesale reversion to Stalinist rule. On the contrary, the array of policies implemented by Brezhnev and Kosygin were in critical respects a continuation of Khrushchev's attempt to evolve a stable, mature socialist system. They continued, for example, to focus intense attention upon agriculture. Huge investments were made in that sector and in agricultural inputs such as fertilizer; peasants' private plots were once again in favor; *kolkhoz* peasants were awarded pensions in 1964; and in 1966 the workday system of payment was replaced, giving peasants regular incomes, and the administration of agricultural production was reshaped yet again. Most important, in 1965 and again in 1970 the state raised dramatically the prices paid to peasants for grain, produce, and meat. In response to these new policies, grain production went from 108 million tons in 1963 to 222 million tons a decade later.

What made it possible to raise agricultural incomes and hence production was the decision to subsidize agricultural prices. The subsidy began as a modest 3.5 billion rubles in 1965, rose to 14.3 billion rubles in 1970, and continued steadily upward thereafter. The effect was to keep food prices low while boosting peasant earnings. Cheap food also meant that industrial workers achieved substantial gains in real income, particularly when the rising value of social consumption is added to increasing wage rates. The simultaneous and sustained improvement in urban and rural living standards was utterly novel in the experience of the Soviet Union, and it did a great deal to stabilize the regime. The leadership traced its policies to the Third Program of the Communist Party—adopted at the Party Congress of 1961 and elaborated in subsequent plans and pronouncements—which called for efforts to equalize conditions between town and country and to improve social services. Underpinning this reorientation was the slow but inexorable transformation of society. It was in 1961 that the population of the cities first surpassed that of the countryside; by 1967 the increase in the size of the work force began to lessen; and labor shortages began to be reported in selected occupations by 1970. Productive employment would grow by just over 1 percent a year in the early 1970s, by less than half that a decade later.[23] The heroic age of "growth through mobilization"—generated by demography, geography, and the quasi-military marshalling of resources—came to an inevitable end in the 1960s.

Further growth would require a different mix of policies and stimuli: specifically, the application of new technologies and attendant increases in productivity. That would in turn depend upon the cooperation of workers motivated by material incentives or at the least by better treatment, more consumption, and greater opportunity.

Initially, the need of the Soviet economy for a better-paid, better-fed, better-educated, and more motivated work-force coincided with the regime's need for popular legitimacy and the requirements of its reproduction as a social and political system. But in critical respects the objectives diverged sharply and over time would come into conflict with one another. As early as 1965 economists, encouraged originally by Khrushchev and later by Kosygin, were warning the leadership of the nation's technological backwardness and locating the source of the gap in the system's rigidity and centralization and the excessive defense burden under which the economy labored. The government sought an answer in high technology and in reforms aimed at decentralizing economic decision making. The State Committee on Science and Technology was established and efforts were directed at acquiring Western technology, but innovation remained largely concentrated in the military and in defense industries and typically was not widely diffused. Devolution of authority to plant managers also produced few results, for the autonomy of enterprises was sharply circumscribed. It never, for example, encompassed the freedom to set prices. Decentralization also threatened the interests of bureaucrats at the center, who became deeply concerned at what they saw as the consequences of reform in Eastern Europe, Czechoslovakia in particular. After 1968 economic reform was in most cases abandoned and, with the establishment after 1970 of "production associations" responsible for the direction of industry, control was again concentrated at the center.[24]

Unwilling or perhaps unable to restructure the economy, the regime could not rely on economic growth to generate political stability. It chose instead to ensure the acquiescence of the population by a combination of repression and bribery. Repression, though muted in comparison with the Stalin era, was unrelenting and carried out by a revitalized and increasingly sophisticated KGB, led by Yuri Andropov. Equally important was the implicit bribe-like arrangement between the people and their rulers, a deal that has recently been labeled the "Soviet social contract."[25] In return for rising living standards, extensive social provision, and almost total job security, workers submitted tacitly to the system's denial of rights. The regime directed scarce resources toward consumption and instituted policies designed to guarantee minimal standards for the entire population.

Wages rates between skilled and unskilled and between rural and urban workers were considerably narrowed under Brezhnev and Kosygin, and although the quality of consumer goods was low, they were increasingly available. The people remained poor, but they were far better off than in previous decades and their poverty was shared. The package contained few incentives, very little variation, and nothing that would encourage risk or increase productivity. It was, however, a quintessentially stable arrangement, or so it seemed for many years.

Buoyed by the domestic stability produced by this unusual "social contract," Soviet leaders looked and felt secure through the late 1960s and into the early 1970s. They could, moreover, boast of growing military strength and increasing diplomatic clout. To the Soviets, therefore, the policy of détente with the United States was a course entered into from a position of strength. That position seemed to get even stronger in the early 1970s as their superpower rival experienced a political crisis at home, the embarrassment of defeat in Vietnam and the onset of a prolonged era of slow economic growth. The contrast between the difficulties of the United States and its allies and the string of outward successes racked up by the "socialist camp," disunited as it might have been, suggested to many the decadence of the former and the potential of the latter. That interpretation would prove to be very, very wrong, but it was not a foolish point of view in the 1970s.

## BEYOND THE SOVIET UNION

Among the many reasons that it was not foolish to regard socialism as the wave of the future was the fact that "actually existing socialism," imperfect though it may have been, seemed to have managed during the quarter century after 1945 to establish itself firmly well beyond the borders of the Soviet Union, both in Eastern Europe and in Asia. Socialism in Eastern Europe was, of course, utterly derivative and dependent, more a projection of Soviet power than a manifestation of socialism's inherent attraction. Nevertheless, once in place it proved for a time quite capable of reproducing itself locally and it hence appeared likely to be more or less permanent. As such, it brought Soviet troops and Soviet interests close to the center of Europe and ensured a Soviet presence in all that occurred within Europe. Eastern European socialism inspired little enthusiasm there or elsewhere—although for a time Yugoslavia seemed to offer a model of a decentralized economy with room for markets and for worker representation—but its resilience seemed to demonstrate socialism's potential even when its origins were external and quite artificial.

The challenge of socialism in Asia was more impressive still. The victory of the Chinese Communists in 1949 was not engineered from outside but in fact achieved in the teeth of strong opposition from forces outside China. The Communists were victorious against the Japanese and, after that, won a decisive victory over Guomindang forces that were aided by the West—this with only modest "fraternal" assistance from the Soviet Union. The triumph of communism in China therefore meant much more than the roughly simultaneous imposition of Soviet domination in Eastern Europe. The Chinese Revolution was the product of perhaps the most successful and thoroughgoing mobilization of peasant discontent in world history. The Communists had brilliantly combined a national struggle against foreign domination with a social revolution of the peasants. It was a model that would have wide appeal in a variety of non-Western settings and seemed to offer an attractive path to modernity and national independence. The relationship between this strategy of national liberation and agrarian revolution and the subsequent effort to build a socialist state and a collectivist economy was, of course, never entirely clear, and the Chinese in particular would find enormous difficulties in reconciling these objectives. Still, the revolution served notice to West and East alike that there was an alternative to Western domination and to the dependent pattern of economic development that seemed to be the normal fate of non-western nations. The model was especially attractive to the leaders of nations just winning their independence from colonial powers and eager to craft economies as strong and self-reliant as they imagined their recently independent states to be.

## "ACTUALLY EXISTING SOCIALISM" IN EASTERN EUROPE

The achievements of socialism in Eastern Europe were not pretty. The Soviets had managed to install regimes more responsive to the great-power interests of their Soviet sponsors than to the needs of local citizens, regimes as willing to bludgeon political opponents as were their Soviet counterparts, and equally at ease in carrying out purges, executions, and various other acts of repression. Indeed, Communists in Eastern Europe quite slavishly responded to cues emanating from Moscow in the last years of Stalin's horrific rule and undertook a purge of the so-called national communists who had come to power under Soviet auspices in the late 1940s. In Czechoslovakia, for example, nearly a dozen high officials and many lesser figures were purged during 1951–1952. Most were Jews, including Rudolf Slánský, the first secretary of the party. Victims were denounced as "Trotskyist-Zionist-Titoist-bourgeois-nationalist traitors, spies and saboteurs, enemies of the Czechoslovak nation, of its People's Democratic Order, and of Socialism." In Poland the resistance leader and loyal Communist, Wladyslaw Gomulka, was removed from office in 1948 for refusing to support a Soviet-style policy of collectivization, and in 1951 was actually arrested. He was not executed, however, and returned to power in 1956. The leading figure of the national deviation in Hungary fared less well: László Rajk, longtime Communist, Spanish Civil War veteran, and later resistance fighter, was executed in 1949. In Rumania Lucretiu Patrascanu and in Bulgaria Traicho Kostov, another leader of the wartime underground resistance to the Nazis, met similar fates in 1948 and 1949. The lesson taught by the purges was clearly expressed by the Czech party newspaper *Rude Pravo*: "Love of the Soviet Union does not tolerate the slightest reservation. The road into the morass of treason begins on the inclined plan of reservations and doubts regarding the correctness of the policy of the Soviet Union."[26]

The normal effect was to keep the leaders of the "People's Democracies," as the regimes called themselves, compliant and eager to implement the Soviet vision. When on occasion, however, these governments proved unable to hold the natives in check, as in Berlin in 1953 or Hungary in 1956, or when their will to serve the Soviets faltered and they opted to take the side of local opinion, as in Czechoslovakia in 1968, the Red Army was there to intervene and to remind Eastern European leaders of the ultimate source of their authority. Intervention served as well to remind the world of the effective reach of Soviet military power and the willingness of the superpower's leaders to make use of it.

The record of the socialist states in Eastern Europe also demonstrated that Soviet hegemony could be exercised with flexibility and some subtlety. None of the regimes—except perhaps Yugoslavia, which from the early 1950s was essentially detached from the "socialist camp"—ever came close to achieving genuine, unforced political legitimacy in the eyes of its citizens. Nevertheless, the Soviets almost always found local surrogates eager to carry out the purges, the policies and the changes of front desired by Moscow. Until at least 1956, as one scholar of East European dissidence acknowledges, "There were quite a few Stalinists and even more Marxists in East-Central Europe."[27] And there were even more ordinary men and women willing to cooperate with whoever held the power to make life a little better or much worse. The combination of Soviet power lurking in the background, a repressive state apparatus, a mass party operating in the foreground and monopolizing political discourse, and widespread collaboration and acquiescence, imparted to the regimes of Eastern

Europe at least the appearance of solidity and authority.

Armed with outward political strength, the "People's Democracies" began in the 1940s to construct what they regarded as socialism. After some brief hesitation about the extent to which to follow the Soviet model, they fell in line with policies that sought to replicate the triumph of socialism in the Soviet Union. Nationalization of industry was pushed forward rapidly; agriculture was collectivized; and the Soviet preference for heavy industry over the production of consumer goods came quickly to be reflected in the development plans of the East European nations. In addition, the Soviets imposed reparations upon the nations that had taken up arms in concert with Hitler and thereby extracted a great deal of wealth during the late 1940s and early 1950s. A further drain on local economic resources was imposed with the outbreak of the Korean War, which diverted further resources from civilian to military use. With Stalin's death, however, the drive to emulate the Soviet model lessened in intensity, and some minor modifications were introduced into economic plans and collectivization efforts. More important modifications, not only in economic policy but also in politics, occurred in 1956. Prompted in large part by Khrushchev's critique of Stalin, East European reformers sought to implement a version of socialism tempered by recognition of the diversity of local circumstance and tradition. The events of 1956 demonstrated in quite precise terms just how far the socialist states in Eastern Europe would be allowed to deviate from the Soviet norm.

The precision came from comparing the differing Soviet responses to the efforts of Polish and Hungarian reformers and, in particular, the fates that befell the two men who in each case came to symbolize the local, slightly deviant, path. Imre Nagy, the Hungarian "national communist," was arrested, tried, and executed in 1958; Wladyslaw Gomulka, his Polish counterpart, was elevated to the post of party leader, dominated Poland's political life through 1970, and died peacefully in 1982. In Poland, the party's morale began seriously to erode with the death of Stalin and the subsequent fall of Lavrenti Beria, head of the Soviet secret police. The leadership responded by letting Gomulka out of jail in late 1954 and loosening controls over political life. During 1955 and 1956 the government released thousands of political prisoners and rehabilitated groups and individuals previously denounced. In the midst of these changes party secretary Boleslaw Bierut died and was replaced by Edward Ochab, who struck a conciliatory tone and proceeded to shift economic priorities further away from the Stalinist model of investment in heavy industry and collectivization of agriculture. He also made concessions to Catholics. Because he did all this without challenging the party's predominance in political life or the government's subservience to the Soviet Union, the Soviet leadership went along with his plans.

Ochab's plans were utterly upset by the general strike that broke out in Poznan on June 28, 1956. The workers' action demonstrated that the ferment by now extended well beyond the party and the intellectuals and had truly popular roots. Though it was sparked largely by economic grievances, the strike had transparently clear political overtones. The government's initial reaction was violent repression and more than seventy people were killed, but its more considered response was an acceleration of reform that led, in turn, to ever-greater mass mobilization, which led in its turn to the setting up of local workers' councils and a pilgrimage of more than a million Poles to Czestochowa. After considerable maneuvering and a meeting with Khrushchev on October 19, Ochab gave up his leadership of the party to Gomulka and a series of further reforms was instituted: collectivization was effectively abandoned; the de facto house arrest of Cardinal Wyszynski was ended; the army leadership was taken away from the Soviet Marshal Konstantin Rokossovsky and given to a loyal Pole; and wages were raised. In return, Gomulka acceded to Poland's continued loyalty to the Soviet bloc and reasserted the party's political preeminence.[28]

If the Poles had thoughts of pressing their case further, they were deterred by what happened at roughly the same moment in Hungary. As in Poland, the Hungarian party responded to the death of Stalin with liberalization and reform. Imre Nagy became prime minister in July 1953 and launched what was called the New Course. The program was intended to rectify the imbalances characteristic of the earlier, Stalinist phase of policy making: heavy industry was deemphasized and the production of consumer goods increased; collectivization was slowed down or reversed; and political prisoners were freed. The New Course was "the sharpest and earliest reversal of mature Stalinism;" and its daring, novelty, and "abruptness" had serious consequences.[29] The new policies did not find support in Moscow and also elicited strong opposition from the "Muscovites" who still largely controlled the Hungarian Communist Party. Nagy was dismissed and the more rigid and orthodox Mátyás Rákosi resumed control of both the party and the government in 1955.

Rákosi attempted to revert to more "Stalinist" economic policies, though by now the regime lacked the repressive power to make them effective. Indeed, Rákosi himself oversaw the rehabilitation of leaders purged just a few years earlier and the grant of amnesty to priests and political prisoners. By midsummer, discontent had become widespread and prompted the timely intervention of the Soviets, who forced Rákosi's retirement and exile to Moscow. He was replaced by his deputy, Ernó Geró, whose appointment pleased nobody. Protest continued into the fall of 1956 and was further encouraged by the Polish example. Things came to a head on October 23, when a march of students in Budapest sparked a more generalized resistance. The Soviet troops stationed in Hungary at first moved to suppress the movement, then pulled back, and it appeared for a time that a compromise solution along the lines of the recent Polish settlement would be adopted.

Geró was replaced by a new leadership that included Nagy and János Kádár, a former resistance fighter who had been purged by the previous leadership. By this time, however, Nagy had moved away from his former position as a reform Communist and had traveled far beyond what the Soviets would accept. He essentially opted for the revolution in progress, which at the moment was dominated by the establishment of workers' councils and the spread of rebellion to the workers and the peasants, and voiced demands for free elections, for economic reform, and for Hungary's withdrawal from the Warsaw Pact. The Soviets simply could not abide the proclamation of Hungarian neutrality in the Cold War and on November 1 began to send fresh troops into Hungary. On November 4 they crushed the uprising. Nagy was ousted and Kádár took the reins of government, from which position he sought to rebuild the party, the economy, and the state. With the revolution effectively suppressed, the Hungarians were allowed over time to move in a direction parallel to that pioneered by the Poles. However, the regime had permanently forfeited its claims to political legitimacy and the new system could never gain the loyalty of its subjects. Acquiescence and sullen resignation perhaps, but nothing more.[30]

For those Eastern Europeans who had dared hope that Stalin's death might open the door to reform and adoption of a more humane path, the events of 1956 were traumatic and utterly depressing. Within a very short span of time, they had been forced to accept two dispiriting facts. First, that Stalinism had been just as bad as its foes had claimed—in fact worse, in that Stalin's crimes had so often been carried out against his erstwhile comrades. And second, that the prospects of escaping from the Stalinist legacy were virtually nonexistent. If Khrushchev's speech had been followed by a sustained effort at reform, it might have sparked a renewal of socialist enthusiasm, but coupled instead with the brutal events in Hungary, its message and effect were far different. The lessons of 1956 were a terrible shock to supporters of socialism, more demoralizing in their combined impact than even the Nazi-Soviet pact of 1939. In the East and in the West, socialism would never quite recover.

The message sent by the Soviet intervention in Hungary would be reinforced in Germany in 1961 and in Czechoslovakia in 1968. The building of the Berlin Wall represented an important further step in the apparent consolidation of the socialist regimes in eastern Europe. What distinguished the development of the East German state from that of other states in the Soviet bloc was that its shape and structure remained provisional for so much longer. Until it was stabilized, moreover, the Soviets could not feel secure in their hegemony over the regime. A permanent settlement was elusive, however, for the Western allies had committed themselves to the emerging West German state and to the existing division of Berlin. Purely domestic considerations were thus never primary in determining the policies of the East German regime. On the front line of the Cold War, its fate was critical, far too critical to be left to the Germans themselves.

The Soviets were spared the embarrassment of being seen to dictate policy openly by the willingness of Walter Ulbricht to act as a surrogate. Throughout the 1950s Ulbricht guided the German SED, the party created from a merger of the Communists and Social Democrats but dominated by the former, along a path very close to that of the Soviet Union. As in other Eastern European countries, the Germans had adopted a "new course" in the aftermath of Stalin's death, but it meant even less in Germany than elsewhere. Indeed, the announcement of the New Course in early June 1953 was greeted not with applause but a general strike, centered in Berlin but affecting other industrial cities as well, on June 17. The strike was quickly suppressed by Soviet troops, but its legacy was a reluctance to experiment and a resolve by the SED leadership, Ulbricht specifically, to retain tight control. Beginning almost immediately in that summer and continuing into 1954, he undertook a purge of potentially disloyal elements in the party. At the Party Congress of March 1954, the SED formally proclaimed its position as the leading force in all spheres of the nation's political and cultural life. The party also persisted in an essentially Stalinist model of economic development, emphasizing heavy industry and collectivization.

The highly orthodox pattern was only minimally disturbed by the events of 1956 and in some respects was accentuated by the leadership's horror at the apparent fragility of the socialist regime in Hungary. "De-Stalinization" was thus very limited, and by late 1956 the leadership was engaged in a renewed effort to repress "revisionists" such as Wolfgang

Harich and various other socialist intellectuals. Soon Ulbricht declared that he was "going over to the offensive," and in 1958 he announced a plan to overtake the West German state economically in no less than three years. The government pushed forward with its ambitious plans for the development of heavy industry and with further collectivization in agriculture.[31]

The rigid character of East German politics was in part a response to the precarious legitimacy of the regime. The state's borders remained unrecognized by the Western powers and the continued talk of reunification, which lasted through 1955 and was revived yet again in discussions between the SED and the Social Democrats in the late 1950s, made the state's very existence seem not quite secure. So, too, did the continued exodus of tens and hundreds of thousands of its citizens to the West. Between 1949 and 1961, an estimated 2.7 million refugees crossed into West Germany, an enormous hemorrhage of some of the East's most productive workers and professionals. It is no wonder, then, that the regime was wary of relaxation and experimentation and that the Soviet leadership came to regard the existing arrangements as fundamentally untenable.

Khrushchev had demanded a resolution of the issue of Berlin and the German states in 1958 and by 1961 was impatient, as he put it to President Kennedy, "to tranquillise the situation in the most dangerous spot in the world...to excise this thorn, this ulcer."[32] Although the United States responded with strong words, the Soviets were given to understand that little would be done if they simply sealed the border from their side.[33] East Berlin was closed off from the West beginning the night of August 12, the actual wall constructed a few months later. The Soviet–East German action served effectively to end the long era of uncertainty about the fate of Germany and the shape of the German state or states. The means chosen to do so, of course, confirmed yet again the illegitimacy of socialism in Eastern Europe, but by the early 1960s that was hardly news. What was news was that yet another option for escape and another potential lever to pry open the increasingly closed regimes in that part of the world had been removed.

Ironically, the harsh resolution of the Berlin question led not to further repressions within the Warsaw Pact nations but to a certain softening in the tenor of politics throughout Eastern Europe. The key was the turn of events in Moscow, where Khrushchev launched a second wave of "de-Stalinization" that found its echoes in the socialist states of Eastern Europe. The push toward collectivization was everywhere lessened; efforts were made to reverse the tendency toward central control over the economy; investment began to be shifted toward the production of consumer goods; and in most countries the government adopted a more tolerant stance toward political dissent. It appeared for a time that the "Polish solution" might become the norm throughout the region.

The problem was that the Polish alternative was itself an unstable compromise that would be difficult enough to maintain even in Poland but almost impossible to export and implant in other nations. The test would come in Czechoslovakia, whose unhappy fate would demonstrate the limited applicability of the Polish model. Socialism in Czechoslovakia was initially more popular and legitimate than elsewhere in Eastern Europe. The country was more industrial than its neighbors, and both its working class and its intellectuals had been initially more sympathetic to socialism. There was also a greater popular identification with the Soviet Union. Perhaps because of these charactertistics and perhaps not, the regime established in Czechoslovakia in 1948 was unusually "Stalinist" in its style of rule and in the policies it imposed on its subjects. It had but the briefest episode of relaxation after the death of Stalin and, when it had passed, reverted to a rigidly orthodox pattern of political repression, centralized direction of the economy, and strenuous efforts to "socialize" industry, agriculture, and distribution.

By 1960 the Novotný leadership in Czechoslavakia felt confident enough to issue a new constitution that asserted the leading role of the Communist Party and officially proclaimed the state not a "people's republic" but a "socialist republic." As of the early 1960s, agriculture was thoroughly collectivized and industry run on supposedly "socialist" principles, while education and cultural policy were "carried out in the spirit of scientific Marxism-Leninism," as the new constitution so subtly expressed it. Economic growth, however, began to falter as the forced mobilization of resources began to produce diminishing returns in both agricultural and industrial production. Indeed, the Third Five-Year Program was formally abandoned in 1962. The growing perception of economic difficulty combined with the Soviet example of continued "de-Stalinization" to tempt party leaders to entertain proposals for reform. Ota Sik, the economist, led a faction that favored decentralization, the use of market mechanisms, and calculations of "profitability" rather than planning, and the group won formal acceptance of its ideas in 1964. Implementation was slowed, however, by the resistance of the more orthodox members of the party and the bureaucracy, who still controlled the top of the party hierarchy. Novotný, in particular, refused to acquiesce to the reformers' innovations and in so doing ensured their failure.

Reform at the center of the state was blocked, but it quickly found a more supportive venue among the Slovak section of the party and its organizations and publications. The Slovaks pressed during the early 1960s for the rehabilitation of comrades purged so brutally a decade before; they insisted as well on greater autonomy and on a political space free from the domination of the Czechs who ruled the party in Prague. Two new leaders arose within the Slovak section of the party—Alexander Dubček and Gustav Husak—and they dominated the next period in the nation's troubled history. The emergence of a rival center of authority among the Slovaks created an alternative to the existing regime that nevertheless professed continued loyalty to socialism, the Warsaw Pact, and Moscow. Gradually, however, it became implicated in a movement that transcended those limitations and threatened the stability of the regime. As the effort to reform the economy and the political system intensified, it also became more popular. By the mid-1960s opposition to the party and its leaders had crystallized among the legal profession, which sought to redress the wrongs that had arisen from the regime's "distortions of socialist legality," and soon after the lawyers were joined by students and by their leaders among the intellectuals. Students demonstrated in 1966 and again in 1967; and in 1967 the writers' congress offered a sharp rebuke to the government. By late 1967 the Novotný regime felt severely challenged and sought escape from the crisis in a military coup. The Soviets refused to countenance it, and Novotný was forced to resign in favor of Dubček in January 1968.

It was Dubček's fate, whether he intended it or not, to preside over a mass movement for political reform that rapidly spilled over the boundaries he tried to impose upon it. By March 1968 censorship was allowed to lapse in practice; in May it was officially abolished. As of April 5, the new Central Committee had adopted an action program that proposed further economic reforms, a federal polity giving more autonomy to the Slovaks, a revived constitution, and reintroduction of civil rights. In the heady atmosphere that came to be associated with the "Prague Spring," countless new organizations arose and innumerable new voices made themselves heard. The Soviets began to sound the alarm in late April, but their mounting pressure only encouraged local resistance. A crucial moment came on June 27, when a cluster of intellectuals signed a public statement known as the "Two Thousand Words." Concern now spread rapidly among not only the Soviet leadership but also the sclerotic leaders of the other Eastern European regimes. On July 3, Brezhnev explained that "we cannot remain indifferent to the fate of socialism in another country." The Warsaw Pact rulers came together shortly thereafter and on July 15 urged Dubček to rein in the forces of reform. Further negotiations got nowhere, and on August 10 the Czechoslovaks signaled their intention of adopting new party rules allowing the election of officials and the recognized right of opposition. On August 20 Soviet and Warsaw Pact troops invaded the country and effectively put an end to the experiment in "socialism with a human face." The denouement was protracted: Dubček was not officially replaced by the more compliant Husak until the following spring, and popular resistance, though largely nonviolent, continued at least that long. Resentment persisted even longer, particularly among the many intellectuals who lost their jobs, but formal opposition waned and the regime regained at least the appearance of stability.[34]

The demise of reform communism in Czechoslovakia had profound intellectual and emotional effects, primarily among those who had once dared hope for a more humane and democratic socialism. The "Prague Spring" had excited the imagination of a new generation of socialists in Western Europe and the United States, many of them students active in contemporaneous protests over the war in Vietnam or civil rights. They fantasized that the movement in Czechoslovakia was somehow all of a piece with their own efforts and were deeply disappointed at the outcome. The impact was still more devastating in Eastern Europe, for it served to discredit all of the socialist regimes in the eyes of their local intelligentsias.

Intellectuals had long played a critical, if ambivalent and contradictory, role in the modern politics of Eastern Europe. Their historic prominence was, if anything, accentuated by the coming to power of putatively socialist regimes in the 1940s. The socialist states had been in some essential way ideologically-dominated systems of rule, and intellectuals had taken a more than incidental part in their creation, staffing, and defense.[35] Inevitably, they chafed under the rigid rule of the party and were less willing to follow the tortuous path of orthodoxy than the politicians who ran the states. But many continued to hope for the transformation of the post-Stalinist states into more open and tolerant polities. The hopes had been dented by events in Hungary in 1956 and by the building of the Berlin Wall in 1961, but they nonetheless lingered. The outcome in Czechoslovakia buried them; subsequently, genuinely critical intellectuals migrated to the West or went into a more or less silent internal exile. In either case, they effectively and definitively withdrew their support from the socialist regimes.

The desertion of the regimes by the intellectuals of Eastern Europe and by those over whom they exerted influence was a critical blow. If it did not immediately produce a crisis of confidence among the region's rulers, that was because the regimes had long known that their survival depended not on the support of the local population but on the sufferance and support of their Soviet patrons. Still, they craved the legitimacy that they so desperately lacked and that they sought wherever possible to engineer. Now they looked in particular for support among the workers. A singular irony of "actually existing socialism" was that it came to power in societies where the workers were a distinct minority of the population. Only in Germany and Czechoslovakia had there been large numbers of urban workers before the imposition of socialist rule. Elsewhere, they were far outnumbered by the rural population. But socialist construction, it was long hoped, could create the very working class the new order was supposed to serve, and it is clear that the social and economic policies adopted across Eastern Europe were meant to privilege the emerging working class. Workers were preferentially recruited into the party and into the management of industry; their children were given special access to education; health and other social services were more readily available in urban, industrial centers than elsewhere; and workers' living standards, though not the first priority in the crafting of economic policy, were with some notable exceptions protected by substantial food subsidies and stable food prices. The exceptions in fact proved the rule, for the occasional protests of workers over increases in food prices or work norms ordinarily brought quick responses and concessions from even the least sympathetic regimes. And the workers took note of this special relationship to the regimes and for the most part withheld their support from the agitations of the intellectuals.

It thus came as a particularly distressing shock to party leaders in Eastern Europe when Polish workers greeted the announcement of increased food prices by the Polish government in December 1970 with widespread protest. Under Gomulka, Poland has charted its own course through the late 1950s and 1960s and remained relatively immune to the reformist impulses coming out of Czechoslovakia and neighboring socialist countries in the late 1960s. Indeed, the main challenge to Gomulka's leadership came not from liberal reformers but from the chauvinist, militarist, and anti-intellectual "Partisans" grouped around Mieczyslaw Moczar. Gomulka's demise, however, came not from these rivals within the leadership but from the workers, who rose en masse in late 1970 against the new regimen of wages and prices. Protests were especially intense and widespread in the Baltic region, and they were brutally suppressed. But the regime also relented: Edward Gierek replaced Gomulka on December 20, and shortly afterwards the December decree on prices and wages was withdrawn. A period of domestic stability ensued Nevertheless, the workers had now signaled their alienation from the system that claimed to rule on their collective behalf.

The record of socialism in Eastern Europe can accordingly be read as indicating a steady erosion of popular support from the alien regimes imposed from the East in the aftermath of the Second World War. But it can be read another way as well. Although these states lacked popular legitimacy, they did not seem about to crumble and seemed relatively impervious to the problem. Nor did they appear in the early 1970s to be nearing economic collapse. They had in fact experienced considerable economic growth during the 1950s and 1960s, benefiting from the crude, if inevitably also wasteful, mobilization of resources that centralized planning made into the highest economic virtue. Growth had slowed during the 1960s, but progress was still visible. On balance, then, the unpopular and largely illegitimate regimes of the East took on by the early 1970s an air of permanence. The impression was confirmed by the German treaties of the early 1970s, by the politics of détente, by the West's apparent deference to the proclamation in 1969 of the "Brezhnev doctrine," and by the Helsinki Accords of 1975. Socialism in eastern Europe had by the 1970s few admirers, but that made its persistence all the more of a challenge to western European and U.S. conceptions of political and social life and of their linked geopolitical interests.

## "CONTINUING REVOLUTION" IN CHINA

With the victory of the Chinese Communists in 1949, socialism was transformed. Until that date, it had been confined to what had long been regarded as the aberrant and backward margin of Europe.[36] Now it had established itself far beyond Europe's borders and in so doing proved its worldwide appeal. More specifically, the triumph of the Chinese Revolution coincided so precisely with the beginning of the end of European colonialism that it inevitably became a model of anticolonial resistance and development that attracted attention, if not always adoption, in countries struggling for independence and postcolonial economic growth.[37]

The Chinese model had three critical features to commend it. First, the Chinese Communists conceived of their revolution as a national liberation struggle, fought first against the Japanese invaders and then against the forces of the Guomindang armed and financed by Western imperialism. Second, it was a peasant revolution that required mass mobilization of the countryside. In theory, the Soviets had created a regime based on a worker-peasant alliance, but in fact its building had required that the cities be mobilized *against* the countryside. The experience of China as a national liberation struggle founded upon the peasantry thus opened up vast new possibilities for revolutionary action.[38] Third, the effort to build the new society in China proceeded in what appeared to be a very different and much more democratic fashion. Peasants were "won" to the campaigns against landlords; workers and peasants were mobilized behind the tasks set by the regime; and the party sought repeatedly to prevent the emergence of a bureaucratic elite within the party and the state. If it was not ultimately successful in these efforts, and if the alternative to bureaucracy was an intrusive and disruptive drive toward ideological conformity, it was nevertheless different from what had occurred in the USSR and from what was being imposed from above and outside upon the nations of Eastern Europe.

Quite apart from its meaning to the Chinese, therefore, the Chinese Revolution had profound effects upon world politics. Its immediate consequence was to make Asia the center of the Cold War and thus to make the Cold War into a more or less permanent principle of world order. It was in Asia, in fact, that the superpower confrontation came closest to turning into thermonuclear war. The mounting frustration of the United States over its inability to achieve a satisfactory solution to the Korean conflict brought about one such moment of crisis. The impending defeat of French forces at Dien Bien Phu produced a second, and very close, call. The Chinese example also influenced events in Indochina and Korea by providing a vision of successful guerilla insurgency and large-scale revolutionary war. In the late 1940s and early 1950s, when insurgencies still battled colonial or neocolonial regimes in Malaysia, the Philippines, and even Indonesia, the lessons of China's Revolution seemed both obvious and ominously important.

Although the most direct consequences of the Chinese Revolution were felt in Asia, it also served to enhance the stature of socialism elsewhere and to make socialism into a model of independent economic development. Here the contrasting images of the Soviet Union and of China under Mao Zedong complemented each other and combined to produce an alluring prospect of economic growth occurring outside the ambit of the capitalist world market. The apparent achievements of the Soviet economy demonstrated the awesome power of planning and the mobilization by command of the human and natural resources that typically constituted the only strategic advantage possessed by developing countries. The decision of the Chinese Communists to import that model wholesale into a rather different environment seemed to indicate its nearly universal applicability and led the leaders of many developing countries to consider some sort of planned economy as the surest path to material progress. The willingness to adopt socialism as a model of development was evident both in nations whose path to political independence was not marked by armed struggle and peasant mobilization and in nations where the road to freedom was drenched in blood. Socialist or at least statist strategies of development had a particular appeal to nationalist regimes in the Middle East such as those in Egypt, Iraq, and Syria; to independence leaders in African states such as Ghana, Algeria, Kenya, and Tanzania; and, in Asia, to the new rulers of India. The appeal did not always last beyond the tenure of particular rulers, such as Nasser in Egypt, but it was nonetheless widespread.

Socialism seems to have held a particular attraction for the first generation of postcolonial political leaders. It was probably inevitable that the leadership of movements for colonial independence would be dominated by elites who shared at least as much culturally with their colonial masters as they did with the peasant masses who numerically dominated the new nations. It was these local elites, often trained by Western missionaries to Western standards and steeped in the values of Western culture, who were in a position to articulate a nationalist and democratic critique of imperialism and a nationalist vision of the future.[39] Their ideological formation was thus profoundly Western and partook of the characteristically Western values of secularism, rationalism, and universalism. Even when given a local inflection, their views remained a part of the modernist discourse of the West. A classic example was pan-Arabism, which in its expansiveness and its modernizing aspirations owed more to the Enlightenment than it did to the Islamic beliefs of most Arabs. Another was socialism itself, which was imported into the Third World from the West and was often inextricably mixed up with visions of national independence and renewal.[40] For precisely this reason, however, the appeal of such secular and universalist philosophies proved limited, both socially and, as ever broader layers of the population were brought into public life in the postcolonial era, in time as well. The turning point probably came in 1967, when Nasser's defeat at the hands of Israel served to discredit the entire tradition of pan-Arab nationalism and to revive the fortunes of leaders and ideologies who held to a far more religious perspective. Even after that, however, socialism continued to have considerable appeal as an ideology and strategy of development, for the prospects of development within the world market remained dim and so offered no serious alternative.

The existence of socialism as simultaneously a strategy of national liberation and a path to economic development vastly complicated international relations. It meant the creation of a genuinely bipolar world order in which the two camps were in rough balance and constant competition. The effect was to put considerable leverage into the hands of non-Western leaders, who could play one superpower off against the other and ratchet up the terms of allegiance to one side or the other. The clearest reflections of this were the emergence in the 1950s of the so-called nonaligned movement, culminating in the famous Bandung Conference of April 1955, and the increasing dominance of the General Assembly of the United Nations and the UN's various commissions and committees by the developing nations. To an incredible degree, the UN ceased after the decision to invade Korea to be a venue for the Cold War and served instead as a forum within which issues of development and decolonization got a genuine hearing. (The price, of course, was that the organization was regularly bypassed on issues of war and peace.)

The establishment of communism in China thus served to enhance the stature of socialism throughout the world and to create political space for various alternatives to capitalist development by means of integration into the world market. This effect persisted even after the Sino-Soviet split became public and made it clear that socialism was neither a monolithic system nor a coherent bloc or alliance, let alone an emerging, rival world order. The split had begun to be visible to careful observers in the late 1950s but broke into the open during the last years of Khrushchev's reign. By the mid-1960s, the Chinese were labeling the Soviet Union an imperialist power, and Mao Zedong himself declared that economic reforms and the growth of bureaucracy in the USSR amounted to a "capitalist restoration."[41] By 1969 the rivalry between the Soviet Union and the People's Republic led to a huge buildup of military forces along the world's most extensive border and several violent, if limited, clashes. The conflict was no doubt in part a reflection of traditional geopolitical antagonisms, but it was also the result of the divergent paths of development in the two nations. As the Soviet and Chinese leaders opted for different mixes of policy, distinct strategies of economic growth, and contrasting styles of rule, they felt it necessary to critique their rivals within the socialist camp and to denigrate their commitment to the goal of building socialism.

The effort to build socialism in China was indeed different from what had occurred in the Soviet Union.[42] Its distinguishing features flowed logically from its origins as a revolutionary struggle for national liberation based upon the peasantry. Chinese communism had begun as an urban phenomenon, but its bases of support within the cities had been crushed in 1927. Henceforth, it was largely a movement rooted in the countryside. This novel strategic orientation sustained the party during the lean years after 1927 and served it well during the struggle against the Japanese and, ultimately, the Guomindang. Once in power the party continued to nurture its ties to the peasants. Indeed, the new regime's first major initiative was land reform. The antilandlord campaign was carried out with considerable skill and moderation. Work teams were sent into the countryside and local villagers were encouraged to participate in the identification and criticism of landlords, whose land was then redistributed to the poorer peasants. In a typical region, roughly 40 percent of the land was redistributed, and approximately 60 percent of the population received some benefit.[43] The effect was to create, or increase, support for the revolution among the peasants. The era of Communist rule began therefore with an impressive store of goodwill toward the party on the part of the overwhelming mass of China's rural population. To that must be added the legitimacy that the party acquired simply by its victory over the Japanese and the Guomindang. The Communists had succeeded, it appeared, in driving out the foreign enemy and reuniting China. The revolution was thus as much an occasion for national revival as it was a moment of social transformation.

The Chinese Communist Party (CCP) could for all these reasons take the first steps toward the construction of socialism with considerable popular support. The contrast with the Soviet experience could hardly have been greater. The Bolshevik regime had taken power with far more support in the cities than among the peasants; it then saw its most fervent backers decimated in a civil war that required, for its effective prosecution, the conscription of grain and men from a peasantry whose loyalty to the regime, never very firm, began quickly to dissipate. The Bolsheviks were forced by such circumstances to back away from whatever plans and hopes they had for transforming society and to adopt instead the New Economic Policy that revived the economy but served to confirm the peasants and many urban entrepreneurs in their commitment to markets and capitalism. When the party finally moved in the late 1920s toward building "socialism in one country," it therefore did so largely against, rather than with, the society over which it presided. The context proved the undoing of the project. The Chinese Communists, on the other hand, could count on more popular support for their initiatives and thus undertake the process of building socialism with a different set of political assumptions.

Central to these assumptions was the sense that the people could be convinced of the superior virtues of socialism. Convincing the people would require education, propaganda, and "struggle" to win converts to the party's "mass line," which would itself be refined and perfected in the effort to enlist the masses on its behalf.[44] The tactics of the CCP were therefore at least "quasi-democratic." As Mao Zedong explained in 1949, "The method we employ is democratic, the method of persuasion, not of coercion." Later Mao would compare the people's will to the "raw material" essential to a factory; without it, the party would have nothing to work with, no idea of the society that had to be acted upon.[45] Elsewhere, Mao waxed euphoric about the malleability of the Chinese people: they were "poor and blank," but fortunately "a blank sheet of paper has no blotches, and so the newest and most beautiful words can be written on it, the newest and most beautiful pictures can be painted on it."[46]

Mao at times went so far as to turn the materialism of Marx and Lenin literally on its head. He argued, for example, that "Lenin said: 'The more backward the country, the more difficult its transition from capitalism to socialism.' Now it seems that this way of speaking is incorrect. As a matter of fact, the more backward the economy, the easier, not the more difficult, the transition from capitalism to socialism. The poorer they are, the more people want revolution."[47] The masses were to be brought into political activity but were expected to follow the leadership of the party and, more specifically, of Mao Zedong. This is a particular vision of democracy that has little to do with standard notions of popular sovereignty. Its aspiration to mass participation and debate, from which will emerge ideological unity, is especially alien to Western traditions of democracy; it is intrusive, illiberal, and in practice often terrifying. Nevertheless, it imparted a unique pattern to the political and social development of China after the revolution, a pattern that would reach a horrible climax in the excesses of the cultural revolution. It was a pattern, however, that for a prolonged period made Chinese socialism appear to be a genuinely popular alternative to the Stalinist model bequeathed to socialism by the Soviet experience.

This peculiar style of rule became visible soon after the revolution. Upon seizing power, the Chinese Communists chose at first to continue the united-front strategy, symbolized by the theoretical commitment to "New Democracy," that had brought them to power. They focused primarily on restoring order and the authority of the central state, and the leadership construed these tasks as requiring above all price stability and the revival of economic activity and as therefore precluding for the time being the active pursuit of social transformation. The exception was land reform, which the party knew should not be delayed and whose successful implementation served to strengthen popular support for the regime.

With land reform under way and the new state consolidating its control over the country, the party leaders proceeded to launch four mass campaigns designed simultaneously to win mass acceptance for party positions and to recruit cadres in the cities and, specifically, among the workers. The first was the "Resist America and Aid Korea" campaign, which took particular aim at Westerners and Christians within China. The second, and linked, campaign was the "Suppression of Counterrevolutionaries" movement, which attacked alleged spies, former Guomindang supporters, and secret societies. These campaigns proceeded through late 1950 and peaked in April 1951. They led to considerable violence and numerous executions, succeeded in drastically weakening the main rivals to the party, and in the process disarmed the population as well. These were followed by the "Three Anti Campaign," which aimed at corruption, waste, and bureaucratic obstruction; and the "Five Anti Campaign," which while officially targeting bribery, theft, and tax evasion, turned into a broad assault upon the bourgeoisie. The last campaign was not in theory directed against capitalists as a class, but it proceeded by eliciting charges of corruption against almost all capitalists, who were denounced and urged to admit to wrongdoing, investigated, and ultimately classified by party activists as "law-abiding" or not. In Tianjin, for example, the campaign pronounced roughly 10 percent of firms "law-abiding," 64 percent "basically law-abiding," 21 percent "semi law-abiding," and 5.3 percent "serious law-breakers."[48] Most businesses were forced to pay fines, and the party made clear its fundamental hostility to capital and to private enterprise. Together, the four mass mobilizations of 1950–1952 served to consolidate the party's control over the economy and to recruit a new generation to membership, which grew from just under 4.5 million in 1949 to 6 million by late 1952.

Most important, the campaigns helped to create both the necessary climate of opinion for the next step in the building of socialism and the cadres essential to carrying it out at the local level. That stage was launched with adoption of the First Five-Year Plan in 1953. The plan was closely modeled on the centralized development plans of the Soviet Union and reflected in its emphases the characteristic Soviet preferences for heavy industry over consumer goods industries and for investment in industry at the expense of agricultural investment and living standards. The results were at first quite impressive as both industry and agriculture responded to the stimuli provided by the additional inputs of labor and capital mobilized by the new regime. The government also encouraged the development of more collective forms of economic organization. Within industry the remaining private firms were nationalized in 1955. Even more progress was made in agriculture. Shortly after the completion of land reform, "mutual aid teams" of roughly half a dozen households had been established to undertake productive labor on a cooperative basis. Peasants for the most part retained title to their individual plots of land and continued to work private plots that, although small, produced a much larger, indeed indispensable, portion of farm income.

The Five-Year Plan envisioned a transformation toward a more collectivized pattern in agriculture over time. Peasants would be urged to pool their resources into still larger units of thirty to fifty households known as "lower-stage cooperatives," and eventually they were encouraged to create still larger units, "higher-stage cooperatives," consisting of two hundred to three hundred households. The movement toward more collective forms gathered momentum slowly, but in July 1955 Mao Zedong himself intervened and argued for faster progress. By 1956 it swept all before it. As late as the end of 1955, a third of peasant households had still worked in mutual aid teams, over 60 percent in lower-stage cooperatives, and only 4 percent in the higher-stage cooperatives. By the end of 1956, by contrast, less than 4 percent remained in mutual aid teams and less than 10 percent in lower-stage cooperatives; roughly 88 percent had entered higher-stage cooperatives. Even in the higher-stage cooperatives, peasants retained formal ownership of land and continued to cultivate their private gardens, but the quickened pace of social transformation indicated the likely course of future development.

Economic revival was accompanied by a degree of political stabilization. The People's Liberation Army (PLA) was reorganized after the severe test it had faced in Korea. The rhetorical emphasis on self-reliance and on the efficacy of revolutionary war persisted, but the army's leadership made sure to acquire new weapons and reintroduced ranks, hierarchy, and discipline as well. Over the same period Communist Party membership rose consistently, reaching 12.7 million in 1957 as the party and the regime began to reap the political benefits of development. With growth and stability, however, came problems and questions about political authority and the direction and speed of social transformation. The attack on Stalin at the 20th Congress in February 1956 was especially troubling, for it forced the party leadership to undertake a major reassessment of its model of development just as the First Five-Year Plan was drawing to a close.

The Political Bureau undertook a protracted discussion and evaluation, summarized by Mao in his note "On the Ten Great Relationships," in which he first outlined an alternative to the Stalinist model. Mao criticized the Soviets for neglecting agriculture and consumer goods, for excessive centralization in economic planning, and for the "arrogance and conceit" with which Moscow treated the nationalities that made up the USSR.[49] But Mao Zedong's stature was itself an issue, however, for the clear lesson of Khrushchev's secret speech on Stalin's crimes was to avoid the "cult of personality" that Stalin had created around himself. In consequence, Mao's views did not at first prevail among the party's leadership. Instead, the leadership proceeded to work up the Second Five-Year Plan that envisioning a more or less steady course of economic policy leading, it was hoped, to consistent but unspectacular growth.

Mao refused to acquiesce and instead went on to elaborate his alternative vision of political and economic development. His foray into mass politics was the so-called Hundred Flowers campaign, which he announced in May 1956 but which did not truly get going for almost another year. The aim was to elicit criticism of the party's "bureaucratism, sectarianism and subjectivism"; the chosen vehicle would be the intellectuals. Once the campaign had properly begun, the response was quicker and more fulsome than Mao had anticipated and centered on the "Democracy Wall" at Peking University, where sharp criticisms of the party and the lack of democracy appeared. The party leaders panicked almost immediately and, with Mao's somewhat reluctant support, pulled back, urged a restoration of order, and began a campaign that ultimately branded 300,000 intellectuals as "rightists." Mao's behavior in this instance would prove to be characteristic: again and again over the next twenty years he rallied the people or some section of the people against his opponents in the party behind a populist and quasi-democratic rhetoric only to abandon those who had heeded his call when their views moved beyond the limits he was prepared to tolerate.

The failure of the Hundred Flowers campaign did not deter Mao from his efforts to alter the course of party policy making. His next effort was even more disastrous, for it affected not merely the intellectuals but the majority of peasants and workers. The battle lines were drawn during the debate over the Second Five-Year Plan. Its drafters were concerned about the decline in agricultural productivity that had accompanied the transition to higher-stage cooperatives and the related difficulty of squeezing any more surplus from agriculture for investment in industry. In 1957 agricultural output had grown by only 1 percent, half the rate of population increase, and it seemed impossible to plan for more than the 5.5 percent goal initially proposed for the next five years. Mao Zedong, on the other hand, was unwilling to accept such a modest goal and cited on his behalf the apparent enthusiasm with which peasants took to collective forms of work organization. From that reading of recent history he concluded that far more ambitious plans, based on intensified ideological commitment and the mobilization of the nation's seemingly inexhaustible human resources, could be realized. His scheme came to be known as the Great Leap Forward.[50]

The Great Leap represented an application of Mao's political practices to economic development. At its heart was a preference for peasants and for local initiative and a rejection of centralized, bureacratic planning and the attendant overemphasis on heavy industry that characterized the Soviet model. The idea was to raise agricultural production through mass mobilization, thereby increasing peasant incomes and consumption and stimulating light industry, whose subsequent growth would bring along heavy industry. It was assumed that much of this growth would be localized within provinces or within the larger, and almost natural, "macroregions" within which the economy had long functioned.[51] Each province was encouraged, for example, to develop "a backbone of basic industries" that could assist the development at the local level of small-scale manufacturing employing "appropriate," intermediate technology. Roughly a hundred million peasants were set to work on irrigation projects that brought 7.8 million hectares under cultivation. An even higher stage form of cooperative labor, the "people's communes"—embracing several thousand households who gave up private plots and made use of communal kitchens, nurseries, and other shared infrastructure—were developed, and by mid-1958 included 99 percent of peasant households. Communes and villages were also urged to undertake industrial work in the countryside, and roughly a million backyard furnaces were soon operating with the aim of increasing metal production. People's communes were also set up in the cities and, by implication, put to work in industry. In addition, over two hundred million people were enrolled in local militias in both the cities and the countryside, thereby carrying the spirit of local self-reliance even into military and internal security matters.

The effort involved in the Great Leap was prodigious and it produced some genuine gains. The expansion of agricultural acreage was an obvious achievement, and there were benefits, too, in the great variety of local initiatives encouraged during these years. If nothing else, the focus on the local and the regional prevented, or at least retarded, the overcentralization of planning and the extreme bureaucratization that plagued the Soviets from the time of Stalin. The Stalinist style of highly centralized planning, adumbrated in China's First Five-Year Plan, was critiqued and abandoned before it could become fully and firmly established, before its flawed operation could become customary, and before a stratum of officials committed to its perpetuation could arise and consolidate their power and perquisites. But neither was a genuine alternative to Stalinist planning worked out, for the policies of the Great Leap were an immediate, practical disaster. There was a colossal waste of effort, and the privileging of ideology over efficiency led to substantial losses. As early as mid-1959, Mao Zedong himself was forced to concede its unfortunate consequences: "The chaos caused was on a grand scale." A reappraisal followed and the party leadership began to back off from Mao's vision. But policy changed far more slowly, and it is estimated that the negative effects were felt through 1962 and were responsible for as many as 20 million deaths from famine. The central policies of the Great Leap were reversed by that year: peasants were allowed to work in smaller groups and private plots were restored, and economic growth resumed in industry and agriculture.

Neither the Great Leap Forward nor its failure and reversal resolved the ongoing debate between Mao Zedong and his opponents over the direction of economic and political development. Resolution was precluded by two key factors. First, there were no institutional mechanisms for adjudicating disagreements. Mao might well write eloquently about the "correct handling of contradictions among the people," but that was precisely what his brand of quasi-democracy and charismatic leadership could not accomplish. Second, it was possible to identify the two contending factions in the struggle—one centered on Mao; his third wife, Jiang Qing; Lin Biao, leader of the PLA; Chen Boda, Mao's longtime personal secretary and ideologue; and Jiang's close ally Zhang Chunqiao; and the other, looser group revolved around Liu Shaoqi; Peng Zhen, the mayor of Peking and local party leader; and, it appears, Deng Xiaoping—but it was far more difficult to discern precise differences in policy. Despite Mao's assertions, there were no "capitalist-roaders," only supposed comrades with slightly different perspectives on how to bring about socialism. The absence of an alternative vision to Mao's was itself a reflection of the fact that no rival center of power had been allowed to develop. There was only the party, whose supremacy both Mao and his opponents proclaimed, and there was no serious ideological alternative to what came increasingly to be called "Mao Zedong Thought."

The growing rift with the Soviet Union discredited any path other than

Mao's and produced a stiflingly conformist critique of revisionism from which none dared dissent. Even when Mao's policies were discredited by practical experience, Mao and Mao Zedong Thought remained unchallenged at the level of political discourse. Indeed, after the failure of the Great Leap the entire party leadership—Liu Shaoqi and his wife, Wang Guangmei, Deng Xiaoping, Zhou Enlai, and Mao Zedong—joined in the quintessentially Maoist Socialist Education Campaign, designed to bring socialist values to the people and to "rectify" the work of the party. Over time it became clear that Mao Zedong's notion of ideological struggle and rectification was more radical and more "democratic" than Liu Shaoqi's, and that Mao was more firmly committed to the idea that in carrying it out, it was "necessary to give the masses a free hand." What was never clear was quite what this populist mobilization was supposed to accomplish, for it was not linked to a program of institution building. On the contrary, its spirit was suspicious of all institutions and of any and all efforts to set up a "normal" and stable set of relationships within which development could proceed over the long term.

Mao Zedong and his supporters were extremely critical of bureaucracy and elitism within the party and, in more extreme formulations, regarded much of the leadership as corrupt, reactionary, and worthy of being overthrown. At the same time, Mao insisted again and again on the need for the party, and he repeatedly backed off when his own initiatives threatened the party's authority. His opponents, by contrast, were well represented in the party hierarchy, but beyond that they had only very weak institutional support in the state apparatus or in the economy. They lacked as well a compelling alternative model of development and an ideological foundation from which to criticize Mao or to resist and counter his attacks. Their deficiencies were Mao's major assets. In addition he could count on support from yet another, powerful quarter: the army. With the appointment of Lin Biao as defense minister, Mao gained a critical ally. The PLA had long had a special role in the history and lore of the Chinese Revolution, and its reputation was enhanced by its heroic efforts in Korea. The reforms of the mid-1950s had largely depoliticized the army, but from the early 1960s Lin Biao had managed to bring it back into politics. It was for the army that he produced the little red book, *Quotations from Chairman Mao*, that helped to transform the army into an ideologically committed weapon in the ongoing political battle. When the PLA exploded China's first atom bomb in October 1964, its prestige reached a peak from which it entered decisively and disastrously into the nation's politics. Lin Biao decided to abolish ranks within the army in 1965, and in the same year he secured effective control over the security apparatus. In 1966 he appointed Jiang Qing to preside over cultural policy for the army.

From these positions of strength Mao would launch the Great Proletarian Cultural Revolution.[52] It began in the fall of 1965 with an attack on "reactionary bourgeois ideology," more specifically, with criticism of the writer Wu Han for his historical drama *The Dismissal of Hai Rui*. The play was not unreasonably read by Mao and his supporters as a parable critical of Mao and the folly of the Great Leap. Wu Han's defenders sought to treat the dispute as an academic matter; the Maoists disagreed and utilized the dispute to launch a much broader assault on Mao's enemies. After considerable debate within the party, Mao's allies prevailed and the Cultural Revolution was formally launched in the spring of 1966 with the setting up of the small Central Cultural Revolution Group, which urged the "masses" to become involved in the struggle. The response was particularly forthcoming among students, especially high school students, who began to form themselves into rival camps of Red Guards. The "radicals" among them appear often to have come from "bourgeois" backgrounds and to have on that account suffered discrimination in favor of the children of party members, who tended to become the core of the "moderate" Red Guard units. The Red Guards were organized initially in the schools and universities, where they did battle with educational authorities, with wayward teachers, and with one another.

Though Red Guard efforts were sanctioned by Mao and the party leadership, the principles by which the Cultural Revolution would be conducted remained a matter of contention. Liu Shaoqi sent "work teams" into the schools and universities and sought to lay down ground rules to control the campaign. The rules strongly favored the party's Youth League, and the moderates clustered around them and restricted the participation of those outside the party and from bad class backgrounds. The result was a series of battles between radical Red Guards and party work teams allied with more moderate students. Mao took the side of the former, and in late July secured the withdrawal of the work teams. On August 1 he created his famous wall poster urging the masses to "Bombard the Headquarters." Ten days later the party leadership published a sixteen-point directive on prosecution of the Cultural Revolution.

Although the Sixteen Points urged reason and moderation on the movement, they also proposed mobilization of the masses "without restraint." With the party explicitly enjoined by Mao from intervening to stop the process, with the work teams withdrawn and the Youth League disbanded, and with the Central Cultural Revolution Group officially urging on the

160

Red Guards, they took their agitation outside the universities and into the factories and countryside. The Cultural Revolution had entered its most extreme and violent phase. Soon there were Red Guards among the workers and peasants, and a pervasive effort to oust the old leaders of the party and replace them with devotees of Mao's vision.

In the mobilization and countermobilization that ensued, the two sides brought rival groups of workers into the fray as well. More often than not, the radicals sought out the underemployed, underprivileged casual workers; the moderates relied for their support upon the more skilled and stable sectors of the working class. The critical confrontation took place in Shanghai, where the radical workers' groups took on the label "Red Rebels" and the moderates called themselves "Scarlet Guards." Late in 1966 the radicals began seizing control of factories and in January took control of the city government and proceeded to establish a regime modeled on their understanding of the Paris Commune. Until that moment, the radicals had enjoyed the support of Mao and his allies at the center. But the Shanghai Paris Commune was a wholly new type of government that threatened to reduce almost to nothing the role of the party. From this prospect Mao Zedong predictably recoiled, and the "Great Helmsman" moved in February 1967 to oppose the commune in Shanghai and to prevent its replication elsewhere. In its stead, he proposed the so-called Revolutionary Committee, one-third of whose members would come from the PLA, one-third from the party, and one-third from the mass organizations. Over the next year and a half, Revolutionary Committees were be set up across China and came to be the dominant form of political authority. The army played the central role in their establishment and, in consequence, in overseeing the stabilization of political authority after the initial phase of the Cultural Revolution.

The consolidation of the Revolutionary Committees would bring about a gradual cessation of the violence and intimidation that marked the Cultural Revolution. It did not end the movement, however, or overturn its effects. That would take several more years and would not really be possible until the death of Mao and the subsequent arrest of the "Gang of Four" in 1976. The stages by which order was restored and the Cultural Revolution reversed were several and contradictory and did not follow in a straight line. The reason for this was the same as the reasons for its outbreak: the absence of institutional fora for conducting and settling disagreements, the lack of a rival intellectual framework to Mao Zedong Thought, and the party's inability to elaborate and opt for a stable model of development other than the two discredited models associated respectively with Stalin and Mao. The Cultural Revolution was reined in by Mao but never repudiated, and it was thus never quite defeated so long as Mao lived; rather, it exhausted itself after running its violent course. By its end it had virtually no defenders, at least not within China and among those who had witnessed its terrifying excesses.

The effects of the Cultural Revolution beyond China were equally odd, ambiguous, and ironic. Numerous ultraleft groups, both in the West and in the Third World, were inspired by its democratic thrust, its refusal to acknowledge the Soviet Union as the only example of socialism, and its militant anti-imperialism. By the early or mid-1970s, however, efforts to turn Maoist inspiration into revolutionary strategy had almost everywhere failed and the small sects and parties embodying such visions had collapsed into insignificance. The Cultural Revolution also served to diminish the appeal of Chinese socialism as a model of development for non-Western countries. Though Mao Zedong's economic thought—with its preference for small scale, for agriculture over heavy industry, for "appropriate" technology, for regarding a large population as an asset rather than a liability, and so on—often ran parallel to more enlightened views about development, the turmoil that accompanied its implementation was anathema to the leaders of developing nations.

The final irony was the curious rapprochement that occurred between China and the leader of world imperialism, the United States, not long after the height of the Cultural Revolution. At the root of this diplomatic reversal was, of course, the increasing tension between China and the Soviet Union, which had led to border clashes in 1969. The Chinese leadership felt seriously threatened by the hostility of the Soviets, who continued the buildup of forces through 1970. Feelers were sent by both sides in 1970, and in April 1971 the U.S. ping-pong team was invited to China. Henry Kissinger went to China in July and met with Zhou Enlai, and President Richard Nixon followed with a visit in February 1972. China was accorded diplomatic recognition by the United States and given Taiwan's seat on the UN Security Council. The gains secured by China and the United States from their newfound friendship were enormous: each had enlisted a powerful ally in its rivalry with the Soviet Union, and the Chinese, in addition, obtained access to Western technology.

Perhaps most important, the Chinese regime won by its dealings with the United States a significant measure of legitimacy. Though the nation was still recovering from the devastating trials of the Cultural Revolution, its main opponent in international politics had come to acknowledge the authority and viability of China's revolutionary government. Socialism was now, of course, deeply divided. Nevertheless, communism had proved its capacity to win converts, to take root in diverse settings, and to endure over much of the world. The challenge of communism remained at the top of the agenda of world politics in the mid-1970s, and in the rivalry between competing world orders and alternative social systems there was as yet no compelling reason to predict that capitalism would eventually prevail.

# 6 \ Liberalism Eclipsed

POLITICS AND ECONOMICS

IN THE ADVANCED

INDUSTRIAL NATIONS,

1968–1989

The project of creating a viable modern capitalism and,
with it, a reasonably democratic political order proceeded
extremely well for two decades after the onset of the Cold
War. Under U.S. tutelage Germany and Japan fashioned
highly successful economic machines and stable polities; so,
too, did the countries of Western Europe. The United States
itself prospered beyond all expectations, and its politics was seen
as essentially consensual and for the most part was conducted that
way. The achievement did not spell victory in the competition of
social systems encouraged by the Cold War, but it did guarantee
that capitalism would not go quietly into the "dustbin of history."
In fact, an entire generation of scholars became convinced that
capitalism had managed to transform itself into something
different, more humane, and manageable. The new system
was labeled variously—neocapitalism, welfare capitalism,
corporate or managed or organized capitalism—but
whichever label was chosen, the notion was that the
crisis-prone, wasteful, and inhumane capitalism of the

prewar era had been reformed out of existence. The new system approximated in many of its particulars the social and political order imagined and advocated by anticommunist liberals in the early Cold War era.

The events of 1968 and of the late 1960s more generally called this achievement into question and raised the possibility that capitalism remained liable to crisis.[1] An extraordinary concatenation of events occurred in 1968, beginning with the Tet offensive in January. The success of the Vietnamese insurgents was deeply affecting and seriously destabilizing in the United States, for it gave the lie to government pretensions about its prosecution of the war in Indochina. The assassinations of Martin Luther King, Jr., in April and then of Robert Kennedy in June had similar effects in that they suggested that political reform might not be possible within the normal workings of the political system. The violence that attended the Democratic National Convention in Chicago during August sent the same message in its display of the resistance of the party of reform to the claims of antiwar and civil rights activists.

An even more dramatic outbreak of unrest occurred in France.[2] It began as "sexual riot" on the new university campus at Nanterre on the outskirts of Paris, took on a more political dimension with demonstrations against U.S. involvement in Vietnam, and soon gave birth to the "movement of March 22," which became the core of subsequent agitation. In April attention turned to government proposals to reform the universities by imposing more selective admissions criteria, and on May 3 the movement spread to the Sorbonne and the heart of Paris. Students occupied the university but were removed with considerable force, adding yet another grievance to the mix of critiques and demands. Very quickly, protest took aim at the regime itself, its "tentacular bureaucracy" and authoritarianism, and at the "blocked society" over which it was said to be presiding, and soon spread to the workers as well. The government responded to the crisis firmly, though it was also willing to negotiate. De Gaulle himself, however, faltered and vacillated. The situation was saved only by the moderation of the French Communists, who did their best to control the outbreak from below.

The May events in Paris inspired the "New Left" across Europe, though students needed little inspiration; they had been active throughout the year in Madrid, in Germany and Italy, and at universities across Great Britain. There had also been militant demonstrations in Japan and in Mexico during the year, and in both countries insurgency blossomed during the summer and early fall. Roughly simultaneous with these events in the democratic capitalist nations was the unfolding of the "Prague Spring," which by the summer of 1968 had been transformed from an effort to give socialism a human face into a more direct challenge to Soviet domination and, implicitly, to socialism as a political and social order. The crushing of that resistance coincided almost precisely with the rough handling of dissidents at the Democratic Convention by police in Chicago. It seemed to some— including both overly optimistic student radicals and overly worried government officials—that East and West were equally threatened by a rebellion of the young.[3]

Such hopes and fears were largely illusory, but at the time the impact of the discontent was enormous. It was exaggerated by the reactions of the authorities, by its context, and by the ideas and movements to which it gave rise. The first is easiest to see: leaders like Richard Nixon and Charles de Gaulle, and even Leonid Brezhnev, were shocked and utterly undone by the events of 1968, and they would be haunted thereafter by their legacy. Brezhnev, for example, was appalled at events in Czechoslovakia and put a decisive end to whatever remained of Khrushchev's economic reforms. De Gaulle was so panicked by the prospect of a Communist-led demonstration planned for May 29 that he fled to a French army outpost in Baden-Baden. He returned in a matter of hours, rallied his supporters, and presided over a major electoral victory a month later, but he was never the same and left office within a year. For Nixon, the antipathy displayed by protesters confirmed his rather paranoid view of politics, in which he saw himself an isolated and embattled victim. His perspective was articulated most forcefully by his vice-president, Spiro Agnew, who railed against the "adversary culture" that, in his mind, embraced radical students and middle-class liberals alike. It was this highly polarized and almost Manichean perspective on the world that tempted Nixon not merely to bend and stretch the rules of ordinary politics but to break those rules outright. It was that behavior, epitomized by the Watergate break-in, routine recourse to "dirty tricks," and the attendant misuse of executive power and privilege, that brought down his presidency.

The extreme reactions of older, conservative leaders like de Gaulle and Nixon—not to mention more liberal politicians like Lyndon Johnson and Hubert Humphrey who were also traumatized—mirrored and mimicked the rhetoric of the young, who tended to see the unrest of the late 1960s in similarly apocalyptic terms. The combination served to intensify the rhetorical antagonisms between the young and the old, the protesters and those in authority, and to establish a highly antagonistic style of political discourse. That discourse has persisted, and its echoes could be detected for more than a quarter century. Its power derived from its ability to connect diverse forms of protest and currents of reform into a broad challenge to established authority in the capitalist democracies and, on the other side, from its tendency to elicit fear and a highly defensive posture from both moderate and conservative defenders of existing arrangements. The rhetorical contest itself largely created the "adversary culture" of which conservatives complained and inspired the defense against it.

The sense that the challenge of 1968 represented something genuinely revolutionary was, of course, not merely a discursive effect. It was also a product of the circumstances in which protest occurred, for the agitations of students and the young coincided with, and at times became intertwined with, the protests and agitations of far more significant social actors and political movements. In the United States, for example, the opposition to the war drew inspiration from the civil rights movement and, in turn, brought questions of racial justice to a much wider constituency. The antiwar and civil rights movements thus reinforced and strengthened each other. There were also important connections with the labor movement. It was the United Auto Workers, for example, who subsidized the early work of the Students for a Democratic Society. Inevitably, the young and the insurgent—mostly students from middle- or upper-middle-class backgrounds—clashed with the older leaders of the labor movement over issues of tactics, on matters of style, and, ultimately, over ideology as well. Conservatives were quick to capitalize on these divisions and did what they could to pit "hard hats" against "long-haired hippie" radicals, but the reality was more complex, and there remained important connections between the largely student resistance to the war, the civil rights movement encompassing blacks of all social classes, and at least some sections of labor. Indeed, in the late 1960s and early 1970s the links appeared to be becoming stronger, as a revival of labor militancy caused a brief but noticeable increase in the number of strikes. Antiwar and civil-rights activists were quick to rally in support of farm workers and black and Hispanic workers in hospitals seeking union recognition; there was considerable sympathy for the postal workers' strike of 1970; and the upsurge of militancy among young, mostly black auto workers in Detroit and in Lordstown, Ohio, evoked an even more enthusiastic response.

In Europe labor militancy was an even more prominent dimension of the upheavals of the late 1960s. From the late 1940s through the early 1960s labor had been relatively quiescent across much of Europe, as the imperatives of reconstruction and growth led workers and their leaders to adopt a more cooperative and less confrontational style of industrial relations. In some countries, of course, the lack of militancy also reflected the organizational weakness of the unions. In Italy and France, for example, the largest unions were closely allied with the Communists; and both the unions and the parties with which they were affiliated were marginalized and in effect ghettoized, routinely excluded from the corporatist bargaining that occurred elsewhere between employers, the state, and more ideologically acceptable representatives of the workers. The great bulk of industrial workers therefore remained unorganized, even as they gave their votes to the parties of the Left.

In Britain and West Germany, on the other hand, strong organization had served to keep ordinary workers in line behind the relatively moderate policies of labor leaders. In Germany, the unions were very well organized and well integrated into the institutional machinery of collective bargaining, and their interests were at least heard by those in power. What discontent existed at lower levels seldom made itself felt and was to a considerable extent discouraged by the fact that it could so easily be tainted with the brush of anticommunism. In Britain the unions were closely allied with the Labour Party, and the leaders of the party and the unions managed in the 1940s to secure workers' grudging acquiescence to a policy of wage restraint in return for government commitment to full employment and to reasonably generous funding of the welfare state. Unions in Germany likewise managed to convince their members that cooperation with capital offered a better prospect for achieving higher living standards.

These constraints on worker militancy did not survive the late 1960s. In Britain, for example, the steady progress of inflation, the gradual widening of horizons and expectations, and the drift of effective power to the shop floor led to a tremendous upsurge in strike activity that was only worsened by efforts of the Labour Party to control it. In Germany, workers and unions were led to expect great things from the increasingly powerful Social Democrats and the sense of restraint ebbed away. Militancy was even more pronounced in France and Italy and succeeded in boosting union membership to levels more in line with those of other European countries. The result was a newfound and long-term increase in workers' ability to strike effectively. French and Italian workers had long supported the left in elections; now they acquired as well the ability to exert leverage over employers in the workplace. Labor relations became again a locus of visible political conflict. The change had little to do with the student unrest with which it coincided, but the combination did much to credit notions of a more general crisis.

So, too, did the intellectual ferment produced by and around 1968. Political debate during the early postwar years was never as sterile as is sometimes depicted, but it operated within certain limits. The behavior of the Soviet Union during the beginnings of the Cold War did much to discredit currents of thought critical of capitalism. As did subsequent revelations of Stalin's brutality. The political legacy of the thirties and forties also restricted the scope of conservative argument. The agitations of the late 1960s broke apart these, typically unspoken, limits on what was considered legitimate political discourse. The effect was most immediately visible on the left, where a new generation of anti-Stalinist Marxists, or neo-Marxists, arose to challenge the hegemony of staid social democrats and unrepentant defenders of Stalin and the Soviet model. This New Left found new heroes in the ranks of Third World revolutionaries such as Mao Zedong, Castro, Che Guevara, or Ho Chi Minh, and intellectual forerunners in Antonio Gramsci, the Frankfurt school, and French existentialists. It scarcely mattered that Mao, for example, proclaimed himself a loyal follower of Stalin or that the Vietnamese and the Cubans aligned themselves closely with the Soviet Union.

This rebirth of Marxism had important, long-term consequences on political and intellectual life in the democratic capitalist nations. Its influence would not go unchallenged, but its anticapitalist critique became in some sense pervasive and served as the common currency not only of the student left and the antiwar movement but also of the emerging feminist movement, the "greens," and the civil rights movement in its more radical manifestations. Most important, it was this new quasi-Marxist perspective that provided the language and concepts within which the upheavals of 1968 were themselves understood. This self-understanding on the part of the generation of 1968 was in many respects extremely perceptive, in other ways off the mark, and on certain matters delusional. The delusions to which the New Left was susceptible became very clear very soon and, in most cases, were quickly abandoned. The most common was a romantic "Third Worldism," whose primary virtue was its consistent opposition to racism and imperial domination but whose folly was its faith that national liberation movements and efforts to use socialism as a tool for national economic development would produce regimes more truly democratic and popular than those already existing within the Soviet orbit. Rather less common was a naive "workerism" that purported to discern the seeds of revolutionary consciousness in the alienation of working-class youth in the advanced countries. There were virtues in this as well—a measure of populism, an identification with avant-garde subcultures, and an engagement with metropolitan goings-on—but folly, too, in confusing anger with class consciousness.

What was genuinely insightful about the New Left, by contrast, was its critique of advanced capitalism and the liberal political order with which it had become so intertwined. Drawing on the writings of the young Marx and of an earlier generation of European Marxists concerned with issues of culture, belief, and human psychology, the New Left evolved a penetrating indictment of postwar capitalism. To the normal array of charges that capitalism was unstable and wasteful, and that it generated poverty and inequality, were thus added powerful arguments about its lack of meaning, its destruction of social relations, its impact on culture, consumption, and aesthetics, its complicity with inequalities of gender and race, and its tendency to despoil the environment. The criticisms were highly effective, for they suggested that capitalism not only kept people poor and unemployed but, even when they had work and money, hindered personal development and poisoned their relationships with one another and with the world they inhabited. Capitalism, then, was not the liberating force its advocates proclaimed it to be but a barrier to freedom and a force for tradition and the repressions of traditional society.

Throughout the early postwar era, anticommunist liberalism had successfully positioned itself as the best defender of personal freedom and choice against the threat of Stalinism and the boring conformism of conservatism. The critique elaborated by the New Left, however, displaced liberalism from that enviable position and placed it largely on the defensive. The New Left went further, in fact, and elaborated a subtle critique of liberal politics as well. What passed for democracy in the advanced capitalist countries, it argued, was deeply and profoundly undemocratic for a number of reasons: the major parties were all compromised by ties to the system or by an unwillingness to break with it; the range of choices offered voters was so limited that voting mattered little; and participation in elections and in political activity more generally was skewed in such a way as to disadvantage the working class and other oppressed groups. The apparent openness and intensity of debate, moreover, were but a sham: the freedom offered in the realm of discourse masked a system weighted toward outcomes that would favor established interests. Hence the concepts of "repressive tolerance," invented by Herbert Marcuse but widely echoed among the New Left, and of "corporate liberalism," a term of more distinctly local American provenance but equally wide appeal.

The force of the New Left critique derived from its ability to get inside liberalism and reveal its limits, biases, and exclusions. At the same time, it was in its assessment of liberalism and its stance toward liberal politics that the New Left was seriously off-the-mark, for its ability to criticize the anticommunist liberalism that had dominated political discourse in the postwar years stemmed not from antipathy but from what the two perspectives shared. Both sides, however, chose to ignore their commonalities and to regard each other with bitter hostility. The developing rift was deepest in the countries where liberals or social democrats held office but were constrained from implementing their cherished plans for reform. The German Social Democrats, for example, came to power for the first time since the war as partners in the "Grand Coalition" with the Christian Democrats in late 1966, and in 1969 they became the senior partners in a new coalition with the Free Democrats. The requirements of coalition, however, precluded anything more than a modest installment of policy innovation until at least the early 1970s. In Britain, the Labour Party was hamstrung by the balance of payments and the "stop-go" pattern of economic growth from implementing its plans for reform, and forced by the difficulties of economic management to impose wage freezes on its working-class supporters. It succeeded only in alienating the left of the party and the unions on whom it was so dependent.

Antagonism between liberal politicians and the New Left was sharpest and most visible, and also most misplaced, in the United States. The New Left had been inspired by, and emerged from, social movements that largely owed their existence to encouragement by liberal politicians and to timely assistance from the Democrats' institutional supporters in the labor movement, the civil rights movement, and the party itself. Once given life and political independence, though, the social movements of the late 1960s and the New Left turned decisively against the Democrats and the official leaders of both labor and the older civil rights organizations. Their main victims were Lyndon Johnson, who was responsible for more social legislation than any American president since Franklin Roosevelt but whose reforming zeal was sapped by the Vietnam War, and Hubert Humphrey, who had promised to extend Johnson's policies still further. The moderate leaders of the trade unions and civil rights organizations also felt the sting of criticism. The bitterness was occasionally reciprocated, most notably by the gruff old men of the labor movement. More often, however, the New Left's critique was met with the same infuriating "repressive tolerance" that made liberal politics so fundamentally unsatisfying in the first place.

The false antimony that developed between liberalism and the New Left had several unfortunate consequences. It deprived liberalism of the infusion of youthful energy it so desperately needed, and it distanced the New Left from its natural, indeed its only possible, mass constituency. Far more important, it prevented both sides from accurately assessing historical trends. The very plausibility of the New Left's arguments hinted at the decreasing salience of Cold War ideology, for example, but the quarrel between liberals and the left led people to believe that the alternatives of the early Cold War era were still viable. Rhetorics that were at least plausible two decades before were rehearsed again, despite their decreasing purchase on events, and thereby reinforced. The effect, it must be presumed, was to prevent either side from evolving new formulas for political and social reform.

The opposition between liberals and social democrats on the one side, and the New Left on the other, also obscured the character and direction of recent political development. The critique of liberalism or social democracy was premised on the notion that the liberal vision had been largely implemented and proved wanting, whereas in practice much of its program had only recently been put in place, with effects yet to be seen, and parts of it were still waiting for legislative approval or practical application. Not only was the liberal/social democratic political order still in process of creation, but the latest stage in its development owed a great deal to the energies and enthusiasms of the 1960s. Indeed, it makes far more sense to regard the political innovations of the late 1960s and early 1970s as the fulfillment rather than the repudiation of the liberal and social democratic project, as an effort to extend the meaning and effective reach of democratic citizenship. But it was seldom understood as such.

A sure sign that contemporary understanding was inadequate was the fact that terms like *citizenship* were so seldom used at the time, either by the generation of 1968 or by those it chose to criticize. Such language was too liberal, too disinterested, and too analytical to serve the inspirational purposes of a political rhetoric of contestation and mobilization. Nevertheless, both the goals and the practical thrust of political reform in the 1960s represented an effort to fulfill the logic of democratic citizenship as described most clearly by T. H. Marshall, the philosopher of the British welfare state.[4] The welfare state, in his view, capped a prolonged struggle over the course of the twentieth century to extend the effective reach of citizenship so that it encompassed ever-broader sections of the population and came to include in its very definition the exercise of not merely civil and political rights but also social and economic rights. The argument was evolved largely out of Marshall's well-informed reflections on British history, where he saw the achievement of civil rights—to property, to freedom from arbitrary state power, to the rule of law—as the product of the eighteenth century; the achievement of the right to political participation for ordinary men and, eventually, women as the result of reform efforts stretching from the early nineteenth through the early twentieth centuries; and the subsequent granting of effective social and economic rights—to education, health care, jobs, pensions, and relief—as the task of the twentieth century. What was most insightful in Marshall's argument was his understanding that the final phase in the extension of citizenship was in many ways the most difficult and controversial, because it depended to no mean extent on public policies that in practice infringed, or at least limited, the exercise of property rights.

Marshall's schema cannot, of course, be transposed to the experience of other nations without qualification. In the United States, for example, the sequencing of rights was complicated by matters of race: blacks had failed to secure effective political rights long after the state had undertaken the provision of various social rights to its white citizens. As a consequence, the civil rights movement found itself fighting simultaneously for elementary political rights and for the granting of effective social citizenship. Nevertheless, there were clear parallels among all the advanced societies in the progressive advance of citizenship, and it was in the late 1960s that the effort to secure a broad package of social rights dominated political life across national borders. Because different nations displayed rather distinct deficits in terms of the model of full democratic citizenship, their preoccupations differed, but the objectives and outcomes were surprisingly similar.

In Europe, typically, social provision was more generous and more universal than in the United States. Political life, by contrast, was more marked by taboos, exclusions, and orthodoxies. In France and Italy, for instance, the "ghettoization" of the communist parties and the close identification that existed between these parties and the institutions of working-class life—unions and voluntary associations and social networks—meant the de facto exclusion of workers from politics. The growth of more powerful trade unions began to redress this imbalance; so, too, did the movement of communist parties toward a rapprochement with other parties—for example, the beginnings of the so-called historic compromise between the Communists and Christian Democrats in Italy, and the efforts to put together an electoral alliance between the PCF and the socialists in France—and the simultaneous movement of workers themselves toward a more variegated pattern of political allegiance. Whatever else the upheavals of 1968–1969 accomplished, they clearly broadened the bases of political participation. So, too, did the apparent decline of political deference and party discipline across a range of political systems, such as

Germany and Britain, and the growth of a genuinely democratic political culture in nations where the commitment to democracy had been somewhat in doubt in the early postwar years. The most obvious example was West Germany. During the 1950s surveys revealed little pride in the nation's political institutions, only modest recognition of their efficacy, great disinterest in politics, and lingering fears of speaking out freely on politics. By the 1970s opinion had come more closely into line with that in older and more robust democracies. To illustrate, 84 percent of West Germans felt they could speak out politically in 1971; over roughly the same period the percentage of Germans who regularly talked politics increased by more than half, as did the number who declared themselves "interested in politics." By 1972, fully 90 percent declared democracy the best form of government; even among those who were dissatisfied with the performance of parliamentary government 86 percent conceded that parliament was essential.[5] Italian politics moved in the same direction, though with rather more local discrepancies and more of a spirit of *contestazione*.

The political culture of advanced democracy thus caught up with the potential for activism, dissent, and participation inherent in the political institutions of democracy. As that happened, the demand for the further extension of the social and economic rights of citizenship increased as well. And, given the faith that still attached to Keynesian policy making and collective provision and the continued strength of organized labor, the demand took the form of sustained efforts to expand the capacity of the state and to legislate entitlements to benefits provided by, or at least mandated by, government.[6] In Germany, for example, the government approved major increases in pensions in 1967 and 1972; expenditures on health and sickness insurance rose steadily over the postwar era but, again, jumped dramatically in the early 1970s; beginning in 1969, the state also adopted "a more active labour market policy" that, inevitably, also cost more; the 1974 replacement of a system of tax credits by a universal child allowance also added considerably to social expenditures; and expenditures on "social assistance" doubled in real terms in the 1970s. In Britain the curve of social expenditures likewise shot up sharply from the mid-1960s as the Labour Party sought to redress what it considered a decade of Conservative neglect. Innovation was even more dramatic in Italy: an ambitious program of social reform had been debated in the late 1940s but had not been implemented, leaving the nation saddled with a social policy legacy inherited from the discredited past. Little changed until the political ferment of the late 1960s transformed the context of policy making and prompted a series of reforms that over the next decade "thoroughly reshaped the welfare state."[7]

Even more impressive was the turn toward social provision in Japan and the United States, where public expenditures nevertheless remained far below the European average. The link between democratic politics and public policy aimed at increasing social welfare was characteristically indirect in Japan and initiative there remained in the hands of elites, but it was nonetheless essential. It was, after all, the trauma of dealing with labor protest and dissent over ratification of the security treaty with the United States that preceded and presumably elicited the Income-Doubling Plan of 1960.[8] Continued elite concern over the rumblings of discontent from below led to a further shift toward welfare in economic plans promulgated in the late 1960s and early 1970s—especially in Tanaka Kakuei's Plan for Remodeling of the Japanese Archipelago, which proposed "to usher in the new era of 'Restoration of Human Rights' where humans, the sun and greens, instead of big cities and industries, become the master of our society."[9]

The advance of the liberal agenda was most dramatic in the United States, but its progress was least recognized. The reason was simple enough: an enormous amount of legislation dealing with poverty, discrimination, and health care was passed during the mid-1960s, but the achievement was overshadowed by the Johnson administration's disastrous decision to prosecute the war in Indochina.[10] Still another cluster of laws and executive orders concerning affirmative action, school busing, and environmental protection were passed and issued while Richard Nixon was president. Because Nixon came to power as the candidate of the right, with a notorious history of anticommunism, because his election campaign was premised on a "southern strategy" designed to take advantage of white resentment at the gains of the civil rights movement, and because he persisted in the brutalization of Vietnam, it was perhaps inevitable that he would be perceived as the antithesis of liberal reform.[11] It was difficult, therefore, to see that his contributions to public policy were in most instances a further development of the program devised and proclaimed by an earlier generation of liberals. The other reason that the completion of the liberal project was missed is that so much of the achievement came not in the form of increases in government spending but through extensions of the regulatory power of the federal government. According to one calculation, government spending on the regulation of business grew by over 16 percent a year from 1966 through 1973.[12] Such efforts greatly extended the role of the state in the governing of the economy, but they were nonetheless far less visible and, initially at least, less controversial than a comparable increase in welfare spending would have been.

It was only in the late 1960s and early 1970s, then, that much of the program of postwar anticommunist liberalism, and hence also of social democracy, became reality. But because the achievement was surrounded by bitter disputes within the left and critiques of the inadequacy of the liberal-social democratic vision, it was neither recognized nor appreciated. The turbulence of the late 1960s thus bequeathed as its legacy a political order and set of public policies that together marked a new and further extension of democratic citizenship: unprecedented levels of political activism, mobilization, and debate; commitments to a broader array of social and economic entitlements than ever before and states confident in their capacity to meet the elevated expectations of citizens in terms of social welfare; and economic managers ready and willing to utilize Keynesian techniques to steer the economy and thus maintain the steady growth required to finance all of this. The irony was that neither the mainstream liberal left nor its New Left critics quite understood what they had wrought. They were in consequence unable to run the system they created, unwilling to unite in its defense, and so incapable of generating the political support that would have been required to maintain it.

The opponents of the mainstream liberal left and the New Left, by contrast, understood how dramatically the events of 1968 and after had transformed the political landscape of the advanced democracies. They responded with an incisive critique that marked, in effect, the revival of conservative thought and political fortunes in the postwar era. The key document was *The Crisis of Democracy*, the report on the governability of democracies to the Trilateral Commission, published in 1975.[13] What exercised the report's authors were the apparent connections between the evident disillusion of the intellectuals and the rise among them of an "adversary culture," the increasing fractiousness of democratic politics, the multiplication of demands upon the polity, government's inability to resist those claims, and the resulting extension of the state's commitments to its citizens. Not only were these phenomena connected, they gave rise to a logic that would only get worse: as citizens came to expect more from the state, they would mobilize for still more; soon their demands would outrun the state's ability to meet them and the result would be an increase in discontent, fumbling efforts by government to appease the discontented, the breakdown of the disciplines that must, it was assumed, underpin political authority, and a growing crisis of "governability." The first casualty and clearest sign of the crisis would be the loss of fiscal discipline. As the report bluntly argued, "Inflation can be considered a direct result of the ungovernability of Western democracies"(37). Asserting the link to inflation was a brilliant stroke, for it allowed the report to connect the upheavals of the 1960s with the most obvious problem of the 1970s, the rapid increase of prices, and to suggest that the former was responsible for the latter. The connection may have been intuitively plausible, but it flew in the face of the far more obvious connection between inflation and the shock of the 1973 oil crisis. And it ignored, of course, the more complicated arguments of economists. Nevertheless, the argument that inflation stemmed from too much government, too much public spending, and too much taxation, themselves the predictable result of too many claims upon the state's resources, would stick, and it would provide the central plank in the political rhetoric of conservatives for at least two decades.

At the time of its publication, the report to the Trilateral Commission was extensively and justly criticized for its undisguised hostility to democracy. But its effectiveness, as diagnosis and as a contribution to political discourse, cannot be doubted. It was, of course, merely one early statement of what would prove a much broader flowering of conservative political thought in the 1970s and 1980s. Taken together, the resurgence of conservatism as a newly compelling political vision and the revitalization of radical thought on the left—first appearing as neo-Marxism and the critique of racism and imperialism, and subsequently bearing the imprint of feminism and the "new social movements," and still more recently manifesting itself in the widespread turn to "identity politics"—reoriented political debate in the advanced democracies. By the mid-1970s, as a result, the anticommunist consensus of the early Cold War years had dissipated and the liberal-social democratic project had lost its place as the primary organizing principle of political mobilization. Liberals and social democrats were instead placed squarely on the defensive, having to defend their achievements from attack on two fronts, from the right and from the New Left, and deeply ambivalent about the task. Conservatives, on the other hand, were emboldened by the fissures opening between liberals and social democrats and the left, inspired by genuine fear about the direction of political change, and guided by a set of arguments that updated conservatism and that seemed to give the right new purchase on the complicated and troubling world around it.

The altered terms of political discourse would tend over the years to favor the right and to place the liberal left at a decisive disadvantage. The new balance would be reflected in the increasing regularity with which conservatives prevailed in national elections, in prolonged periods of conservative rule in Great Britain, Germany, and the United States, and in the utter inability of those few liberals and social democrats who did manage to win power to implement their programs—for example, Jimmy Carter and Bill Clinton in the United States; François Mitterand in France; Felipé Gonzalez in Spain.[14] Conservatives' success was not due solely or even primarily to the coherence of their arguments or to the practical utility of the programs they advocated. It was due also, and more importantly, to the inherent intractability of the problems confronted by governments, many of them operating with prescriptions and techniques put in place by liberals and social democrats but largely accepted by conservatives during the quarter century of boom and stability from 1947 through 1972, and to the largely fortuitous manner in which the most salient political issues of the 1970s and 1980s—inflation and the deterioration in relations between the superpowers—reinforced the conservative critique of the liberal and social democratic heritage.

The ability of political actors to make particular issues salient and thus to define and control the political agenda is, of course, in part a measure of the intellectual power of their basic vision, but it is also in part a matter of the sequence and drama of events themselves. It was, after all, not merely a perverse conservative construction of reality that helped to focus attention on inflation and on the apparent loss of Western, especially U.S., world hegemony. Inflation was real, and cried out for explanation and redress. And the defeat of pro-Western forces in Indochina and parts of Africa and the Middle East and the growing nuclear parity between West and East were also real, even if they did not necessarily cry out for a particular, or particularly conservative, response. Both events and ideological predispositions thus combined to make inflation and the revival of the Cold War into the most salient issues of the era of conservative political advance, and with devastating and politically asymmetrical effects.

Inflation was without doubt the dominant domestic concern, for it appeared to threaten the most basic premises of the postwar political order: steady economic growth and rising living standards. The causes of inflation were complex and much debated. Clearly, the structural characteristics that distinguished the economy since the Second World War all tended to impart a slight inflationary bias to the system's normal workings. The increased concentration of capital, the diminished magnitude of cyclical fluctuations, the protections wrung from employers by more powerful labor movements and hence the increased rigidities of wages and working conditions, as well as the impact of the more or less automatic, countercyclical stabilizers such as unemployment insurance and increased welfare spending put in place in the late 1940s and expanded steadily thereafter—all worked to cushion the effects of recession in pushing down prices and therefore probably intensified the inflationary push imparted by recovery. To this must surely be added the inflationary effects of the Vietnam War and the loosening up of the international monetary system with the collapse of the Bretton Woods arrangements in 1971 and their replacement by a system of floating exchange rates. By the early 1970s, therefore, inflation was increasing at a rate that began to worry policy makers both in Europe and in the United States. Successive governments in Britain had already been forced to adopt formal incomes policies to combat the rise in prices, and other European countries were attempting to use the informal patterns of "corporatist" bargaining, evolved since the war, to get management and the unions to agree to hold down prices and wages. President Nixon responded with a wage freeze in 1971 and managed to hold inflation in check through his subsequent reelection campaign. Neither of these expedients would withstand the effect of the oil price shocks of 1973–1974 and 1979.

The first oil price shock was caused by the decision of the Arab oil exporters to restrict supplies and raise prices in retaliation for Western support of Israel during the Yom Kippur War of 1973. World oil prices quadrupled in November 1973, and the OPEC (Organization of Petroleum-Exporting Countries) nations' earnings from oil exports leapt from $33 billion in 1973 to $108 billion in 1974.[15] The second oil price shock occurred as a consequence of the Iranian Revolution in 1979 and caused a tripling of prices. Overall, the cost of importing oil from OPEC producers rose by nearly twentyfold over the decade.[16] It took several years for the effects of the staggering increase to work themselves out. Over the course of this adjustment governments tried numerous expedients in a vain effort to control the world economy and recreate the conditions that had facilitated nearly a quarter century of growth. As those efforts were seen successively to fail, the premises on which the postwar political order had been constructed were steadily eroded. Assumptions about the role of the state in economic management, about the propriety of public solutions to social problems, about the very scope of political action—many of which had seemed decisively settled in the early postwar years—were reopened and the political landscape was utterly transformed.

With the first oil shock, inflation soared to the top of the political agenda in the advanced countries, virtually displacing other economic concerns, and it remained a predominant issue for well over a decade.[17] It was particularly traumatizing to bankers and the financial markets over which they presided and led many to advocate restoration of financial stability as the central goal of economic policy. Politicians and government economists could not afford to focus so single-mindedly on a single indicator. They had to worry about the political consequences of their actions and so continued to fret about growth and jobs as well as prices. The dissonance between policy makers and the financial community was further complicated by the complexity of the problems besetting the world economy and the inadequacy of the tools available for handling them. The symptoms of economic distress were especially confounding and could easily produce quite contradictory diagnoses and recommendations. The most obvious problem was inflation, but it was by no means clear how much of that should be ascribed to the effect of the oil shocks, how much to more structural factors. The easing of inflationary pressure in the 1980s, in close response to the decline in energy prices, suggests that the oil shocks were by far the most significant cause of rising prices. By that time, however, governments elected to solve the crisis were busy attacking unions and dismantling the welfare state.

Inflation was not the only economic problem even in the 1970s, for inflation coincided with a general slowing down of growth in many countries. By the late 1960s, it appears, demand was beginning to ebb for the products on which the postwar boom had been based. The contraction was accompanied, moreover, by a distinct lessening in the economic domination of the United States. The United States had lost its decisive edge in manufacturing productivity over Japan and Germany, and they were beginning to challenge its domination of world markets in virtually all manufactured products. The effect was a more genuinely competitive world economy in which American products and U.S. policies would both be challenged. The full extent of the challenges inherent in the emergence of a new international economic environment were envisioned by very few in the 1970s, but the notion that something very basic had changed was widely grasped. The character of the transformation defied categorization, however, and produced by way of analysis nothing more creative than the concept of "stagflation," an inexplicable combination of stagnation and inflation, which merely announced the confusion of its popularizers.

The difficulty of understanding the economy's problems was compounded by the inability of policy makers to agree on solutions. At the root of the disagreements was the gap between the prescriptions of Keynesian theory and the willingness and ability of governments to implement them.[18] Over the course of the postwar boom, Keynes's ideas became

utterly hegemonic among economists, who accepted not only his arguments about effective demand but also his injunction about the responsibility of government for insuring a high and stable level of demand and,
hence, of employment. In practice, however, on very few occasions did
states actually choose to intervene along the lines indicated by Keynesian
theory. The reason was simple enough: Keynes developed his ideas and
policy prescriptions against the background of the interwar depression
and, as he saw it, a prolonged lack of effective demand. The postwar economy was by contrast marked by strong and sustained demand that
required occasional dampening rather than stimulation. The bankers and
bureaucrats who controlled fiscal and monetary policy and oversaw such
adjustments made use of the concepts and the methods worked out by
Keynes and his followers, but the context was vastly different. In practice,
policies worked out to counter slump by government intervention and
deficit spending came to be exercised for the opposite purpose of countering inflation. The only significant exercises in truly Keynesian policy
making were the decisions of Kennedy and Johnson to cut taxes in order
to stimulate the economy. The effect was spectacularly effective and helped
to produce the long boom of the 1960s, but it was an isolated event that
was not emulated by other governments.

When the economic difficulties of the 1970s arrived, therefore, the policy makers charged with running the world's major industrial economies
were ill-prepared for decisive or effective intervention. They confronted
the baffling complex of problems labeled "stagflation" armed with a theory evolved in a deflationary era and with tools applied intermittently in
an era of mild inflation and steadily, if cyclically, rising demand. The only
moment during which Keynesian techniques had been used to control serious inflation had been during the Second World War, and the extensive
physical controls imposed then were clearly unacceptable in peacetime.
Otherwise, the difficulties faced by policy makers were virtually unprecedented. Never in the postwar era had Keynesian methods been used to
counter such a sharp rise in prices; never in postwar had the world economy displayed such a systematic slowing down of demand and growth as
that to which Keynesian policy makers were now asked to respond.

Policy makers therefore faced a series of difficult choices over how to
interpret the conflicting signs of economic crisis, over which problems to
regard as pressing and which merely passing, and over what means to use
to address them. Inevitably, policy was itself confused and inconsistent.
Because the onset of inflation had followed rapidly upon the collapse of
the Bretton Woods system, bankers and finance ministers expended enor-

mous energy trying to patch together a new regime to coordinate exchange rates. At the same time, however, protectionist sentiments rose and states threatened to pull back from, and thus further disrupt, the international system. Neither policy took hold, as exchange rates continued to fluctuate and international trade continued to expand. At the same time a number of nations experimented with more formal and *dirigiste* planning efforts related to incomes policy, energy conservation, and industrial policy, but success was rare. The Japanese engineered a decisive shift toward a more efficient use of energy, but elsewhere the impact was minimal; industrial policy continued to produce results where it had been tried before, but it did not work in new settings; and incomes policies produced meager results except where combined with more activist employment policies, as in Germany, Austria, and Scandinavia.[19]

On balance, the policies adopted during the 1970s worked poorly against inflation and still less well in reversing the long-term slowdown in growth. By the time of the second oil price shock there was an emerging consensus among bankers, businessmen, politicians, and many economists that the prescriptions of the past had failed and that the largely Keynesian assumptions that underpinned them had been disproved by experience. In response, policy makers fell in line with the increasingly insistent demands of the financial community for fiscal rectitude and instituted policies directed primarily at the control of inflation. The impact was especially clear in the United States: "As a new 'memorable alliance' between the power of state and capital was forged, the looseness of US monetary policies that characterized the entire Cold War era gave way to an unprecedented tightness."[20] The turn was signaled by the appointment of Paul Volcker, "a paragon of financial orthodoxy," as chairman of the Federal Reserve in July 1979 and by the "austerity program" and inordinately high interest rates that followed. A similar shift occurred almost simultaneously in Great Britain under Margaret Thatcher's leadership, and other nations had no choice but to respond in kind. The transformation soon made itself felt throughout the world economy.[21]

The collapse of Keynesianism in the late 1970s proved disastrous for the political fortunes of liberal and social democratic parties, already on the defensive over the unrest of the 1960s and early 1970s. The criticisms of the New Left had been deeply wounding and had begun to sap the confidence of the moderate left in its commitment to the so-called politics of growth. The assumption of growth had been the cornerstone of reform politics throughout the postwar era, for it allowed liberals and social democrats to argue that redistribution was not a zero-sum game, that collaboration with capital could produce gains for both employers and workers, and that rising prosperity could in addition generate the tax revenues needed to address the structural causes of inequality.[22] But the politics of growth came under increasing criticism. First, because it supposedly neglected issues of redistribution and equity and of the quality of life, especially in the workplace; then, because growth was blind to the destruction of the environment and to the dangers of rising population and depletion of the earth's resources; and finally, because it seemed no longer possible for governments to deliver on the promise of steady growth. The effect of such critiques was a profound rethinking of the politics and policies of growth—in 1972, for example, the Club of Rome produced its famous report "The Limits to Growth."[23]

By the mid-1970s even previously committed advocates of growth had to concede that control of inflation was now the top priority. As the so-called McCracken Report, "Full Employment and Price Stability," put it in May 1977, governments must in the future make it absolutely clear that *"they will not—and, in the end, cannot—pursue policies which will permit or accommodate high rates of inflation"* (italics in original), and that they therefore "cannot guarantee full employment regardless of developments in prices, wages and other factors in economic life."[24] By the late 1970s, then President Carter was delivering moralizing speeches urging his fellow citizens to learn to live with less, with predictably catastrophic consequences for his political future. Sadly, it fell to liberal and social democratic governments in Germany, Britain, and the United States to preside over the end of the Keynesian era and to take the first serious steps toward austerity and curtailment of the welfare state. When these liberal regimes were succeeded by conservative governments that pushed the same policies still further, it was difficult for liberals and social democrats to mount effective criticism.

It was the politics of inflation, then, that eased passage to the era of conservative political hegemony. This did not mean that conservatives had a better understanding of inflation or any better plan to combat it. They possessed an effective rhetoric linking inflation to their critique of the welfare state, Keynesian economic policy, the power of labor, and the irresponsibility of the intellectuals, but the rhetoric translated poorly into specific policies for running the economy and controlling prices. In practice, conservative policy was as confused and contradictory as that of earlier governments. Britain under Thatcher and the United States under Reagan, for example, pursued utterly contrasting strategies.[25] Thatcher built upon a long-standing tradition of fiscal rectitude and focused intently on reducing public-sector borrowing. To do so required that cuts in the income tax had to be more than offset by rises in the value-added tax (VAT) and in local rates and that expenditures be genuinely squeezed. The policies of the Reagan administration, by contrast, flouted the tenets of fiscal responsibility and led to mounting deficits. Taxes were cut, military budgets increased and painful cuts in entitlements avoided. In Reagan's worldview, of course, "Keynes was the demon of profligacy incarnate. But...Reagan—whatever he calls his macroeconomic policy—could not have followed the fiscal precepts of Keynes better if he had studied at the feet of the master."[26]

Both Thatcher and Reagan benefited, however, from the coincidence of two things: they both promised to control inflation and inflation, for reasons that had little to do with policy, subsided. Inflation lessened because oil prices fell and because the extremely high interest rates imposed, in effect, by the Federal Reserve but reinforced by government and financial authorities in Germany, Britain, and Japan, drove the world economy into a deep recession. But the fact that conservative governments presided over the return to stable prices seemed to confirm their diagnoses and gave a notable boost to their sense of economic competence. That they did little or nothing to deal with the long-term structural problems affecting the economies of the advanced nations was scarcely noticed by the middle and upper classes, who profited handsomely from the tax cuts and, in the United States, from the increased military spending and the easing of inflation and interest rates after 1982—and who happily reelected Reagan in 1984, Margaret Thatcher and the otherwise uninspiring Helmut Kohl in 1987, and the equally uncharismatic George Bush, Reagan's vice president, in 1988.

There were many who did not prosper during the 1980s, but the losers faced enormous difficulties: they had first to figure out what was happening to them and then had to find a means to voice their concerns. Especially hard to detect were the shifts in income distribution brought about by conservative fiscal and social policies. In the most advanced nations, where the welfare state had been most developed and most generously funded, the slowing of growth slowed or reversed the growth of spending on welfare and social services. These adverse trends were much accentuated in countries where conservatives succeeded in altering the shape of the tax structure. In Britain, for example, the Thatcher government drastically lowered the top rates of the income tax, lowered standard rates overall, and shifted the burden onto levies that fell upon consumers. The United States under Reagan experienced two huge installations of tax reform in 1981 and 1986 that vastly diminished the share of taxes paid by the wealthy. The distributional consequences were highly regressive: between 1977 and 1988 the after-tax incomes of the top 10 percent of American families grew by over 16 percent in real dollars, while the share kept by the bottom tenth fell by nearly 15 percent. Overall, 80 percent lost out due to the combined effects of changes in taxes and earnings.[27] The net effects of conservative policies affecting taxes and the welfare state were everywhere in the same direction, but seldom as strongly so as in Britain and the United States.[28] The major exceptions to the pattern of lower, or less rapidly growing, public expenditures were in southern Europe—Spain, Portugal, Italy, and Greece—where spending on government and social services had previously been very low by European standards, and growth was especially dramatic in countries undergoing a transition from authoritarian to democratic government.[29] The laggards in public spending thus caught up with the norm, but the norm itself became considerably less generous.

The biggest and most visible losers during this decade of conservative dominance were of, course, the workers, especially those who had previously earned good money at jobs whose terms and conditions were protected by strong labor unions. They knew very well what was happening to their wages and their jobs, but their close identification with parties of the left gave them little clout with the ruling parties of the center-right. Unions suffered as well from a growing antipathy among the middle and upper classes generally, and from employers in particular, who resented the apparent growth of union strength and militancy. Unions had in fact grown stronger over the long postwar boom and in some countries, such as Germany and Great Britain and Scandinavia, had become virtual partners in government, routinely consulted on issues affecting the economy and social policy. Though they had often enough agreed with employers and the state to urge wage restraint upon their members and might on those grounds be held to have bargained for rather less than the market would bear, they nonetheless managed to secure steadily rising real wages and expanding employment opportunities for the workers they represented. The unrest of the late 1960s and early 1970s, moreover, had produced significant membership gains in France and Italy, the two nations where unions had been numerically weakest, and a "pay explosion" across all of the advanced industrial countries.[30] Between 1965 and 1973 real wages increased by 3.5 percent annually in the "advanced capitalist countries." As wages rose, profit margins fell, and over the same span of years profit rates actually decreased by 2.8 percent a year.[31] In response, employ-

ers and the state became progressively more hostile to the claims and pretensions of labor and stiffened their resistance to further advances. And
in the contests that followed, workers and unions found themselves
severely disadvantaged by the altered political climate, the lack of support
from the state, and the dismal labor market. They suffered disastrous
defeats in confrontations directly involving the state, as with the air traf-
fic controllers (PATCO) in the United States and the miners in Britain, but
even routine negotiations with employers resulted in concessions, "give-
backs," or, at best, minimal gains.[32]

What held together, and to some extent justified, these conservative initiatives in taxation and industrial relations was the connection to inflation. Of course, business interests regularly sought to escape the constraints of collective bargaining, and middle and upper classes had long
resented the imposition of progressive taxes. They needed little encouragement to support such policies and worried little about justifying them.
Nevertheless, it was under the banner of fighting inflation that conservatives moved to tame the labor movement and to shift fiscal burdens onto
those least able to afford them. Conservatives managed to fix a major
share of the blame for inflation onto the unions and argued forcefully that
it was high taxes that permitted a "runaway growth of...spending" and
led to inflation.[33] The master in this sort of rhetorical linkage was Ronald
Reagan, whose strange eloquence smoothly reconciled the irreconcilable
at the level of discourse.[34] But Reagan played on themes that had been
announced earlier—witness the links and leaps in the argument of the
Trilateral Commission—and were repeated often.

Inflation, then, was the essential precondition for the ability of conservatives to dominate the domestic political agenda of the late 1970s and
1980s and, once in office, to impose their vision upon publics who typically
remained unconvinced about the actual program of resurgent conservatism. The revival of the Cold War served much the same function for
the discourse surrounding defense and foreign policy, although in this
realm conservative arguments were more effectively contested. Still, events
seemed to conspire to prove the conservative case: the Soviet invasion of
Afghanistan in 1979 and the downing of the Korean Air Lines jet (KAL-
007) that strayed over Sakhalin Peninsula on September 1, 1983, for example, confirmed the most negative portrayals of the Soviet Union as an "evil
empire." The interpretation of events and strategic developments was not
always so clear-cut, but overall the evidence that the Soviets were not content with nuclear parity and that they were intent on an aggressive pursuit of essentially imperial goals mounted over the course of the late 1970s.

The starting point was the blossoming of détente in the Nixon-Kissinger era. The agreements of the early 1970s recognized the mutual spheres of influence of the United States and the USSR, their relative equality in nuclear weapons, the willingness of leaders on both sides to refrain from development and deployment of antiballistic missile systems, and, with the Paris Peace Accord of 1972, the stalemate in Indochina. The Soviet Union had finally been acknowledged as the superpower equivalent of the United States, and its geopolitical reach had been granted de facto international legitimacy. With the opening to China, however, the United States had gained a critical lever to be used against the USSR in future contests in Asia and elsewhere and had in effect made the Soviets vulnerable to disturbance along a border of many thousands of miles. On balance, détente represented a reasonable compromise on both sides.

The deal looked rather less good to the Americans a decade later. In the intervening years the West had suffered greatly from the oil-price shocks of 1973–1974 and 1979, while the Soviets, with their enormous oil reserves, had been able to take advantage of the high prices to increase export earnings, which in turn had been used to import large amounts of Western machinery.[35] The West, or at least the United States, had also experienced a string of losses in the Third World. The most visible was the fall of Saigon in 1975; others included the overthrow of Emperor Haile Selassie in Ethiopia in 1974; the collapse of the Portuguese Empire in Africa and the emergence of leftist regimes in Mozambique and Angola, the latter defended by Cuban troops; and in 1979 the fall of the shah of Iran and the Sandinista triumph in Nicaragua. Even more ominous to conservatives in the United States and Europe was the steady buildup of Soviet nuclear forces, culminating in the stationing of SS-20s within easy range of Western Europe in 1977.[36] And finally, there were the words of the Soviet leader himself. Speaking to a group of Soviet veterans in 1975, Brezhnev looked back over the history of the Cold War and declared that a "new situation" existed and that even "the leaders of the bourgeois world have...come to realize that the Cold War has outlived itself and that there is need for a new, more sensible and realistic policy." At the base of such a new policy must be a recognition of "the simple truth: in our time, attempts to suppress the people's liberation movement are doomed to failure. And the best evidence of this comes from the fine victory scored by the Vietnamese people in the struggle against foreign interventionists and their henchmen."[37] The implication was clear enough. The new "correlation of forces" favored the advance of socialism, and the balance of tactical advantage had tipped away from the West and in favor of the Soviets and their allies.

The apparent aggressiveness of the Soviet Union and the equally apparent defensiveness of the West gave rise to a prolonged and bitter debate. The debate would in fact outlast the period of Soviet advance, which ended with Afghanistan, the new arms race that marked the so-called Second Cold War of the early 1980s, and, indeed, the very collapse of the Soviet Union. What embittered and prolonged the argument was its entanglement with the legacy of Vietnam. The protracted effort of the United States to suppress revolution in Vietnam produced deep fissures in both elite and popular opinion and shattered the liberal anticommunist consensus that had prevailed with minimal dissent during the first twenty years of the Cold War. What was perhaps most remarkable about the political consequences of Vietnam was that the experience proved equally traumatic to the left and the right, to the military, to the foreign policy establishment, to political leaders and to ordinary citizens alike.[38] The earliest critics were student radicals and liberal intellectuals, but they were soon followed by politicians such as Senator William Fulbright, who sponsored hearings critical of the government's policy in Indochina as early as February 1966.[39] The presidential campaign of 1968 caused more defections from the ranks of the Democratic Party, as first Eugene McCarthy and then Robert Kennedy challenged Johnson on precisely this issue. As the publication of the Pentagon Papers made clear, discontent had by that time begun to infect even the Defense Department.[40] It was discontent among the Democrats themselves, leading to an inability in the end to vote for Johnson's designated successor, Hubert Humphrey, that brought Nixon to power in the November election. Opposition to the war also took more direct forms: demonstrations were widespread and attracted mass support from students and young men of draft age inspired by varying mixes of altruism, political principle, and personal fear. Protests peaked in the spring of 1970, with the outpouring of anger over the bombing of Cambodia. Particularly impressive was the increasing prominence of Vietnam veterans in the antiwar movement. Their activity out of uniform confirmed and furthered the deterioration of morale inside the armed forces, a phenomenon deeply upsetting to U.S. military leaders.

Those who opposed the war did so, of course, for different reasons and with different points of view. On balance, the debate moved millions to the left, toward a politics critical of the Cold War, of militarism, imperialism, and racism. Anger over Vietnam was so pervasive, however, that it affected many whose perspectives were otherwise quite conservative. They had no little or no sympathy for foreigners, no problem with the anticommunist thrust of foreign policy, and no guilt over the use of military force. They simply did not want American soldiers sacrificed in a losing cause. Such was the attitude of many in the military and of what might be called the "populist right" among voters, not a few of whom were lured away from the Democrats by the demagogic appeal of George Wallace in the 1968 election.[41] These two quite diverse currents of opinion—the new antiwar consensus and the somewhat less novel "populist" patriotism—would often be found arguing the same, essentially "isolationist," position in the decades after Vietnam, but the de facto alliance was extremely unstable and liable to break down over support for the most blatantly aggressive military actions, like Grenada, Panama, and the Gulf War, where the margin of U.S. superiority was so great as to preclude serious casualties.

Elite opinion manifested a slightly different set of divisions. From 1968 the mainstream swung sharply away from anticommunism and military intervention in the Third World. Even Nixon and Kissinger shared in this turn from what had been standard practice in the first quarter century of the Cold War. The move toward détente with the Soviet Union and the opening of China were premised on the recognition that the United States lacked the military capability and the political will for global policing and so were coupled with articulation of the so-called Nixon doctrine, which called for a devolution of the policing function onto regional powers approved and armed by the United States. An unlikely array of regimes were accorded this honor: Iran under the shah, Pakistan, Japan, and, in Africa, Zaire and South Africa.[42] Military leaders largely agreed with the effort to restrict the commitment of U.S. ground troops and preferred instead to build upon superior technology and firepower and to allow others to lose their lives in direct combat. The experience of Vietnam thus turned the most conservative leaders—Nixon, Kissinger, and the generals, to be precise—away from routine support for foreign intervention. More liberal politicians and policy makers moved still further and questioned the basic rationale of an anticommunist foreign policy, the logic of the arms race and the theory of nuclear deterrence, and the generally hostile stance toward the aspirations of the Third World for independence and development. Their critique was more effective than their counterproposals for peaceful coexistence, arms control, a foreign policy guided by considerations of human rights, and the creation of a "new international economic order" that would provide a better deal for less developed nations. These liberal initiatives were reflected in various policies of the Carter administration, but they remained inchoate and never truly cohered into an integrated vision of a new, post–Cold War world order.

They were, in any event, crucially dependent on continued public support for détente, and that had begun to ebb as the memory of Vietnam faded. It was further undermined by the accumulating record of U.S. reversals in the Third World and by the apparent aggressiveness of the Soviet Union.[43] Support for a new North-South bargain that would institutionalize a regime of international trade more advantageous to the Third World also ebbed throughout the 1970s, largely in response to the economic impact of the oil shocks.[44]

Advocates of a new, post–Cold War liberal internationalism had to contend as well with the increasingly effective efforts of what might be termed the "new cold warriors." The group took organizational form with the founding of the Committee on the Present Danger in 1976 founded to press the case against détente upon the incoming Democratic administration. The membership list was replete with longtime supporters of the Cold War like Paul Nitze, the historian Richard Pipes, Walt Rostow, Dean Rusk, William Casey, Norman Podhoretz, and others who refused to concede that the central lesson of Vietnam was the obsolescence of the Cold War. On the contrary, they insisted, as Eugene Rostow explained in 1976, that "the program of Soviet imperialism is based upon a military build-up without parallel in modern history.... In many significant categories of military power," he asserted, "the Soviet Union now has more military strength than the United States."[45] In response, the United States must overcome the effects of the "Vietnam syndrome"—a supposed psychological malady leading to a reluctance to use armed force for national purposes. More specifically, it should back off from détente, work to regain its edge in nuclear weapons, rebuild its conventional forces and the morale of its military, and begin to apply pressure on the Soviet Union and its surrogates, extensions, and allies.

The program of the new cold warriors did not become policy until after the election of Reagan, and even then it met strong and effective opposition that precluded its thorough implementation. During the late 1970s, however, opinion among the policy-making elite remained sharply polarized and neither program could muster consensus. The division was embodied and symbolized at the heart of the Carter administration, where the unrepentant cold warrior Zbigniew Brzezinski as national security adviser did regular battle with Cyrus Vance, the prototypical post–Cold War liberal as secretary of state. It was reflected as well in Carter's schizophrenic foreign policy, in which liberal initiatives on human rights, arms control, peace in the Middle East, and a more nuanced stance toward the Third World and Third World revolutions went hand-in-hand with increased pressure on the Soviet Union over Jewish emigration, the decision to station cruise and Pershing missiles in Europe, an increased defense budget, and, in response to the Soviet invasion of Afghanistan, a visible deterioration in Soviet–U.S. relations and the announcement of the "Carter doctrine" pledging intervention to counter any Soviet move in or toward the Persian Gulf.

The disagreement over the nation's role in the world after Vietnam was thus deep and abiding. Even after the election of 1980 it was not in any intellectual sense resolved. Nevertheless, the balance clearly tipped toward the new cold warriors in 1979, when the debacle in Iran discredited Carter's entire foreign policy. The fall of the shah, the progressive radicalization of the Islamic revolution and regime, the hostage crisis, and the failed attempt at a rescue were disastrous for the besieged Democratic administration. The fact that these events coincided with yet another oil crisis and another, seemingly uncontrollable, bout of inflation served to convince Americans that, as even Carter noted at the time, "we were impotent" and effectively "reminded them all of the negative results of OPEC price increases, over which we had no control—and the hostages being seized, over which we had no control."[46] That perception in turn made the election of Reagan a near inevitability.[47] His triumph brought into office the most determined proponents of a renewed hostility toward the Soviet Union. The ensuing period of tension, the so-called Second Cold War, confirmed the enormous political advantage derived by conservatives from their unrelenting focus on anticommunism and the threat of Soviet power.[48] It probably did not yield quite the rich harvest of votes that the parallel fixation on inflation had produced, but it was nonetheless highly effective in providing the right with a clear and unhesitant rhetoric at a moment when liberal politicians, and the nation's political establishment more broadly, were trying desperately to cope with the demands of an increasingly complex and ambiguous world, full of intractable problems and conflicts, by developing a genuinely new vision of a post–Cold War world order.

The atmosphere of international tension that the Second Cold War reflected, and to which it made a further contribution, was intensified as well by the supposed rise of terrorism, especially in the Middle East. The perception was based on very little, but the phenomenon was not wholly imagined. The Israeli victory in the Six-Day War in 1967 and the roughly simultaneous founding of the Palestinian Liberation Organization altered the terms of the conflict between Israel and its Arab neighbors. What had been since 1948 a problem between rival states was transformed: Israel now became an occupying power ruling over Arab lands and a hostile Arab population, and thus vulnerable to attacks from within its historic borders and from the occupied territories as well as from bases in Jordan (at least until 1970), Lebanon, and Syria. The Arab states, on the other hand, had been badly beaten and forced to accept, along with the loss of face, the loss of land to their sworn enemy. For help they turned to the Soviet Union, which, somewhat hesitantly and inconsistently, nevertheless provided the necessary arms, training, and diplomatic support.[49] With that assistance the "front-line" Arab regimes had regained sufficient strength by 1973 to launch the Yom Kippur War, which caught Israel uncharacteristically unprepared and succeeded for a time in pushing back the Israeli armed forces and inflicting serious losses. The Yom Kippur War also came dangerously close to drawing in the United States and USSR, and it was the occasion for the Arab oil boycott that so aggravated the worldwide economic downturn.[50] The effect on Middle East politics was to give Egypt the respect and leverage needed to make peace with Israel four years hence. Already in 1972 Egypt had begun to question the value of the Soviet connection, and by 1975 it had gravitated into the U.S. orbit. That would ultimately make possible the Camp David Accords, agreed to in September 1978.[51] The arrangement left the Palestinians even more isolated and desperate. For a decade they had carried on sporadic guerilla warfare against Israel; now it was more or less the only option available to the PLO.

Middle Eastern politics would be complicated further by the Iranian revolution in 1979 and the subsequent hostage crisis. The image of U.S. powerlessness during the seizure of the embassy in Tehran became a nightly rebuke to the foreign policy of President Carter and an unpaid advertisement for the Reagan campaign. More concretely, it produced a regime in the Middle East openly contemptuous of the U.S. presence in the region and willing to support militant attacks against its varied manifestations. In addition, the invasion of the embassy had apparently resulted in the almost accidental capture of secret documents detailing the U.S. intelligence network throughout the area. The United States therefore emerged from the episode traumatized, angry, and vulnerable. In response, the Reagan administration became preoccupied with the real and imagined terrorist threat and sought desperately to link terrorism to the Soviet Union. Though the evidence was slim and the reasoning highly implausible, the focus on terrorism contributed to the rhetoric with which Reagan and his allies sought to elicit popular support for the Second Cold War.

Actually waging the Second Cold War was, of course, an altogether different challenge, and it was one on which the conservative record proved much more mixed.[52] The outcome of this final phase of the Cold War was indeed profoundly ironic: the Reagan and Bush administrations failed more often than they succeeded but emerged utterly triumphant by the late 1980s. The new administration prosecuted the Second Cold War on two distinct fronts: it confronted the Soviet Union directly with a new arms race, and it sought at the same time to put pressure on the periphery of the Soviet sphere of influence. Neither effort was notably successful. It was easy enough to restart the arms race. Reagan boosted military spending by a third over the already increased levels projected by the Carter administration; over the course of his first term, expenditures rose by 40 percent and consumed more than 7 percent of national income. The administration also proceeded with the plan to deploy intermediate-range missiles in Europe. More ominously, Reagan and the planners he gathered around him began to talk about the possibility of fighting and winning a nuclear war.[53] The combined effects of these actions generated great fear and a storm of protest. Already in the late 1970s Europeans had mobilized over "Euromissiles," arguing that their installation would turn their countries into "launching platforms…expendable in the interests of 'Western' defence."[54] Opposition spread to the United States in the form of the movement for a "nuclear freeze," first proposed in 1980 and nearly approved by Congress in August 1982.[55] Hundreds of thousands marched across Europe and the United States against what was perceived as a renewed threat of nuclear war. The opposition displayed an impressive breadth, for it brought together veterans of the movement against the Vietnam War and the "new social movements," feminists and "greens" in particular. Its size and intensity forced the administration to temper its rhetoric and to at least feign an interest in arms control negotiations while nevertheless moving forward with plans to install new missiles at the end of 1983. The missiles were deployed, but the momentum of the arms race had been blunted.

It was in the context of the resistance to the new arms race that Reagan proposed in March 1983 the building of an antiballistic missile defense system known popularly as "Star Wars" and bureaucratically labeled the "Strategic Defense Initiative." The "Star Wars" speech contained disturbing echoes of the plot of his 1940 movie "Murder in the Air," and the plan itself was an odd mixture of fantasy and frightening military strategy. The proposal was very expensive, and most scientists regarded the program as far beyond the scope of existing technology. Precisely because the program's stated aims were not feasible, however, people worried over what the initiative portended. For their part, Soviet strategists "saw no prospect of a truly effective defense against an enemy first strike, as President Reagan had described his goal." But they did envision the possibility that the United States could develop a defense strong enough to withstand a Soviet counterattack. This would afford the Americans with the capacity and confidence to launch a preemptive first strike.[56] What attracted Reagan, it appears, was the prospect of escape from the dilemmas of nuclear war altogether; his advisers, it might be assumed, were less naive and grasped its offensive possibilities. But whatever the goal, the response was negative all around. U.S. allies were skeptical at best, the Soviets denounced the plan, and domestic opposition grew to encompass even the Catholic bishops.[57] Funding was in fact approved, but at levels far below what was proposed, and the administration began to back off from its more ambitious designs.

Proponents of the Second Cold War thus found that they derived less political advantage from pursuing the battle against "the evil empire" than they had from criticizing Carter and others for not doing so. They would soon discover, in addition, that the Soviet Union did not necessarily respond as they had imagined and predicted. Indeed, the most remarkable consequence of the new arms race was that it had very little impact upon Soviet policy regarding nuclear weapons. The best estimates suggest that the growth of Soviet military spending leveled off about 1975–1976 and that the Soviet leaders, though worried over the U.S. buildup, did not undertake a comparable buildup of their own. They decided, in particular, "not to attempt to emulate the SDI program."[58] Despite severe provocation, Soviet policy was not significantly altered until Mikhail Gorbachev came to power in March 1985, and at first even he merely continued the policies that had been put in place by Yuri Andropov and maintained by Konstantin Chernenko.

The Reagan administration did not have any more success in its efforts to probe the weak points of the Soviet "empire." The policy took as given that the United States should avoid entanglements like Vietnam, in which large numbers of American troops would be put at risk in dubious ventures in distant parts. Indeed, Reagan's defense secretary Caspar Weinberger was even more insistent than his predecessors on the importance of keeping U.S. forces out of harm's way. What the United States should do instead was to foster a series of "low-intensity conflicts" that would pin down the Soviets and bleed their strength and resolve.[59] To this end funds, training, and logistic support were provided to anti-Soviet forces in Afghanistan, Nicaragua, Angola, and Cambodia. With the exception of Afghanistan, where the United States allied itself with Islamic fundamentalists and where the terrain and the culture proved inhospitable to the Soviets, these efforts were quite unsuccessful. The campaign against the Sandinistas was especially disastrous: the U.S.-backed "contras" were distinctly unpopular and the involvement of the United States was utterly transparent and, after Congress banned further aid to the "contras," illegal as well. Desperate to proceed despite congressional restrictions, Reagan's top advisers concocted a scheme to divert funds from arms sales to Iran, which were also illegal, to the "contras." The plan was discovered in late 1986 and the ensuing "Iran-Contra Scandal" put an inglorious end to this phase of the campaign against the Soviet Union.

Overall, then, virtually every initiative of the Reagan administration in waging the Second Cold War met with serious and unanticipated obstacles. By late 1986 and 1987, in fact, its foreign policy was in disarray, its architects and fiercest spokesmen in disgrace. Hence the official U.S. response to the sudden ending of the Cold War was confusion. Gorbachev proposed a summit meeting for November 1985, where he and Reagan agreed to a 50 percent reduction in strategic forces. At Reykjavik, Iceland, a year later they decided to eliminate intermediate-range missiles from Europe and briefly contemplated even more radical cuts. With the signing of the INF treaty in 1987, the Second Cold War could be said to have been definitively brought to a close. At the same time, the Soviets began to terminate their role in Afghanistan and arranged for Cuba to extract its troops from Angola. When the Soviets decided in 1989 to stand by and watch as revolutions swept the rulers of the Warsaw Pact countries from power, the Cold War was truly over.

To this remarkable transformation the policies of the United States and its allies made only a minor contribution. Overall, of course, the U.S. strategy of containment had countered the worldwide challenge of communism and provided the geopolitical framework within which the long-term competition between the two systems unfolded. But what brought that protracted contest to a decisive end was the determination of the leaders of the Soviet Union that the game was not worth fighting. Rather than responding in kind to the most recent U.S. challenge, they called off the rivalry. This was the last thing U.S. planners expected. In retrospect, of course, partisans have asserted that this had been their aim all along.[60] If so, why did the Reagan and Bush administrations display such an utter inability to grasp what was happening in the late 1980s? Even as they were signing historic agreements ending the Cold War on largely U.S.

terms, U.S. policy makers kept insisting that Gorbachev's reforms were a ruse, that *perestroika* and *glasnost* were fraudulent and superficial and that the Soviets would never voluntarily abandon previous positions of strength. The Bush administration was particularly unimaginative, and George Bush failed fundamentally to derive political advantage from victory in the Cold War.

It was an ironic note on which to end the first full decade of conservative political domination. Conservative parties and leaders had seized and held onto power largely by focusing on two issues—inflation and the "Soviet threat"—and on both issues they had prevailed completely. By the late 1980s inflation was beaten, the Cold War had been won, and the Soviet Union was visibly disintegrating. But success on these issues had not translated, at least not yet, into long-term political advantage, and in no country did conservatives feel politically secure. They still held office in most of the advanced capitalist democracies—or would do so shortly, as in France—but their hold on office seemed tenuous. More important, they lacked a vision of the future and a program with which to inspire their supporters and by which to guide policy making. They made good use of issues like crime and their calls for "law and order" and "family values" served well enough to rally the faithful, but they were not an effective substitute for the issues that had dominated the politics of the 1970s and 1980s but which were no longer the central concerns of most voters. Particularly obvious by the end of the 1980s were the limitations of conservative economic policy: inflation was down and there had been a modest revival in the mid-1980s, but unemployment had become a permanent feature of the industrial landscape in the advanced countries, especially in Europe, and there seemed little or no likelihood of a return to the pattern of growth that had prevailed during the early postwar era. If liberal policies had failed to cope with the unexpected economic disasters of the 1970s, conservative policy had proved itself unable in the 1980s to engineer a long-term solution to slow growth.

What was becoming clear, then, was that while conservatives and their opponents had been arguing about how to manage an economy of whose logic and needs each side claimed a superior understanding, the economy itself changed beyond recognition. As the economic indicators moved up and down and policy makers fixed upon controlling one or another measure of performance or well-being, the very structure of the world economy had been transformed. It was more global and less local; its centers of innovation had moved; its technical bases had been greatly upgraded; its forms of industrial organization had mutated; its use of labor had been reshaped; and its workings had become far less amenable to the efforts of states to control it. The changes had been in the making for many years and more than a few commentators had taken note of their direction and importance. But just as the discourse of the Cold War had lasted far beyond the time when its terms yielded a plausible picture of the world order, so the discourse of politics and policy making that had been established after the Second World War and had served to order and interpret the "golden age" of capitalist growth and to structure its politics had outlasted its usefulness. So long as the geopolitical lineaments of the Cold War world order remained in place, however, it was impossible fully to comprehend the new world emerging from the old. That task was perhaps beyond the capacity of those for whom the Cold War world defined the limits of their imagination and would necessarily fall to others, who would seek to define and shape the post-Cold War world.

# Communism's
## 7 \ Endings

In late spring 1976 George Bush, then director of the Central Intelligence Agency, commissioned a review of the agency's estimates of Soviet military strength by a group of outside experts who would come to be known as "Team B." Chaired by the "Russophobe" Richard Pipes, Team B asserted that current CIA reports had been too optimistic about the Soviet Union, underestimating its capabilities and overlooking its aggressive intentions. The report's conclusions were leaked in December 1976 in an obvious effort to push the incoming Carter administration away from détente and toward a confrontation with the Soviet Union.[1] The manuever hardly seems to have been necessary, though it did contribute marginally to the growing pessimism about U.S.–Soviet relations. The interesting point about the exercise is therefore not its impact, nor its deeply flawed findings, nor what it says about Bush and the post-Watergate gloom of loyal Republicans but, rather, what it reveals about the assumptions surrounding the state of communism in the USSR and about the continued saliency of Cold War ideology.

By the early 1970s, Soviet leaders could boast confidently that the nation had achieved strategic parity with the United States, that its military and political strength had forced the West to recognize the legitimacy and permanence of its domination of Eastern Europe and to acquiesce to the "Brezhnev doctrine," that its economic record had made these accomplishments possible, and that continued economic growth would sustain these positions of strength and allow further advances. It was indeed "this shift of the balance of forces in the world arena" that had made "peaceful co-existence and mutually advantageous cooperation" possible, according to Soviet spokesman Georgii Arbatov. Assumptions about the vitality and stability of the Soviet system were thus at the basis of Soviet foreign policy and of U.S. responses. Arbatov, again, made the connection explicit: "The possibility of successful talks with the U.S.A. and of positive changes in Soviet-American relations is ensured by the activity of our party, the Soviet state and the entire Soviet people in strengthening the homeland's economic and defensive might, strengthening the ideological and political unity of our society and consolidating the Socialist Commonwealth."[2] Although U.S. experts debated whether this reality constituted the basis for peace and stability or the promise of confrontation, they agreed fundamentally on the underlying strength of the regime. Years later Pipes would insist that conservatives like him had perceived the mounting crisis of the Soviet system in the early 1980s, and that it was this perception that underpinned the foreign policy initiatives of the Reagan administration.[3] But there is no evidence that they or anyone else detected the flaws in the Soviet economy or the fragility of its political system in the 1970s. On the contrary, the left, the right, and and the center shared a view that Soviet achievements were real, that they would persist, and that U.S. policy would have to take Soviet power into account as a structural feature of the system of international relations.

Where policymakers differed was over Soviet intentions. Here the enduring power of ideology made itself felt. Since the Cuban missile crisis, the behavior of the Soviet Union had been characterized by caution. Its most aggressive move was the suppression of dissidence in Czechoslovakia, and the motive was clearly defensive. The Soviet Union persisted in offering both rhetorical support and arms for "national liberation" movements in the Third World, but in practice Soviet influence was ordinarily exercised on behalf of moderation and compromise.[4] But the ideology of the Cold War continued to inform relations between the United States and the USSR, and even when the substance of relations improved, suspicion and antipathy remained. Despite the fact that détente was initiated by veteran cold warriors like Nixon and Kissinger, who could hardly be charged with sympathy toward the Soviet regime, the policy was nevertheless the subject of repeated attacks that in the end forced its abandonment. The ideological antagonisms of the early Cold War therefore long outlasted the occasion for their generation and the time when they might plausibly have led to military confrontation. And they were reciprocated, for Soviet leaders proved as trapped in their ideological discourse as U.S. leaders were in theirs.[5]

The lingering effects of ideology guaranteed that when the rivalry between the superpowers temporarily lessened in the 1970s, it would not translate into a stable and cooperative relationship but would soon revert to hostility, renewed arms competition, and a pattern of nasty local confrontations known as the Second Cold War. Indeed, the very origins of the Second Cold War seem to have been more ideological than geopolitical. Of course, there were political changes in the Third World that could be interpreted as defeats for the West: the overthrow of Haile Selassie; the fall of Vietnam; the collapse of the Portuguese Empire in Africa; revolutions in Iran and Nicaragua. But it required an intensely ideological view of world politics to construe all of these events as U.S. losses and Soviet gains. And the issues that preoccupied policy makers and that drove foreign policy debate were not, in any event, shifts of regime on the periphery but debates over missiles, compliance with arms agreements, and human rights. It was a discourse, moreover, that was not focused outward and empirically on the world but inward on questions of national identity, which in the 1970s became intimately bound up with political economy but which came to be fought out in terms of ideology. Events were of marginal importance, and the event that might have made a real difference—the Soviet invasion of Afghanistan—came only at the end of the process that led to the Second Cold War.

The worsening of Soviet–U.S. relations may not have had much to do with the behavior of either superpower during the 1970s, but the deterioration would have consequences for their subsequent actions and policies. The United States under Reagan committed itself to policies of active intervention in the Third World and to a large arms buildup. The Soviet Union, in consequence, found itself pinned down in conflicts on several continents and locked into at least the beginnings of a new and more expensive arms race. The burden on its economy was considerable, but what was perhaps more important was the impact of the Second Cold War on the prospects for reform within the Soviet Union and on the balance of forces for and against economic restructuring.[6] A serious program of structural reform was probably out of the question so long as Brezhnev dominated Soviet politics. Early in his rule he had committed himself to a strategy of achieving political stability by raising standards of living and guaranteeing security for workers, for peasants, and, most important, for officials. Successive Five-Year Plans during the Brezhnev era devoted increasing resources to "social consumption," wages were steadily increased for workers, and substantial subsidies were granted to peasants in the form of higher prices.[7] Party leaders, and state and industrial bureaucrats whose positions appeared threatened by Khrushchev's penchant for administrative restructuring, became firmly entrenched under Brezhnev. Behind his slogan "Respect for Cadres," officials of all sorts acquired substantial privileges and came close to becoming a "new class," which by 1980 had earned its new name, the *nomenklatura*.[8]

Attempts to reform the system while Brezhnev presided over it would have meant a dramatic reversal of these policies and would have encountered fierce resistance from those the policies served. The pressures to undertake reform were, in any case, not particularly intense, for the Soviet economy was still growing, albeit at a diminishing rate. The discovery and initial exploitation of huge oil reserves at a time of high international oil prices was further cause for complacency because oil sales provided the currency needed to purchase Western technology and, when necessary, foodstuffs. The incentives to undertake structural reform were thus insufficient to move the largely unmovable system. Given his own failing powers, moreover, it is unlikely that Brezhnev would have been capable of responding. In consequence, reforms were limited in their scope and effectiveness under Brezhnev. The most important were the 1979 decree "Strengthening the Economic Mechanism," which sought to reshape the system of targets and quotas with the aim of improving quality, and the simultaneous effort to group workers into "industrial brigades" as a means of introducing more incentives.[9] Neither was particularly successful, and as the Brezhnev years drew to a close, it became clear that more radical restructuring would be necessary. The onset of a new phase of the arms race further fueled this perception, for the military came to understand the need to modernize the economy in order to compete successfully with the United States.

The widespread recognition of the need for reforming the economy was a major factor behind the selection of Yuri Andropov as Brezhnev's successor over his rival, Konstantin Chernenko. Andropov, former director of the KGB, was convinced that it was essential to modernize the economy and reform the political system. He pursued a vigorous campaign against idleness and corruption and, at a more basic and theoretical level, sought to think through the problem of restructuring the economy. To this end, he appointed Mikhail Gorbachev to head a special task force on economic reform; he and Gorbachev were largely responsible for a series of studies and analyses that were highly critical of previous economic policy. The central text was Tatyana Zaslavskaya's famous "Novosibirsk paper," which proclaimed boldly: "The complexity of the economic structure has long since overstripped the threshold of its efficient regulation from a single center." The existing system, she went on to complain, caused an "inhibition of market forces" and was therefore at odds "with the new demands of the productive forces." Bringing them into conformity could not, however "be realised without confict," for reforms would be resisted by the ranks of bureaucrats that "have sprouted like mushrooms in recent years."[10]

Unfortunately, Andropov was old and quite ill when he took office, and he would not live long enough to see through his intitiatives and reforms. He was succeeded by Brezhnev's rightful heir and former drinking companion Chernenko, under whose decrepit leadership little occurred. It required yet another change of leadership, resulting in Gorbachev's selection as party leader in the spring of 1985, for reform to rise once again to the top of the political agenda. By that time the conditions were far less favorable: the Soviet Union was locked into an expensive competition with the United States in the development and production of nuclear arms and bogged down in a series of regional conflicts that sapped morale and resources and diverted attention from domestic problems. The economic problems had grown worse as the potential for further "growth through mobilization" became exhausted and the rate of growth dropped to virtually nil. And the collapse of oil prices drastically reduced the leadership's flexibility in economic affairs, making it impossible to rely on the import of Western technology to spark increases in productivity or, even, to buy foodstuffs or consumer goods on the international market. The arrogant complacency of the Brezhnev era—brought about by détente, by the achievement of nuclear parity with the United States, by gains in the Third World, and by recognition of the nation as a genuine superpower—had thus turned within a decade to a growing paralysis. Over the intervening ten years, whatever opportunity might have existed for resolving the crisis had passed. But it was surely no accident that the leaders of the Soviet Union had failed to perceive or act upon the crisis until it was too late: their world had yet to fall apart; their interests were still too well served by the system; and they remained trapped within the ideological discourse whose mastery legitimized their status while rotting their brains.

## RETRENCHMENT AND REFORM IN CHINA

Complacency was not an option for Communists elsewhere. In both China and Eastern Europe the need to reshape or recast socialism was much clearer much sooner. While the Soviets were settling into their status as a roughly coequal superpower during the mid-1970s, the Chinese were still dealing with the convulsions of late, indeed increasingly senescent, Maoism. The worst excesses of the Cultural Revolution had ended with the intervention of the army in 1967–68 and the disbanding of the Red Guards, and a measure of stability was restored with the Ninth Congress in April 1969. But the damage done by the upheaval was not easily repaired, for the Cultural Revolution had ravaged the party and the state bureaucracy, and at its close political leadership was shared uneasily between the PLA and what remained of the party and the state. It was thus almost inevitable that the leader of the army, Lin Biao, should aspire to succeed Mao, even as he sycophantically praised "the Great Helmsman," and that the most serious challenge to Mao's leadership should therefore come from his chosen successor. Even when Lin's coup failed in 1971, however, the course of Chinese politics remained very much in doubt. The army's representation was diminished but still very important, and the party leadership was split three ways between the few old comrades who had survived the Cultural Revolution, those on the left who had intitiated and led the movement, and those who had been thrown up by the turmoil and taken the positions of those deprived of office.[11] None of these groupings proved capable in the short run of providing effective leadership: the survivors were too few and too timid; the left too ideologically driven and intemperate; and the new entrants to the top levels of the party too inexperienced to run the party and the state.

Over the next five years Mao himself played the central role in elevating the fortunes of one group or individual and casting down others, but he did so inconsistently and ineffectively. He first acquiesced in the ascendancy of Zhou Enlai, whose stature rose in the aftermath of the Lin Biao debacle, and in the rehabilitation of Deng Xiaoping, who had been criticized during the Cultural Revolution as the number-two capitalist roader in the party. Deng returned to Beijing in March 1973, took over much of Zhou's work when the latter took ill in 1974, and became first vice premier in January 1975. Also in January, Zhou addressed the Fourth National

People's Congress on what would become known as the Four Modernizations. By committing the party to carrying out the Four Modernizations—of agriculture, industry, defense, and science and technology—Zhou, with Mao's support, reaffirmed the party's adherence to the nationalist project above all else. It was under the guise of advancing the Four Modernizations that the party would adopt a fundamentally new course after the death of Mao, and it was under that rubric that the turn to capitalist methods of organizing the economy would be justified.

As late as 1975, however, the issue of what direction Chinese politics and economic development would take was still quite unresolved. Mao's support for Zhou and Deng, in particular, wavered and at the time of his death in September 1976, it was the left that was momentarily in the ascendant. The left, gathered around Jiang Qing, Mao's wife, and Zhang Chunqiao, had been placed on the defensive by Lin Biao's treachery, and was forced during 1972 and early 1973 to accept the dominance of Zhou and the return to good graces of Deng. Mao sought to balance his tilt toward the survivors by bringing Wang Hongwen, a close ally of the left from Shanghai, into the leadership in Beijing. Wang was to emerge as the fourth and most highly placed member of the so-called Gang of Four. He was brought onto the Politburo in May 1973; by the party's Tenth Congress in August, the left was again predominant. From their positions of power on the Central Committee and with the support of Mao, they began to reshape the campaign against Lin Biao into a campaign against both Lin Biao and Confucius, which, by the convoluted logic of Chinese political discourse, meant Zhou Enlai.

Throughout 1974 and 1975 survivors and radicals battled for the soul of the party, with an increasingly infirm and incoherent Mao Zedong maintaining the balance while leaning toward the left. The death of Zhou Enlai in January 1976 forced a choice, and the decision was made to replace Zhou not with Deng, the logical candidate, but with Hua Guofeng, a beneficiary of the Cultural Revolution though not one of its leaders or major proponents. The passing over of Deng was an obvious continuation of the Gang of Four's campaign against Zhou; appropriately enough, the subsequent mass demonstration of mourning over Zhou Enlai at Tiananmen Square in April was understood correctly as a demonstration of support for Deng as well as Zhou and a sign that the left and the Gang of Four could not count on mass support. The Gang was not deterred, however, and Deng was again dismissed.

The Gang of Four was nevertheless still not satisfied and sought to press its advantage while Mao was still alive. It regarded Hua Guofeng as a "nice gentleman of Malenkov's ilk," and hence woefully unworthy of inheriting the mantle of Mao Zedong. The effect was to drive Hua into a reluctant alliance with the survivors within the leadership, especially the generals, and to create a united front against the left. The Gang of Four was safe until Mao died in September 1976, but within a month the four were arrested. With the fall of the Gang of Four, the Cultural Revolution was finally over, and the rebuilding of the state, the party, and the economy could begin anew. Hua was left in charge and could quote Mao's words—"With you in charge, I'm at ease"—on his own behalf, but his position was institutionally weak and he lacked both a theme for legitimating his political authority or a plan to revive the economy, which by one estimate had suffered losses of over 28 million tons of steel production and of 100 billion yuan of industrial production as a result of political disruptions over the previous three years. Hua was forced by July 1977 to bring Deng back yet again and uneasily shared leadership with him over the next year. The ensuing contest between Hua and Deng echoed the debates of the previous decade, but with Mao gone and the Gang of Four in jail, the case for a continuation of the policies of "class struggle" and recurring episodes of cultural revolution lost out and the argument for a pragmatic approach to the "Four Modernizations" prevailed.

Hua staked his future on the mandate of Mao, the almost blind adherence to Mao Zedong Thought, and a new and more ambitious version of the Ten-Year Plan (1976–1985). His position was summarized in the "two whatevers": "Whatever policy Chairman Mao decided upon, we shall resolutely defend; whatever directives Chairman Mao issued, we shall steadfastly obey." Deng's rather different preferences had long been known, if only from the denunciations of his enemies. He was more practical, did not worship at the cult of Mao, and did not believe that politics and class struggle could guide every action. Even before Mao's death, Deng had argued that "the view that once revolution is grasped, production will increase naturally and without spending any effort is believed only by those who indulge in fairy tales." In the ideological struggle with Hua Guofeng, Deng countered the reliance upon Mao's Thought with the injunction to "seek truth from facts." As he coyly put it, "Comrades, let's think it over: Isn't it true that seeking truth from facts, proceeding from reality and integrating theory with practice forms the fundamental principle of Mao Zedong Thought? Is this fundamental principle outdated?... How can we be true to Marxism-Leninism and Mao Zedong Thought if we are against seeking truth from facts?" Prior to Mao's death such a commonsensical appeal might have fallen flat, but in 1978 the party and presumably the Chinese people were ready for a more practical politics that would begin the process of rebuilding the economy.

It soon became clear that Hua's economic policies were failing to deliver the promised growth, and at the meeting of the Third Plenum of the Central Committee, held in December 1978, the policies were reversed. China would move away from collectivized agriculture through novel "production responsibility systems" allowing greater freedom to production teams and permitting work groups to contract with the larger teams, by supporting private plots and village fairs, and in general by increasing incentives and overcoming "equalitarianism"; industry would be reoriented away from huge investment in heavy industry; and the economy overall would be subjected to a steady effort at "readjusting, restructuring, consolidating and improving" while abandoning the Ten-Year Plan so recently trumpeted by Hua Guofeng.

It would take another two years for Deng's victory to be complete and a bit longer for the implications of his new program to become clear. By the time of the Twelfth Party Congress in September 1982, however, the direction the Dengist reforms would take was evident, and so were the likely consequences and the debates to which they would give rise. The Congress resolved to "intensify socialist modernization...[with] economic construction at the core," but the decision to press forward with economic reform was coupled with two further commitments to "socialist legality" and to the creation of a "socialist spiritual civilization."[12] The emphasis upon law represented a concession by the party that it would not engage in the arbitrary exercise of power that had characterized the recent past and that it would permit a "gradual, though not uninterrupted, depoliticization of the Chinese economy, polity and culture."[13] The affirmation of the importance of law led also to a sustained effort to reshape the legal environment within which economic reform would occur. The notion of a "socialist spiritual civilization" has a quite peculiar ring, though it was perhaps anticipated in Mao's conception of cultural revolution. Its use seems to have been quite alien to whatever Mao might have meant, however, for it served as a kind of prophylactic device that allowed the leadership to proceed with reform, to anticipate its negative effects, and to offer an immediate antidote and corrective. The turn to the market would inevitably lead to values and practices inimical to socialism: individualism, inequality, corruption, "bourgeois liberalism," and other forms of "spiritual pollution." Deng and his allies clearly foresaw these likely consequences but were not deterred, and instead sought preemptively to inoculate society against them.

The parallel commitments to market reforms and to combating the cultural side effects of capitalism represented a brilliant stroke by Chinese reformers and set in motion a pattern that was to be played out repeatedly over the next decade. The state adopted a series of liberalizing initiatives aimed at generating economic growth; successive spurts of growth were accompanied by increases in crime, corruption, conspicuous consumption, decadence, increasing inequality, and, more ominously, inflation; the party and the state responded with intensified efforts to root out and punish corruption, to combat "spiritual pollution" and "bourgeois liberalism," and to inculcate the values of a "socialist spiritual civilization." But the economic reforms remained in place and, if anything, were pushed ahead. The logic was a cyclical pattern of "relaxation and control," of *fang* and *shou*.[14]

The effect was a spectacular record of economic growth accompanied by a curious political evolution. The reforms affected both agriculture and industry, though in slightly different fashion. Within agriculture, the commune was effectively abolished and individual peasant households were accorded increasing freedom. The adoption of "Central Document #1" in June 1984 granted to individuals the ability to engage in private economic activity and gave peasant households the right to sign land-use contracts that came close to making land into their private property. Capitalism thus came to the Chinese countryside by reorganizing existing units of production and encouraging the growth of market relations within the rural sector.[15] Economic reforms within industry took a rather different form, with market-oriented industry growing up alongside or within the interstices of state-owned industry. Thus, although the leadership decided to restructure industry at roughly the same moment as it chose to reshape agriculture and along comparable lines, capitalist styles of industry took root more selectively in the Special Economic Zones and in the coastal cities. New forms of cooperative ventures, some involving foreign capital, were often established in these areas, with an explicit orientation to export markets. Regional and local governments were also allowed to become partners in new enterprises. In both industry and agriculture the results of economic reform were impressive: agricultural output grew by more than 9 percent annually during 1978–1984, and peasant incomes increased roughly fivefold from 1978 to 1990; between 1979 and 1989 total output increased by nearly 11 percent a year and industrial output by an annual average of 12.4 percent, wages even in state-owned industries tripled, and urban living space doubled; and exports increased nineteenfold from 1979 to 1991.[16]

The success of reform in China, particularly in contrast to the sorry results of reform in Eastern Europe and the Soviet Union, has yet to be fully explained. Perhaps the critical facilitating factor, however, was that the starting place was very different. The command economy was never as firmly established in China as in other socialist countries, and the Chinese model was consistently more decentralized than the Soviet model developed in the USSR and copied elsewhere. Mao's deep suspicion of bureaucracy contributed to this resistance to Soviet-style overcentralization; so, too, did the peasant base of the revolution, which ensured that the preference for heavy industry, though evident in China, would be more muted than elsewhere and that investment would not be financed by the superexploitation of the agricultural sector. These characteristics of the Chinese model of socialism were reinforced by, and themselves reinforced, the distinctive economic geography of China, in which a "cellular pattern of organization" on the local level was linked into "quite far-flung networks" to create large, quasi-natural economic regions.[17] The Great Leap Forward and the Cultural Revolution, for all their disruptive effects on industry and agriculture, accentuated this localism and added a drive to create self-sufficient regional economies. The Dengist reforms built upon these traditions and structures and, by all accounts, were energized by the unleashing of local and regional entrepreneurial zeal.[18]

China's economic revolution has benefited as well from the consistency with which it has been pursued by the political leadership. The cycle of relaxation and control of politics and cultural life has had little effect on economic policy, which has become steadily more "capitalist" and market-oriented. From the beginning, it seems clear, China's leaders understood the risks and consequences attendant upon economic reform. They spoke openly about using capitalist methods to advance the cause of socialism, and the stress laid upon the development of "socialist spiritual civilization" was meant to offset the dangers. It also provided a discourse through which to deal with the inevitable objections and resistance to traveling down the "capitalist road," a discourse that turned social critique into attacks upon crime and corruption and that deflected criticism from the emerging system to guilty individuals or "spiritual pollution." Hence the readiness of party leaders to denounce crime and corruption and to prosecute at least its less-well-connected practitioners.

Deng Xiaoping seems to have been willing to go even further in allowing his closest allies to be sacrificed so long as his policies were continued. Political and economic reform raised the hopes of students and liberal intellectuals in the mid-1980s and led to a wave of student demonstrations in December 1986. Deng was utterly unsympathetic to the protesters and quite willing "to shed some blood," if it was necessary to keep order. It was not, for the protests waned in the new year, but someone had to take the blame for letting "spiritual pollution" and "bourgeois liberalism" thrive and allowing students to be misled. Hu Yaobang, the general secretary of the party and a strong advocate for Deng's policies, was the victim. He was removed from his position at the top of the party, denounced by the Politburo, and pressured into "self-criticism."

A similar, and still more unpleasant, fate would ultimately befall Hu's replacement, Zhao Ziyang. Zhao presided over the next installment of reform, in which the party accepted that the "central task" of the era was economic development and that in this "primary stage of socialism" the market would have a large role to play: "The state regulates the market; the market guides the enterprise," he explained. Zhao actually elaborated his own variation of the "whatever" principle, announcing that "whatever is conducive to the growth [of the productive forces] is in keeping with the fundamental interests of the people and is therefore needed by socialism and allowed to exist."[19] Closely related to Zhao's vision of the enhanced role of the market was a project for the "reform of the political structure." Zhao was thus moved to propose a package of reforms that, taken together, revealed a strong preference for depoliticization and decentralization, and included proposals for severing the ties between politics and economics; for establishing clear institutional boundaries to separate the party, the state, and the economy; for "strengthening the socialist legal system"; and for replacing the bureaucracy with a civil service system. The proposals called for "consultation" rather than democracy, and Zhao explicitly warned that "we shall never allow the kind of 'great democracy' that undermines law and social stability."

Zhao's plan for political reform quickly acquired the label "neoauthoritarianism," and Zhao did not disavow the term. The plan's authoritarian aspect derived not from its basic suspicion of democracy but from the perception of its proponents that the transition to a modern economy and polity required strong, almost "Bonapartist," leadership that could resist pressure from both left and right, from those who wanted further reform and from those wanted less of it, and therefore move ahead with economic modernization. Indeed, Zhao and his allies followed up their proposals for political change with an attack upon the those deeply entrenched practices that stood out as major obstacles to reform: the so-called iron rice bowl that guaranteed more or less permanent employment to workers and the "common pot" of benefits to which all members of enterprises felt entitled. At the same time a new "enterprise reform" was passed and a new bankruptcy law took effect.

The cumulative effect of these reforms was an economic upsurge that, like previous fits of growth, produced high levels of inflation, which in turn generated public concern about the impact of economic reform and yet another wave of "moral panic" over corruption. With this the political cycle turned toward control as party conservatives again began fretting over "spiritual pollution" and urging retrenchment. Students and liberals, by contrast, took Zhao's proposals about political reform as a signal to argue for a more thorough democratization. Political debate intensified during 1988–1989 and climaxed in the spring of 1989. Hu Yaobang, whose career Deng had already sacrificed, returned to Beijing in April and took part in a sharp exchange over education within the Politburo, during which he suffered a heart attack from which he soon died. His death produced another outpouring of support at the Revolutionary Heroes Monument at Tiananmen Square that soon grew to extremely large proportions. The confrontation escalated and soon encompassed not merely students but workers as well. Deng denounced the "turmoil," but this hard-line response only emboldened the protesters, who were energized as well by the prospect of Mikhail Gorbachev's visit, planned for May 15. Gorbachev's presence would attract world attention to what was happening in Beijing, and protesters believed that fear of incurring the opprobrium of the international community would deter the leadership from undertaking outright repression of the movement. Leaders of the prodemocracy movement ratcheted up the stakes still further by declaring a hunger strike. The government held off until Gorbachev departed on May 18, and Zhao used the intervening period to urge compromise. He failed, however, and martial law was declared at midnight on May 19. Troops encircled the capital and prepared to enter but were blocked by the spontaneous obstruction of local residents. The soldiers stopped their advance and withdrew to the outskirts of the city. Meanwhile, Zhao Ziyang was removed from office and denounced by his opponents in the leadership. Gradually, the ranks of the protesters gathered in Tiananmen Square began to diminish. By early June the government apparently felt that it was opportune to act and on June 3–4 sent in the troops, whose advance to the center resulted in the deaths of several hundred, possibly a thousand, Beijing residents but just a few students, most of whom evacuated the square as the soldiers prepared to enter. Mass arrests followed a week or so later, and several exemplary executions were staged.

The government thanked the troops for their bravery and blamed Zhao

Ziyang and an excess of "bourgeois liberalization" for the unrest. Zhao was replaced by Jiang Zemin, former mayor of Shanghai. But neither Jiang nor Deng repudiated the policies of the previous decade. Deng publicly asked, "Is there anything wrong with the basic concept of reform and openness?" "No," he replied to himself, and explained that the source of the problem lay in the failure to apply the "four cardinal principles"—the socialist road; the dictatorship of the proletariat; the leadership of the Chinese Communist Party; and Marxism-Leninism and Mao Zedong Thought—and to combat "spiritual pollution." To rectify the situation, the party undertook yet another campaign against corruption and crime, hoping in the process "to inspire satisfaction among the people," as Deng put it. But there would be no turning back, no retreat from the economic reforms that Deng and his allies had obviously decided were essential to China's "modernization" and to its achievement of wealth and power.[20] By 1989 far too many had benefited from reform for it to be abandoned.[21] Deng's great achievement, then, was to have created a constituency for economic reform and thus to have linked the fate of China as a nation state to the continuing success of his economic policies and to the political power of the Communist Party.[22] The outcome should come as no surprise, confirming as it does the identity of interest between the party and the nationalist project. What is perhaps surprising is that the party's leaders still feel compelled to use the words "*communism*," or "*socialism*" or even the enigmatic "socialism with Chinese characteristics" to describe their project, their methods, their goals, or their values.

## DISINTEGRATION IN EASTERN EUROPE

If the continued viability of Communist power in China derived ultimately from the party's successful identification of its interest with the national interest, it was the complete failure to connect socialism with nationalism that fatally undermined the communist regimes of Eastern Europe. Those regimes were conceived in Moscow and considered illegitimate from birth, but for roughly two decades they tried to accomplish the impossible task of simultaneously rooting themselves in local conditions and traditions and demonstrating their fealty to the Soviet bloc and the Soviet model. What made it possible even to imagine the possibility were three features of the region's history: the discredit attaching to parties of the right for their failure to support democracy between the wars and for their common, if by no means universal, support of the Nazis during the war; the prestige of the Soviet Union for its role in defeating fascism; and the fact that socialist parties had attained a measure of support in the past and had compiled credible records of opposition to authoritarianism and to Nazism. These traditions gave the socialist regimes at least a glimmer of hope in their efforts to achieve popular legitimacy. A further cause for hope was the prospect of reform within the Soviet Union under Khrushchev. Khrushchev's denunciation of Stalin and his vision of a prosperous and even humane socialism inspired a generation of Eastern European "revisionists" to think that Eastern Europe, with its closer ties to the West and greater appreciation of Western traditions of democracy, would be the ideal location to create "socialism with a human face."[23]

These plans and proposals proved illusory, however, and did not survive the Soviet interventions of 1956 in Hungary and 1968 in Czechoslovakia. By the 1970s serious thinkers had abandoned whatever hopes they might have entertained about reforming socialism. The Polish philosopher Leszek Kolakowski spoke for an entire generation when he complained in 1971 that "the dead and by now also grotesque creature called Marxism-Leninism still hangs at the necks of the rulers like a hopeless tumor."[24] Given the service that Marxism routinely rendered to irresponsible power by adorning and justifying the repressive practices of the regimes, faith in even the most humane vision of socialism became impossible for Eastern Europeans and could no longer serve as a viable framework within which to work out a philosophy of reform or resistance. In response, the intelligentsia across much of Eastern Europe chose a form of "internal exile," of alienation, and of resigned indifference to the rulers of their countries and the rituals and rhetorics in which they so frequently and pathetically indulged. The strategy was to act and speak, at least to one another, "as if we were grown up and legally independent" (Ludvík Vaculík), to "live within the truth" (Vaclav Havel), and to behave "as if" one were a citizen of a democratic state. In Poland this "internal exile" was given a name, "antipolitics," and so named it became something more: a decision to create a "real day-to-day community of free people" (Adam Michnik) and thus gradually to undertake what would come to be called the "self-organization of society."

But the advocates of "antipolitics" confronted an enormous difficulty, for the principled refusal to engage the regime was nearly impossible to distinguish from the isolation and outward conformity on which the regimes depended. It was in the very nature of communist polities to deny the distinction between the public and the private, to insist that the personal was political and to admit to no social and political space between the state and the individual. Communist politics, at least as practiced in those nations modeled initially on the Soviet experience, was premised on the irrelevance and effective absence of an autonomous "public sphere" in which political discourse could proceed in relative freedom as well as of those intermediate institutions that make up "civil society." The attempt to recreate the conditions for democracy in Eastern Europe has encouraged a heightened sensitivity to the importance of civil society as its essential prerequisite.[25] In the socialist states, of course, there were plenty of organizations, and cultural and social life was extremely well organized. But because "Communist civil society was patronized and controlled by the Party," it could not play the role assigned to it in democratic theory.[26] The choice of "internal exile" did not help, for although it might deprive the approved organizations of "communist civil society" of a measure of legitimacy, it did little or nothing to build the autonomous civil society needed to overcome the existing regimes or to replace them with functioning democratic political systems. Dissidence was hence disengaged, if understandably so, and resistance was displaced into the realm of discourse and parody and toward the struggle for "straight talk" and against the official language of the regime.[27]

These limits, self-imposed but nonetheless based upon a reasonable calculation of the strength of the state versus the strength of its erstwhile opponents, were visible and operative across Eastern Europe and governed the tactics of opposition even when protest went beyond the normal bounds. In Czechoslovakia, for example, intellectuals founded two organizations, Charter 77 and VONS (the Committee for the Defense of the Unjustly Persecuted), both of which sought legitimacy by identifying with the Helsinki Accords while declaring themselves to be fundamentally "apolitical." But party leaders were not fooled, and chose to regard them as oppositional and hence liable to repression, which followed swiftly and effectively circumscribed the groups' activities and limited their appeal and effectiveness.[28] Elsewhere, dissidence and opposition remained largely underground, private, and therefore without noticeable political effect.

Opposition was also made marginal by the efforts of the regimes to confine dissent to the intelligentsia and to undercut potential support among workers. The unrest of Polish workers in 1970 was almost as upsetting to party leaders throughout Eastern Europe as the "Prague Spring," for it signaled a loss of legitimacy among the very class whose interests the state claimed to represent. In response, the regimes began to implement a Brezhnev-style social contract with the working classes. At the center of the contract was a bargain: an improved standard of living, with enhanced security, was exchanged for political acquiescence. The economic basis of the compromise required two shifts in policy: an increase in imports from the West financed partially by exports but largely by borrowing; and a shift in investment strategy from heavy to light industry and from producer to consumer goods. In the short term, the deal was facilitated by détente and by the fact that Western banks were awash in funds as a result of the oil crisis and inflation and for that reason were eager to lend. Over the long term, the profligacy of the 1970s would overwhelm the initiatives of the 1980s and cause increasing economic stagnation in all the Eastern European economies. Nevertheless, both the increased living standards and job security of the working class were protected, even at the cost of growth, and served to immunize most workers from the infection of dissent.

The relative quiescence of labor in Eastern Europe probably did more to prevent the emergence of civil society in the region than the intellectuals' preference for "internal exile" over overt dissent. The organizations created by middle-class intellectuals and professionals typically make up the bulk of the array of associations that normally constitute civil society, but they are seldom the most effective or powerful groups within the polity. Where they exist and are allowed to flourish, genuinely independent trade unions and churches routinely exert more clout, even if their internal workings and subcultures display rather "illiberal" and even "uncivil" characteristics. Throughout the 1970s and early 1980s unions did not exist and the churches were mostly tame. That would change in the late 1980s, but only in response to changes in the structure of political opportunity opened up by the weakening and fissuring of the regimes and their leadership.

The exception was Poland, where the "self-organization of society" proceeded further than anywhere else in Eastern Europe. Three remarkable developments underpinned the rise of an autonomous civil society in that nation. The first was the founding by reformist intellectuals of KOR, the Committee for the Defense of Workers, to organize legal defense and financial assistance for workers who had engaged in a series of strikes and protests over the government's decision to raise food prices in June 1976. Again, the initial stimulus to organization was "compassion" and the aim "apolitical," but KOR and its talented leaders—Adam Michnik, Jacek Kuron, and others—quickly grasped the political implications of their initiative and by 1977 had changed the group's name to Social Self-Defense Committee, in a clear recognition of their oppositional status, and had set up "the Flying University." In 1978 they undertook the far more daring and potentially threatening step of creating the Founding Committee for the Free Trade Unions of the Coast and encouraged the establishment of similar committees across the country.[29]

Even at this early stage the opposition to the regime enjoyed at least the passive support of the Polish Catholic Church. In the aftermath of 1956 the church had evolved a *modus vivendi* with the regime that conceded it "a *minimum* of freedom from which," as the future pope argued, "a clever pastor can build a maximum."[30] In return for increased space within which to conduct its pastoral activities, the church muted its public criticism of the regime while nonetheless providing succor and occasional cover for those who opposed it, particularly after 1968. The role of the church increased enormously and its stance became more critical toward the government in 1978, when the Polish Cardinal Karol Wojtyla became Pope John Paul II. The pope's subsequent visit to Poland in June 1979 proved utterly catalytic. In the presence of Edward Gierek, the party secretary, he denounced "all forms of political, economic and cultural colonialism"—an obvious reference to Soviet domination—and convinced masses of discontented Poles "that they were not alone."[31]

The third, and by far the most important, step in the "self-organization of society" in Poland was the creation in August 1980 of Solidarity, an independent workers' union founded in the Gdansk shipyard and led by Lech Walesa.[32] The strikes from which Solidarity grew were aimed in the first instance at countering the rise in food prices, but the movement quickly transcended economic grievances and demanded recognition of workers' rights to form free and independent unions and to strike. Stunned and momentarily overwhelmed by Solidarity's success, the government and the union signed a series of agreements, the so-called Social Accords, at the end of August and the beginning of September 1980, which not only granted the strikers' demands but also provided "that the state radio system broadcast Catholic Sunday Mass" and conceded a host of reforms previously thought to be incompatible with continued Communist rule.[33] The accords added up to a comprehensive list of rights whose effective exercise was fundamentally incompatible with the Leninist model of party domination of state and society. In this sense, Jacek Kuron was right in saying of Solidarity's achievement, in retrospect, "I thought it was impossible, it was impossible and I still think it was impossible."[34] Perhaps inevitably, Gierek was quickly sacked as party secretary and replaced by Stanislaw Kania on September 6. Kania's leadership lasted only a few months; he was to be replaced by General Wojciech Jaruzelski, who became prime minister in early February 1981.

If Solidarity's founding and initial success were remarkable, its evolution over the next year was equally astounding. Within two weeks of the signing of the Social Accords, representatives from union organizing committees around the country gathered together to become the Independent Self-Governing Trade Union, "Solidarity," and to demand recognition and formal registration, which was finally granted in November. Solidarity mushroomed rapidly into something much more than a trade union but less than a political party, and by the beginnning of the new year the locus of activity had shifted to the countryside and to the effort to create Rural Solidarity. By spring 1981 the movement could plausibly claim 10 million members, but at that point it was beset by a mounting crisis of identity. Its founders persisted in the claim that their creation was something beyond or outside politics and insisted that it was also "self-limiting" and therefore not a threat to the state. The pretense was not accepted by the government nor by Solidarity's increasingly defiant membership.

Throughout the summer of 1981 Solidarity continued to extend its reach while engaging in often bitter internal debate about the future. Debate intensified during the extended Solidarity convention in the fall and the movement edged closer to becoming a genuine political party with the adoption of the "October Program" calling for "social, political and cultural pluralism...[as] the foundation of democracy." The government, now thoroughly dominated by Jaruzelski and urged on by the impatient Soviet party leaders in Moscow, resisted Solidarity's demands and moved toward a confrontation.[35] Solidarity's leaders, apparently mesmerized by their rhetorical triumphs and unwilling to accept the government's willingness to use force against the movement, kept on debating strategy into December 1981 and were still at it on the night of December 12, when Jaruzelski declared martial law and had Solidarity's leaders arrested.

Despite sporadic resistance, the repression was well prepared and depressingly effective. It was not, by and large, especially brutal, nor was it prolonged. Solidarity's leaders were freed relatively quickly and "martial law" was officially ended in July 1983, shortly after the pope's second visit. By the mid-1980s Solidarity was much weakened and Jaruzelski felt secure enough to declare a general amnesty in 1986. The church played a part in this stabilization and chose to distance itself from Solidarity and to urge moderation and restraint upon its more enthusiastic supporters. The lesson seemed to be that the system, however discredited and illegitimate in the eyes of its subjects, was not easily changed.

Nowhere in Eastern Europe did disillusion lead to political change, and in most countries the system was so rigid that even relatively minor economic reforms were not possible. The exception, on this score, was

Hungary, where the severity and effectiveness of the prior repression seems to have allowed the regime greater leeway to experiment with market-oriented reforms. But elsewhere the implicit "social contract" between the party and the working class precluded experimentation, for even the smallest moves toward liberalization threatened to raise prices, to lower real wages, and to reduce employment security. Political and economic stasis became the norm across Eastern Europe, and the result was deepening economic stagnation.[36] Despite this, reform and restructuring were put off by timid and unimaginative party leaders and in the end it was the accession to power of Mikhail Gorbachev that pried open the politics of eastern Europe.

Gorbachev was himself preoccupied with domestic matters during his first two years as leader and so his presence had little immediate effect on events in Eastern Europe. By 1987–1988, however, he had committed himself to political transformation within the Soviet Union and to ending the Cold War. Both choices had serious implications for the socialist states of Eastern Europe: clearly, Gorbachev would not intervene to protect unpopular local regimes; and no longer would the Soviet Union serve as a model for socialism. Gorbachev's new orientation toward the Warsaw Pact nations was communicated to local party leaders soon enough, but they were slow to catch on, or perhaps reluctant to confront what lay ahead. When Gorbachev spoke to the Council of Europe on July 7, 1989, and formally renounced the "Brezhnev doctrine," however, it was obvious that Eastern European socialism would soon face its supreme challenge.

The end of Communist power came first in Poland. Jaruzelski moved toward economic reform in a referendum held in November 1987, but his plan was rebuffed. In the following spring a new wave of working-class unrest erupted and threatened not only economic stability but Solidarity's and Walesa's claims to represent the unrepresented. Walesa moved to tame this outbreak and to contain yet another wave of strikes in August 1988, and Jaruzelski responded by offering "round-table" talks on the economy and on the role of Solidarity. The talks were difficult but issued in April 1989 an agreement to hold elections in June. The rules surrounding the vote ensured that the party would maintain its domination of the Sejm, but the contest for the minority of contested seats in the parliament and for the Senate, where no seats were reserved for the government, ensured that the election would constitute a genuine test of support and legitimacy. The result was an overwhelming defeat for the party and the government and a complete triumph for Solidarity. Though Jaruzelski was voted in as president in July, he was unable to form a government. In August, Tadeusz

Mazowiecki became prime minister and began putting together the first non-Communist government in Poland's recent history.

In rapid succession the socialist regimes in Hungary, Czechoslovakia, East Germany, Bulgaria, and Romania collapsed or were overthrown.[37] Yugoslavia was not transformed so much as it disintegrated. By December 1989 the Soviet bloc had virtually ceased to exist. The transition was perhaps smoothest in Hungary, where economic reform had begun as early as 1968 with adoption of the New Economic Mechanism, and where political reform was not so long delayed as elsewhere. Party leader János Kádár was replaced by Károly Grósz in May 1988, and the shift at the top stimulated creation of a wide array of new political movements and organizations that Grosz chose to tolerate under the slogan "socialist pluralism." Popular discontent became more visible and widespread in June 1989, when a mass movement arose to rebury Imre Nagy, the leader of the 1956 uprising. The party leadership was persuaded to participate in "round-table" talks analogous to those just concluded in Poland, but the talks failed to result in a clear plan for transition to non-Communist rule. Instead, the party's power crumbled. In September the government allowed thousands of East Germans to escape through Hungary to the West. In October the Communist Party changed its name to the Socialist Party, selected a new leader, and asked its membership of 700,000 to reenlist under the new banner of humane, democratic socialism. A mere 30,000 chose to do so. Thus transformed and exposed as a hollow shell, it held power formally until the elections of March–April 1990, but the era of Communist rule had already ended during the previous fall.

The exodus of East Germans via Hungary—and later via Prague and a sealed train traveling through East Germany to the West—was a sorry commentary on what was once seen as the most prosperous and stable, as well as the most ideologically solid, of the socialist states of central and Eastern Europe. The Achilles heel of the East German state had always been its proximity to the West, the temptations this location offered to its citizens, and their tendency to give in to that lure and to risk great loss to attain it.[38] But the timing of this latest wave of emigration was particularly distressing to the regime's leaders, for it came as preparations were under way for the celebration on October 7, 1989 of the fortieth anniversary of the state's founding, whose ceremonies would be graced by the presence of Mikhail Gorbachev.

Gorbachev's visit came amid growing protests. Prior to 1989 political opposition to the East German regime had centered primarily in the churches and in a scattering of pacifist, feminist, and environmentalist groups whose numbers were estimated by the State Security Service (Stasi) not to exceed 2,500.[39] But the ferment across the region and the revival of emigration prompted the founding of a new and larger organization, New Forum, on September 10. Meanwhile, the regular demonstrations for peace held at Saint Nikolai Church in Leipzig began to grow; by late September and early October crowds of 8,000 to 10,000 were marching; and a still larger demonstration was planned for October 9, the day after Gorbachev's departure. For his part, Gorbachev had used his visit to tell the aging party leader, Erich Honecker, that "life punishes those who come too late." In response to an appeal orchestrated by the conductor Kurt Masur, the authorities backed off from their plan to crush the October 9 march and 50,000 turned out. Protests became more frequent and consistently larger until roughly 500,000 paraded through East Berlin on November 4. Honecker was forced to step down and was replaced by his protégé, Egon Krenz, who undertook rapid reforms that were nevertheless too late. The regime's de facto end came on November 9, when a Politburo decision to allow "private trips abroad" was taken as a signal to tear down the Berlin Wall. The East German state and its moribund socialist economy quickly evaporated; and the rush to reunite the two Germanies began.[40]

The end of Communist power was equally abrupt in Czechoslovakia, where memories of 1968 had kept the opposition cowed, isolated, and demoralized. The liberal opposition groups, Charter 77 and VONS, had remained small and marginalized, though they were joined from the mid-1980s by the hitherto rather quietist and complacent Catholic Church, which was especially important in mobilizing discontent in Slovakia. Still, the forces of "civil society" and of resistance were not very formidable. Gustáv Husák, who ruled the nation for almost two decades after the Soviet invasion, was finally replaced in 1987 by Milos Jakes, but Jakes was no more enlightened and his appointment signaled no significant change. Inspired largely by events in neighboring East Germany, however, mass protest gathered strength in mid-November and two new, broad-based political movements were founded: Civic Forum, led by the writer Vaclav Havel; and the Public against Violence (VPN), which had similar aims and played a similar role in Slovakia. On November 25, three-quarters of a million people rallied in Prague and a general strike two days later marked the consummation of the link between the liberal intellectuals and the workers. The Communists resigned in December and Havel took over as president.[41]

December 1989 also witnessed the bloody end of Communist rule in

Romania, which by this time had become the dynastic property of the Ceausescu family. Even before that, the longtime Communist leader in Bulgaria, Todor Zhivkov, had been replaced and the party had indicated its willingness to reform. Throughout the region, therefore, the system that had predominated since the onset of the Cold War more than forty years earlier had disappeared. The revolutions of 1989 had brought about a "mass extinction of Leninist regimes" and a "clearing-away process" that could mean only the beginning of a new era dominated by the effort to build viable national states and stable economies in places where neither had existed for a very long time.[42] The effort will inevitably be protracted, marked by setbacks and messy detours, and it is likely that the borders and ethnic mixtures of the emerging states will not always coincide with those of the states they have replaced. Indeed, within a few short years of the liberation from communism the former German Democratic Republic was but a memory, submerged within memories of a larger and more historic German nation; Czechoslovakia had been supplanted by separate Czech and Slovak republics; Yugoslovia had been brutally destroyed, its component communities "ethnically cleansed," and it populations widely displaced. Nor had the early years of the transition to the market been uniformly prosperous.[43] Still, the Communist era was over; and however successful parties nostalgic for the old certainties might be in the "post-Communist" competition for votes, there would be no going back to the system that had so thoroughly failed.

## THE END OF THE SOVIET UNION

The disappearance of socialism in Eastern Europe had not been predicted, but once it occurred it was not difficult to understand or assimilate to what had long been recognized about the region's history. Socialism had come to Eastern Europe with the Red Army and, despite sporadic efforts by "national Communists" to lay down roots, establish links to the national past, and acquire some retrospective legitimacy, the regimes established in the late 1940s never won the spontaneous allegiance of more than a very small proportion of the local population. When the ultimate guarantor of the system's authority withdrew its support, collapse was probably inevitable. No such logic applied to the Soviet Union, where socialism was a product of indigenous political development and where the state, the social order, and the nation appeared to share a profound and deeply rooted identity, perhaps brutally imposed at first but tested in war and long years of armed peace. The end of Soviet communism was thus neither predicted nor very well explained by those who claimed expert knowledge of this unique political and social system.

What surely doomed the Soviet Union was the fact that it was truly a system, and a system with universal pretensions and aspirations to world-historic significance. Its coherence, its comprehensiveness, its drive for ideological hegemony, and its efforts to merge public and private, to merge politics and economics, and to organize and control everything precluded partial reform because it was impossible to fix part of the system without disturbing the whole. The Soviet Union, in this regard, was a "structural-functionalist" nightmare, quite unlike the advanced capitalist societies for which the concept and the analysis were originally crafted.[44] Not only was it a "totality," it was a "totality" in motion whose legitimacy depended in large part on its supporters' and leaders' continuing faith that the final victory of socialism was assured. The Marxian notion of dialectics was, of course, muddled enough to give socialists a trope with which to explain away momentary setbacks and to counter the "adverse currents" that slowed progress toward socialism. Nevertheless, the rulers of the Soviet Union were long sustained by a heroic reading of the past and of the achievements, attained against great odds and a series of determined adversaries, of the party and the state it had created. When that sense of forward movement was lost, ideological certainty began to evaporate and the system suffered a rapid "delegitimation."

The concept of movement and its centrality to the socialist project suggests a set of metaphors with which to capture the recent history of the Soviet Union. A particularly effective metaphor was offered by Yurii Boriev, who wrote of Soviet history as a train:

> The train is speeding into a luminous future. Lenin is at the controls. Suddenly—stop, the tracks come to an end. Lenin calls on the people for additional, Saturday work, tracks are laid down, and the train moves on. Now Stalin is driving it. Again the tracks end. Stalin orders half the conductors and passengers shot, and the rest he forces to lay down new tracks. The train starts again. Khrushchev replaces Stalin, and when the tracks come to an end, he orders that the ones over which the train has already passed be dismantled and laid down before the locomotive. Brezhnev takes Khrushchev's place. When the tracks end again, Brezhnev decides to pull down the window blinds and rock the cars in such a way that the passengers will think the train is still moving forward.[45]

Like all metaphors, this one becomes strained when pushed too far. Still, it seems not unreasonable to extend it just a bit further and say that when Gorbachev took control, he sought simultaneously to lift the blinds, to ask the passengers to discuss the direction in which the train should move, and to put down tracks to get it there. What he failed to reckon with were the forces of inertia and of self-interest, which kept the train moving in the same old way even when the track led nowhere, so long as the rights and perquisites of the conductors were safeguarded. Leaving metaphor to the side, the record of Gorbachev's effort to turn the Soviet Union around met with great resistance and produced few results, and what little was achieved worked to elicit more opposition and to undermine rather than to strengthen the system.

Part of the problem was that few among the leadership shared Gorbachev's understanding of what was wrong. Andropov, Gorbachev's patron, seems to have been well aware of the need for reform, but neither his successor nor his entourage were so inclined. It was under Chernenko's geriatric leadership that Gorbachev began to emerge as a future leader, but he was forced to sit through Politburo meetings at which his fellow members persisted in the vilification of Khrushchev and his failed effort to reform the system. As late as July 1984 Defense Minister Dmitri Ustinov asserted confidently that "Khrushchev did us a lot of damage. Think," he went on, "about what he did to our history, to Stalin." Gromyko, the most senior among the group, concurred: Khrushchev, he declared, "rendered an irreversible blow to the positive image of the Soviet Union in the eyes of the outside world." Prime Minister Nikolai Tikhonov continued, "And what he did to our economy! I myself have had to work in a Sovnarkhoz." Even Gorbachev went along with the critique, chiming in, "And to the party, breaking it into industrial and agricultural organizations."[46] The antipathy to reform was thus consensual, and Gorbachev had to be aware of the complacency that pervaded the party, which he nonetheless expected to lead in the effort to renew Soviet politics and society. What, then, accounts for his faith? He was presumably the victim of the lore of the party itself, which ascribed enormous authority to the leader and elided the fact that Khrushchev fell from power precisely because he threatened the job security of party cadres, and that Brezhnev owed his longevity to his craven support for the rights of the *nomenklatura*. Gorbachev was thus misled by the aura surrounding the leader, which was all the more beguiling once he could envision himself in that role.

Gorbachev was to be sorely disappointed, for he was spectacularly unable to make the party and the bureaucracy respond to his wishes: "Throughout his first two years," in fact, "he issued commands and replaced key personnel, yet nothing changed."[47] His frustrations were an indirect testimony to the resilience, indeed imperviousness, of the Soviet system of rule by party bureaucracy. That system, however, was not entirely unresponsive. In certain spheres Gorbachev had his way and in others he was blocked; overall, the response to his multiple probings precisely delineated the contours of the regime. In foreign policy and matters of defense, for example, the power of the general secretary was immense and so Gorbachev was able to dismiss opponents, appoint supporters, and change course dramatically. On the economy, where bureaucratic power was deeply entrenched, his initiatives evoked the strongest and most effective resistance and he made very little progress. In politics proper, his plans and proposals provoked both the most enthusiastic support and the most bitter opposition; and in the end the forces unleashed by Gorbachev's political reforms utterly destroyed the state. The results were not accidental but demonstrated in clearest form the structure of the Soviet system. It was a regime that was highly centralized overall, with the powers of life and death and war and peace vested in a tiny elite. Underpinning this state was an economy that was equally centralized but in which an entire class of bureaucrats had carved out comfortable niches and which, for that reason, could not and would not be reformed without threatening the wealth and perquisites of those in charge. And all of this was surrounded by a political order based upon an approved language that obscured reality and sustained by the passivity of the Soviet masses—a fragile construction highly vulnerable to an outbreak of candor and the lifting of repression.[48]

The structure of Soviet power thus made it logical for Gorbachev to turn his immediate attention to foreign relations. He quickly called for a summit meeting with the United States and began a series of negotiations that would lead to the winding down of the Cold War. The summit was held in Geneva in late 1985, but the breakthrough came in the subsequent meeting held at Reykjavik in October 1986, where Reagan and Gorbachev came close to agreeing on a wholesale ban on nuclear weapons. The obstacle to a deal was "Star Wars," the Strategic Defense Initiative, to which Reagan was wedded and the Soviet Union was strongly opposed. Within a year, however, the Soviet leader had decided to ignore the issue of "Star Wars," perhaps because he was told by his scientists that the scheme was too fantastic to worry over, and the two sides concluded the INF treaty banning intermediate-range nuclear weapons across Europe. The arms race that so exacerbated the Cold War came suddenly to an end, and over the next two years the peripheral confrontations that kept the superpowers at odds were ended as well. The Soviet Union wound up its involvement in Angola and Ethiopia, reduced its commitments to Nicaragua and Cuba, and withdrew from Afghanistan. By 1988–1989, Gorbachev was

222

addressing the United Nations about "universal values" and asserting that the Soviet Union shared with Western nations a "common European home" and, by implication, a common set of principles for ordering domestic affairs and internal politics.

The Soviet decision unilaterally to call off the Cold War utterly shocked Western political leaders, but it was not unprecedented in Soviet or, indeed, Russian history. The clearest parallel was Brest-Litovsk, where Lenin gave up huge chunks of what had been the tsarist empire in order to save the embattled Soviet state.[49] Gorbachev's aim was similar, for he understood that the Soviet Union needed to disengage from the furthest extensions of its military and diplomatic reach in order to concentrate resources and attention on more urgent matters closer to home. Indeed, Gorbachev was at one with the military in perceiving that the weakness of the Soviet economy would ultimately undermine Soviet power and thus required drastic reform. Making that reform a reality was more difficult, however, because it meant confronting the bureaucrats within the party/state and within industry, whose job it was to manage the economy and whose privileges, meager as they were by Western capitalist standards, depended upon the system's continuing to function as it had over the years.

Nor was Gorbachev himself clear about what form restructuring, or *perestroika*, would take or just how thoroughgoing it would be. Prior to assuming leadership he had been in dialogue with the Novosibirsk group of economic reformers, Abel Aganbegyan and Tatyana Zaslavskaya in particular, and had served as a sponsor of their publishing activities. Their critique of the command economy was devastating, but their remedy was what Zaslavskaya called a "second socialist revolution" that would democratize and decentralize and make greater use of markets but would not be dominated by markets and private capital.[50] Gorbachev himself spoke in December 1984 of the link between maintaining the Soviet Union's role as a superpower and the need for a more productive and efficient economic system. He explained, "Only an intensive, highly developed economy can safeguard a reinforcement of [the] country's position on the international stage and allow her to enter the millennium with dignity as a great and flourishing power."[51] So reasoning, he proposed to reignite growth through yet another "breakthrough of scientific-technical progress," a rather familiar refrain among forward-looking Soviet planners, but Gorbachev seems not at first to have envisioned more than limited use of markets. Soon enough, reformers would become convinced that private entrepreneurship (euphemistically labeled "cooperative" enterprise) had a more substantial role to play, though initially it would be confined in large part to the woefully neglected and thus virtually nonexistent service sector.

The limited character of Gorbachev's vision of economic reform combined with the tactical realization that it would take time to prepare adequate plans for reshaping the economy to delay serious efforts at economic restructuring. But the economy was nevertheless lagging. Gorbachev turned therefore to a characteristically Soviet set of measures to improve performance by exhortation and harassment. The slogan used was *uskorenie,* or acceleration, the methods reminiscent of earlier efforts to boost production: increased investment in "machine-tools"; a program to intensify "scientific-technical" advance; a major emphasis on *gospriemka,* or quality control; measures to improve discipline, like the "antialcohol" campaign, and to crack down on "unearned income"; and, most inappropriately, yet another attempt to increase government leverage over agriculture through the consolidation of various agricultural ministries into *Gosagroprom.*[52]

The measures produced a brief, minor upturn in 1986 but no long-term improvement in productivity or the rate of growth. More important, they were counterproductive in that they accentuated central control over the economy, prolonged the tradition of inducing growth by command, and reinforced the popular suspicion and hostility to private economic activity. The socialist critique of capitalist culture and of individualism had evolved by the 1970s and 1980s into a pervasive cynicism toward innovation and resentment directed at those guilty of excessive entrepreneurial zeal and successful enough to accumulate personal wealth. Antipathy was increased by the fact that most private enterprise was illegal, even if it was tolerated by the regime and essential to its routine functioning. An extensive black market provided scarce goods and services to consumers and served as well to lubricate the cumbersome machinery by which industry was operated. It reached from the bottom to the top of the economy and permeated the party and the bureaucracy.[53] Such activity remained illegal, however, and those who practiced it and profited from it were defined as criminals and in many cases acted as such, and in the popular mind private economic activity came to be identified with crime and corruption.

Gorbachev's early interventions into the economy made these links between capitalism, crime, and corruption firmer, both in reality and in the imaginations of ordinary citizens. The drive for higher growth led managers both to inflate production statistics and to engage in hoarding, bribery, and other means of circumventing bureaucratic controls to obtain higher output. The antialcohol campaign was especially effective at spread-

ing corruption, for it encouraged the production and distribution of spir-
its outside official, established channels, produced huge profits for those
who did so successfully, and led as well to a huge demand for the sugar
essential for home brewing, which in turn produced inflated prices, "wind-
fall" profits, and irregular production and importation. Meanwhile, efforts
to enforce the new policy generated only contempt for the authorities. The
campaign's great achievement, it seems, was to increase the profits of the
so-called mafia.[54] But they were the only winners, for the government's
misguided campaign did nothing to boost morale or improve discipline
among industrial workers while depriving the state of badly needed revenues. It also confirmed popular stereotypes against capitalists and guaranteed that ordinary Russians would remain suspicious and resentful of
the "new Russians," who managed to make money from doing business,
even after private property and entrepreneurial activity became fully legal
in the late 1980s and even after 1991.[55]

The economy's failure to respond to administrative bullying and its
stubborn refusal to "accelerate" led Gorbachev to contemplate reforms
of a more drastic and structural character. As early as February 1986 he
spoke of "radical economic reform," but concrete proposals were largely
absent until 1987–1988.[56] The new Law on State Enterprises was finally
ready by mid-1987; it provided for the freeing up of state enterprises in
two stages (half in 1988, half in 1989) by removing them from the control
of *Gosplan* and by according them "self-management" and "self-financ-
ing." Joint ventures with foreign investors also received offical sanction
in 1987 and the Law on Bank Specialization allowed the growth of banking from 1988. Cooperative enterprise was legalized as of May 1988,
though cooperatives were limited to "services" and often hemmed in and
harassed by the local governments, whose approval they required and
whose officials used their authority to extort bribes from aspiring entrepreneurs.

The difficulties encountered by cooperatives were indicative of a much
broader, indeed institutional, resistance to implementing economic
reforms. Even as Gorbachev eliminated Central Committee offices concerned with the economy, obstruction became endemic lower down in the
bureaucratic hierarchy and came to permeate the regional authorities and
individual enterprises, whose managers had learned how to operate within
the old system with its peculiar rules and incentives and who feared the
uncertainties of the market and genuine competition. As of 1988 the economy was organized in huge, grossly inefficient enterprises, with more than
70 percent of workers employed in enterprises employing more than a

thousand.[57] These enterprises would not disappear or become leaner or more efficient in response to a decision taken in Moscow. When the plan ceased to operate in 1988–1989, therefore, it was merely replaced with state orders that in 1989 still accounted for 90 percent of production. Agriculture, brutally collectivized decades before and subjected to repeated and demoralizing reorganizations, remained largely unaffected by reforms and responded with continued lethargy. The scope for markets accordingly continued to be limited, and as reform loosened the control of the center and the planning bureaucracy, no mechanism of economic coordination arose to replace it. Economic power became almost "feudalized," the economy itself "cellularized." Local autarchy asserted itself, and instead of trade or planned exchange there was a reversion to barter.

The economy, which had been in a prolonged "precrisis" throughout the 1980s, entered into genuine crisis during 1990, with food and essential consumer goods increasingly scarce and government forced to impose rationing or to pay workers in coupons redeemable in kind. The data would show that in 1990 the "net material product" of the country fell by 4 percent, labor productivity by 3 percent and foreign trade by 7 percent, while prices were increasing at a rate of nearly 20 percent by the end of the year. The crisis worsened in 1991, with output declining by 15 percent, and it was estimated that in that year alone Soviet consumers in the aggregate spent 86 billion hours waiting in queues.[58]

And Soviet consumers were not happy about it. In response, political leaders began to contemplate a more drastic set of reforms that would add up to a thorough transformation to a market economy. Gorbachev called on Prime Minister Nikolai Ryzhkov, who in May 1990 presented a plan for a transition over five years. Boris Yeltsin, by now Gorbachev's main political rival, commissioned what became Stanislav Shatalin's famous 500-Day Plan for a rapid conversion to the market. The economist Aganbegyan prepared yet a third plan designed to accomplish the transition "with the least social and economic costs."[59] In the early fall of 1990 Gorbachev and Yeltsin seemed ready to opt for a dramatic move toward the market, but Gorbachev backed off and produced yet another compromise plan—a series of "Guidelines for the stabilisation of the economy and the transition to a market economy"—which the Supreme Soviet approved in October. The deal represented a retreat from reform and marked the effective end of Gorbachev's effort to transform the economy.

The ensuing stasis was, of course, itself destabilizing, and by the following spring it was evident that the government had forfeited its capacity to guide the nation's economy. In response, the leadership sought to reimpose stability through highly unpopular measures to control runaway inflation by calling in notes worth fifty rubles or more. Vladimir Kryuchkov, the head of the KGB, began to place the blame for the country's problems on a CIA plot to destroy the economy and weaken the Soviet state. The effect was to deepen the crisis and to put off still further into the future the adoption of reforms that might have proved difficult in the short run but that could have at least initiated the process of reinvigorating the economy.

The basic reason for the stalemate over economic transformation was that by late 1990 Gorbachev had lost control of Soviet politics. He seems to have been deluded by the trappings of absolute power into believing that, as leader, he could modernize the party and its outlook without abandoning its domination over the state or the state's role in running the economy, overseeing culture, and superintending the pace and pattern of social change. Perched atop the party hierarchy in Moscow, moreover, he surveyed the political landscape from a uniquely remote and peculiarly unrevealing perspective, unable to see that below its surface tranquility were fissures, antagonisms, identities, and interests that could neither be articulated in the language of socialism nor, given the narrow space for independent politics within the Soviet system, be expressed institutionally.[60] Some Western analysts spoke wishfully of an emerging pluralism within the Soviet Union, but the organization and representation of interests within the polity was anemic, artificial, and ineffective.[61] This essentially "bureaucratic pluralism" therefore gave no real voice to those beyond the ranks of rival factions within the bureaucracy. The real split was between "the 'ruling strata'...and 'everyone else,'—that is, between state and society."[62] In the Stalin era the divide between rulers and ruled was bridged by terror, by policies that intruded violently into everyday life and social organization. The removal of terror allowed society to develop outside the direct control of the state, but the closed character of the political system prevented social change from registering within the polity. By the 1980s the Soviet Union had become a complex "urban-industrial society," with a large and well-educated professional class, but its political system remained a kind of "bureaucratic absolutism."[63] This new society represented the fundamental social base for reform: its emergence made a reshaping and modernization of politics a necessity; its values and beliefs served to undercut faith in the ideology that still guided the state; its material aspirations created a demand for consumer products common in the West but scarce and expensive in the USSR; and it provided Gorbachev not only with a constituency but also with activists and publicists prepared to advance *perestroika* and *glasnost* (openness) and to resist efforts to retard or reverse its progress.[64]

This complex "urban-industrial" society, with its increasing numbers of well-educated professionals, was nevertheless itself fractured and to some extent misshapen. It harbored within its ranks what Zaslavskaya labeled a "socially degenerate stratum of officials," the elite of managers and party and state officials (*nomenklatura*) whose status depended on the mainte-nance of the old system of political and industrial power.[65] This new class had become secure in its dominance in the post-Stalin era and its role was fully secured under Brezhnev. It was therefore strategically placed to thwart implementation of reform proposals adopted at Gorbachev's insistence and to organize resistance within the party and the *apparat*. Its opposi-tion was extremely damaging to Gorbachev's project, for he had conceived of the party as the agency that would transform the state and the econ-omy and was deeply disillusioned when the party itself became the chief obstacle to reform. The transformation of the Soviet system into a more open economy and polity was further hindered by the fact that "urban-industrial society" in the USSR was, at least by Western standards, deformed. The service sector was grossly underdeveloped, private employ-ment was basically unknown, and the professions were inadequately rewarded, uniquely regulated, overtly patronized, and systematically denied the autonomy typically accorded to professionals in advanced industrial societies. It was an emerging social order that, at least in its mid-dle and lower ranks, desperately craved a more open political regime and a more flexible and productive economy, but it was not particularly well suited to implementing or facilitating the transition.

None of this was apparent to Gorbachev and other reformers when they charted the course of *perestroika* in the mid-1980s. Nor did they even dimly perceive the likelihood that their intitiatives would produce enor-mous unrest in the republics on the periphery of the Soviet Union. On the contrary, Gorbachev regarded the imperial character of the USSR as a strategic asset and a major achievement: "The Soviet people," he declared in February 1986, "represent a new kind of social and international com-munity."[66] Again, Gorbachev took the surface calm for reality and, having spent his career entirely in Russia, failed to notice that stability in the republics was premised upon the center's acquiescence to accumulations of local power that in crucial respects undermined central authority. Soviet nationality policy had long been contradictory: it was a unitary state that nonetheless pretended to grant local autonomy even to regions that pos-sessed little historic or ethnic/national identity.[67] What autonomy meant in practice was the encouragement and sponsorship of local cultural traditions together with an understanding that the party headquarters in Moscow would share political control in the republics with local strongmen. These local elites created political machines along ethnic or clan lines and, freed from central supervision, they often became extremely corrupt and thoroughly criminalized.[68]

In his zeal to revitalize the political system and to give it a measure of integrity, Gorbachev sought to replace holdovers from the Brezhnev era with figures loyal to the new regime. The largely unintended result was to make the composition of the Politburo more purely Russian and thus to deprive the republics of representation at the center. Gorbachev also adopted Yegor Ligachev's principle of "exchange of cadres" between regions and thereby broke with customary understandings that had prevailed under Brezhnev (and perhaps even earlier). The critical episode occurred in Kazakhstan in 1986, when the corrupt Dinmohamed Kunayev was removed as secretary of the Kazakh Communist Party and replaced by Gennadi Kolbin, a Russian reformer. The decision provoked riots in Alma-Ata in December 1986 and forced the appointment of a Kazakh as second secretary in January 1987. The confrontation had no good outcome: it convinced the republics that Gorbachev was committed to Russian domination within the Soviet Union and reinforced for reformers the image of the republics as corrupt, clannish fiefdoms deeply in need of radical reform but unwilling to undertake it.

The visible decay of central authority to which *perestroika* and *glasnost* gave rise encouraged the nationalities throughout the Soviet Union to press their grievances and assert local rights and control. Violence broke out between Armenians and Azerbaijani over the disputed territory of Nagorny Karabakh during 1988. In 1989 there was agitation among the Abkhazians and the Georgians and, in short order, a movement among Georgians for independence from the center. A mass demonstration in Tbilisi in April 1989 was suppressed by the army at the cost of a hundred dead. To the north, the Baltic states also began to demand political sovereignty. Nationalists there based their claim on the historically intriguing argument that because the incorporation of the Estonia, Latvia, and Lithuania into the Soviet Union had been accomplished through the workings of the notorious 1939 pact with the Nazis, it was not legal. By 1989, of course, the socialist regimes in Eastern Europe had disintegrated and their example served as both inspiration and warning to those who favored and to those feared and resisted the various movements for national independence.

230

Despite his profound understanding of the crisis of the Soviet system and his brilliance in international affairs, Gorbachev was utterly unaware of the fragility of the political regime whose leadership he assumed in 1985. He did not understand the depths of antagonism toward the system nursed by its subjects and victims; he vastly underestimated the tenacity with which the *nomenklatura* would fight to retain their power and privileges; and he did not anticipate the centrifugal tendencies inherent in the relationship between the center and the provinces and republics. Underlying all of these mistakes and misperceptions was perhaps his fundamental weakness: he still believed in an ideology that was increasingly meaningless to the great mass of the population. Gorbachev still professed his faith in Marxism and his continued reliance upon the "works of Lenin," which for him and supposedly for the party as a whole constituted "an inexhaustible source of dialectical creative thought, theoretical wealth and political sagacity."[69] His was clearly "the ideology of reformism," as Andrei Amalrik described it in 1969, which was founded on the belief that a "humanization of socialism" was genuinely possible.[70] It was thus benign and flexible, but it was still ideological in that it represented an obvious case of "false consciousness," for reform was just what the Soviet Union could not survive.

Gorbachev's political reforms began with an acceleration of turnover at the apex of the system. Because the old and infirm were overrepresented on the Politburo and in the Central Committee Secretariat, it was not difficult through retirement and natural attrition for Gorbachev to put in place a core of supporters at the top. At the Twenty-Seventh Congress held in February 1986, moreover, less than 60 percent of the old Central Committee was reelected. Still, the party balked at Gorbachev's initiatives and he responded by raising the banner of *glasnost* as a way of shaking the party out of its lethargy. The impact was minimal at first, but the disaster at Chernobyl in April 1986 stimulated debate, discussion, and the beginnings of independent political organizing. From roughly the middle of 1986 Soviet writers and intellectuals seem to have decided that Gorbachev was serious about reform and they responded with an outburst of criticism, analysis, argument, and proposals that quickly outpaced those emanating from the top. Gorbachev moved to release the dissident scientist Andrei Sakharov in December, and over the next year the increasingly bold Russian intelligentsia began to recover its voice: films like *Repentance* were released; novels such as Anatoli Rybakov's *Children of the Arbat* finally appeared; and a sustained effort was launched to rediscover and honestly to rewrite the Soviet past. This "return of history" was often painful, for it meant not merely counting up the victims of Stalin's purges and tracing their fates but confronting the complicity of so many who participated in the crimes of the regime or conspired to keep them secret.[71] The result was a veritable cultural revolution, a liberation of the truth about the state whose fate was now becoming a matter for the public to decide.

The party, or large parts of it, remained immune to the spirit of reform, and its recalcitrance pushed Gorbachev into support for a broader effort at "democratization" during 1987. At the Central Committee Plenum in June he proposed that the party should lead rather than dominate, argued for the independence of the judicial system, and called for genuine elections to the soviets. But action was put off until a special party conference to be held in 1988, and in the meantime, Gorbachev was forced to acquiesce in a series of malicious attacks on Boris Yeltsin, who had been made Moscow party leader in 1986 and who had emerged as the most prominent and impatient proponent of reform. The general secretary's speech in November at the celebration of the seventieth anniversary of the Revolution was, appropriately, an uninspiring compromise.

But while Gorbachev wavered, as was increasingly his wont, the enemies of reform did not. In March 1988, for example, his rivals within the leadership conjured up and publicized a letter from a chemistry teacher named Nina Andreeva denouncing the reforms and proclaiming: "I Cannot Compromise My Principles." Gorbachev responded with a forceful refutation, but in the subsequent elections to the special party conference the forces of reform did poorly. Nonetheless, Gorbachev managed to bully the meeting into approving a set of "theses," whose centerpiece was a plan to democratize the political system by bypassing the party and electing a new Congress of People's Deputies—essentially a revival of the soviets—and which also included proposals for contested elections within the party, term limits for party leaders, and a broad commitment to the establishment of a "socialist state based on the rule of law." In the fall of 1988 Gorbachev went still further and drove his opponents from office, packing Ligachev off to Agriculture, reducing the size and authority of the party secretariat, and having himself selected as president of the Presidium of the Supreme Soviet in place of the aging and conservative Andrei Gromyko.

A complicated electoral system was devised to select representatives to the new Congress of People's Deputies, with a third of the seats reserved for representatives of the "nationalities" and another third for "public organizations" like the Communist Party, the trade unions, the Academy of Science, and other quasi-official and thus controlled associations. There were some spectacular victories for the democratic forces, such as Yeltsin's triumph in Moscow where he won nine of ten votes. Overall, however, the outcome of the elections of March 1989 gave disproportionate weight to the party bureaucrats. When the Congress met in June 1989, it turned out that roughly 85 percent of deputies were party members, and the body elected a Supreme Soviet that was extremely orthodox and resistant to Gorbachev's reforms. Reformers were thus grossly outnumbered, but they were numerous enough to force real debate within the body, and toward the end of the proceedings Sakharov managed to get the floor to read a "Decree on Power" that would have "abrogated" Article 6 of the Constitution, the clause formally acknowledging the "leading and guiding role" of the party. The convening of the Congress and the taking of sides led reformers to expand their organizing still further, and out of the meeting emerged the so-called Inter-Regional Group that brought together Yeltsin, Sakharov, and other reformers and put them in alliance with reformers in the Baltics and other dissident republics. The cause of reform also began to spread among the workers as miners went on strike in July 1989 and called for an end to the party's monopoly of political power.

From the summer of 1989 Soviet politics became a genuine three-way competition, with Yeltsin and the advanced reformers seeking to end the party's political dominance and intensify economic restructuring, with the party *apparat* aroused and organized to defend its position and to slow down or reverse *perestroika*, and with Gorbachev leaning toward the reformers but desperate to preserve the basic structure of the Soviet system and to keep reform within some expanded definition of socialism. The contest took place not only within the emerging system of democratic elections but also in the streets and in the mines and factories. In February and March 1990 local and regional elections gave the reformers big victories in the major cities, but returned parliaments that were far from fully committed to political and economic transformation. Strikes continued and became ever more political. The press was increasingly free and lively, and debate came to center on the effort to remove the party from its "leading role" in politics. The Central Committee Plenum met in Moscow in February 1990 to consider the issue, and the gathering was greeted by a demonstration of roughly 300,000 demanding that Article 6 be eliminated. In March the Congress of People's Deputies agreed not only to terminate the party's special status but also to create the post of executive president for Gorbachev. Not to be outdone, Yeltsin got himself elected as chair of the Presidium of the Supreme Soviet of the Russian Federation, and hence president, at the end of May. As party authority weakened and the party and the state fragmented at the center, disintegration proceeded on the periphery. Lithuania declared its independence in March 1990; Russia proclaimed itself sovereign in June 1990; and a "parade of sovereignties" followed as the republics declared themselves formally independent. Amid the chaos, Gorbachev made a final attempt to reform and revitalize the party at its 28th Congress held in July 1990. His efforts were to no avail, as the resignations of Yeltsin, Gavril Popov (the mayor of Moscow), and Anatoli Sobchak (the mayor of Leningrad) signaled and stimulated a hemorrhage of party membership.

The Soviet Union entered its terminal crisis in the summer of 1990. The economy was worsening and it seemed that a choice would have to be made between a reversion to command, a policy in which nobody truly believed, and a dash to the market, which few were willing to risk. The transition programs prepared and debated over the summer were testimony to the depth of the problems; the shelving of these plans in the fall offered equally strong evidence that there was no leadership capable of carrying out the transition. The political framework of the system was also coming apart, and the declarations of political independence over the summer of 1990 led to a "war of laws" between the Union and the republics. In a country where political and economic power were merged and where the state owned the means of production, the battle proved deadly serious. It was no longer a matter of giving "voice" to those previously excluded but of controlling the lives and livelihoods of the entire population. Thus when the miners went on strike again in the spring of 1991, Yeltsin brokered a deal that not only met the workers' economic grievances but also transferred ownership of the mines from the Union to the Russian Federation. The "war of laws" came therefore to encompass not merely questions of symbolic significance and issues concerning the distribution of tax revenues, however important these might have been, but economic matters as well. The struggle over sovereignty and the very shape of the state accordingly came to dominate the final days of the Soviet system and would provide the occasion for the failed coup of August 1991.

Confronted with the problem of the very survival of the Soviet Union, Gorbachev backed away from reform and appeared to side with the forces of resistance. The Soviet military sent a signal to Gorbachev with a series of maneuvers around Moscow in September 1990. A meeting with the so-called Peasant Union in October helped to dissuade Gorbachev from supporting Shatalin's 500-Day plan for the transition and made him aware that restructuring would not meet with approval from the managers of the state's collective farms. Shortly after, he met with a group of roughly a thousand army officers, who delivered a similar message. In December the liberal Interior Minister was replaced by Boris Pugo, a KGB general, and, in another conservative move, Gennadi Yanaiev became vice-president; in January 1991, Prime Minister Ryzhkov was removed in favor of Valentin Pavlov. Alarmed at the drift away from reform and toward what he perceived as "dictatorship," Edvard Shevardnadze resigned in December. In January the army and KGB moved ineffectively to seize control of communications in Latvia and Lithuania. A tense stalemate ensued while the government adopted its misguided policy of calling in large-denomination rubles and blaming the nation's economic woes on the West and the CIA. A countermobilization by Yeltsin and his allies led the conservatives to back off, but politics remained completely polarized and government largely paralyzed, unable to move forward or backward and capable only of standing by as the economy deteriorated still further and as the centrifugal forces unleashed by Gorbachev pulled the state apart.

For his part, Gorbachev became preoccupied with maintaining the Union and undertook to do so through negotiations with the republics. A draft treaty was tentatively agreed to in November 1990, but it was ultimately rejected. Gorbachev countered by staging a referendum on continued union in March 1991. Seventy percent voted in favor of a "renewed federation of equal Soviet republics," a formulation that obscured more than it revealed, but an even larger share of voters within Russia supported an amendment for the popular election of the Russian president, a choice that implictly ratified the sovereignty of the Russian Federation. When Yeltsin scored a decisive victory in the June 12 voting, he emerged with authority at least equal to Gorbachev's, who had not been popularly elected and who presided over a political system whose powers were ebbing by the day. Yeltsin's growing authority was already being deployed during April 1991 in the negotiations that produced the "9 plus 1" agreement, which provided for a new Union that devolved real power to the republics. The agreement was codified into a draft treaty in July, and August 20 was set as the date for signing and for the de facto creation of a new state.

The forces arrayed against reform panicked. Already in June Pavlov had asked the Supreme Soviet for emergency powers, but Gorbachev prevailed and the request was denied. After securing agreement on the details of the union treaty Gorbachev sought external support in the form of a "grand bargain" with Western leaders assembled in London. He got rather little, returned to the Soviet Union, and went off to the Crimea on vacation. His opponents, many of whom Gorbachev had himself appointed, decided to move against him and planned a "coup" for August 19. The "coup" was terribly botched, the army and the KGB hesitated long enough for Yeltsin to organize opposition in Moscow, and in four days the "coup" collapsed. Its leaders were arrested or committed suicide and Gorbachev was brought back to Moscow, where he was put back in office but never restored to power. Political power had flowed from Gorbachev to Yeltsin, who was eager to make use of it. He presided over the suppression of the Communist Party and, in December 1991, the abolition of the Union of Soviet Socialist Republics as a sovereign state. It was therefore Yeltsin who would take the lead in cobbling together the loose confederation that replaced the USSR, the Commonwealth of Independent States; and it was Yeltsin who would appoint the Russian government, led by Yegor Gaidar, which finally understook serious economic reform.

The outcome was genuinely tragic in every dimension. The rather minor personal tragedy was that the man who began the process of opening up and transforming Soviet socialism should have so little a part to play in its reconstruction. The more serious social tragedy was that reform was delayed so long that its consequences were sure to be dire, and the path to a new society, a market economy, and a functioning system of democratic politics would inevitably be dangerous, troubled, and protracted. And the great political tragedy was that the death of the Soviet Union proved once and for all that socialism, as a comprehensive vision of how to organize society, was not merely impractical but truly undesirable. From tragedy comes knowledge, of course, but the lessons learned from the failure of socialism cannot help but produce a renewed awareness of human limitation, of what cannot be done, rather than a liberating sense of expanding possibilities and multiple alternatives. This is not an altogether uplifting conclusion. Still, on the existing record it appears irrefutable.

# 8 The World after the Cold War

The dissolution of the Soviet Union marked the effective end of the socialist project and of the Cold War.[1] The Cold War world order was a structure unprecedented in world history: it had been at one and the same time a confrontation between social systems, a contest over competing principles of world order, and a rivalry between superpowers of colossal, indeed continental, proportions.[2] The division of the world to which the Cold War gave rise, moreover, had been unusually stable and effective and virtually defined the second half of the twentieth century. As a whole, the present century can be said to have been dominated by two great choices: between democracy and the varieties of authoritarian, and often also imperial, systems of rule, and between capitalism and socialism. The permutations and complications flowing from these options defined the era's main conflicts and passions. It is possible in a very rough sense to suggest that it was the resistance to democracy among European elites that dominated the extended period of war, unstable peace, and renewed war from 1914 to 1945, the so-called Thirty Years' War of the Twentieth Century.[3] But what made the contest so very violent was that it overlapped with, and was intensified by, the struggle between capitalism and socialism, whose more prolonged rivalry constituted a parallel "seventy-years' crisis" that would end only with the definitive eclipse of socialism.[4] The antipathies of the Cold War era proper would also be fueled by the intermingling of politics and economics, for by the late 1940s it was obvious that capitalism, whatever its flaws and however embarrassing its entanglements with local dictators, was most thoroughly compatible with a democratic polity, and socialism fundamentally was not. But the contest was overall simpler, for it pitted capitalism as an economic and political system against socialism as a system for organizing both production and politics. The meaning of its resolution was therefore quite unambiguous: liberal capitalism had prevailed, and socialism could no longer be regarded as a viable alternative for ordering economics or politics.[5]

While the contest proceeded, the Cold War dominated world politics and the world economy. From that conflict emerged an international order that provided the basic framework for international relations, that established the critical institutions governing the world economy, and that penetrated and shaped domestic politics within the rival blocs and limited the options available to the nations and peoples not fully integrated into either camp. The Cold War world order was an "international settlement" built upon a "set of...transactions" that kept "interstate conflict short of war" and "a series of domestic group compromises that allow[ed] for the generally peaceful conduct of politics and economic life at home."[6] Its enormous reach was testimony to the scope of the geopolitical vacuum left by the Second World War; its staying power proof of the viability, at least for this particular stage of industrial development, of the economic systems in competition; its recurring intensity evidence that truly great differences and choices were at stake.

Precisely because the Cold War was an order, a settlement that integrated international relations, the framework of the world economy, and domestic political arrangements, its passing is of truly world-historic significance.[7] A transformation this dramatic, even if it is mostly peaceful, inevitably opens up new possibilities, though the first reaction, predictably enough, is often a sense of loss.[8] Lost with the passing of the Cold War were two central features of the preceding era: the sense of mission and the certainty that sprang from ideology; and the widespread commitment to an alliance system through which the use of force was controlled, and occasionally applied, and by which local and regional conflicts were kept within bounds. With the turn to the market in China, the revolutions in Eastern Europe, and the collapse of the Soviet Union, the socialist vision ceased to inspire. And as communist faith evaporated, the fervor behind anticommunism dissipated as well. Intellectuals have felt the loss of ideological fervor keenly and speak apocalyptically about "the end of history," when what they mean is the obsolescence of the discourses in which they were trained and whose mastery constitutes their main cultural capital and underpins their claims to status and authority. Political parties, organized around popular and simplified versions of the discourses of the intellectuals, have also had cause to lament the passing of the familiar world of Cold War politics. Somewhat surprisingly, though, parties of the liberal left were perhaps less affected than those on the right, for long before 1989 the left had been forced to distance itself programmatically and emotionally from the disasters that marked "actually existing socialism." It was, in any case, already on the defensive over the apparent crisis of the welfare state and the failure of Keynesian prescriptions for economic growth.[9]

Conservatives, by contrast, had done well from the late 1970s into the 1980s, and at least a part of their success had been based on the revival of anticommunism. The ending of the Cold War deprived conservatives of a convenient foe and so removed a central plank from their political program without providing a substitute. The effect was a sense of drift and confusion that overcame conservative politicians like John Major, who barely secured reelection in 1992, and George Bush, who did not. Even more seriously affected were the ruling conservative parties in Italy and Japan. The Christian Democrats in Italy and the Liberal Democrats in Japan were electoral coalitions knit together by convenience, patronage, and clientalism, and held firm by the ideology of the Cold War. Absent the latter, the ties of mutual advantage could not survive the exposure of the corruption endemic in both parties' operation and therefore could not prevent their rapid dissolution.

The difficulties experienced by right-wing parties should not be exaggerated, however, for they did not indicate a shift to the left and were in most cases short-lived. Despite the wildly optimistic hopes of Bill Clinton and his "policy-wonk" friends, for example, the defeat of George Bush did not begin a transformation in U.S. public policy. In Italy, the immediate effect of the demise of the traditional center-right party was the emergence of a slicker and slightly more right-wing political formation led by Silvo Berlusconi, and only after his further disgrace was there a genuine opening for the left and for reform; in Japan, the fall and rise and regrouping among parties and factions seems to have had virtually no impact on

the complexion or practice of government.[10] Still, the end of the Cold War
left conservatives at least temporarily stunned and caused them to stumble
electorally at precisely the moment when they ought to have been proclaiming victory over their historic enemy.[11]

The system of military alliances that had been built up around the
superpower rivals was the second obvious casualty of the ending of the
Cold War. That system was routinely denounced over the years for the
way it turned local conflicts into ideological battles, threatening to involve
the entire world, and for the expensive and terrifying arms race it had
spawned. In retrospect, it has been praised for keeping the peace so long,
for having managed conflict rather than escalating it, and for imposing
discipline upon rogue states and leaders. Particularly upsetting to security
experts is the fact that nothing has come to replace the old, Cold War system of blocs and pacts and alliances. For a time, hope was placed in an
enhanced role for the United Nations and the principles of world order
that it embodied. That prospect was quickly diminished by the decision
of the United States to assume leadership in the crisis produced by the
Iraqi invasion of Kuwait in 1990, and the body has since then been made
to seem ineffectual by its demonstrated impotence in Bosnia.[12]

The coalition put together to fight the Gulf War seemed momentarily to
suggest an alternative pattern for a "new world order," but success in that
venture was to prove utterly exceptional. The regime of Saddam Hussein
was uniquely repugnant, a Mesopotamian variation on National Socialism
whose actions were indefensible; success in the recently concluded war
with Iran had left the Iraqi leadership wildly over-confident but financially
desperate; Iraq was without allies throughout the Middle East; the Soviet
Union, which might ordinarily be expected to check U.S. incursions into
the region, was entering its terminal crisis as a state; and the rulers of
Kuwait and Saudi Arabia were largely willing to foot the bill. Such a favorable conjuncture cannot ever be expected to recur and did not do so over
the next few years. Circumstances differed greatly in Somalia, for example,
where a few American deaths produced an embarrassingly rapid withdrawal, and almost everything about the conflict in the former
Yugoslavia—culture, religion, geography, and especially the balance of
military force—combined to make intervention there less effective and
less attractive. The outcome in Bosnia was indeed horrendous and dis-
graceful, though it was perhaps slightly naive to imagine that an alternative policy, forceful enough to deter the Bosnian Serbs and their backers in
Serbia yet sufficiently restrained as to have avoided the potentially dangerous commitment of large numbers of Western troops, could have been

devised and implemented any sooner or more effectively than it was.[13]

The end of the Cold War has therefore meant the loss both of ideolog- [241] ical certainty and of a structure for managing international conflict. If the end of ideology is on the whole liberating, the absence of a mechanism for insuring international order is rather more frightening. Balancing these losses, however, are the unprecedented opportunities opened up by the Cold War's passing. The most important surely is the chance to renegoti- ate the Western domination of the world. It is not completely accurate to describe liberal capitalism and revolutionary socialism as quintessentially Western products and ideologies, but the rival perspectives did share a great deal: a common European origin, a similar vision of material progress achieved by technical rationality, and an emphasis on the secular and the human rather than the spiritual and supernatural.[14] The Cold War world order, in which two superpowers armed with universalistic ideolo- gies of Western provenance dominated the globe, was in this respect merely the final phase in the protracted domination of the non-Western world by capital, military forces, and culture emanating from, and anchored in, the West.[15]

The characterization of capitalism, socialism, and liberalism as "West- ern" is, of course, contentious and, if true, only partly and contingently so. Capitalism, after all, may have begun in the West, but in the 1980s and 1990s its most ardent and successful practitioners were to be found in the East. Innovation and rapid growth have relocated to the Pacific Rim and to the coastal regions of East Asia, and not a few in the West wonder openly whether those economies do not embody the better model for cap- italism's future. Communism, too, found fertile ground in the East, and professedly communist governments still cling to power in Asia. Those regimes were established, moreover, as the outcome of movements against Western imperialism; and socialism's broad appeal in the Third World stemmed directly from its promise of an alternative, non-Western, non- capitalist path to economic and social progress. Whatever its origin and whatever it signified to Europeans and North Americans, elsewhere "Com- munism offered a new principle of order to societies which western inter- vention had thrown into the melting pot." As Geoffrey Barraclough has argued, "Its bold solutions, its willingness to cut through tangles, above all its dynamic belief in itself and its mission, raised it, for Asian purposes, above the cautious pragmatism, linked with a crippling respect for entrenched interests, which seemed to mark the western approach to Asian interests." Nor are the geographical roots of liberal democracy uniquely Western, for Europe has proved itself capable of nurturing and sustaining the most brutal and authoritarian regimes. The conservative historian Lord Skidelsky has recently asserted that "Western European civilization could produce a Marx or a Hitler, but not a Lenin or a Stalin." Whether this is taken as a cause for shame or a reason to celebrate, it hardly suggests a close connection between the West and political democracy.[16]

So neither liberal capitalism or its less liberal Asian variations, nor communism can be fulled comprehended in terms of West and East. Nevertheless, the ending of the Cold War does represent a new opening for non-Western peoples and nations and an opportunity for the center of dynamism in world history to move still further away from its historic, modern locations in Western Europe and North America and toward Asia and the Pacific.[17] Just what new order will be bargained out remains, of course, undetermined. It seems distinctly unlikely, however, that the next phase of world history will be dominated by a single hegemon, as has commonly happened in the past. Whatever world order is constructed will nevertheless of necessity be built upon the economic and political structures bequeathed to the present by the era that has just been concluded. Those emerging structures will also shape the possibilities for economic development and for domestic politics. To assess these diverse possibilities, then, it is essential to look in more detail at the structure of the world economy and the polities left in place when the Cold War ended.

## THE NEW WORLD ECONOMY

The two greatest historians of capitalism, Marx and Schumpeter, agreed on one central proposition: capitalism was the first truly revolutionary mode of production, the first economic system to make change, rather than stability, its driving force and whose very structure guaranteed recurring crises and periodic "gales of creative destruction." The obvious corollary is that the ups and downs, the booms and busts of capitalism, not only determine the momentary well-being of individuals, firms, and entire societies but also serve further to transform the system itself. Thus the long postwar boom—"the golden age of capitalism"—worked to undermine the very conditions that made growth during that era so spectacular, and the ensuing period of "stagflation" and slow growth has continued to reshape the geography, the technology, the industrial structure, and the products of the contemporary economy.

Informing and dominating all such change has been a steady increase in competition across the world economy and within its component national and regional networks. Intensified competition has determined the location of production and consumption, the pace and direction of technical change, the pressures that have restructured the labor market, and the very form of business organization itself.[18] The structure of the postwar economy was, in fact, bound to generate competition as Western Europe and Japan rebuilt their economies and began to catch up with the United States. U.S. domination of the world economy was often denounced in terms that derived from the critique of empire, and the role of the United States in international affairs did at moments seem to be based on a model of imperial privilege. But at the heart of the U.S. vision for the postwar economy was a plan that was the antithesis of a genuinely imperial economic system: the United States did not seek to impose an international division of labor, with different nations and regions specializing in production for a metropolitan or imperial market. Instead the national units, at least within the advanced nations, were encouraged to emulate the United States in its forms of industry, its patterns of production and consumption, even its social structure and styles of labor-management relations.

The U.S. political economy of that era has been usefully labeled "Fordism," to denote the combination of mass production, mass consumption sustained by the fruits of hard bargaining between strong unions and large, powerful, and profitable corporations, and income redistributed by progressive systems of taxation and expenditure.[19] What was so unique about the "golden age of capitalism" was that the model's pioneers sought not to protect and monopolize it but to propagate and export it. With obvious and important variations from one nation to another, this is roughly what happened during the 1950s and 1960s. The nations of Western Europe and Japan all moved toward the mass production of goods consumed through mass markets. Germany and Japan made the shift more quickly and fully than other countries, for their industry had been so thoroughly damaged during the war that they were forced to build it anew and did so deploying the latest technology, which was typically American, and organizing production along the lines pioneered by the United States. The trend was aided by, and reflected in, patterns of trade. Trade grew enormously in the quarter century after 1945, but it grew primarily between the more advanced countries who penetrated one another's markets with essentially similar goods produced by comparable methods.

The economic interrelationships between the advanced nations were thus not complementary but basically competitive. Competition began in earnest in the mid- and late 1960s, when Japan, Germany, and other advanced economies achieved the ability to match U.S. producers in quality and price and so rapidly entered into the U.S. domestic market. The data are unambiguous: between 1965 and 1973 the U.S. share of world manufacturing exports fell from roughly 24 percent to 18 percent; the Japanese share grew from 8 percent to 14 percent. In 1960 imports accounted for less than 5 percent of the U.S. market; in 1970 they constituted more than 10 percent of sales and by 1979 more than 20 percent. The "import penetration ratio" thus increased by nearly three times from the early 1960s to the early 1970s, and it was in precisely those industries where international competition was keenest that profit rates started to decline, at least in the United States.[20] Companies that had previously exerted a seemingly effortless domination over their competitors now faced challenges from rivals at home and abroad.[21]

What made the impact of increased competition so serious was that it coincided with the running down of the sources of growth generated from within the Fordist model itself. Fordist prosperity had been self-sustaining in that its structure of demand fit so well with the prevailing techniques of production. Mass production of cars and consumer appliances depended on the existence and steady expansion of a market composed of consumers with moderate incomes and relatively undifferentiated tastes. The labor-capital accord at the heart of the postwar settlement ensured the reproduction of precisely that market as well-organized workers captured a share of rising productivity and living standards rose accordingly.

Over time the rate of expansion of the market for mass-produced goods of medium quality slowed. Three developments inherent in the further development of Fordism contributed to this slowing down of the engine of growth. First, the market for cars and refrigerators and televisions and the like began to be saturated. Second, the evolution of the economy of mass production led to a modest increase in the number of manual workers but to a much more dramatic rise in the numbers of supervisory, technical, and professional jobs and in the ranks of those who earned their keep providing services rather than producing goods. As the occupational structure changed, so did the structure of incomes: on the whole, supervisory and technical workers within industry were better paid than production workers; within the service sector wages were more bifurcated between those with professional credentials, who tended to earn relatively high salaries, and those without recognized skills, who worked at wages well below the standard prevailing among unionized factory workers. The effect on demand was to erode the socioeconomic middle while simultaneously expanding the markets for cheap consumer products, typically produced at substandard wages in "union-free" environments, and those for high-quality products made by more skilled workers using the latest techniques and sold at a premium.

The third critical limitation upon the continued growth of demand for the products of Fordist industry was the failure of the Fordist model of industrialization to spread beyond the advanced capitalist countries into the developing regions of the Third World. The growth of trade in industrial goods far outpaced the increase in primary products and, with the exception of the petroleum-exporting countries, the terms of trade for developing countries deteriorated steadily from the early 1950s to the early 1960s and then stabilized at this relatively low level throughout the 1960s boom.[22] In consequence, developing countries lacked the capital to create modern industry and economic growth remained limited. The leaders of Third World countries were also extremely ambivalent about participation in the world market. They understood from experience the dangers of depending too much on exports, and their doubts about the world market were reinforced by theorists of development. As a result, politicians and their economic advisers in many countries opted instead for a strategy of "import-substitution industrialization."[23] The objective was to escape the trap of selling commodities at low prices and using the earnings to purchase expensive manufactured imports by imposing tariffs to reduce imports and encourage domestic production. Where protection alone did not suffice, the state itself should intervene and use its own resources to invest in manufacturing.[24] The assumptions behind the model of growth through "import-substitution industrialization" echoed the prejudices of Fordism, with its preference for heavy industry and mass consumption, but they were also compatible with socialist programs of state-led national development.

"Import-substitution industrialization" had very mixed results. Most Third World nations were too small or too poor, or their social structures too unequal, to serve as sufficient markets for industrial production. Larger countries with more substantial markets, such as Mexico and Brazil in Latin America and India in Asia, fared better and achieved more substantial rates of growth. The Mexican economy grew annually by more than 6 percent through the 1950s and by close to 8 percent in the 1960s; Brazil did still better. Both countries managed over the postwar era to shift labor and capital from agriculture to industry and to build up a diversified industrial structure, more than 90 percent of whose products were consumed domestically.[25] Growth was even more spectacular in India: the output of industry more than tripled between 1950 and 1970 and, in the process, India "acquired a comprehensive structure of industrial production" that "has endowed the Indian case with a degree of self-reliance rare among noncommunist developing countries." Grain production in India also doubled over the two decades, as did national income overall.[26] Ironically, however, whatever success this quasi-Fordist industrialization had in developing nations was achieved outside the world market. The Indian share of world trade actually decreased during the period of highest growth in the 1960s.[27] In aggregate, then, the contribution of Third World markets to the expansion of world trade and markets overall remained quite limited.

Increased international competition coincided with, and accentuated, the exhaustion of the internal sources of growth within Fordism and its limited geographical extension to produce a genuine crisis. But policy makers responded with confusion, avoidance, and a mix of policies that was often contradictory and self-defeating. At the root of the difficulty was what, to lift a phrase from a different context, might be termed "money illusion": the fixation of public policy on inflation rather than on the underlying structural difficulties confronting the advanced economies. The focus on battling inflation not only preoccupied and misled political and economic leaders, it also tended to rule out responses to the crisis that called for a substantial expenditure of funds or an extension of government involvement in the economy.

The promising debate on industrial policy that began during the 1970s was a particularly unfortunate casualty of the new mood of austerity, for while it served to open up important lines of inquiry on the sources of economic dynamism, it had little practical impact on government policy. Even the most cursory examination of comparative rates of growth, for example, revealed that Germany and Japan were outpacing the United States and the United Kingdom in rates of technical innovation and utilization.[28] When these aggregate trends were examined more closely, it became clear that differential rates of growth could not be explained simply by different factor endowments and that the rather simple dichotomies used to categorize policy making—for example, planning, state control, and public ownership versus free markets—were too crude to capture the variety of policy mixes and institutional arrangements that had been practiced in the advanced capitalist countries and within specific industries and that had produced such differences in performance. The central finding was that institutions, social structures, and cultural patterns mattered enormously. Japan, Germany, and the United States might equally well be labeled capitalist and were equally committed to private ownership, but they displayed marked differences in the structure of firms and the relationships that existed between and within firms, in the prevailing style of management, in the connections between finance and industry and in the very role of profits within the business culture. Differences also existed in rates of investment, in the conduct of industrial relations and in the definition of the contract between employers and employees, in attitudes toward technology, and in the scope and character of the links between the state and the economy.[29]

These findings led logically to arguments about the potential value to the economy of government initiatives in research and development, indicative planning and the mobilization of capital, and manpower training, to be accompanied in some cases by selective import controls. They argue as well for new forms of business enterprise, more flexible links between businesses, and more cooperative models of industrial relations and workplace organization. Fiscal considerations, however, kept options based upon such arguments largely off the political agenda in the world's largest economy, while the straitened finances of governments effectively doomed the feeble industrial policy initiatives undertaken in Britain during the 1970s and the more ambitious program undertaken by French Socialists. More generally, the weakening of labor organization across the capitalist world diminished the appeal of labor-sponsored plans and programs.[30] Indeed, the ascendancy of conservatism meant in many cases a reversion to laissez-faire and a dismantling of previous government policies and the institutions set up to implement them. Instead of a more activist industrial policy, then, states moved toward "deregulation" and "privatization" during the 1980s.[31] The Thatcher government in Britain was the most enthusiastic proponent of privatizing state assets and reaped fiscal and electoral rewards for doing so; the Reagan and Bush administrations took the lead in efforts to free up business from what were seen as intrusive and stifling government regulations. The effects of both policies on economic performance seem to have been modest, but the effect on the debate over public policy was considerable. By lessening the state's involvement in the economy, privatization and deregulation reduced the long-term capacity of government to influence economic performance. Diminished state capacity meant that the range of policy options that could be plausibly debated and realistically implemented became ever more narrow and restricted.

More aggressive efforts at industrial policy thus failed to develop during the 1970s and 1980s. Rather more appealing to both businesspeople and politicians was the temptation to retreat from the world economy behind trade barriers and restraints upon the mobility of labor and capital. The move toward a "new protectionism" was particularly strong during the 1970s and primarily took the form of various "grey area measures": voluntary export restraints, orderly marketing arrangements, antidumping provisions, "gentlemen's agreements," and countervailing duties. The most important were quantitative import restrictions and the imposition of selective duties to counter alleged "dumping" and "unfair competition." The United States took the lead in pressuring the Japanese and other exporters to acquiesce in voluntary quotas on textiles, steel, televisions, and cars. And the Trade Act of 1975 established a more general policy allowing all sectors of U.S. industry to apply for import duties to fight off unfair competition. The European Community did likewise, and the growing tolerance for interfering in the free flow of trade was indirectly recognized in the agreements issuing from the Tokyo Round of GATT negotiations in 1979. The effort to create a more liberal international trading system thus slowed measurably during the 1970s.[32]

The movement toward a more open world economy reasserted itself during the 1980s, however, as the dangers of protectionism became clearer. By then, the world's leading industrial economies had become thoroughly interdependent and the world's leading firms were transnational in scope. Between 1972 and 1991, it has been estimated, imports grew 65 percent more rapidly than home demand and exports grew twice as fast as the economy as a whole.[33] Neither multinational corporations nor the national economies in which they operated could therefore retreat from the global economy without forfeiting their ability to participate in the growth of world trade. In consequence, governments began to back off from efforts to insulate their economies from competition and sought instead to prevail in the increasingly competitive environment. The United States, for example, gained a considerable advantage for its exports from the decision to lower the value of the dollar, begun with the Plaza Accord in 1985 and leading to a 30 percent devaluation over just two years. For their part, the members of the Common Market chose at roughly the same time to further the process of integration and set for themselves the goal of creating a "Single European Market" by 1992.[34]

The desire to capture the benefits that seem to have accrued to Europe from regional integration and to compete with exports from Europe and the East Asian countries has spurred efforts at economic integration in other regions, particularly in North and South America. The most visible achievement was the signing of the North American Free Trade Agreement; more successful, at least initially, was the creation in 1991 of Mercosur, a common market linking the economies of Argentina, Brazil, Paraguay, and Uruguay.[35] On the surface, the trend toward the formation of such regional trading blocs might seem to threaten the broader trend toward a more open, global economy, but in most instances it appears to have furthered rather than retarded the growth of trade worldwide.[36]

The emergence of a truly global economy was aided by two dramatic transformations during the 1980s: the collapse of socialism and the abandonment by Third World countries of economic strategies that envisioned development outside the world market. Communism's varied endings left in place regimes presiding over vastly different political economies. Everywhere the legacy of socialism meant state ownership of industries, government control over prices and wages, and popular cultures inhospitable to central features of modern capitalism. The transition to greater private ownership, free markets in goods, capital, and labor, and a culture geared to mass consumption and tolerant of the inequalities and insecurities characteristic of advanced capitalist society might be inevitable, but the pace at which the new order has emerged has varied widely.

The nations of Eastern Europe will surely come to approximate Western norms more rapidly than the states of the former Soviet Union; and, within that region, eastern Germany, the Czech and Slovak republics, Poland, and Hungary have experienced the transformation with the least dislocation and resistance. The terms on which these new states and new economies have entered the world market have been harsh, however. They were told by Western advisers that the road to success was through exports, but the IMF, the World Bank, and the European Community insisted that the first step was to break up the trading relations that existing within Eastern Europe and between Eastern Europe and the Soviet Union. The consequence was a dramatic drop in trade and hence in aggregate output and economic activity. Only then, and only on a country-by-country basis, would trade links be established with the West. These tough conditions were imposed, morever, in the presence of a global recession and in the absence of a new Marshall Plan to smooth the transition.[37] It should have come as no surprise that after a couple of years of such "shock therapy," voters in the East should have turned to those representatives of the old regime who promised a less painful path to economic progress.[38] Equally obviously, continued progress will also require stable political regimes and secure national identities, which means that growth will be close to impossible in nations where disputed borders and rival ethnicities threaten the legitimacy of states.

Within the former Soviet Union, the overriding question is how the smaller states will renegotiate their relationship with the formerly dominant Russian center. The highly centralized nature of Soviet planning and development, in which regions were forced to specialize as part of a quasi-

**250**

imperial economic order and to neglect the development of local infrastructure and networks of distribution and supply, makes the relationship
between Russia and the rest far more important than their relationships
with the rest of the world economy.[39] Political independence nevertheless
almost guarantees that the links will not be reestablished until it is in the
clear interest of the smaller states to do so. Indeed, the economic difficulties experienced by the Russian Federation in the first few years after 1991
meant that "going it alone" made sense economically and that the decision to break from the center was economically rational as well as politically popular.[40] Over time the prospect of a revival of trade, investment,
and other relations with Russia will become more attractive, but if and
when economic ties are renewed, they will be based on a more equitable
exchange than they were previously, and the resulting re-creation of a post-
Soviet trading sphere should serve to enhance, rather than to hinder, the
continued emergence of global markets. That has already happened farther
east. In Asia proper, China's decision to reenter the market has impacted
the supply side of the world economy far more than the demand side,
while China's hybrid authoritarianism casts a pall of uncertainty over its
economic future. Nevertheless, it does not seem unreasonable to consider
at least the coastal regions of China, with their strong ties to Hong Kong
and to overseas Chinese investors, as having created in economic terms a
"greater China" that has decisively entered the world market and
expanded its global reach.[41]

Over the long term, the addition of the formerly socialist countries to
the world market will constitute the greatest extension of the scope of capitalism since the age of discovery and the initial establishment of the capitalist world system.[42] Its effects will not be fully manifest, however, until
capitalism sinks deeper roots within these nations. It may well be, therefore, that the consequences of the increasing integration of the Third World
into the global economy will be more dramatic in the short term. The turn
away from efforts to develop through strategies of export-led growth outside, or in opposition to, the world market happened very quickly but
nonetheless decisively. The change was brought about by five factors: the
decreasing relevance of the socialist model of development, which preceded the actual collapse of socialist regimes by at least a decade; the utter
failure of the campaign to establish a "New International Economic
Order," which would have meant the success of efforts to negotiate a new
global bargain over the terms of trade and created international institutions and policies compatible with strategies of "import-substitution industrialization" (ISI); disillusion with the effectiveness of ISI models them-

selves; the debt crisis of the 1980s, which provided international finance with the lever necessary to pry open national economies that had sought to close themselves off from foreign penetration and domination; and, most important, the rise of the so-called Four Tigers—South Korea, Taiwan, Hong Kong, and Singapore—as "newly industrializing countries" that achieved remarkable rates of growth through exports.

The debt crisis of the 1980s grew directly from the oil crises of the previous decade. Increased energy prices confronted less developed countries with a series of short-term difficulites and a tempting opportunity to achieve a temporary solution with enormous costs over the long term. What made economic life difficult for those countries was the slowdown in the world economy, which reduced the demand for exports and hence lowered export earnings, the rising cost of energy imports on which strategies of industrial development were crucially dependent, and the desire of better-off consumers to continue the importation of increasingly expensive manufactured products. Aside from oil exporters, none of the less developed economies could cope with these difficulties without loans from Western banks, who were awash in funds newly available from higher oil prices and the general inflation. With interest rates not much above the rate of price increase, debt made sense. But real interest rates shot up in response to the actions of the U.S. Federal Reserve in 1979, and by 1982 most Third World countries were left with unprecedented levels of debt. The worldwide recession of the early 1980s undermined their ability to pay even the interest, and it is estimated that levels of indebtedness reached $1 trillion by 1986.[43] The debt crisis lingered throughout the 1980s and was largely responsible for the disastrous decline in income for Latin America and Africa: between 1980 and 1989 per capita income decreased by 15 percent in Latin America and by fully 30 percent in Africa.[44]

The debt crisis, at least partly political in origin, was resolved only after prolonged negotiations that proceeded simultaneously among the leaders of the developed nations and between the debtors, their creditors, and the International Monetary Fund. Gradually, policy makers in the advanced countries realized that large amounts of debt would have to be forgiven or taken over by state agencies. The outlines of a resolution began to emerge at the Toronto economic summit in 1988, with the decision to grant relief to the poorest countries, and became clearer with the announcement in 1989 of the Brady Plan (named after the U.S. Secretary of the Treasury Nicholas Brady), which offered relief to "middle-income" debtors, primarily in Latin America. This was followed in June 1990 by the announcement by the Bush administration of the so-called Enterprise for the Americas Initiative, which offered further debt relief to be coupled with efforts to liberalize trade from Alaska to Argentina and to encourage privatization.[45] These policies did not actually reduce debt—in the four years following the Brady Plan, debt increased by almost a quarter, to $1.5 trillion—but they did manage to control its increase and, more important, successfully reduced the exposure of the big banks and so lessened the chances of financial collapse. By October 1993 the IMF could ask rhetorically, but meaningfully, "Is the Debt Crisis Over?"[46]

Before it was declared over by financial journalists and policy makers, the debt crisis had worked a revolution on Third World economic policy. Despite the global character of the discourse over debt, each debtor country had to work out its own deal with its creditors and with the International Monetary Fund. Invariably, the settlements imposed "adjustment policies" that called for budget cuts and fiscal austerity, leading to sharp declines in public spending on social welfare and to the abandonment of state support of industrial development, and that insisted upon the privatization of state-owned industry and the dismantling of import controls. Already, policies of "import-substitution industrialization" and state-led development were losing support, especially among the growing middle classes, but the decisive push away from this model of growth was provided by the debt crisis and the decisions of bankers, the leaders of the developed countries, and the IMF to make debt relief conditional on economic liberalization.[47]

As strategies for development outside the world market lost credibility, the success of the four East Asian "tigers" appeared to confirm that the path to growth led through exports and thoroughgoing integration into the world economy and thus "to vindicate the promise of free-market economics. Before the four existed," it has been suggested, "it had been necessary to invent them in order to justify the theory; and after they expanded, not a little invention went into rendering the facts of their performance consistent with the postulates of the free market."[48] A little invention and a lot of forgetting, for the East Asian "economic miracles" had occurred in strong states that had played a major role in directing and sustaining industrial development and in creating the social conditions that encouraged growth. Equally obscured by the fearful response of Western leaders and businesspeople to the threat of competition from the East was the fact that it had long been U.S. policy to encourage Japan to orient itself toward East Asian markets and to build up in that region a peaceful variation of the "Greater East Asia Co-Prosperity Sphere" that Japan had earlier sought to impose by force, and also that the growth of the "Four Tigers" has been largely a reflection of the emergence of Japan as the world's most successful engine of development. But what was not obscure and what has not been lost on other countries in what used to be called the Third World is that the East Asian route to prosperity has led through the world market and that it has worked. The example of East Asia, then, has been a decisive spur toward the liberalization of world markets and yet another deterrent to efforts to engineer growth, in either the developed or developing world, the prosperous North or the relatively impoverished South, through protectionism and hence in isolation from the global economy.[49]

The prolonged crisis of growth during the 1970s and 1980s did not, therefore, produce either a renewed effort at government intervention in industrial development or a reversal of the commitment of leading states and economies to the increasingly open system of multilateral trade that had produced the increasingly competitive global economy. Planning and industrial policy initiatives failed or at least failed to win public support and therefore became distinctly less fashionable; national economies became ever more enmeshed in the world economy; and the prospects of state-led development occurring outside the world market diminished to next to nothing.

What did change over these years was the organization of production and the place of labor within the system of production. The move away from or beyond Fordism took different forms, some rather benign but others extremely harsh. Among the former were the efforts to deploy the latest technology without necessarily laying off workers. This was, unfortunately, rather rare, limited essentially to companies already enjoying a substantial technical edge over their competitors or those with assured markets, such as defense contractors. It happened most often in Japan, where companies had made commitments of lifetime employment to workers and where the use of robots, numerically controlled machinery, and automated production was most advanced. Even more benign were those instances where a style of production recently labeled "flexible specialization" allowed for substantial growth in productivity, income, and even employment. Scholars looking for paths out of the Fordist impasse have been struck by the apparent success of regions and industries where mass production never really took hold and where earlier patterns of artisanal production persisted into the industrial and even "postindustrial" eras. Three regions have attracted most attention: Silicon Valley and the Route 128 complex of computer-related industries in the United States and the Emilia-Romagna region around Bologna in what has been called "the Third Italy." What has distinguished these regions is the accumulation of a substantial reservoir of human capital upon which industry could draw and the nurturing of informal networks within and between firms along which information could flow and around which production could be organized and reorganized. These resources made it possible for these regions to grow without adopting bureaucratic forms of business organization and thus to respond quickly and efficiently to shifts in world markets based upon changes in consumer taste and advances in quality and in the techniques of production.[50] The third benign alternative to Fordism developed as numerous large firms began to rediscover the virtues of production carried out by small groups of skilled workers cooperating on a common task and to adopt various mechanisms for incorporating the principles embodied in "flexible specialization" to the needs of multinational companies through the use of "quality circles," "production teams," and joint committees of labor and management.

The eclipse of Fordism also meant the spread of rather more harsh methods of recruiting and managing workers and organizing the workplace. For many firms, the most visible manifestation of the crisis of growth was a profits squeeze generated by the steady growth of wages during the long boom. The obvious answer was to lower wages or lay off workers, and employers did both. Unemployment had remained at historically low levels throughout the 1950s and 1960s, and labor shortages had encouraged mass migration from the countryside to the cities as well as the importation of labor from abroad. After 1970, by contrast, unemployment began to rise and approached or exceeded 10 percent in several advanced economies by the recession of 1981–1982. Worse yet, it tended to stabilize at such high levels. Even when growth resumed, as it did in the mid-1990s, it produced what was labeled, with some exaggeration, "a jobless recovery."[51] Levels of unemployment were highest in the European Community, where benefits, entitlements, and real wages were relatively high; unemployment was lower and job creation higher in the United States, where lower wages and benefits, for both the employed and the unemployed, prevailed; and in Japan continued expansion meant steady work, although even in that favored environment offers of lifetime security became less routine.[52]

Not only did work become increasingly scarce, but the wages paid for it declined. Real wages had grown in all of the advanced economies during the 1960s and the so-called wage explosion of the early 1970s, but since then the pattern has been more varied: real wages have continued to rise in Germany and Japan; grew slowly in France, Italy, and Britain;

and declined in the United States. These national aggregates disguise, of course, enormous variation within countries: typically, a core of well-paid workers in the most profitable and technically sophisticated industries has done well, while large numbers of less skilled workers in industries with less secure market niches have seen their earnings stagnate or have suffered actual losses. Many of these less skilled workers are immigrants or racial and ethnic minorities. Compounding, and contributing to, the decline in real wages and conditions has been the spread of part-time work, which has reached epidemic proportions in certain occupations and which typically carries either lower wages or fewer benefits or both. Despite the fact that part-time work is often the preserve of women workers who have supposedly been the beneficiaries of legislation mandating equal work for equal pay and an end to employment discrimination, the gap between the wages and conditions of part-time and full-time workers has not diminished since 1970, and has in some instances probably widened.

Underpinning the deterioration of job prospects and living standards for workers, and preventing the transformation of irregular employment with low wages, few benefits, and fewer prospects into good jobs at high wages has been the steady erosion in the power of unions.[53] Union membership peaked in most advanced countries in the early and mid-1970s, when union shop-floor bargaining power was also impressive. Both bargaining power and crude membership figures have declined subsequently. Two distinct processes have produced this result. The first is structural change, which has led to a decline in the proportion of manual employees in the occupational structure overall and to a precipitous fall in the numbers employed in manufacturing. The second is the deliberate attack on unions by employers and the state. The Reagan and Thatcher governments manifested the most intense antipathy to trade unions and presided over the most severe losses of union power and membership, but unions were placed on the defensive everywhere, as employers stiffened their resistance to wage demands and as the state began to withdraw its support from the effort to ensure industrial peace through corporatist bargaining. The effect was to give employers a relatively free hand in restructuring industrial relations, the workplace, and the market for labor.

Surely the most dramatic method of restructuring was to relocate, to parcel out sections of the manufacturing process to workers in different plants in different regions or even different countries. The aim in this dispersal of production is to take advantage of the lower wages prevailing in new, and predominantly union-free, environments. The labor force in

256

these settings is often made up largely of women, whose rates of pay are extremely low.[54] The most notorious instances are the enclaves of manufacturing (*maquiladoras*) established in less developed countries south of the Rio Grande where foreign investors not only get the benefits of cheap labor but are also given tax breaks, tariff exemptions, and direct state assistance in the recruitment of workers and the suppression of unions. Put starkly, "The *maquiladoras* pay no taxes, they pollute the environment, and their working conditions are unsafe."[55] Workers in these zones of unfettered but nevertheless state-sponsored "free enterprise" produce large quantities of goods for the U.S. market, especially in textiles, automobiles, and consumer electronics; and almost all of the major transnational firms have come to depend to some degree on production carried on under these harsh conditions.

Typically, restructuring takes less dramatic forms, even if the result is equally clear-cut. Industrial workers have long been used to periodic layoffs, followed by moments of frenzied overtime and tight labor markets. During the 1970s and 1980s, however, these cycles masked trends, with relatively fewer workers being called back during successive booms, new generations of machinery requiring fewer hands, and more and more jobs subcontracted or permanently moved away. Over time, the structure of the labor force became more fragmented, with a small number of "core" workers with high skills, good wages and benefits, and established rights to union representation or employee participation, and a much larger number of workers lacking in these traits and perquisites.[56]

A similar process has recently begun to affect middle management and white-collar workers. In the United States, the recession of the early 1990s had its most devastating employment effects not upon blue-collar workers but on employees who had been largely immune to the transformation of work during previous downturns. Several factors have combined to undermine the protected niches of nonmanual employees. Most obvious is the simple fact that as the competitive pressure to raise profits continues, firms find diminishing returns in restructuring work among manual employees and turn instead to redeploying better-paid, but not necessarily more productive, employees located higher up the organizational hierarchy. This rather natural process has been accentuated by the rise among managers of an ideology of "re-engineering."[57] And making it all possible has been the steady progress of technology. For decades the promise of computers has been that they would increase productivity among both manual and nonmanual workers. Until recently, however, the promise has remained particularly unfulfilled for clerical, professional, and supervisory jobs. The latest wave of technical innovation seems finally to have delivered: the rapid advance in the networking capability of firms and individuals and the increasing sophistication of software, itself made possible by advances in both the processing power and the storage capacity of personal computers, have allowed firms to reorganize nonmanual work through the same sorts of relocation, devolution, subcontracting, and outsourcing that have been applied so profitably to manufacturing.[58]

The passing of the era of Fordist mass production has resulted, therefore, in a series of sharply contrasting outcomes, linked despite their diversity to a common and powerful logic of intensified competition on a global scale.[59] The balance sheet is difficult to draw up, if only because an accurate accounting would necessarily have to be global rather than national and the available data are simply inadequate for the task.[60] Roughly speaking, however, it is clear enough that the world's economic and social geography has been recently and dramatically transformed. As recently as the early 1970s, the geography of development appeared starkly obvious: the capitalist West and the socialist East represented two rival paths that seemed to lead with equal assurance, indeed inevitability, to the creation of modern industrial economies. The so-called Third World was not merely backward economically and technically but was viewed as an open social space to be colonized, in an age of "decolonization," by capitalism or socialism and brought by one or another path to modernity. The oil crises of the 1970s utterly destroyed this simple and comfortable understanding of the world economy. Neither East nor West proved immune to the tightening up of energy supplies, and the ability to control the flow of oil put the economic fate of the most advanced economies in the hands of an array of quasi-feudal rulers bent on keeping the modern world at bay, or at least out of the reach of their subjects. The sense of outrage and anger that accompanied the oil price shocks of 1973–1974 and 1979 owed more than a little of its animus to this sudden reversal of roles, dependencies, and accompanying advantages and liabilities.

Since the 1970s the world's economic geography has been transformed by the effective ending of socialism as a rival system for organizing national economies, by the fragmentation of the Third World as an economic force, and by the further differentiation of the advanced capitalist economies. When socialism ended, it left in place a set of gargantuan monuments to Fordism in its least efficient, dirtiest, and most inflexible forms. The gains to be realized by the crude mobilization of people and natural resources had long since ceased to yield significant advances in production and led to actual declines in productivity. In consequence, growth lagged and socialism came to be equated with stagnation and inefficiency, made bearable only by the fact that the system's meager fruits were shared out on a roughly equal basis and that the future seemed secure, if rather bleak. The wreckage of socialism also included a despoiled environment; tremendous neglect of infrastructure and services, which, according to the crude assumptions of socialist development theory, were unproductive and parasitic activities; and a culture that was deeply suspicious of inequalities of wealth, of individualism, and of property rights. The formerly socialist economies possessed relatively few advantages with which to offset these liabilities. Russia, China, and some of the successor states in the former Soviet empire inherited substantial endowments of natural resources that could be profitably exploited, but only if the proper infrastructure were in place. The other great resource available to the postsocialist economies is an enormous reservoir of labor, some of it extremely skilled and well educated but all of it cheap by international standards.

The mixed legacy of socialism has left the formerly socialist societies in a very ambiguous relationship to the world economy and the global division of labor. In the aggregate, the abandonment of the socialist alternative means an inevitable expansion in the reach of capitalism and the world market. But the integration of the postsocialist economies into the world economy has proved a slow process. In China, for example, the coastal regions have secured for themselves a distinctive niche, producing relatively inexpensive goods for export markets in Asia and elsewhere. The style of production remains distinctly labor-intensive, a sort of pre-Fordism or "dirty Taylorism," made effective by the absence of unions and the availability of large reserves of cheap labor.[61] Export-led growth has helped to generate a broader boom in these same regions, in part because there exists a relatively wide base of local trade and commercialized peasant agriculture on which to build. More distant and inland regions of China have fared less well, and industry there more often remains state-owned and unprofitable. The effect is a new type of dualism likely to give rise to political instability, which could in turn affect the prospects for all regions and sectors. Still, the power of the center is strongly rooted and might well allow a more gradual integration of the entire economy into the world market, even if the less developed regions do so on less advantageous terms.

Proximity to European markets has had a similar effect on the economies of Eastern Europe.[62] Hungary, the Czech and Slovak republics, and Poland have made the greatest progress toward integration into the world market, seeking to secure niches as relatively low-cost producers of

goods destined for markets in Western Europe. Here, too, the style of production is best characterized as pre-Fordist, although the participation of
Western European firms has brought with it a higher technological level
than might otherwise have been expected to emerge in these societies.
Several countries deviate from this pattern significantly, though in opposite directions. Bulgaria and Romania, more backward economically and
culturally and more distant from European markets, remain overall less
prosperous and technically advanced, although actual declines in production and employment have largely been avoided; and the warring states
that emerged from what once was Yugoslavia have experienced economic
ruin as the price of national strife. Eastern Germany, by contrast, was
almost forcibly integrated into the newly unified Germany on terms that
promised to bring wages, living conditions, and social services quickly
into line with those prevailing in the West. The immediate effect in the
East was the loss of jobs. For the West, the cost was primarily fiscal and it
was more than many wanted to bear and required a tax burden decried
by bankers and businesspeople. But the will to create a new Germany
united economically and socially as well as politically overrode narrowly
economic considerations; its long-term consequence will most likely be to
erase the differences between East and West and move both into the post-
Fordist future.

The states that have arisen from the former Soviet Union face more formidable problems in adjusting to the world market.[63] They have inherited not merely outdated industries and cultures inimical to the workings
of capitalist markets but also distorted local and regional economies and
extremely underdeveloped infrastructures.[64] Investment in distribution
and local transportation networks was a low priority under Soviet planning. Central planning also imposed excessive concentration on the regions
that have now often become separate states. The implosion of central
authority thus led rapidly to the decline of interregional trade and to the
odd and frustrating combination of regional surpluses and shortages and
the fragmentation of markets. Stabilization will have to occur separately
in the different republics, though success hinges overall on the experience
of Russia.

The transition to capitalism in Russia has not been easy. Reform had
not proceeded terribly far before the collapse of 1991: in that year, it has
been estimated, well over 80 percent of employees still worked in the state
sector or on collective farms.[65] When Yeltsin consolidated his authority
in the fall of 1991, he appointed as prime minister Yegor Gaidar, who was
committed to reform and ready to move forward decisively. Prices were

decontrolled at the beginning of 1992; scarce consumer goods became quickly available but at much higher prices, and real wages fell by 40 percent in four months. Prices recovered by fall 1992 and remained at roughly 80 to 90 percent of the prereform level after that.[66] Popular discontent manifested itself quickly, however, and found willing expression in the Russian parliament. Gaidar was out of office before the end of the year, although he returned the following summer. Yeltsin, who in choosing not to call for new elections in the fall of 1991 forfeited the opportunity to obtain a mandate for his leadership and for reform, responded to criticism ineptly and in a manner reminiscent of the nation's authoritarian past. Relations with Parliament continued to deteriorate until the bloody confrontation in the fall of 1993. Though Yeltsin prevailed, he emerged from the episode with diminished stature and support, and in the elections of December 1993 the new constitution was approved but the "liberal" parties fared poorly.[67]

The effort to reform Russia's economy has proceeded despite the continuing troubles of the government, but it has been marked by hesitations and contradictions: official encouragement of foreign investment and exports, for example, coexisting with the protection of major industries like automobiles through high tariffs and state subsidies; food prices free of control together with enormous subsidies for public transportation; a housing market partially privatized but mostly controlled; product markets let loose in one sector and hampered by restrictions elsewhere; and fancy shops lining the main streets of Moscow and St. Petersburg and filled with expensive Western goods but without customers. The prospects for growth within the former Soviet Union are thus not overly bright in the short or the medium term. The absolute declines in output that began in 1990 and persisted after the breakup of the Soviet state had ended by mid-1995, but sources of genuine growth were still very few. For a considerable period growth will presumably be centered in the very small sector of technically advanced industry, much of it previously devoted to defense, in extractive industries that produce relatively few jobs, and in filling in the gaps in infrastructure, transportation, communication, and marketing especially. Growth in manufacturing exports, for which these nations' reserves of labor might prove an ideal resource, will be limited by the fact that China, Eastern Europe and many newly industrializing economies will be pursuing growth through precisely that strategy but with fewer hindrances and historical liabilities.

Engineering growth will be further hampered by continued political instability, as the hardships and inequities associated with the creation of a market economy recreate popular support for former Communists and nationalists eager to slow, if not actually to reverse, the transformation. The revival of the political fortunes of the left in the post-communist states is both curious and interesting. When the socialist states and systems began to come apart there was widespread speculation, and some hope, that they would be replaced by some sort of market or democratic socialism that would allow greater scope for markets and enterprise while preserving the extensive protection, services, and social rights proclaimed and, to some extent, provided by the old regimes. Nowhere across Eastern Europe or the former Soviet Union did this happen, for the records of those governments had served to discredit any and all notions of socialism. Even the industrial workers, in whose interests the system was supposed to operate, opposed socialist policies. Likewise women, who allegedly achieved equal rights under socialism, refused to support programs, policies, and institutions of socialist provenance or inspiration.[68] But as the transition to a market economy progressed, this initial rejection of the socialist heritage was gradually reconsidered, and citizens began to vote in large numbers for communists and former communists. When they take office or achieve control of parliament, however, the former communists confront the same problems as do the liberals they replace. The option of market socialism, if it was ever feasible, no longer makes practical sense when what remains under state control are the oldest, least efficient industries and when the more advanced and competitive industries and most of the networks of distribution are in private hands. The former communists can marginally slow down the pace at which the transition occurs, and can probably lessen the pain and disruption, but the possibility of choosing a genuinely different path for economic reform is exceedingly remote. The market is the future; although just what niche the formerly socialist economies will fill within the world market remains very unclear. The problem is especially acute for the states of the former Soviet Union, Russia in particular, which have retreated from the dirty and inefficient Fordism of the past but have yet to evolve a viable alternative.

The world's economic geography has also been radically redrawn by the divergent outcomes reached by Third World countries that, a quarter century ago, seemed to share a similar trajectory and a common predicament of underdevelopment. Prior to the onset of the global economic slowdown of the 1970s, the best hope for such nations seemed to lie in the strategy of state-led industrial development. And, in fact, growth was impressive among a group of "late-industializing" countries that applied strategies of state-sponsored development and that included India,

Turkey, Brazil, Mexico, and Argentina as well as Korea and Taiwan. After 1970, however, the distinctions within this cluster of states became clearer and their fates begin significantly to diverge. The so-called four tigers—Korea and Taiwan, together with Hong Kong and Singapore—rapidly mastered the tricks of mass production. Because their relatively small size limited the capacity of domestic markets, however, these economies turned outward and soon captured export markets in both the advanced and the less developed countries. More recently, they have proved adept at using the most sophisticated technologies in the production of a wide range of industrial goods. Their industrial structures are heavily weighted toward manufacturing, which is carried on with a mix of advanced techniques and cheap labor, and away from services, which have nonetheless grown steadily. Relatively few people are employed in agriculture in any of these countries, and so their occupational and social structures approximate rather closely the norm of the advanced industrial societies, though with somewhat fewer professionals engaged in the provision of services and with rather more engineers and a labor force enjoying fewer rights and earning less money than in Europe or North America.[69]

Nations like Mexico, India, Brazil, Argentina, and Turkey, which chose until recently to pursue state-led strategies of development based on import substitution, have evolved in recent years so as to present more fragmented industrial and social structures.[70] Some of these countries have relatively large agricultural populations, who in some cases wrest a living through very primitive forms of cultivation and who in other regions and settings provide the labor for more modern agricultural production. Here the favorable results of various "green revolutions" coexist alongside peasants whose relationship to the soil and its products has not changed in a very long time.[71] Industrial development in these nations has typically proceeded through the spread of mass production, though modern industries paying reasonable wages were often surrounded by marginal producers exploiting abundant and inexpensive supplies of labor. As these economies were forced to become more open during the 1980s and 1990s, the more advanced sectors faced stiff competition from imports and did not fare well. The effect has been to weed out the better jobs and more "progressive" firms or to force them to push wages and conditions downward. In Turkey, for example, the turn to the market in January 1980 reversed two decades of development policy and led to a realignment of prices and wages such that, over the decade 1977–1987, the share of wages in the national income was halved.[72] In response, exports grew rapidly and manufacturing expanded. Inequality increased greatly, as the middle and upper classes enjoyed the fruits of a regressive redistribution and of cheaper imports. Tourism also grew enormously, tying the nation ever more firmly into the world economy.

The move from planning and "import-substitution industrialization" toward exports, consumer goods, and the world market came more than a decade later in India, and even then more hesitantly and inconsistently, and the resulting social and economic adjustments were likewise delayed. But the decision to compete in the world economy has created the same pressure to lower wages and intensify the work process.[73] The stagnation, or decline, of wages has been equally dramatic across Latin America: in Argentina real wages declined by nearly a quarter between 1970 and 1982; in Brazil and Mexico the value of real wages in 1984 was less than 85 percent of the value in 1970.[74] The decline thus occurred whether or not governments chose to open the economy to the pressure of the world market, and it seems that delay did not produce better terms. Thus, the opening up of the Mexican economy came relatively late but, perhaps for that reason, was even more dramatic in its effects. NAFTA was not the first movement toward liberalization, but the combination of NAFTA and successive devaluations of the peso served further to impoverish the working class and to encourage foreign investment and export-oriented production based upon cheap labor. The Turkish, Indian, and Mexican cases thus differed in timing and undoubtedly will produce marginally different outcomes, but their common trajectory exemplifies the broader trend, which is better regarded as a retreat from Fordism rather than a move beyond it.

Still other nations in what used to be called the Third World have stagnated or even regressed in the face of recent changes in the world economy, and thus their social and economic structures have taken on a more distorted and unbalanced character. In the least developed nations, especially in Africa, population has increased but agricultural employment has stagnated or declined. The effect has been overwhelming urban migration but, again, few jobs and little development. At the root of these nations' difficulties is the sustained weakness of demand for the agricultural products and raw materials that constitute their major natural endowments. This structural deficit, together with the increased cost of energy and industrial imports, has produced growing impoverishment. The problems are compounded by the instability of states in the region, the rampant corruption of elites, and the failures of strategies of state-led economic growth. The effect has been to make such regions unattractive for investment, but without the resources with which to generate autonomous development, and it conjures up the real prospect that they will remain for some time "millennial losers." The growth of even old-style Fordist industry would be a great boon, but pre-Fordist, Fordist, or post-Fordist development is not on offer.[75]

The diversity of economic outcomes outside the developed nations—what might be termed the OECD (Organization for Economic Cooperation and Development) economies—is thus considerably greater than that within these more favored regions. Still, the various OECD economies have responded differently to the challenges of the 1970s and 1980s and so emerged from that era of slow growth with different profiles and orientations. Job creation was greater in the United States and Japan, though the path to expanded employment varied. Overall, employment grew by 1.6 percent annually in the United States and Canada over the years 1979–1990, by 1.1 percent in Japan, but by only 0.5 percent in the European Community.[76] Japan, the only major OECD economy to sustain growth in manufacturing employment, continued to generate well-paid jobs in industry, where technical innovation remained rapid and styles of work organization increasingly flexible; the East Asian economic giant also saw steady growth in employment in services. The United States, by contrast, moved more decisively into services, where a majority of jobs were skilled, professional, and reasonably well-paid, if not as secure as such employment had been in the past, but where a substantial minority of positions were low-skilled, poorly paid, and insecure. Manufacturing employment has also remained strong in the United States, declining by only half as much as in Europe, but the trend has nevertheless been toward a more heteregeneous pattern of employment: the more advanced firms have deployed new technologies and post-Fordist principles, but other firms have relied on the intensified exploitation of relatively unskilled and increasingly cheap labor, often working part-time or on irregular schedules. When Wal-Mart boasts about buying American products made by American workers and portrays communities saved by its enlightened policies, for example, it is not saying that it has created any particularly good or secure jobs. Nor can it pretend that the workers it has momentarily rescued from the dole can transfer their skills to other firms or industries when the huge distributor gives the next contract to another impoverished small town with an abandoned factory in which it can employ even cheaper labor deployed according to distinctly pre-Fordist principles. The United States was historically a high-wage economy; more recently, job growth has come at the expense of wages.

Job growth in other OECD countries has been less robust, though overall the quality of employment has been maintained or even enhanced. The willingness of most of the European Community to endorse the so-called social charter, which guarantees rights to workers and even to citizens who are not in full-time employment, indicates that such rights are largely the norm across the rest of Europe. The reluctance of the United Kingdom to accept the "social charter" is equally clear evidence of the decision of successive Conservative governments to cope with slow growth by lowering wages, removing the protections previously won by labor, and of their understanding that this strategy inevitably means a retreat from prior commitments to social and economic rights. For most European economies, however, the price of maintaining a high-wage, high-skill economy and generous social provision has been fewer new jobs.[77] During the long postwar boom the numbers of unemployed in the OECD countries averaged roughly 10 million, and unemployment rates across the developed economies hovered around 5 percent and were often lower; the norm for the 1990s was 35 million unemployed, which was closer to 10 percent of the labor force and, in some nations, slightly higher, and it often stayed at that elevated level even during upswings in the business cycle. There was a clear trade-off, then, between the quality and quantity of employment; by implication, the transition to a post-Fordist economy in Europe has meant, and in all likelihood will continue to mean, fewer jobs in total, especially in industry. It will also probably mean less generous social provision. Based upon the most recent experience, future employment growth should come predominantly in services, especially commercial and banking services and in personal and community services provided privately. But the major European economies, Germany in particular, have lagged well behind the United States and even Britain in the creation of these jobs.[78] Ironically, the trend toward post-Fordism as a strategy of production has proceeded further in Europe, while the trend toward "postindustrialism," defined as the shift from manufacturing to services, has been greater in North America and in Great Britain; over the same time, Japan has become a model of post-Fordism while services remain distinctly less developed, constrained by the nation's reluctance to open its systems of distribution and communication to genuine competition.

Overall, of course, the OECD economies look more alike than different, and they have progressed along a similar trajectory toward a society characterized by fewer manufacturing jobs, by a steadily increasing share of industrial jobs organized according to post-Fordist principles, by a shrinking agricultural sector, at least in terms of employment, and by constant growth in services. The occupational structure has thus become less industrial, less "proletarian," less rural, more urban, more skilled and professional, and more prosperous in general but not uniformly so. It is also slightly older, as birth rates decline and the population and work force age, and also more female, because the mix of job opportunities, both good and bad, and corresponding skill requirements favor the increased employment of women.[79] The labor force has also become steadily more diverse ethnically and racially. Similar social transformations have affected the less prosperous and technically advanced nations, but variations in starting points and rates of change make for quite different impacts upon social structure. Even relatively poor countries, for example, have experienced an increase in white-collar and professional occupations, particularly in the public sector, and it is at least in part the growth of these new middle classses that lies behind the pressure to open up the economy to the world market. More important quantitatively has been the widening stream of migrants leaving agriculture and the villages that has flooded the cities and industrial districts with cheap labor.

The economic and social consequences of the decline of agriculture have been particularly enormous. World agricultural production has on the whole increased substantially, for technology has ensured rising output with fewer workers, though in the poorer nations population has often increased as rapidly. The move to cities typically begins the process that leads to lower fertility and reduced rates of population growth, but there is a considerable time lag during which numbers can outrun resources and, even more dramatically, the availability of jobs. The central problem is that developing nations offer great reserves of labor available for industrial work at a moment when the returns to be gained from either pre-Fordist, labor-intensive manufacturing or from classic Fordist mass production are diminishing in the face of more advanced techniques in use within the OECD economies and within the industrial sectors of the "newly industrializing countries." There is thus a mismatch that has produced massive unemployment in the sprawling and impoverished cities of the least developed societies.[80]

Still, the process of urbanization continues unabated and with it the decline of ways of life rooted in agriculture. The most obvious example is the weakening of patriarchal authority, which has ordinarily been stronger in the countryside than in the cities, and whose atrophy has produced often fierce reactions from men and from defenders of tradition. It is surely a major factor behind the rise of religious fundamentalism, particularly in Islamic countries, where the devout have become convinced that the invasion of western culture represents the growing power of evil,

*Jahalliya,* threatening the heart of Muslim society.[81] Even the most remote parts of the world are now routinely exposed to the products of Western, especially American, culture, their populations flooded with images of consumer culture and the secular, indulgent lifestyles that seem to accompany the acquisition and enjoyment of material wealth. The unattainability of such affluence is one spur to its rejection; probably more important is the fact that the products of the consumer culture emanate from the same metropolitan regions whence came earlier generations of colonial governors, slave traders, rapacious businessmen, crusaders, and missionaries bent on eradicating error and local faith. Hence the deep ambivalence toward the West and its modernizing culture and the attractions of orthodoxies that lay claim to deeper local roots and of moralities strong enough to resist the onslaught of decadent modernity.[82]

## RESHAPING THE WORLD OF POLITICS

Understanding the contours of contemporary politics requires a procedure much like the one needed to probe the nature of the world economy. Beneath, or alongside, the ups and downs of the economy during the 1970s and 1980s there was occurring a profound restructuring that went largely unremarked. Similarly, while the eyes of the world remained riveted alternately on summit meetings, rituals of state, electoral spectacles, or, for the more "concerned" observers, on the human horrors of fierce local conflicts, both the international system of states and the balance between democratic and authoritarian forms of rule have been dramatically transformed over the past quarter century. The change is likewise structural and hence likely to persist, even if the trend is marked by occasional outbreaks of violence and reversions to undemocratic rule.

How best to characterize the emerging structure of states? To begin, it is useful to take note of the contradictory forces that have been remaking political life within and between states. The passing of the Cold War has expanded the range of possibilities for national political development, for it is increasingly improbable that the choices made locally will occasion the direct intervention of either the remaining superpower or the community of states. Throughout the Cold War era the superpowers chose to regard local changes of regime as opportunities to advance the reach of their respective blocs or alliances or, more ominously, as occasions when states might well shift their allegiance. Such worries did not often lead to outright intervention, but it did prompt the United States and the Soviet Union to offer arms and aid to the rulers of emerging states in return for their support in the global contest for influence. The effect was to confer upon indigenous elites enormous advantages in dealing with their own subjects, endowing them with added authority, legitimacy, and guns. In consequence, elites were under less pressure to bargain with their domestic opponents and to secure the "consent of the governed," and so regularly resorted to authoritarian forms of rule.[83] Though the trade in arms continues to provide local dictators with weapons they do not need, the ending of the rivalry between superpowers has removed a crucial external support for local strongmen and allows a more natural process of bargaining and contestation to determine political development.

Only in extreme cases, therefore, will outside powers get involved in shaping the domestic politics of states. The Iraqi invasion of Kuwait provided a useful test case, demonstrating just how flagrantly illegal regional conflict had to be before prompting international action, and suggesting at the same time that involvement is much more likely when crucial economic issues are at issue. The breakdown of order in the former Yugoslavia serves to define another boundary, indicating how much violence can be tolerated so long as the economic and security stakes are relatively low. The West bestirred itself only when the contending forces had achieved a rough military parity and the lines of a possible geopolitical settlement had begun to emerge, neither of which happened until after the worst incidences of "ethnic cleansing" had been carried out and the forcible relocations of local populations had devastated communities across the land.[84] The clear message sent by these events is that there is now a much greater latitude afforded to states that can make a plausible claim to legitimacy.[85]

The retreat of the superpowers produced by the ending of the Cold War can also, of course, rearrange the incentives for peace or war so as to lessen the intensity of local and regional conflicts. The winding down of the Cold War was surely a facilitating factor in the bargaining that led to majority rule in South Africa. Likewise in the Middle East, it appears that the main protagonists have been readier to accept the need for a compromise solution now that the conflict is removed from the agenda of U.S.–Soviet or U.S.–Russian relations. As the Cold War was winding down, the *intifada*, which began in December 1987, effectively demonstrated to Israelis that the Palestinian problem would not go away, despite severe repression, and that Israel's fond hope that a moderate Palestinian leadership would emerge was but a fantasy. The PLO, for its part, came over time to realize that Israel was not going to be defeated militarily, at least not by any Arab state currently in existence, and that with the defeat of Iraq in the Gulf War, it had no credible allies ready to do battle on its behalf. This mutual recognition of what was possible led Yassir Arafat and Yitzak Rabin to begin the process of bargaining over the shape and scope of an eventual Palestinian state, or quasi-state, on the West Bank. Whether the process will succeed, whether it can survive the death through assassination of the figure whose military record lent legitimacy to the effort, remains to be seen. What is not in doubt is that the entire development depended for its success on the ending of the Cold War and the removal of the Soviet Union as a factor in Middle East politics.

Whether the greater autonomy allowed to local elites and states serves the ends of peace and democracy or produces continued strife in any particular case, the net effect is nonetheless a devolution of power whose overall long-term consequence should be an empowerment of local populations. The increased freedom accorded national states and peoples by the ending of the Cold War is and will continue to be counterbalanced, however, by the altered nature of the world economy. What now seems increasingly to constrain the choices and behaviors of states, both in terms of the policies they pursue and also the extent to which they allow citizens a voice in the making of policy, is the market. Growing economic interdependence means, almost by definition, that autarchy cannot succeed; the liberalization of trade and the opening up of domestic markets mean likewise that the judgments of international capital, represented most visibly by the International Monetary Fund and the World Bank, will largely determine the success or failure of national economic policies.[86] Given the preference of bankers for fiscal responsibility and for market mechanisms, states and their rulers have less and less scope for policies that ignore, overrule, or counteract the dictates of the market. The effect is a hollowing out of the meaning of democracy, for if putatively democratic polities cannot prevail over markets, then democracy cannot effectively translate public opinion into control over social and economic questions.[87] On the contrary, powerful economic interests are much better placed to make effective use of the increasingly sophisticated techniques of modern mass communications in order to shape and elicit public opinion. They are abetted in this effort by the supposed atrophy of the organizations of civil society, as citizens in ever-larger numbers come to find that their relationships with one another are tenuous, indirect, and dependent upon mass media over which they have little or no control. To the extent that this is so, the adoption of democratic forms and procedures in the current era might be rather less meaningful than a comparable advance in political democratization might have been at an earlier moment in the development of communications technology and the evolution of civil society.[88]

Political development is thus less constrained by the structure of international relations but more hemmed in by the dictates of the global division of labor. On balance, the external context allows for lots of debate and contention over the borders and identities of states while effectively blocking states, old or new, from choosing a path of development outside the existing system of states or the world market with which it is inextricably intertwined. Contests over the shape of the state thus continue and even intensify as the quasi-imperial blocs that structured the Cold War era are replaced by alliances that are less coherent and that do not serve the interests of one or another hegemonic power. Russia and the United States still wield enormous influence, but the wishes of the two great powers do not prevail as they once did. Instead, states in large measure choose their own forms of political organization and ally with whom they wish. As they do, the world political order becomes more and more dominated by national states and those states typically become more democratic. Two basic trends thus characterize contemporary political development: the formation of ever more national states and steady, if not entirely uniform, progress toward political democracy. The two processes often go together, but not always, and when they come momentarily into conflict it is usually the effort to create a viable national state that takes precedence, and the struggle for democracy that is sacrificed. The dilemma is intrinsic to the very notion of the national state and to the ideology of nationalism that routinely accompanies it. Nationalism, the banner behind which democratic states and more inclusive polities were created in the nineteenth century, appears in the post–Cold War world a far less attractive and less liberal outlook, for it so often serves to justify exclusion, repression, and ethnic or religious antipathy.[89]

The devolution from a world of quasi-imperial blocs of rival states to a world of national states remains nevertheless much of a piece with nineteenth- and early twentieth-century developments and might well be regarded as "the unfinished business of 1918–1921," when the system of states was recast by the roughly simultaneous collapse of the Russian, German, Austro-Hungarian, and Ottoman empires.[90] The business must be tackled in a new context, however, in which it is mixed up, first, with the transition from command to market economies and, second, with another bit of "unfinished business," the establishment of stable national states in lands formerly ruled as European colonies. As Ryszard Kapuscinski has rightly explained, "The twentieth century is not only the century of totalitarianisms and world wars, but also history's greatest epoch of decolonization."[91] The Cold War could not and did not prevent decolonization, but it did profoundly affect the pace of metropolitan disengagement and the terms on which colonial rule was ended. The ending of the Cold War, in turn, has speeded the process of creating independent states by freeing up enormous regions from the quasi-imperial domination of the former Soviet Union and has also brought to a close the era when postcolonial politics was contained within the discourse of the West, or of the East-West conflict, and flowed along channels largely defined by the related choices between capitalism and socialism and between democracy and dictatorship.

Well before the Cold War ended, actual political development in the Third World had begun to overflow the boundaries of that discourse and ceased to be informed by those choices. The change was partly generational. The political leaders who had dominated the early struggles for independence had passed from the scene by the late 1960s and 1970s, and the political assumptions that guided their actions did not command assent from their successors. The effort to throw off colonial rule could perhaps be undertaken only by local elites schooled in the language of the colonizers, for to be successful they needed to ground their critique of imperial domination within the discourse of Western political and economic thought.[92] The task was made much easier by the transformation of Western opinion wrought by the war against fascism, which highlighted the liberal and democratic elements in Western political thought. The increasingly prominent role of the Soviet Union in international affairs helped as well, for in Soviet hands Marxism became a critique of imperialism as much as of capitalism and it presented itself to colonial peoples as a strategy of national liberation. Equally important, socialism seemed to offer a path to modernization that would avoid dependence on the former colonial powers. So whether postcolonial elites chose to position themselves as supporters of capitalism and parliamentarism or to renounce liberalism in favor of socialism, the sources of their ideas remained very much within the Western political tradition, broadly conceived.

The peoples over whom they ruled seldom shared in that tradition, however, and were often relatively impervious to the efforts of their imperial masters to penetrate their worldviews and alter their beliefs and customs. Imperialism surely mattered to those upon whom it was imposed, but its effects were felt first and foremost over questions of political authority, then over economic issues, and only at some remove did it impact local religions, personal behavior, and social mores. The devastating indictments of the psychological consequences of colonial rule elaborated by writers like Frantz Fanon and Albert Memmi and Aimé Césaire and of the violence inflicted on indigenous traditions were effects felt primarily by elites, and their grievances were appropriately communicated to the literate classes in the colonizing states.[93] Ordinary people, by contrast, remained enmeshed in older patterns of belief, customs inherited from the past and allegiances based on connections that were parochial and familial. If nationalism requires an "imagined community," it was not the logical or typical form through which the popular political imagination expressed itself in large parts of the colonial or postcolonial world.[94] The political and social visions articulated initially by postcolonial elites therefore resonated hardly at all with the sentiments of ordinary people. The nationalisms espoused by the leaders of new states meant little to peasants whose loyalties were bounded by local ties of kinship and ethnicity, and the claims of legitimacy uttered by nationalist politicians likewise failed to move subjects who might well belong to thoroughly disenfranchised ethnic groups but whose fates had been coupled with those of their historic enemies by the accidents of colonial map making. Even less plausible were the claims, so common and so insistent in the 1960s and 1970s, of ideologies like Pan-Arabism and other quasi-universal interests and identities evoked by terms like "the Third World" or "the global South."

The failure of such political projects was in retrospect inevitable, for they lacked social roots. Equally inevitable, it seems, was the turn to a politics of local attachments, of ethnicity, of traditional communities of faith, of "blood and belonging" and *ressentiment*.[95] In countries as culturally distinct and geographically dispersed as Serbia, India, Rwanda, and Algeria, the trend of recent politics has led away from rational, secular, and liberal ideologies of hope and inclusion and toward irrational, sacred, and illiberal ideologies of fear and exclusion. There is nonetheless a continuity between these successive and contrasting outlooks such that they might best be regarded as the first and second stages in the evolution of postcolonial political cultures. The move from national or even universal ideologies toward visions more easily grasped by ordinary citizens represents a democratization, perhaps a sort of vernacularization, of political discourse. And at the center of these competing political rhetorics is a focus on the state and the effort to create viable and effective national states. It is a commonplace of contemporary political commentary that national states have less and less control and that, with the global communications revolution, the age of the nation-state has passed, but in a world defined by the crumbling of empires and quasi-imperial hegemonic blocs, the desire to create a state that can offer some modicum of protection in an alien and frequently hostile environment becomes more insistent than ever.[96] As the Israelis have learned to their advantage, and as the

Palestinians, the Catholics of Northern Ireland, the Tamils of Sri Lanka, and the Kurds scattered across three separate states, each dominated by others, have learned to their sorrow, controlling even a small state matters enormously; and it is worth fighting for its creation.[97]

The turn away from secular and universalist outlooks has been, of course, most marked in the Arab countries and dates effectively from the Six-Day War of 1967.[98] The defeat of Gamal Abdul Nasser's Epypt decisively discredited the vaguely socialist and implicitly secular Pan-Arabism to which he and an entire generation of Middle Eastern leaders subscribed.[99] It is unlikely that Nasserism, or its variations elsewhere, ever sunk very deep roots into the consciousness of the Egyptian masses, but it did provide a language for the military officers, state bureaucrats, and urban professionals to articulate a vision of progress and modernity. Even Nasser's critics on the left spoke a similar language. Hence the dialogue between Pan-Arabism and socialism, which between them seem to have exhausted for a time the truly viable alternative paths to the future and kept political debate within an ideological framework that was basically Western, secular, and modernist. After 1967 that framework came apart and opened the way for a discourse dominated by Islam.

The Islamic revival long predates the discrediting of Pan-Arabism, but its political manifestation was delayed by the apparent success of reforming nationalists like Nasser in the early years of independence.[100] But the inability of postcolonial elites to generate economic growth over time or to fashion truly competent states that could effectively deliver services and field armed forces capable, in particular, of confronting Israel, undermined confidence both in the personnel and the vision that inspired them. Increasingly, leaders and led turned instead to Islam. The attractions of Islam were multiple: sociological and political as well as cultural. Ordinary people throughout the Middle East, North Africa, and large parts of Central and South Asia were believers and thus available for mobilization based on appeals to the traditional faith. That tradition, moreover, was extremely vital. Faced with the incursion of Western power and capital into the Middle East, the slow, painful decline of the Ottoman Empire, and the consolidation of European imperial authority in Asia, Islamic scholars undertook periodic revivals aimed at reinvigorating Islamic society and Islam's political fortunes. The effect was an intense intellectual engagement with the West that resulted in the elaboration of a harsh but penetrating critique of Western culture and the articulation of Islamic alternatives to Western models of social and political development. The critiques and counterproposals partook of Islam's historic aspiration

274

toward theocratic rule and orthodoxy and are thus easily categorized as "fundamentalist," but the designation fails signally to convey the creativity with which these deeply conservative thinkers have responded to modernity.

The enduring vitality of Islam has taken institutional form as well. The claims of Islam to a central place in politics and culture have been acknowledged by generations of rulers and the effect has been to blur the distinction between the state and religion wherever Islam has gained predominance. Across the nations of the Middle East, Islamic universities enjoy privileged status and public support; mosques and religious schools abound; Islamic charities work closely with the state; and, of course, Islamic law is often public law. These links between Islam and politics are not new, but they have been supplemented in recent years by sustained and successful efforts further to expand the range of Muslim institutions. The most notable has been undertaken by the Muslim Brothers (or Brotherhood), founded by Hasan al-Banna in the 1930s. The organization based itself on al-Banna's notion of the "comprehensiveness of Islam," in which the construction of mosques, schools, and clinics would provide the framework in which an urban Muslim could live much of his life without reference to the western and secular influences around him."[101] After the Second World War, the Muslim Brotherhood established itself throughout the Middle East, expanding from its original base in Egypt to Syria, Palestine, Jordan, and Sudan, and everywhere the Brotherhood has created dense networks of social and educational organizations that serve simultaneously to spread its philsophy, train political recruits, and provide services to local populations ill served by the institutions of the state. Similar groups have been organized in Algeria and Tunisia and proclaim the same approach to religion and politics. As Rashid al-Gannushi, leader of the Islamic Association of Tunisia, explained, "It is not enough to pray five times a day and fast in order to be worthy of Islam. Islam is activism...it is on the side of the poor and the oppressed."[102] The Muslim Brotherhood was a Sunni movement that does not have a strict counterpart in the Shi'i community, but it was among Shi'a Muslims in Iran after the revolution of 1979 that the most thorough effort to organize all of society on Islamic principles and to apply Shari`a, the Islamic law, to public and private affairs was undertaken.[103]

Augmented by militants who admit no distinction between state and society, the infrastructure of Islam has thus come to rival, and often to surpass, the bureaucratic reach of the state; and to some extent the two have been combined. The merging of state and religion leaves virtually no room for the creation of civil society or of a "public sphere" that is not dominated by faith or controlled by the state.[104] Paradoxically, radical Islamic groups denounce their political opponents, often the rulers of the states in which they are organized, as "unIslamic" and evil, and call for their overthrow and replacement by leaders faithful to Islamic teachings. The very states and leaders so ruthlessly criticized proclaim their adherence to Islam with equal vehemence and order the review of laws and state policies to bring them into conformity with the Shari`a. Islam, in short, literally constitutes the framework of political discourse and in so doing allows very little space for ideas that cannot find some justification within the tradition. Advocates of more secular visions like socialism or liberalism thus lack institutional niches within Islamic polities and remain impotent at best.[105]

The problem, however, is not the rebirth of religious sentiment but, rather, the difficulty of postcolonial states in finding a basis for legitimacy. That dilemma is common not only throughout the Middle East and across North Africa but also in Africa, where it is if anything more intractable.[106] It even affects seemingly more "mature" states such as India. The troubling intensification of communalism and of violent conflict between Muslims and Hindus, for example, stems less from the waxing of religious fervor than from a deepening crisis of the Indian state.[107] The Congress's vision of a secular state standing aloof from religion and from communal antagonisms and guiding national economic development has proved chimerical, and as its purchase on events and popular loyalties has decreased, especially since 1977, so alternative projects for building the state and its economy have arisen and begun to compete with increasing effectiveness. The most serious challenge comes from the Bharatiya Janata Party, which is linked to a broader Hindu brotherhood, the Rashtriya Swayamsevak Sangh (RSS), and which has profited enormously from the agitation over possession and ultimately the destruction of the Babari Masjid, the mosque at Ayodhya built on the site of the temple to the Hindu god Lord Rama.

Militant Hindu nationalism has been less a religious than a political phenomenon, however. The offical Congress ideology of secularism led to state policies that sought to regulate communal conflict by recognizing institutional niches for different faiths and, in particular, conceding the authority of Muslim personal law and maintaining "endowments, mosques and other institutions and aspects of Muslim culture."[108] The policies operated in much the same way as the policy of "reservation," which sought to build in preferences in public employment and education for "Scheduled" and "backward" castes and tribes. The state therefore did not stand above local loyalties but was implicated in maintaining a delicate balance of privileges and preferences. The rise of Hindu nationalism has been premised on the perceived failure of that effort, on the claim that Congress's policy was really a "pseudosecularism" that benefited Muslims and other non-Hindus, and on the promise to create a stronger, more united "Hindu" state. The very usage of the term Hindu is in this context only partly religious, for the word has referred historically both to the wide array of local cults and rituals centered on various Hindu gods and to people "native to India," in contrast to their foreign Muslim and later Christian rulers. "As a concept," one author argues, Hinduism "is India's twin," and its usage has often been contentiously political. [109] What therefore appears from a distance to be a revival of primitive religious antagonisms that threatens to destroy the Indian state proves on closer inspection to be a by-product of the state's desperate lack of legitimacy and a militant, and potentially divisive, strategy for capturing and strengthening the state.

The construction of stable, locally rooted, national states has been less troubled elsewhere, at least since 1980. Prior to that, progress toward democracy had been slow, halting, and frequently reversed; since then, it has been steadier and more widespread. It is easy enough to identify the factors that weakened the hold of democracy and retarded its development during the first quarter century of the Cold War era. The competition of the superpowers produced a logic of intervention, alliance building, and cooptation that placed a low priority on the internal character of regimes and that often impeded the process of building support, bargaining, and striking compromises that democratic politics seems to require. Internally, many Third World countries were distinguished by social structures that entrenched interests hostile to democracy and were dominated by cultures that were equally traditional and resisted democracy and modernity.[110] The most consistent brake upon democracy was a powerful landlord class, *latifundists* in Latin American usage. Landlords have brought to modern politics a historic and cultural antipathy to democracy, to which has been added a compelling economic incentive: their desperate need to keep control of the land and to keep the cost of rural labor low in order to maintain systems of "labor-repressive agriculture" on which their fortunes have long depended. They understood instinctively that democracy would sooner or later produce electoral majorities pledged to advance peasant interests and would lead ultimately to land reform. With almost equal inevitability peasant revolutionaries eschewed the path of political reform and opted for revolutionary mobilization in the countryside, a choice that guaranteed with comparable certainty the imposition of harsh regimes armed with "emergency powers" and weapons provided by the United States. The cycle of resistance to democracy, peasant mobilization, and further repression seemed for a time to constitute a logic from which there was no escape.[111] Escape appeared blocked in part because of the lock that the old rulers maintained on both the state and on civil society. Conservative agrarian elites, and their educated children and clients, have routinely staffed the state administration and the military, especially in Latin America, and from such positions of institutional strength were able to blunt and distort virtually all efforts to introduce political reform. They have also dominated local cultural institutions, including the press, and have had close relations with the Catholic Church, which for long periods abetted their rule and legitimated the brutality required to maintain it.

The undeveloped character of Third World economies weighted local structures toward agriculture and thereby gave landlords rather more political weight than would have been the case in a more modern, industrial society. Nonetheless, the landlords were not alone in resisting democracy. In most of the Third World business elites displayed an almost equal antipathy toward democracy. They, too, sensed that the grant of democratic rights would enfranchise workers eager to organize unions and bent on using their votes to support parties and policies of redistribution. In consequence, authoritarian regimes could routinely count on the support of big business. Predictably enough, workers could be expected routinely to support democracy, although they were not immune to the attractions of populist strongmen like Juan Perón. Rather more contradictory and contingent, and hence of great importance in determining the shifting balance of forces arrayed for and against democracy, has been the stance of the middle classes. Though different strands of political theory predict different behavior on the part of the middle classes, they are most often regarded as supporters, or potential allies, of the movement toward democracy. In the context of underdevelopment, however, the middle classes have reason to fear and oppose democracy. The extreme poverty of workers and peasants ensures that political democracy translates readily into redistributive politics, which, to be successful, must lower the incomes or restrict the perquisites enjoyed by the middle classes. Therefore the middle classes, who in other settings are said to be the breeding ground and source of recruits for the innumerable organizations that make up "civil society," whose existence is considered critical for effective democratic politics, turn away from the uncertainties of democracy. Instead, they rally behind military men and aspiring dictators who promise, as Augusto Pinochet did so effectively in Chile, to protect the middle classes from the predations of the poor and oppressed.[112]

Taken together, the external and internal constraints on democracy combined to make the establishment and maintenance of effective democratic rule difficult and relatively rare in those regions of the world where it had not been achieved by the onset of the Cold War. Nevertheless, since the late 1970s both sets of obstacles have been removed or at least diminished in their ability to block progress toward democracy. Thus even before the Cold War ended, the international community had begun to take questions of human rights a bit more seriously and, within limits, the superpowers had acquiesced to the new emphasis, if only to embarrass rivals whose clients and allies were deemed worse than one's own.[113] The Helsinki Accords, signed in 1975, were surprisingly important in this process: in return for mutual de facto recognition of Soviet and U.S. spheres of influence and for implicit Western acceptance of the "Brezhnev Doctrine," the two sides committed themselves to a broad array of human rights and to a process of regularly monitoring the implementation of such rights.[114] The subsequent onset of the Second Cold War led rather surprisingly to a greater emphasis on human rights, as the United States realized the ideological gains to be reaped from a focus on violations of rights within the Soviet bloc. The accession of Ronald Reagan and his appointment as UN ambassador of Jeanne Kirkpatrick, who crafted the infamous distinction between the merely "authoritarian" regimes allied with the United States and the hopelessly "totalitarian" states linked to the Soviet Union, did lead to a temporary deemphasis on rights, but the process was difficult to reverse, and over the course of the 1980s the Republicans were pushed into reaffirming U.S. support for human rights. In 1986 they had no choice but to sit idly by and watch pro-U.S. dictators fall from power in Haiti and the Philippines;[115] and by the late 1980s, the United States was forced to go along with sanctions against apartheid in South Africa. The decisive ending of the Cold War, followed by the disappearance of one of its protagonists, has further loosened the constraints imposed by the international alliance system upon the progress of democracy.

Internally, economic and cultural developments have likewise removed or lessened the effectiveness of the main obstacles to democracy in many less developed nations. The land question, on which so many democratizing projects have foundered, has perhaps not been solved, but it has become less salient. Agriculture has become less dominated by local landlords, more dominated by multinational agribusiness and by the spread of capitalist farming. Over the same period, peasant rebellions have been effectively suppressed and peasants themselves have moved in large numbers from rural to urban regions. The threat posed by the unmet needs of peasant communities to established interests has thus diminished, even if the extent of need remains enormous. The threat posed by organized labor has also lessened, if only because the worldwide depression of the 1970s and the subsequent slow growth of the 1980s and early 1990s has undermined unions' ability to organize and to bargain collectively. Peasant and worker radicalism has been further weakened, of course, by the discrediting both of socialism and of state-led national industrial development as strategies for economic progress. The decline of popular insurgency has, in turn, removed the incentive for the middle classes to ally with the opponents of democracy. In addition, the continued urbanization that accompanies economic growth and the increasing technical sophistication of modern industry and communications have led to the steady expansion in the size of the middle classes and to the increased predominance of well-educated and highly skilled professionals, with cosmopolitan tastes and cultural predispositions, within the middle classes. The effect has been a consolidation of middle-class urban culture, the spread of consumer culture among both the middle and working classes, and the elaboration and proliferation of the networks of institutions that make up "civil society."

As this more modern or even "postmodern" culture thrives, older cultural traditions are compelled to respond. In Islamic nations, the response has been a reaffirmation and reimposition of orthodoxy and a frantic effort to create a world of social institutions bound up with religious authority. Elsewhere, the traditional cultures have chosen to adapt. The most interesting and politically important case is Catholicism. Since Vatican II, the political and social role of the Catholic Church has evolved significantly. The initial shift was toward modernity and democracy, and it is clear that the withdrawal of church support from authoritarian regimes in southern Europe and in Latin America furthered the cause of democracy.[116] The Catholic Church has also acquitted itself well in Africa, where it refused to compromise with apartheid and has chosen to cast its fate with the opposition to corrupt and undemocratic rule.[117] The spirit of Vatican II inspired many Catholics, clerics in particular, to go still further and to argue that the church had a moral duty to exercise a "preferential option for the poor." The notion became the basis for what came to be known as "liberation theology," a movement that spread widely in Latin America and that placed the church, and its rank-and-file clergy especially, on the side of the poor in their struggles with landlords, capitalists, and dictators. With the accession of John Paul II as pope, the church turned away from liberalism, at least in matters of personal and social morality, and from the radicalism of "liberation theology." But it did not turn fully to the right. Instead, John Paul articulated a vision that was populist in social and economic policy, democratic in its politics, but conservative in doctrine and reactionary in its view of women and the family.[118] The combination might well be regarded as inherently contradictory and the inspiration behind it as opportunistic; but the effect has been to place the church more squarely at the center of ordinary people's lives and in the forefront of efforts to make democracy real.

The dismantling of the structures of international politics and of local interests, traditions, and practices impeding democracy has produced a corresponding turn to democratic politics. By the mid-1990s, democratic regimes prevailed across southern Europe and in much of Latin America. More important, democracy had become the norm against which local politics was assessed and toward which the international community insisted regimes make progress. The tremendous uncertainty that attends both the creation of new national states out of the rubble of the central and East European empires, as people in this vast region take up "the unfinished business of 1918," and the consolidation of effective and locally rooted polities in the postcolonial states, as people in the former colonies take up what might be termed the "unfinished business of 1947–60," makes it distinctly unwise to predict continual triumphs for democracy. Nevertheless, the balance for and against democracy has shifted decisively and made the chances of creating and sustaining democratic polities more likely than ever before.[119]

Whether these democratic polities can cope effectively with the problems they will face is a different matter. The dilemma of all national states in the post–Cold War world is that although their capacities have weakened, the demands placed upon them have in no way diminished. Citizens desperately seek local remedies, or scapegoats, for ills visited upon them from outside, by the world economy especially, but states have typically lost the ability to predict and regulate the economy and have fewer resources to aid its victims. Even in the established democratic nations, therefore, there is an urgency and stridency to political conflict that stems from the indisputable fact that the politics of growth and the rather happy task of allocating the fruits of prosperity have been replaced by a series of zero-sum contests in which there will be losers as well as winners. The transformation guarantees, or at least makes it more likely, that the politics of social inclusion, of state expansion, and of widening citizenship, so central to the construction of stable democratic regimes during the 1950s and 1960s, will be replaced by a politics marked by exclusions, by states shedding social commitments and denying the entitlements that recently seemed inherent in the very concept of citizenship. That will not make the possession of citizenship any less cherished, nor will it dissolve the loyalties vested in national states. As the faltering movement toward the single market in Europe suggests, citizens are unwilling to entrust their fates to political institutions over which they have little or no control.[120] But the states in which citizens do put their trust are increasingly constrained by participation in the international economy and its institutions. In the effort to meet the standards of fiscal rectitude for monetary union, for example, both France and Germany have been forced to begin seriously to cut back on social spending. The irony, then, is that democracy and the national state have come to define the norm in politics even as they have come to mean rather less.[121] The difficulties confronting democratic states do not make the alternatives to democracy or, practically speaking, to democratic capitalism, any more plausible. They do mean, however, that the turn toward political democracy remains incomplete, that alternatives to democracy and to democratic capitalism will continue to attract popular support and to tempt embattled leaders, and that those attractions and temptations will periodically win out. In politics, therefore, there is no "end of history" in sight, but rather continual efforts not only to make effective choices but to determine who will make those choices and by what set of rules they will do so.

# Notes

Introduction   *The Cold War As Structure and History*

1. Although the bulk of "Sovietologists" failed utterly to anticipate the collapse of 1989–1991, there were exceptions. The most important was Zbigniew Brzezinski, whose *The Grand Failure: The Birth and Death of Communism in the Twentieth Century* (New York: Scribner, 1989) went to press in August 1988. A second exception was a group engaged in "scenario planning" at Royal Dutch Shell who in 1984 supposedly envisioned a "greening of Russia." See Daniel Yergin and Thane Gastafson, *Russia 2010 — And What It Means for the World* (New York: Random House, 1993), 10–11. A third and important exception was Francis Fukuyama, whose article "The End of History" appeared in *National Interest* in the summer of 1989, as the regimes in Eastern Europe were entering their terminal crisis. Since Fukuyama's focus was largely on the end of socialism as an idea, its relationship to actual events is necessarily of secondary importance. Indeed, the idea of the "end of history" has had a rather long career, especially in Europe, and first achieved currency on the left rather than the right. For the lineage, see Lutz Niethammer, *Posthistoire: Has History Come to an End?* (London: Verso, 1992; first published in German in 1989). See also Perry Anderson's brilliant and critical review of the discussion in "The Ends of History," in *A Zone of Engagement* (London: Verso, 1992), 279–375. For a penetrating critique of Sovietology articulated even before the recent collapse, see Patrick Cockburn, *Getting Russia Wrong: The End of Kremlinology* (London: Verso, 1989).

2. The historiography of the Cold War is rich and varied, though it is primarily focused upon the origins of the Cold War and is inevitably weighted toward considerations of foreign policy and defense. The so-called revisionists brought to the subject a needed balance and a concern for the economic dimensions of foreign policy and the sense that the Cold War was more of a structure than a mere policy. Their work constitutes therefore an essential precondition for the analysis proposed here. Prior to the ending of the Cold War, however, it was difficult fully to

grasp the systemic nature of the contest and to appreciate its persistence well beyond the years of greatest antagonism. The literature is far too extensive to cite fully, but some recent summaries and assessments might serve as a starting point. See John Lewis Gaddis, "International Relations Theory and the End of the Cold War," *International Security*, XVII (Winter 1992–1993), 5–58; Lynn Eden, "The End of United States Cold War History," *International Security*, XVIII (Summer 1993), 174–207; Bruce Cumings, "'Revising Postrevisionism', or, The Poverty of Theory in Diplomatic History," *Diplomatic History*, XVII (1993), 539–569; Michael Hunt, "The Long Crisis in U.S. Diplomatic History: Coming to Closure," *Diplomatic History*, XVI (1992), 115–140; and Jacob Heilbrunn, "The Revision Thing," *New Republic* (August 15, 1994), 31–39. For the most comprehensive and judicious rendition of the early history of the Cold War, see Melvin Leffler, *A Preponderance of Power: National Security, the Truman Administration and the Cold War* (Stanford: Stanford University Press, 1992); for a review of the Cold War era more generally, see Thomas McCormick, *America's Half-Century: United States Foreign Policy in the Cold War* (Baltimore: Johns Hopkins University Press, 1989). The "systemic" aspect of the Cold War is discussed most explicitly and helpfully in Anders Stephanson, "The United States," in David Reynolds, ed., *The Origins of the Cold War in Europe: International Perspectives* (New Haven: Yale University Press, 1994), 23–52.

3. See Fred Halliday, "The Cold War and its Conclusion: Consequences for International Relations Theory," in Richard Leaver and James Richardson, eds., *Charting the Post–Cold War Order* (Boulder: Westview, 1993), 11–28; and Charles S. Maier, "Empire or Nations? 1918, 1945, 1989...," paper presented to the Center for European Studies, Harvard University, April 1995.

4. Gordon Craig and Alexander George, *Force and Statecraft: Diplomatic Problems of Our Time*, 2nd ed. (New York: Oxford University Press, 1990), 116–133.

5. See Alan Milward, *The European Rescue of the Nation State* (London: Routledge, 1992).

6. Abbott Gleason, *Totalitarianism: The Inner History of the Cold War* (New York: Oxford University Press, 1995), chapter 4 and passim. There is a fitting irony in the fact that Communists, both in the USSR and in Europe, should have derived an enduring political advantage from their association with antifascism. See François Furet, *Le Passé d'Une Illusion: Essai sur l'Idée communiste au XXe siècle* (Paris: Laffont/Calmann-Lévy, 1995). Much the same argument is made, though from a very different perepective, by Eric Hobsbawm, *The Age of Extremes: A History of the World, 1914–1991* (New York: Pantheon, 1994), chapter 5.

7. Andrei Amalrik, *Will the Soviet Union Survive until 1984?* (New York: Harper and Row, 1970), 27–28. A slightly different translation is rendered in Martin Malia, *The Soviet Tragedy: A History of Socialism in Russia, 1917–1991* (New York: Free Press, 1994), 405.

8. See, for example, Daniel Moynihan, *Pandaemonium: Ethnicity in International Relations* (New York: Oxford University Press, 1993); and Zbigniew Brzezinski, *Out of Control: Global Turmoil on the Eve of the Twenty-first Century* (New York: Scribner, 1993).

9. Francis Fukuyama, *The End of History and the Last Man* (New York: Free Press, 1992).

10. Daniel Chirot, "After Socialism, What? The Global Implications of the Revolutions of 1989 in Eastern Europe," *Contention* (Fall 1991), 29–49; and Chirot, *Modern Tyrants: The Power and Presence of Evil in Our Age* (New York: Free Press, 1994), 16–23.

## Chapter 1    *The Legacy of Depression and War*

1. For a broad review of the relationship between material resources and "great-power" status, see Paul Kennedy, *The Rise and Fall of the Great Powers* (New York: Random House, 1988).

2. Jean Lacouture, *De Gaulle: The Rebel, 1890–1944* (New York: Norton, 1990), 559–579.

3. Corelli Barnett, *The Audit of War: The Illusion and Reality of Britain as a Great Nation* (London: Macmillan, 1986).

4. Arno Mayer, *Why Did the Heavens Not Darken?* (New York: Pantheon, 1989).

5. Jonathan Haslam, *The Soviet Union and the Threat from the East, 1933–41* (Pittsburgh: University of Pittsburgh Press, 1992), 132–133, 149–150.

6. On the uniquely inhumane character of the German invasion of the Soviet Union, see Omer Bartov, *Hitler's Army* (New York: Oxford University Press, 1991).

7. See the essays in Susan Linz, ed., *The Impact of World War II on the Soviet Union* (Totowa, N.J.: Rowman and Allanheld, 1985).

8. Harriman, quoted in Walter LaFeber, *America, Russia and the Cold War, 1945–1992*, 7th ed. (New York: McGraw-Hill, 1993), 21.

9. See Daniel Yergin, *Shattered Peace: The Origins of the Cold War and the National Security State* (Boston: Houghton Mifflin, 1978); and Martin Sherwin, *A World Destroyed: Hiroshima and the Origins of the Arms Race* (New York: Vintage, 1987).

10. See Robert Dallek, *The American Style of Foreign Policy: Cultural Politics and Foreign Affairs* (New York: Knopf, 1983), 138–142; LaFeber, *America, Russia and the Cold War*; and Melvyn Leffler, "The American Conception of National Security and the Beginnings of the Cold War, 1945–1948," *American Historical Review*, LXXXIX (April 1984), 346–381.

11. Alan Brinkley, "The New Deal and the Idea of the State," in Steve Fraser and Gary Gerstle, eds., *The Rise and Fall of the New Deal Order* (Princeton: Princeton University Press, 1989), 85–121; and, more generally, Brinkley, *The End of Reform: New Deal Liberalism in Depression and War* (New York: Knopf, 1995).

12. Barry Eichengreen, *Golden Fetters: The Gold Standard and the Great Depression, 1919–1939* (Oxford: Oxford University Press, 1993); and Charles Kindleberger, *The World in Depression, 1929–1939* (Berkeley: University of California Press, 1973).

13. Fred Block, *The Origins of International Economic Disorder: A Study of United States International Monetary Policy from World War II to the Present* (Berkeley: University of California Press, 1977), 29.

14. Cordell Hull, quoted in ibid., 40; and Kathleen Burk, "The Lineaments of Foreign Policy: The United States and a 'New World Order,' 1919–39," *Journal of American Studies*, XXVI, 3 (1992), 387–388.

15. The notion of a "grand area" was formulated under the auspices of the Council of Foreign Relations. On the general trend of "geopolitical" thinking in these years, see G. John Ikenberry, "A World Economy Restored: Expert Consensus and the Anglo-American Postwar Settlement," *International Organization*, XLVI, 1 (Winter 1992), 305–306.

16. *The General Theory of Employment, Interest and Money* (London: Macmillan, 1936). On the evolution of Keynes's thought, particularly in relation to the practical and theoretical objections of the British Treasury, see Peter Clarke, *Before the Keynesian Revolution* (Oxford: Clarendon, 1989).

17. See Keynes's two famous books: *The Economic Consequences of the Peace* (New York: Harcourt, Brace and Howe, 1920), which criticized the Versailles settlement; and *The Economic Consequences of Mr. Churchill* (London: Leonard and Virginia Woolf, 1925), which criticized the British decision to return to gold in 1925.

18. Alvin Hansen, "Stability and Expansion," in P. T. Homan and F. Machlup, eds., *Financing American Prosperity: A Symposium of Economists* (New York: Twentieth Century Fund, 1945), 199, quoted in Ikenberry, "A World Economy Restored," 296.

19. The extent and timing of Keynes's influence in Britain has been much debated. For a review of the discussion, see J. Cronin, *The Politics of State Expansion: War, State and Society in Twentieth-Century Britain* (London: Routledge, 1991). On the reluctance of policy makers elsewhere, see Bradford Lee, "The Miscarriage of Necessity and Invention: Proto-Keynesianism and Democratic States in the 1930s," in Peter Hall, ed., *The Political Power of Economic Ideas: Keynesianism across Nations* (Princeton: Princeton University Press, 1989), 129–170.

20. Margaret Weir, "Ideas and Politics: The Acceptance of Keynesianism in Britain and the United States," in Hall, *Political Power of Economic Ideas*, 55–56. See also Jonathan Hughes, *The Vital Few*, 2nd ed. (New York: Oxford University Press, 1986), on Eccles.

21. Acheson and Clayton quoted in Block, *Origins of International Economic Disorder*, 40–41.

22. On the bargaining with Great Britain, see Ikenberry, "A World Economy Restored." On the realities of postwar politics, see below.

23. Hence the phrase "embedded liberalism" as a description of the postwar settlement. See John G. Ruggie, "International Regimes, Transactions and Change: Embedded Liberalism in the Postwar Economic Order," in Stephen Krasner, ed., *International Regimes* (Ithaca: Cornell University Press, 1983), 195–231. On the long process required to establish such a regime, see Charles Maier, "The Two Postwar Eras and the Conditions for Stability in Twentieth-Century Western Europe," *American Historical Review*, LXXXVI (April 1981), 327–352.

24. See Gerhard Weinberg, *The World at Arms: A Global History of World War II* (Cambridge: Cambridge University Press, 1994), 894–920.

25. The statement is from *An Investigation of Global Policy with the Yamato Race as Nucleus*, a document prepared by the Research Bureau of the Ministry of Health and Welfare in 1943, cited in John Dower, *War without Mercy: Race and Power in the Pacific War* (New York: Pantheon, 1986), 263, and, more generally, 262–290.

26. Quoted in Dower, *War without Mercy*, 277.

27. See, among others, R. F. Holland, *European Decolonization, 1918–1981* (New York: St. Martin's, 1985), chapter 2; Theodore Friend, *The Blue-Eyed Enemy: Japan against the West in Java and Luzon, 1942–1945* (Princeton: Princeton University Press, 1988); Jan Pluvier, *South-East Asia from Colonialism to Independence* (New York: Oxford University Press, 1974); W. Roger Louis, *Imperialism at Bay: The United States and the Decolonization of the British Empire, 1941–1945* (Oxford: Oxford University Press, 1977); and André Nouschi, "France, the Empire and Power (1945–1949)," in Josef Becker and Franz Knipping, eds., *Power in Europe? Great Britain, France, Italy and Germany in a Postwar World, 1945–1950* (New York: de Gruyter, 1986), 475–484.

28. E. Roosevelt, *As He Saw It* (New York, 1946), 115, quoted in John Young, *France, the Cold War and the Western Alliance, 1944–49* (New York: St. Martin's, 1990), 4.

29. Norman Naimark, "Revolution and Counterrevolution in Eastern Europe," in Gary Marks and Christiane Lemke, eds., *The Crisis of Socialism in Europe* (Durham: Duke University Press, 1992), 61–83; Czeslaw Milosz, *The Seizure of Power* (New York: Farrar, Straus and Giroux, 1982); Gale Stokes, "The Social Origins of East European Politics," *East European Politics and Societies*, 3 (Spring, 1989), 30–74; and Jan Gross, "Social Consequences of War: Preliminaries to the Study of the Imposition of Communist Regimes in East Central Europe," ibid., 198–214. For a comparative view, see Gregory Luebbert, *Liberalism, Fascism or Social Democracy: Social Classes and the Political Origins of Regimes in Interwar Europe* (New York: Oxford University Press, 1991); and John Stephens, "Democratic Transition and Breakdown in Europe, 1870–1939: A Test of the Moore Thesis," *American Journal of Sociology*, XCIV, 5 (March 1989), 1019–1077.

30. See Lacouture, *De Gaulle*.The French did make a modest military contribution during 1944–1945 and managed to secure for themselves a share in the occupation of Germany.

31. See Jean-Pierre Rioux, *The Fourth Republic, 1944–1958* (Cambridge: Cambridge University Press, 1987); Stanley Hoffmann, "The Effects of World War II on French Society and Politics," *French Historical Studies*, II, 1 (Spring 1961), 28–63; John Young, *France, the Cold War and the Western Alliance*; and Irwin Wall, *The United States and the Making of Postwar France, 1945–1954* (Cambridge: Cambridge University Press, 1991).

32. John L. Harper, *America and the Reconstruction of Italy, 1945–1948* (Cambridge: Cambridge University Press, 1986); and Gianfranco Pasquino, "The Demise of the First Fascist Regime and Italy's Transition to Democracy, 1943–1948," in Guillermo O'Donnell, Philippe Schmitter, and Laurence Whitehead, eds., *Transitions from Authoritarian Rule: Prospects for Democracy* (Baltimore: Johns Hopkins University Press, 1986), Part I: "Southern Europe," 45–70.

33. Peter Weiler, *Ernest Bevin* (Manchester: Manchester University Press, 1993), chapter 4.

34. The report itself dealt only with social security, but in so doing it elaborated a broader vision of state responsibility for welfare, health, and employment. See

William Beveridge, *Social Insurance and Allied Services* (London: Macmillan, 1942); and, for the broader vision, *Full Employment in a Free Society* (New York: Norton, 1945).

35. Paul Addison, *The Road to 1945: British Politics in the Second World War* (London: Quartet, 1977).

36. John Morton Blum, *V Was for Victory* (New York: Harcourt Brace Jovanovich, 1976); and Barry Karl, *The Uneasy State: The United States, 1915–1945* (Chicago: University of Chicago Press, 1983), 205–223; and Brinkley, *The End of Reform*.

37. David Brody, *Workers in Industrial America* (New York: Oxford University Press, 1980), 112–116.

38. Franklin Roosevelt, "Economic Bill of Rights," excerpted in Walter Laqueur and Barry Rubin, eds., *The Human Rights Reader* (New York: New American Library, 1989), 313–314.

39. On the application of these notions to Japan, see Michael Schaller, *The American Occupation of Japan: The Origins of the Cold War in Asia* (New York: Oxford University Press, 1985), 30–51.

40. John Gimble, *The American Occupation of Germany: Politics and the Military, 1945–1949* (Stanford: Stanford University Press, 1968).

41. See Gregory W. Sandford, *From Hitler to Ulbricht: The Communist Reconstruction of East Germany* (Princeton: Princeton University Press, 1983); and Norman Naimark, *The Russians in Germany: A History of the Soviet Zone of Occupation, 1945–1949* (Cambridge: Harvard University Press, 1995).

42. Douglas MacArthur, *Reminiscences* (New York, 1964), quoted in Schaller, *The American Occupation of Japan*, 20.

43. On the politics of history in Germany, see Charles Maier, *The Unmasterable Past: History, Holocaust, and German National Identity* (Cambridge.: Harvard University Press, 1988); Andreas Huyssen, *Twilight Memories: Marking Time in a Culture of Amnesia* (New York: Routledge, 1995); and Ian Buruma, *The Wages of Guilt: Memories of War in Germany and Japan* (New York: Farrar, Straus, and Giroux, 1994).

44. See Schaller, *American Occupation of Japan*; John Dower, "Japan: Legacies of a Lost War," Center for Studies of Social Change, New School for Social Research, Working Paper Series, #66, May 1988; and Carol Gluck, "The Past in the Present," in Andrew Gordon, ed., *Postwar Japan as History* (Berkeley: University of California Press, 1993), 64–95.

## Chapter 2  *Nations, Boundaries, and Cold War Realities*

1. The scholarly understanding of the formation of nations and of the blindnesses inherent in perspectives that take the nation-state for granted has been greatly advanced by the work of, among others, Benedict Anderson, John Breuilly, Ernest Gellner, Anthony Giddens, Liah Greenfeld, Eric Hobsbawm, Miroslav Hroch, Tom Nairn, Charles Tilly, and Immanuel Wallerstein. See, in particular, Anderson, *Imagined Communities: Reflections on the Origins and Spread of Nationalism,* rev. ed. (London: Verso, 1991); Breuilly, *Nationalism and the State* (New York: St. Martin's, 1982); Gellner, *Nations and Nationalism* (Ithaca: Cornell University Press, 1983), and *Culture, Identity and Politics* (Cambridge:

Cambridge University Press, 1987); Giddens, *A Contemporary Critique of Historical Materialism*, vol. II, *The Nation-State and Violence* (Berkeley: University of California Press, 1987); Greenfeld, *Nationalism: Five Roads to Modernity* (Cambridge: Harvard University Press, 1992); Hobsbawm, *Nations and Nationalism since 1870*, 2nd ed. (Cambridge: Cambridge University Press, 1993); Hroch, "From National Movements to Fully-formed Nations: The Nation-Building Process in Europe," *New Left Review*, no. 198 (March/April 1993), 3–20; Tom Nairn, "Breakwaters of 2000: From Ethnic to Civic Nationalism," *New Left Review*, no. 214 (November/December 1995), 91–103; Tilly, *Big Structures, Large Processes and Huge Comparisons* (New York: Russell Sage Foundation, 1983); and Wallerstein, "The Concept of National Development, 1917–1989," *American Behavioral Scientist*, XXXV, 4/5 (1992), 517–529.

2. The most comprehensive account, written from an American perspective, is Melvyn Leffler, *A Preponderance of Power: National Security, the Truman Administration, and the Cold War* (Stanford: Stanford University Press, 1992).

3. Michael Hogan, *The Marshall Plan: America, Britain and the Reconstruction of Western Europe, 1947–1952* (Cambridge: Cambridge University Press, 1987), 414ff.

4. Alan Milward, *The Reconstruction of Western Europe, 1945–51* (London: Methuen, 1984), 15. Milward is himself skeptical about the economic crisis of 1947, but the evidence he presents seems more than sufficient to explain the contemporary perception of crisis.

5. Marshall, cited in Walter LaFeber, *America, Russia and the Cold War, 1945–92*, 7th ed. (New York: McGraw-Hill, 1993), 52.

6. The senator was Arthur Vandenberg, quoted ibid., 56.

7. Charles S. Maier, "Issue Then Is Germany and with It Future of Europe," in Maier and G. Bischof, eds., *The Marshall Plan and Germany* (Oxford: Berg, 1991), 17–26.

8. J. Bradford De Long and Barry Eichengreen, "The Marshall Plan: History's Most Successful Structural Adjustment Program," in R. Dornbusch et al., eds., *Postwar Economic Reconstruction and Lessons for the East Today* (Cambridge: MIT Press, 1993), 189–230.

9. Truman and Stimson quoted in LaFeber, *America, Russia and the Cold War*, 26–27. Whether the United States was justified in dropping the atomic bomb continues to generate debate. See Gar Alperovitz, *The Decision to Use the Atomic Bomb: And the Architecture of an American Myth* (New York: Knopf, 1995); and Ronald Takaki, *Hiroshima: Why America Dropped the Atomic Bomb* (Boston: Little, Brown, 1995).

10. Marshal Vershinin in 1949, quoted in Lawrence Freedman, *The Evolution of Nuclear Strategy*, 2nd ed. (New York: St. Martin's, 1989), 61.

11. Bruce Cumings, *The Origins of the Korean War* (Princeton: Princeton University Press, 1981); William Stueck, *The Korean War: An International History* (Princeton: Princeton University Press, 1995). On the question of who actually provoked the war, see Kathryn Weathersby, "Korea, 1949–50: To Attack, or Not to Attack? Stalin, Kim Il Sung and the Prelude to War," *Cold War International History Project Bulletin*, #5 (Spring 1995).

12. Many such "liberals," though not all, would move to the right during the 1950s and 1960s and become founding members of "neoconservatism." See John Ehrman, *The Rise of Neoconservatism: Intellectuals and Foreign Affairs, 1945–1994* (New Haven: Yale University Press, 1994).

13. LaFeber, *America, Russia and the Cold War*, 96–98; Freedman, *Evolution of Nuclear Strategy*, 69–71; Ernest May, ed., *American Cold War Strategy: Interpreting NSC 68* (Boston: Bedford Books, 1995).

14. Sheila Fitzpatrick, "Postwar Soviet Society: The 'Return to Normalcy,' 1945–1953," 129–157, and Jerry Hough, "Debates about the Postwar World," 253–282, in Susan Linz, ed., *The Impact of World War II on the Soviet Union* (Totowa, N.J.: Rowman and Allenheld, 1985).

15. Tito, December 1942, quoted in Ivo Banac, "Political Change and National Diversity," in S. Graubard, ed., *Eastern Europe...Central Europe...Europe* (Boulder: Westview, 1991), 154. This collection was originally published as the January 1990 issue of *Daedalus*.

16. Beneš and Jaszi were both writing in the April 1946 issue of *Foreign Affairs*, and are quoted in Norman Naimark, "Revolution and Counterrevolution in Eastern Europe," in Gary Marks and Christiane Lemke, eds., *The Crisis of Socialism in Europe* (Durham: Duke University Press, 1992), 66–67.

17. See Joseph Rothschild, *Return to Diversity: A Political History of East Central Europe since World War II*, 2nd ed. (New York: Oxford University Press, 1993); and Zbigniew Brzezinski, *The Soviet Bloc: Unity and Conflict*, rev. ed. (Cambridge: Harvard University Press, 1967).

18. William Roger Louis and Ronald Robinson, "Empire Preserv'd: How the Americans Put Anti-communism before Anti-imperialism," *Times Literary Supplement*, May 5, 1995, 14–16.

19. Warren Susman, *Culture As History: The Transformation of American Society in the Twentieth Century* (New York: Pantheon, 1984), 150–210.

20. See, for example, Elaine Tyler May, "Cold War—Warm Hearth: Politics and the Family in Postwar America," in Steve Fraser and Gary Gerstle, eds., *The Rise and Fall of the New Deal Order, 1930–1980* (Princeton: Princeton University Press, 1989), 153–181; and, more generally, Stephen Whitfield, *The Culture of the Cold War* (Baltimore: Johns Hopkins University Press, 1991). The Cold War also affected legal discourse and civil rights. See, for example, Mary Dudziak, "Desegregation As a Cold War Imperative," *Stanford Law Review*, 41 (1988).

21. Abbott Gleason, *Totalitarianism: The Inner History of the Cold War* (New York: Oxford University Press, 1995), chapter 4; and David McCullough, *Truman* (New York: Simon and Schuster, 1992).

22. Alan Wolfe, *America's Impasse: The Rise and Fall of the Politics of Growth* (New York: Pantheon, 1981), 19–23.

23. Margaret Weir, *Politics and Jobs: The Boundaries of Employment Policy in the United States* (Princeton: Princeton University Press, 1992), chapter 2; and R. Alton Lee, *Truman and Taft-Hartley: A Question of Mandate* (Lexington: University of Kentucky Press, 1966).

24. Robert Zieger, *American Workers, American Unions, 1920–1985* (Baltimore: Johns Hopkins University Press, 1986), 114–119.

25. Bert Cochran, *Labor and Communism: The Conflict That Shaped American*

*Unions* (Princeton: Princeton University Press, 1977), 248–331.

26. See Nelson Lichtenstein, "From Corporatism to Collective Bargaining: Organized Labor and the Eclipse of Social Democracy in the Postwar Era," in Fraser and Gerstle, *Rise and Fall of the New Deal Order* , 122–152; and Lichtenstein, *The Most Dangerous Man in Detroit: Walter Reuther and the Fate of American Labor* (New York: Basic Books, 1995).

27. Robert Collins, *The Business Response to Keynes, 1929–1964* (New York: Columbia University Press, 1981), Part III; Howell John Harris, *The Right to Manage: Industrial Relations Policies of American Business in the 1940s* (Madison: University of Wisconsin Press, 1982); and Weir, *Politics and Jobs*, 47–53.

28. Richard Du Boff, *Accumulation and Power: An Economic History of the United States* (Armonk, N.Y.: M. E. Sharpe, 1989), 98–99.

29. See Ernest May, "The U.S. Government, A Legacy of the Cold War," in Michael J. Hogan, ed., *The End of the Cold War: Its Meaning and Implications* (Cambridge: Cambridge University Press, 1992), 217–228; and Michael Sherry, *In the Shadow of War: The United States since the 1930s* (New Haven: Yale University Press, 1995), 140–143.

30. Josef Becker and Franz Knippings, eds., *Power in Europe? Great Britain, France, Italy and Germany in a Postwar World, 1945–1950* (New York: de Gruyter, 1986).

31. On the origins, extent, and limits of Labour's postwar reforms, see J. Cronin, *The Politics of State Expansion: War, State and Society in Twentieth-Century Britain* (London: Routledge, 1991).

32. Peter Weiler, *Ernest Bevin* (Manchester: Manchester University Press, 1993).

33. Richard Vinen, *Bourgeois Politics in France, 1945–1951* (Cambridge: Cambridge University Press, 1995).

34. See John Gimbel, *The American Occupation of Germany: Politics and the Military, 1945–1949* (Stanford: Stanford University Press, 1968); Michael Ermarth, ed., *America and the Shaping of German Society, 1945–1955* (Oxford: Berg, 1993); Mary Fulbrook, "Nation, State and Political Culture in Divided Germany, 1945–90," in John Breuilly, ed., *The State of Germany: The National Idea in the Making, Unmaking and Remaking of a Modern Nation-State* (London: Longman, 1992), 177–200; and Michael Schaller, *The American Occupation of Japan: The Origins of the Cold War in Asia* (New York: Oxford University Press, 1985).

35. Norman Naimark, *The Russians in Germany: A History of the Soviet Zone of Occupation, 1945–1949* (Cambridge: Harvard University Press, 1995).

## Chapter 3    *American Power, American Dreams*

1. Herman van der Wee, *Prosperity and Upheaval: The World Economy, 1945–1980* (Berkeley: University of California Press, 1986), 62–63.

2. Robert Payne, quoted in David Halberstam, *The Fifties* (New York: Villard, 1993), 116.

3. Anthony Carew, *Labour and the Marshall Plan: The Politics of Productivity and the Marketing of Managerial Science* (Manchester: Manchester University Press, 1987); Charles Maier, "The Politics of Productivity: Foundations of American International Economic Policy after World War II," in *In Search of Stability:*

*Explorations in Historical Political Economy* (Cambridge: Cambridge University Press, 1987), 121–152.

4. Michael Bernstein, "Why the Great Depression Was Great: Toward a New Understanding of the Interwar Economic Crisis in the United States," in Steve Fraser and Gary Gerstle, eds., *The Rise and Fall of the New Deal Order, 1930–1980* (Princeton: Princeton University Press, 1989), 32–54; and Bernstein, *The Great Depression: Delayed Recovery and Economic Change in America, 1929–1939* (Cambridge: Cambridge University Press, 1987).

5. Calculated from data presented in Table 39.2 in Stanley Lebergott, *The Americans: An Economic Record* (New York: Norton, 1984), 498.

6. Nelson Lichtenstein, "From Corporatism to Collective Bargaining: Organized Labor and the Eclipse of Social Democracy in the Postwar Era," in Fraser and Gerstle, *Rise and Fall of the New Deal Order*, 140–142.

7. The argument is especially well put in Kim Moody, *An Injury to All: The Decline of American Unionism* (London: Verso, 1988), chaps. 2–3.

8. See Bernstein, "Why the Great Depression Was Great," 32–54.

9. Michael Piore and Charles Sabel, *The Second Industrial Divide: Possibilities for Prosperity* (New York: Basic Books, 1984).

10. The phenomenon was not confined to the United States. See Philip Armstrong, Andrew Glyn, and John Harrison, *Capitalism since 1945* (Oxford: Basil Blackwell, 1991), esp. 122–124; and, for a more theoretical formulation, Samuel Bowles and Robert Boyer, "A Wage-Led Employment Regime: Income Distribution, Labour Discipline, and Aggregate Demand in Welfare Capitalism," in Stephen Marglin and Juliet Schor, eds., *The Golden Age of Capitalism: Reinterpreting the Postwar Experience* (Oxford: Clarendon, 1990), 187–217.

11. Richard Du Boff, *Accumulation and Power: An Economic History of the United States* (Armonk, N.Y.: M. E. Sharpe, 1989), 104, 111.

12. David Gordon, Richard Edwards, and Michael Reich, *Segmented Work, Divided Workers: The Historical Transformation of Labor in the United States* (Cambridge: Cambridge University Press, 1982).

13. Mike Davis, *Prisoners of the American Dream* (London: Verso, 1986); and Robert Zieger, *American Workers, American Unions, 1920–1985* (Baltimore: Johns Hopkins University Press, 1986), chapter 2.

14. Nicholas Lemann, *The Promised Land: The Great Black Migration and How It Changed America* (New York: Knopf, 1991).

15. Gerald Epstein and Juliet Schor, "Macropolicy in the Rise and Fall of the Golden Age," in Marglin and Schor, *Golden Age of Capitalism*, 126–152.

16. Cited in Du Boff, *Accumulation and Power*, 100. The section relies heavily on Du Boff's useful analysis, esp. 93–107.

17. Despite the enormous need for relief and support, transfer payments remained at less than 4.5 percent of GNP in the 1930s. During the 1950s, they averaged a bit over 6 percent. See ibid., 98.

18. Kenneth Jackson, *Crabgrass Frontier: The Suburbanization of the United States* (New York: Oxford University Press, 1985), 195–218. It was surely no accident that so much of the effort of government was directed to providing benefits for veterans. For earlier but important precedents, see Theda Skocpol, *Protecting Soldiers and Mothers* (Cambridge: Harvard University Press, 1992).

19. Jackson Lears, "A Matter of Taste: Corporate Cultural Hegemony in a Mass-Consumption Society," in Lary May, ed., *Recasting America: Culture and Politics in the Age of Cold War* (Chicago: University of Chicago Press, 1989), 38–57.

20. Steven Mintz and Susan Kellogg, *Domestic Revolutions: A Social History of American Family Life* (New York: Free Press, 1988), 184.

21. The standard account is Jean-Claude Chesnais, *The Demographic Transition: Stages, Patterns and Economic Implications* (Oxford: Clarendon, 1993).

22. Walter Nugent, *Structures of American Social History* (Bloomington: Indiana University Press, 1981), 126–135.

23. Ibid., 127; and Mintz and Kellogg, *Domestic Revolutions*, 178–179.

24. Amram Scheinfeld, "Motherhood's Back in Style," *Ladies Home Journal* (September 1944), cited in Elaine Tyler May, *Homeward Bound: American Families in the Cold War Era* (New York: Basic Books, 1988), 159.

25. Quoted in Mintz and Kellogg, *Domestic Revolutions*, 178–180.

26. For Stevenson's intervention, see ibid., 181; on Hoover and Nixon, see May, *Homeward Bound*, 137, 162–164.

27. The argument here is strongly influenced by Richard Easterlin's *Birth and Fortune: The Impact of Numbers on Personal Welfare*, 2nd ed. (Chicago: University of Chicago Press, 1987), esp. 37–60.

28. May, *Homeward Bound*, 140–141.

29. Mintz and Kellogg, *Domestic Revolutions*, 181.

30. Hard, unambiguous data on class differences in fertility in the United States are scarce. Easterlin does cite one important study—Glen Elder, *Children of the Great Depression* (Chicago: University of Chicago Press, 1974)—and offers surrogates that seem to measure the phenomenon at least indirectly. See Easterlin, *Birth and Fortune*, 39–53.

31. On Keynesian economics as political theory, see the essays in Peter Hall, ed., *The Political Power of Economic Ideas* (Princeton: Princeton University Press, 1989).

32. Gabriel Almond and Sidney Verba, *The Civic Culture: Political Attitudes and Democracy in Five Nations* (Boston: Little, Brown, 1965).

33. Martin Wattenberg, *The Decline of American Political Parties, 1952–1980* (Cambridge: Harvard University Press, 1984), 23–24; Walter Dean Burnham, "American Politics in the 1970's: Beyond Party?" in Burnham and W. N. Chambers, eds., *The American Party Systems*, 2nd ed. (New York: Oxford University Press, 1975), 308–357; and Angus Campbell et al., *The American Voter* (New York: Wiley, 1960).

34. On Eisenhower, see Stephen Ambrose, *Eisenhower*, 2 vols. (New York: Simon and Schuster, 1983–1984).

35. See Michael Hogan, "Partisan Politics and the End of the Cold War," in Hogan, ed., *The End of the Cold War: Its Meaning and Implications* (Cambridge: Cambridge University Press, 1992), 232–237. Hogan sees the turn away from isolationism as rooted less in the exigencies of the Cold War and more in the gradual, structural transformation of industrial structure. The two factors may well have interacted, however, and both may have been required for the turn to have been executed so smoothly and thoroughly.

36. On Eisenhower, see Ambrose, *Eisenhower*.

37. Richard Chase, *The Democratic Vista* (1958), 145, quoted in Alan Matusow, *The Unraveling of America: A History of Liberalism in the 1960s* (New York: Harper and Row, 1984), 8.

38. Aspects of this birth are well rehearsed in Gary Gerstle, "The Protean Character of American Liberalism," *American Historical Review*, IC, 4 (October 1994), 1043–1073.

39. See Arthur M. Schlesinger, Jr., *The Vital Center: The Politics of Freedom* (Boston: Houghton Mifflin, 1949), for a highly articulate statement that attempts to make the disenchanted, worldly-wise, and cynical stance of liberalism into a sign of intellectual maturity and political virtue. For a useful analysis, see Richard Gid Powers, *Not Without Honor: The History of American Anticommunism* (New York: Free Press, 1995), 199–213.

40. Cited in Zieger, *American Workers, American Unions*, 184.

41. Cited in Moody, *Injury to All*, 81.

42. The links between Martin Luther King, Jr., and the Kennedys were especially important, if occasionally strained. See David Garrow, *Bearing the Cross: Martin Luther King, Jr., and the Southern Christian Leadership Conference* (New York: Random House, 1992).

43. Thomas Edsall has recently asked whether the identification was wise for the Democrats. The implication of this argument is that it was, but the question is undoubtedly worth asking. See Edsall, with Mary Edsall, *Chain Reaction: The Impact of Race, Rights and Taxes on American Politics* (New York: Norton, 1991).

44. President's Commission on the Status of Women, *American Women* (Washington, D.C.: Government Printing Office, 1963).

45. Ethel Klein, *Gender Politics: From Consciousness to Mass Politics* (Cambridge: Harvard University Press, 1984), 17–23; William Chafe, *The Paradox of Change: American Women in the 20th Century* (New York: Oxford University Press, 1991), 195–202; and Cynthia Harrison, *On Account of Sex: The Politics of Women's Issues, 1945–1968* (Berkeley: University of California Press, 1988).

Chapter 4    *Economic Miracles, East and West*

1. Sidney Verba, "Germany: The Remaking of a Political Culture," in Lucian Pye and Verba, eds., *Political Culture and Political Development* (Princeton: Princeton University Press, 1965), 170.

2. See Richard Rosecrance, *The Rise of the Trading States* (New York: Basic Books, 1986); and Thomas Berger, "Norms, Identity and National Security in Germany and Japan," in Peter Katzenstein, ed., *Culture and Security: New Directions in World Politics* (New York: Columbia University Press, forthcoming, 1996).

3. The executive was apparently Friedrich von Bülow, nephew of the Wilhelmine chancellor. Deutscher's article appeared in *Nova Polska* in January 1946 and is quoted in Alan Kramer, *The West German Economy, 1945–1955* (New York: Berg, 1991), 158–159.

4. Quoted in Wolf Gruner, "Germany in Europe: The German Question As Burden and As Opportunity," in John Breuilly, ed., *The State of Germany: The*

*National Idea in the Making, Unmaking and Remaking of a Modern Nation-State* (London: Longman, 1992), 202.

5. Timothy Garton Ash, *In Europe's Name: Germany and the Divided Continent* (New York: Random House, 1993). See also Alan Milward, *The European Rescue of the Nation-State* (London: Routledge, 1992).

6. See Karel van Wolferen, *The Enigma of Japanese Power: People and Politics in a Stateless Nation* (New York: Knopf, 1989), 41; and John Dower, "Peace and Democracy in Two Systems: External Policy and Internal Conflict," in Andrew Gordon, ed., *Postwar Japan As History* (Berkeley: University of California Press, 1993), 7–14.

7. Michael Hogan, "European Integration and German Reintegration: Marshall Planners and the Search for Recovery and Security in Western Europe," in Charles Maier, ed., *The Marshall Plan and Germany* (New York: Berg, 1991), 115–170.

8. Both documents are cited in Michael Schaller, *The American Occupation of Japan: The Origins of the Cold War in Asia* (New York: Oxford University Press, 1985), 137, 143.

9. Alan Milward, "The Marshall Plan and German Foreign Trade," in Maier, *Marshall Plan and Germany*, 452–487.

10. The question of the legacy bequeathed by past relations between state and society has been confronted most directly in the German case. See Simon Reich, *The Fruits of Fascism: Postwar Prosperity in Historical Perspective* (Ithaca: Cornell University Press, 1990); and, more generally, Mancur Olson, *The Rise and Decline of Nations: Stagflation and Social Rigidities* (New Haven: Yale University Press, 1982).

11. Erhard (1953), cited in Garton Ash, *In Europe's Name*, 244.

12. See Herbert Giersch, Karl-Heinz Paqué, and Holger Schmieding, *The Fading Miracle: Four Decades of Market Economy in Germany* (Cambridge: Cambridge University Press, 1992), 26–36; Volker Berghahn, "Ideas into Politics: The Case of Ludwig Erhard," in Roger Bullen, Hartmut Pogge von Strandmann, and Antony Polonsky, eds., *Ideas into Politics: Aspects of European History, 1880–1950* (Totowa, N.J.: Rowman and Littlefield, 1984), 178–192; Ludwig Erhard, *Prosperity through Competition* (New York: Praeger, 1958); and Anthony Nicholls, *Freedom with Responsibility: The Social Market Economy in Germany, 1918–1963* (Oxford: Clarendon, 1994).

13. Röpke, "Guiding Principles of the Liberal Programme," quoted in Christopher Allen, "The Underdevelopment of Keynesianism in the Federal Republic of Germany," in Peter Hall, ed., *The Political Power of Economic Ideas: Keynesianism across Nations* (Princeton: Princeton University Press, 1989), 281.

14. Jens Alber, "Germany," in Peter Flora, ed., *Growth to Limits: The Western European Welfare States since World War II* (New York: de Gruyter, 1988), vol. II, *Germany, United Kingdom, Ireland, Italy*, 15–22.

15. Graham Hallett, "West Germany," in Andrew Graham with Anthony Seldon, eds., *Government and Economies in the Postwar World: Economic Policies and Comparative Performance, 1945–85* (London: Routledge, 1990), 89.

16. Reich, *Fruits of Fascism*, asserts that this was particularly the case in the car industry, where the Finance Ministry ensured that Volkswagen would get the financing it needed throughout the postwar era.

17. Giersch et al., *Fading Miracle*, 79–80.

18. Kramer, *West German Economy*, 171.
19. Hanes's views were expressed in a January 21, 1950, reply to a German memorandum of December 15, 1949. Cited in Thomas Schwartz, "European Integration and the 'Special Relationship': Implementing the Marshall Plan in the Federal Republic," in Maier, *Marshall Plan and Germany*, 196–198.
20. Schwartz, "European Integration and the 'Special Relationship,'" 202–211; Kramer, *West German Economy*, 167, 170.
21. Werner Abelshauser, "The First Post-Liberal Nation: Stages in the Development of Modern Corporatism in Germany," *European History Quarterly*, XIV (1984), 285–318.
22. Peter Hall, *Governing the Economy: The Politics of State Intervention in Britain and France* (New York: Oxford University Press, 1986), 236–239.
23. Andrei Markovits and Christopher Allen, "Trade Unions and the Economic Crisis: The West German Case," in Peter Gourevitch et al., eds., *Unions and Economic Crisis: Britain, West Germany, Sweden* (London: Allen and Unwin, 1984), 107.
24. Kramer, *West German Economy*, Table 5.6.
25. The share of the labor force engaged in the primary sector (agriculture and mining) thus fell from 25 percent to 9 percent between 1950 and 1970. See Karl Hardach, *The Political Economy of Germany in the Twentieth Century* (Berkeley: University of California Press, 1980), 218. In addition, roughly 3.6 million refugees—many highly skilled and almost all extremely motivated—moved from the German Democratic Republic to West Germany between 1950 and the building of the Berlin Wall in 1961. See Kramer, *West German Economy*, 213.
26. Giersch et al., *Fading Miracle*, 63.
27. Hardach, *Political Economy of Germany*, 228; Hans-Joachim Braun, *The German Economy in the Twentieth Century* (London: Routledge, 1990), 237–254.
28. The importance of labor supply in postwar growth was first and best argued by Charles Kindleberger, *Europe's Postwar Growth: The Role of Labour Supply* (Oxford: Oxford University Press, 1967). Increasingly, the need for labor was met by immigration for southern and eastern Europe and the former colonies. On impact see Stephen Castles and Godula Kosack, *Immigrant Workers and Class Structure in Western Europe*, 2nd ed. (Oxford: Oxford University Press, 1985). On capacity utilization, see Kramer, *West German Economy*, 168–169. On the Nazi legacy, also see ibid., 17–24.
29. The different arguments are well summarized in the various contributions to R. Dornbusch et al., eds., *Postwar Economic Reconstruction and Lessons for the East Today* (Cambridge: MIT Press, 1993). See, in particular, the essays by Giersch et al., "Openness, Wage Restraint and Macroeconomic Stability: West Germany's Road to Prosperity 1948–1959," which largely adopts the "ordoliberal" position; J. Bradford De Long and Barry Eichengreen, "The Marshall Plan: History's Most Successful Adjustment Program," which argues that the key to German growth was the implicit social contract, which allowed Germans to avoid divisive distributional conflicts and to keep labor costs low, and which was made possible by Marshall Plan aid; and Holger Wolf, "The Lucky Miracle: Germany, 1945–1951," which takes a more agnostic position. Erhard's argument about Korea is made in *Prosperity through Competition*, chapter 3.

30. Edwin O. Reischauer, *Japan: Past and Present* (New York: Knopf, 1964), 233.
31. R. P. Dore, *Land Reform in Japan* (Berkeley: University of California Press, 1959).
32. T. A. Bisson, *Zaibatsu Dissolution in Japan* (Berkeley: University of California Press, 1954).
33. Kyoko Sheridan, *Governing the Japanese Economy* (Cambridge: Polity Press, 1993), 121–136; Janet Hunter, *The Emergence of Modern Japan* (London: Longman, 1989), 99–100, 257–260; and Koichi Hamada and Munehisa Kasuya, "The Reconstruction and Stabilization of the Postwar Japanese Economy: Possible Lessons for Eastern Europe?" in Dornbusch et al., *Postwar Economic Reconstruction*, 158–160.
34. For the positive evaluation of the impact of the reforms, see Hamada and Kasuya, "Reconstruction and Stabilization"; for the alternative, see Wolferen, *Enigma of Japanese Power*, chapters 14, 15.
35. Sheridan, *Governing the Japanese Economy*, 126–131. For Tsuru's own view of Japan's postwar economic record, see Shigeto Tsuru, *Japan's Capitalism* (Cambridge: Cambridge University Press, 1992).
36. Ian Nish, "Japan," in Graham and Seldon, *Government and Economies*, 254–256.
37. Chalmers Johnson, *MITI and the Japanese Miracle: The Growth of Industrial Policy, 1925–1975* (Stanford: Stanford University Press, 1982).
38. Wolferen, *Enigma of Japanese Power*, 390–391.
39. John Zysman, *Governments, Markets, and Growth* (Ithaca: Cornell University Press, 1983), chapter 5.
40. Eleanor Hadley, "The Diffusion of Keynesian Ideas in Japan," in Hall, *Political Power of Economic Ideas*, 296–299.
41. Quoted in Schaller, *American Occupation of Japan*, 289.
42. Philip Armstrong, Andrew Glyn, and John Harrison, *Capitalism since 1945* (Oxford: Basil Blackwell, 1991), 129.
43. Sheridan, *Governing the Japanese Economy*, 139.
44. Armstrong et al., *Capitalism since 1945*, 132–135.
45. Sheridan, *Governing the Japanese Economy*, 154.
46. As De Long and Eichengreen argue in "The Marshall Plan," the real contribution of the Marshall Plan to economic growth was its contribution to the "negotiation of the social contract" that allowed for the creation and maintenance of "relatively inflation-resistant labor markets." (214, 219).
47. See Lawrence Beer, "Japan (1947): Forty Years of the Post-War Constitution," in Vernan Bogdanor, ed., *Constitutions in Democratic Politics* (Aldershot: Gower, 1988), 173–205; and Kyoko Inoue, *MacArthur's Japanese Constitution: A Linguistic and Cultural Study of Its Making* (Chicago: University of Chicago Press, 1991).
48. See Francis Fukuyama, *The End of History and the Last Man* (New York: Free Press, 1992), 240–241, on the formal character of Japanese democracy.
49. Beer, "Japan," 177.
50. Robert Scalapino and Junnosuke Masumi, *Parties and Politics in Contemporary Japan* (Berkeley: University of California Press, 1962), 37–39.
51. Hideo Otake, "Defense Controversies and One-Party Dominance: The Oppo-

sition in Japan and West Germany," in T. J. Pempel, ed., *Uncommon Democracies: The One-Party Dominant Regimes* (Ithaca: Cornell University Press, 1990), 128–161.

52. Wolferen, *Enigma of Japanese Power*, 133.

53. The CIA's support for Japanese conservatives began in the 1940s and apparently continued into the early 1970s. See *New York Times*, October 9, 1994.

54. Wolferen, *Enigma of Japanese Power*, 60–65, 132–133; Scalapino and Musumi, *Parties and Politics*, 86–92.

55. See Meirion Harries and Susie Harries, *Sheathing the Sword: The Demilitarization of Japan* (London: Heinemann, 1987); and J. K. Emmerson, *Arms, Yen and Power: The Japanese Dilemma* (New York: Dunellen, 1971).

56. On the recurring tendency to resolve political conflict through growth, see Laura Hein, "In Search of Peace and Democracy: Japanese Economic Debate in Political Context," *Journal of Asian Studies*, LIII, 3 (August 1994), 752–778; and Hein, "Growth versus Success: Japan's Economic Policy in Historical Perspective," in Gordon, *Postwar Japan As History*, 99–122.

57. Foreign Minister Shiima, quoted in Martin Walker, *The Cold War: A History* (New York: Henry Holt, 1994), 188.

58. Kurt Sontheimer, "The Federal Republic of Germany (1949): Restoring the *Rechtsstaat*," in Bogdanor, ed., *Constitutions in Democratic Politics*, 229–240.

59. On politics in West Germany, see Peter Katzenstein, *Policy and Politics in West Germany: The Growth of a Semisovereign State* (Philadelphia: Temple University Press, 1987); H. A. Turner, *The Two Germanies since 1945* (New Haven: Yale University Press, 1987); and Michael Balfour, *West Germany: A Contemporary History* (London, 1983).

60. Peter Katzenstein, "Industry in a Changing West Germany," in Katzenstein, ed., *Industry and Politics in West Germany* (Ithaca: Cornell University Press, 1989), 7.

61. Whether Stalin's proposal offered a real prospect for reunification has been the subject of considerable debate. See Rolf Steininger, *The German Question: The Stalin Note of 1952 and the Problem of Reunification* (New York: Columbia University Press, 1990); and the literature cited in Garton Ash, *In Europe's Name*, 455.

62. Lothar Wilker, *Die Sicherheitspolitik der SPD, 1956–1966* (Bonn: Neue Gesellschaft, 1977); and Otake, "Defense Controversies and One-Party Dominance," 149–154.

63. Markovits and Allen, "Trade Unions and the Economic Crisis," 129. See also Allen, "The Underdevelopment of Keynesianism in the Federal Republic of Germany," in Hall, *Political Power of Economic Ideas*, 263–289.

64. See the data gathered together in David Conradt, "Changing German Political Culture," in Gabriel Almond and Sidney Verba, eds., *The Civic Culture Revisited* (Boston: Little, Brown, 1980), 212–272.

65. Peter Breit, "Culture As Authority: American and German Transactions," in Reiner Pommerin, ed., *The American Impact on Postwar Germany* (Providence: Berghahn, 1995), 139.

66. See Marilyn Ivy, "Formations of Mass Culture," in Gordon, *Postwar Japan As History*, 239–258; Volker Berghahn, "West German Reconstruction and Amer-

ican Industrial Culture, 1945–1960," in Pommerin, *American Impact on Postwar Germany*, 77; and Arnold Sywottek, "The Americanization of Daily Life? Early Trends in Consumer and Leisure-Time Behavior" in Michael Ermarth, ed., *America and the Shaping of German Society* (Oxford: Berg, 1993), 132–152. The problem was, of course, not confined to the defeated nations but to other advanced societies as well, particularly in Europe. See Richard Kuisel, *Seducing the French: The Dilemma of Americanization* (Berkeley: University of California Press, 1993); and Victoria de Grazia, "Mass Culture and Sovereignty: The American Challenge to European Cinema, 1920–1960," *Journal of Modern History*, LXI (March 1989), 53–87.

67. See William W. Kelly, "Finding a Place in Metropolitan Japan: Ideologies, Institutions and Everyday Life," in Gordon, *Postwar Japan As History*, 193–194; and Uta Poiger, "Rebels with a Cause? American Popular Culture, the 1956 Youth Riots, and the New Conception of Masculinity in East and West Germany," in Pommerin, *American Impact on Postwar Germany*, 93–124.

Chapter 5   *The Cold War and the "Socialist Project"*

1. Robert V. Daniels, *The End of the Communist Revolution* (London: Routledge, 1993), 155.

2. For the text and the context, see Strobe Talbott, ed., *Khrushchev Remembers* (Boston: Little, Brown, 1970), Appendix IV: "Khrushchev's Secret Speech," 559–618, 341–353.

3. The description and implicit judgment come from Eric Hobsbawm, *Age of Extremes: The Short Twentieth Century, 1914–1991* (New York: Pantheon, 1994), 242–243.

4. David Holloway, *Stalin and the Bomb: The Soviet Union and Atomic Energy, 1939–1956* (New Haven: Yale University Press, 1994).

5. Martin Walker, *The Cold War: A History* (New York: Holt, 1994), 213–219.

6. Alec Nove, *Stalinism and After* (London: Allen and Unwin, 1986), 107. For a fuller assessment, see Nove, *An Economic History of the U.S.S.R.* (Harmondsworth: Penguin, 1976), chapters 11 and 12; and James Millar, *The Soviet Economic Experiment* (Urbana: University of Illinois Press, 1990).

7. Fred Halliday, *The Making of the Second Cold War* (London: Verso, 1983).

8. There remains, of course, considerable debate on how seriously to attribute the characteristics of the Soviet system to the ideology that purportedly inspired it. On the skeptical side, see Moshe Lewin, *Russia/USSR/Russia: The Drive and Drift of a Superstate* (New York: New Press, 1995), esp. chapter 8; for the alternative view, see Martin Malia, *The Soviet Tragedy: A History of Socialism in Russia, 1917–1991* (New York: Free Press, 1994). On socialism as a principle of world order, see Paul Dukes, *World Order in History* (London: Routledge, 1996).

9. J. N. Westwood, *Endurance and Endeavour: Russian History, 1812–1992* (Oxford: Oxford University Press, 1993), 364–365.

10. See *Khrushchev Remembers*, 245–320; and Malia, *Soviet Tragedy*, 293–294, 310–312.

11. The debate on what was systemic and what was incidental in the Soviet system was, of course, the central question in the field, for upon its resolution rested all

estimates of the prospects of reform. Among the more useful attempts to define the Soviet system, both during and after Stalin, were those of Seweryn Bialer. See his *Stalin's Successors: Leadership, Stability and Change in the Soviet Union* (Cambridge: Cambridge University Press, 1980), 49–61; and *The Soviet Paradox: External Expansion, Internal Decline* (New York: Knopf, 1986), especially chapter 1. The long discourse about totalitarianism was another way of discussing the same set of issues, with advocates of the totalitarian thesis emphasizing the systemic, and opponents the contingent, aspects of the Soviet system. Ironically, the totalitarian thesis has fared poorly among Western academics but has been taken up by writers in the formerly communist lands as an almost self-evident and common-sensical description of the system.

12. See, for example, Khrushchev's discussion of collectivization in *Khrushchev Remembers*, 71–75; and his further reflections in Strobe Talbott, ed., *Khrushchev Remembers: The Last Testament* (Boston: Little, Brown, 1974), 107–110.

13. See Sheila Fitzpatrick, *Stalin's Peasants* (Oxford: Oxford University Press, 1994); and Alec Nove, *The Economics of Feasible Socialism Revisited* (London: Harper Collins Academic, 1991), 92–97.

14. Nove, *Economic History*, 323.

15. Ibid., 322–360.

16. See János Kornai, *The Socialist System: The Political Economy of Communism* (Princeton: Princeton University Press, 1992), on the tendency of socialism's defenders to undertake repeated, but consistently ineffective, efforts to "perfect our system of planning," 396–408.

17. Bialer, *Soviet Paradox*, 42.

18. Lewin, *Russia/USSR/Russia*, 163. On the mature Soviet system as an extreme and distorted version of rule by professionals, see Harold Perkin, *The Third Revolution: Professional Society in International Perspective* (London: Routledge, 1996), chapter 6.

19. See Mikhail Voslenskii, *Nomenklatura: The Soviet Ruling Class* (Garden City, N.J.: Doubleday, 1984; first published in German in 1980); and Milovan Djilas, *The New Class* (New York: Praeger, 1957).

20. The case for the structural limits to reform is made convincingly by Malia, *Soviet Tragedy*, chapter 9.

21. In addition to works by Sakharov and Medvedev, see Andrei Amalrik, *Will the Soviet Union Survive to 1984?* (New York: Harper and Row, 1970).

22. In addition to his other offenses, Tvardovsky apparently also ran afoul of *Russity*, the shadowy ultranationalist group. See Lewin, *Russia/USSR/Russia*, 259.

23. Anders Åslund, *Gorbachev's Struggle for Economic Reform*, 2nd ed. (Ithaca: Cornell University Press, 1991), 18.

24. Westwood, *Endurance and Endeavour*, 434–442; Malia, *Soviet Tragedy*, 358–361.

25. Linda Cook, *The Soviet Social Contract and Why It Failed: Welfare Policy and Workers' Politics from Brezhnev to Yeltsin* (Cambridge: Harvard University Press, 1993).

26. Joseph Rothschild, *Return to Diversity: A Political History of East Central Europe since World War II*, 2nd ed. (New York: Oxford University Press, 1993), 132–140. The quote from *Rude Pravo* appears on page 133.

27. Tony Judt, "The Dilemma of Dissidence: The Politics of Opposition in East-Central Europe," *Eastern European Politics and Societies*, II, 2 (Spring 1988), 188.

28. For a contemporary account, see Flora Lewis, *A Case History of Hope: The Story of Poland's Peaceful Revolution* (New York: Doubleday, 1958); and, for insight into the heads of key participants, see the documents included in L. W. Gluchowski, "Poland, 1956: Khrushchev, Gomulka, and the 'Polish October,'" *Cold War International History Project Bulletin*, no. 5 (Spring 1995). See also Nicholas Bethell, *Gomulka: His Poland, His Communism* (New York: Holt, Rinehart and Winston, 1969); and Zbigniew Brzezinski, *The Soviet Bloc: Unity and Conflict*, rev. ed. (Cambridge: Harvard University Press, 1967), 239–268.

29. Rothschild, *Return to Diversity*, 154.

30. For a review of the events and their consequences, see Bela Kiraly and Paul Jonas, eds., *The Hungarian Revolution of 1956 in Retrospect* (Boulder: East European Monographs, 1978).

31. David Childs, *The GDR: Moscow's German Ally*, 2nd ed., (London: Unwin Hyman, 1988), 37–65, esp. 53, 59–65.

32. Quoted in Childs, *GDR*, 60.

33. Walker, *Cold War*, 153–159. See also R. Garthoff, "Berlin 1961: The Record Corrected," *Foreign Policy*, no. 84 (Fall 1991), 142–156.

34. See H. Gordon Skilling, *Czechoslovakia's Interrupted Revolution* (Princeton: Princeton University Press, 1976); Milan Simecka, *The Restoration of Order: The Normalization of Czechoslovakia* (London: Verso, 1984); and Rothschild, *Return to Diversity*, 166–173.

35. See especially George Konrad and Ivan Szelenyi, *Intellectuals on the Road to Class Power* (New York: Harcourt Brace, 1979); and Alvin Gouldner, "Marxism As Politics of the New Class," in *Against Fragmentation* (New York: Oxford University Press, 1985), 28–51.

36. See Larry Wolff, *The Invention of Eastern Europe: The Map of Civilization on the Mind of the Enlightenment* (Stanford: Stanford University Press, 1994), on the modern history of the distinction between Eastern and Western Europe.

37. Lowell Dittmer, "China's Search for Its Place in the World," in Brantly Womack, ed., *Contemporary Chinese Politics in Historical Perspective* (Cambridge: Cambridge University Press, 1991), 230–246.

38. See Eric Wolf, *Peasant Wars of the Twentieth Century* (New York: Harper and Row, 1969).

39. On the critical role of such local, "Creole," elites in the origins and development of nationalism, see Benedict Anderson, *Imagined Communities*, 2nd ed. (London: Verso, 1991), chapter 4.

40. B. Womack, "In Search of Democracy: Public Authority and Popular Power in China," in Womack, *Contemporary Chinese Politics*, 65–67.

41. Mao Zedong, "On Khrushchev's Phony Communism and Its Historical Lessons for the World," *Peking Review* (July 17, 1964).

42. For a useful comparison, see William Rosenberg and Marilyn Young, *Transforming Russia and China: Revolutionary Struggle in the Twentieth Century* (New York: Oxford University Press, 1982).

43. The data apply specifically to south China. See Jonathan Spence, *In Search of*

*Modern China* (New York: Norton, 1990), 516, for this and for much of what follows.

44. Tang Tsou, *The Cultural Revolution and Post-Mao Reforms: A Historical Perspective* (Chicago: University of Chicago Press, 1986), 28–29, 269–273.

45. The quotes come respectively from Mao Zedong, *On People's Democratic Dictatorship* (1949) and "Talk at an Enlarged Central Committee Conference," (January 1962), both cited in Tony Smith, *Thinking Like a Communist* (New York: Norton, 1987), 134–135.

46. Mao, cited in Spence, *In Search of Modern China*, 577–578.

47. Mao Zedong, cited in Nigel Harris, *The Mandate of Heaven: Marx and Mao in Modern China* (London: Quartet, 1978), 286.

48. Spence, *In Search of Modern China*, 538–539.

49. "On the Ten Great Relationships" was not published until after Mao's death. On the discussion in general, see Jack Gray, *Rebellions and Revolutions: China from the 1800s to the 1980s* (Oxford: Oxford University Press, 1990), 301–303.

50. Gray, *Rebellions and Revolutions*, 306–317.

51. G. William Skinner, *The City in Late Imperial China* (Stanford: Stanford University Press, 1977). On the continued importance of regions and provinces in organizing the Chinese economy, see David Goodman, "State Reforms in the People's Republic of China since 1976: A Historical Perspective," in Neil Harding, ed., *The State in Socialist Society* (Albany: SUNY Press, 1984), 292–293; and Audrey Donnithorne, *Centre-Provincial Economic Relations in China* (Canberra: Contemporary China Centre, Australian Nationaly University, 1981).

52. On the Cultural Revolution, see especially Tang Tsou, *The Cultural Revolution and Post-Mao Reforms*; Lynn White, *Policies of Chaos: Oganizational Causes of Violence in China's Cultural Revolution* (Princeton: Princeton University Press, 1989); and Jean Daubier, *A History of the Chinese Cultural Revolution* (New York: Random House, 1974).

Chapter 6    *Liberalism Eclipsed*

1. David Caute, *The Year of the Barricades: A Journey through 1968* (New York: Harper and Row, 1988), is probably the most comprehensive survey. On the contemporaneous economic crisis, see Robert Collins, "The Economic Crisis of 1968 and the Waning of the 'American Century.'" *American Historical Review*, CI, 2 (April, 1996), 396–422.

2. There are any number of accounts that explore the crisis from many points of view. Perhaps the most interesting, and least appreciated, is the view from the top. For this, see Jean Lacouture, *De Gaulle: The Ruler, 1945–1970* (New York: Norton, 1992), 527–558.

3. The naiveté of student revolutionaries who imagined an international youth revolt against both capitalism and bureaucratic socialism is well known, but politicians and policemen were just as deluded. The author, for example, traveled innocently to the Soviet Union on a student tour in the summer of 1968 but discovered later that the CIA had used the occasion to open a file in which it was alleged that the purpose of the trip was to make contact between radicals in the United States and their counterparts in Moscow. Alas, it was fantasy.

4. T. H. Marshall, *Citizenship and Social Class* (Cambridge: Cambridge University Press, 1950).

5. David Conradt, "Changing German Political Culture," in Gabriel Almond and Sidney Verba, eds., *The Civic Culture Revisited* (Boston: Little, Brown, 1980), 212–272.

6. Göran Therborn, "Classes and States: Welfare State Development, 1881–1981," *Studies in Political Economy*, no. 13 (Spring 1984), 7–41; and Alexander Hicks, Joya Misra, and Tang Nah Ng, "The Programmatic Emergence of the Social Security State," *American Sociological Review*, LX, 3 (June 1995).

7. Peter Flora, ed., *Growth to Limits: The West European Welfare States since World War II* (New York: de Gruyter, 1988), vol. II, chapters on Germany, Britain, and Italy. See also James E. Cronin, *The Politics of State Expansion* (London: Routledge, 1991).

8. Kyoko Sheridan, *Governing the Japanese Economy* (Cambridge: Polity, 1993), 145–148; and Robert Scalapino and Junnosuke Masumi, *Parties and Politics in Contemporary Japan* (Berkeley: University of California Press, 1962), 125–153.

9. Tanaka Kakuei, "The Plan for Remodeling of the Japanese Archipelago," (1972), quoted in Shigeto Tsuru, *Japan's Capitalism: Creative Defeat and Beyond* (Cambridge: Cambridge University Press, 1993), 120–121. See also Sheridan, *Governing the Japanese Economy*, 171–178.

10. The folly of the choice is now openly acknowledged. See Robert McNamara, *In Retrospect: The Tragedy and Lessons of Vietnam* (New York: Times Books, 1995); and also Collins, "Economic Crisis of 1968," 412–422.

11. It is also not unreasonable to suggest that Nixon's support for busing and affirmative action was part of his cynical, but widely acknowledged, effort to use race to weaken his Democratic opponents. See Thomas Edsall and Mary Edsall, *Chain Reaction: The Impact of Race, Rights and Taxes on American Politics* (New York: Norton, 1991); and Michael Lind, *The Next American Nation: The New Nationalism and the Fourth American Revolution* (New York: Free Press, 1995).

12. David Gordon, "Chickens Home to Roost: From Prosperity to Stagnation in the Postwar U.S. Economy," in Michael Bernstein and David Adler, eds., *Understanding American Economic Decline* (Cambridge: Cambridge University Press, 1994), 63–65, esp. Table 2.5.

13. Michel Crozier, Samuel Huntington, and Joji Watanuki, *The Crisis of Democracy* (New York: New York University Press, 1975). The Trilateral Commission had been founded in 1973 and was directed by Zbigniew Brzezinski, who played a major role in the evolution of the report.

14. For the weaknesses that bedeviled European socialists, see Herbert Kitschelt, *The Transformation of European Social Democracy* (Cambridge: Cambridge University Press, 1994).

15. See Herman Van der Wee, *Prosperity and Upheaval: The World Economy, 1945–1980* (Berkeley: University of California, 1986), 494–495; Robert Kuttner, *The End of Laissez-Faire: National Purpose and the Global Economy after the Cold War* (New York: Knopf, 1991), 69–72; and, more generally, Daniel Yergin, *The Prize: The Epic Quest for Oil, Money and Power* (New York: Simon and Schuster, 1992).

16. Paul Bairoch, *Economics and World History* (Chicago: University of Chicago Press, 1993), 158–163.

17. Ronald Inglehart, *Culture Shift in Advanced Industrial Society* (Princeton: Princeton University Press, 1990), 93–99.

18. See Peter Hall, ed., *The Political Power of Economic Ideas: Keynesianism across Nations* (Princeton: Princeton University Press, 1989); Andrew Graham and Anthony Seldon, eds., *Government and Economies in the Postwar World: Economic Policies and Comparative Performance, 1945–85* (London: Routledge, 1990). The most thoroughly studied case is, of course, that of Great Britain, which is reviewed in Cronin, *The Politics of State Expansion*.

19. Sweden and Germany succeeded well enough in restraining inflation and in keeping official rates of unemployment low, but there were less favorable consequences in terms of the overall rate of growth of employment. See Gören Therborn, *Why Some People Are More Unemployed than Others* (London: Verso, 1986); and Gosta Esping-Andersen, *The Three Worlds of Welfare Capitalism* (Cambridge: Polity Press, 1990).

20. Giovanni Arrighi, *The Long Twentieth Century: Money, Power and the Origins of Our Times* (London: Verso, 1994), 314.

21. Kuttner, *End of Laissez-Faire*, 75–81.

22. See Charles Maier, "The Politics of Productivity: Foundations of American International Economic Policy after World War II," in Peter Katzenstein, ed., *Between Power and Plenty* (Madison: University of Wisconsin Press, 1977), 23–49; and Alan Wolfe, *America's Impasse: The Rise and Fall of the Politics of Growth* (New York: Pantheon, 1981).

23. D. H. Meadows, ed., *The Limits to Growth* (New York: Universe Books, 1972).

24. Paul McCracken et al., *Towards Full Employment and Price Stability* (Paris: OECD, 1977), 184–185.

25. See Joel Krieger, *Reagan, Thatcher and the Politics of Decline* (New York: Oxford University Press, 1986); and Paul Pierson, *Dismantling the Welfare State? Reagan, Thatcher and the Politics of Retrenchment* (Cambridge: Cambridge University Press, 1994).

26. Stephen A. Marglin, "Lessons of the Golden Age," in Marglin and Juliet Schor, eds., *The Golden Age of Capitalism: Reinterpreting the Postwar Experience* (Oxford: Clarendon, 1990), 34–35.

27. Kevin Phillips, *The Politics of Rich and Poor* (New York: Random House, 1990), 17.

28. Paul Pierson and Miriam Smith, "Bourgeois Revolutions? The Policy Consequences of Resurgent Conservatism," *Comparative Political Studies*, XXV, 4 (January 1993), 487–520.

29. From 1960 to 1992 public expenditure as a share of GDP increased from 28.2 percent to 53.6 percent in Italy, from 20 percent to 46.3 percent in Greece, from 17 percent to 52.7 percent in Portugal, and from 19.9 percent to 44.5 percent in Spain. See David Cameron and Kathryn McDermott, "The Expansion and Contraction of the Public Economy, 1960–1992," paper presented to the Center for European Studies, Harvard University, April 1995, Table 1. On the phenomenon of democratic transition in this region, see Guillermo O'Donnell, Philippe Schmitter, and Lawrence Whitehead, eds., *Transitions from Authoritarian Rule,*

Part I: "Southern Europe" (Baltimore: John Hopkins University Press, 1986); and Samuel Huntington, *The Third Wave: Democratization in the Late 20th Century* (Norman: University of Oklahoma Press, 1991).

30. Peter Lange, George Ross, and Maurizio Vannicelli, *Unions, Change and Crisis: French and Italian Union Strategy and the Political Economy, 1945–1980* (London: Allen and Unwin, 1982); and G. S. Bain and R. Price, *Profiles of Union Growth* (Oxford: Basil Blackwell, 1980).

31. These estimates come from Philip Armstrong, Andrew Glyn, and John Harrison, *Capitalism since 1945* (Oxford: Basil Blackwell, 1991), 248.

32. See, among others, Kim Moody, *An Injury to All: The Decline of American Unionism* (London: Verso, 1988).

33. The phrase comes from Reagan's speech before the International Business Council, September 9, 1980, reprinted the next day in the *New York Times*.

34. Reagan himself could say and believe anything quite independent of data, particularly if it was similar to the script of one of his movies. For numerous examples, see Mark Green and Gail McColl, *Ronald Reagan's Reign of Error* (New York: Pantheon, 1984); Garry Wills, *Reagan's America* (New York: Doubleday, 1987); and Michael Paul Rogin, *Ronald Reagan: The Movie* (Berkeley: University of California Press, 1987).

35. Martin Walker, *The Cold War: A History* (New York: Holt, 1994), 235–236. The advantage provided to the Soviets by the oil crisis would be only temporary, and was soon squandered. See, for example, Paul Kennedy, *The Rise and Fall of the Great Powers* (New York: Random House, 1987), 493–494.

36. Lawrence Friedman, *The Evolution of Nuclear Strategy* (New York: St. Martin's, 1989), chapters 23–24.

37. Leonid Brezhnev, quoted in Walker, *Cold War*, 236–237.

38. Kennedy, *Rise and Fall*, 404–405.

39. Allen Matusow, *The Unraveling of America: A History of Liberalism in the 1960s* (New York: Harper and Row, 1984), 376–394.

40. U.S. Department of Defense, *United States–Vietnam Relations* (1968). The papers were leaked by Daniel Ellsberg and published by the *New York Times*.

41. On the roots and broader significance of this populist strain in American political culture, see Michael Kazin, *The Populist Persuasion: An American History* (New York: Basic Books, 1995). On the racial dimensions of Wallace's appeal, see Thomas Edsall and Mary Edsall, *Chain Reaction*.

42. At the center of the policy was, of course, the plan for the "Vietnamization" of the war in Indochina or, more cynically, "changing the color of the corpses." See Walter LaFeber, *America, Russia and the Cold War, 1945–1992*, 7th ed. (New York: McGraw-Hill, 1993), 264–265.

43. For the details, see Raymond L. Garthoff, *Détente and Confrontation: American-Soviet Relations from Nixon to Reagan*, rev. ed. (Washington, D.C.: Brookings Institution, 1994).

44. The effort to put in place a "New International Economic Order" was led by the Brandt Commission, established in 1976. See Willy Brandt, *North-South: A Program for Survival*, report of the Independent Commission on International Development Issues (Cambridge: MIT Press, 1980). Its basic recommendations had already been rejected by the time they appeared in print. See Geoffrey Bar-

raclough, "Waiting for the New Order," *New York Review of Books* (October 26, 1978); Wolfe, *America's Impasse*, chapters 7–8; Nigel Harris, *The End of the Third World* (London: I. B. Tauris, 1987); and the important study by Stephen Krasner, *Structural Conflict: The Third World against Global Liberalism* (Berkeley: University of California Press, 1985).

45. See Rostow's presentation to the Platform Committee of the Democratic National Convention, May 19, 1976, cited in Wolfe, *America's Impasse*, 138.

46. Carter's views were recorded in his diary on election day. See Jimmy Carter, *Keeping Faith: Memoirs of a President* (New York: Bantum, 1982), 568.

47. Was the victory actually sealed by a deal with the Ayatollah Khomeini? After the Iran-Contra arms deal was exposed in 1986, substantial circumstantial evidence emerged to suggest that the Reagan campaign struck some sort of a bargain with the Iranians to the effect that Iran would delay the release of U.S. hostages until after the election, in return for which Iran would receive U.S. arms for use in its war with Iraq. Whether such charges can or will ever be proved may well be doubted, given William Casey's timely death from a brain tumor. But see the account of Carter's Middle East expert, Gary Sick, in the *New York Times*, April 15, 1991, which is further elaborated in his book, *October Surprise: America's Hostages in Iran and the Election of Ronald Reagan* (New York: Random House, 1991).

48. Fred Halliday, *The Making of the Second Cold War* (London: Verso, 1983) is the best, near-contemporary account.

49. Richard Herrmann, *Perceptions and Behavior in Soviet Foreign Policy* (Pittsburgh: University of Pittsburgh Press, 1985), 66–69, 91–101, 142–148.

50. Walker, *Cold War*, 226–227.

51. For the diplomatic background, see Garthoff, *Détente and Confrontation*, 640–644.

52. Raymond Garthoff has again compiled the definitive record in *The Great Transition: American-Soviet Relations and the End of the Cold War* (Washington, D.C.: Brookings Institution, 1994).

53. See Colin Gray and Keith Payne, "Victory Is Possible," *Foreign Policy*, no. 39 (Summer 1980), for an example and, more generally, Robert Scheer, *With Enough Shovels: Reagan, Bush and Nuclear War* (New York: Random House, 1982).

54. Edward Thompson, in Thompson and Dan Smith, eds., *Protest and Survive* (London: Penguin, 1980), quoted in Friedman, *Evolution of Nuclear Strategy*, 401.

55. See Randall Forsberg, "A Bilateral Nuclear-Weapon Freeze," *Scientific American* (November 1982). The House of Representatives rejected the proposal on August 5, 1982, by just two votes: 204–202.

56. Garthoff, *Great Transition*, 515.

57. National Conference of Catholic Bishops, "The Challenge of Peace: God's Promise and Our Response," *Origins*, XII (May 19, 1983). More broadly, see David Hollenbach, *Justice, Peace, and Human Rights: American Catholic Social Ethics in a Pluralistic World* (New York: Crossroad, 1988).

58. Garthoff, *Great Transition*, 517.

59. Michael Klare and Peter Kornbluh, eds., *Low-Intensity Warfare: Counterinsur-*

*gency, Proinsurgency and Antiterrorism in the Eighties* (New York: Pantheon, 1988).

60. See Richard Pipes, "Misinterpreting the Cold War," *Foreign Affairs* (January/February 1995).

## Chapter 7   *Communism's Endings*

1. Raymond L. Garthoff, *Détente and Confrontation: American-Soviet Relations from Nixon to Reagan*, rev. ed. (Washington, D.C.: Brookings Institution, 1994), 607–608; and John Ehrman, *The Rise of Neoconservatism: Intellectuals and Foreign Affairs, 1945–1994* (New Haven: Yale University Press, 1995), 111–112.
2. Arbatov, "The Strength of a Policy of Realism," *Izvestia*, June 22, 1972, quoted in Richard K. Herrman, *Perceptions and Behavior in Soviet Foreign Policy* (Pittsburgh: University of Pittsburgh Press, 1985), 79–80.
3. Richard Pipes, "Misinterpreting the Cold War," *Foreign Affairs* (January/February 1995).
4. Herrman, *Perceptions and Behavior in Soviet Foreign Policy*, 72–74, 110–113.
5. Joseph Schull, "What Is Ideology? Theoretical Problems and Lessons from Soviet-type Societies," *Political Studies*, XL (1992), 728–741; Rachel Walker, "Marxism-Leninism as Discourse: The Politics of the Empty Signifier and the Double Bind," *British Journal of Political Science*, XIX (1989), 161–189; and Walker, "Language and the Politics of Identity in the USSR," in Michael Urban, ed., *Ideology and System Change in the USSR and East Europe* (New York: St. Martin's, 1992).
6. The argument that the U.S. challenge during the 1980s precipitated the terminal crisis of the Soviet Union is made most explicitly in Peter Schweitzer, *Victory: The Reagan Administration's Secret Strategy That Hastened the Collapse of the Soviet Union* (New York: Atlantic Monthly Press, 1994).
7. Linda Cook, *The Soviet Social Contract and Why It Failed: Welfare Policy and Workers' Politics from Brezhnev to Yeltsin* (Cambridge: Harvard University Press, 1993), esp. chapter 2.
8. J. N. Westwood, *Endurance and Endeavour: Russian History, 1812–1992* (Oxford: Oxford University Press, 1993), 466; Mikhail Voslenskii, *Nomenklatura: The Soviet Ruling Class* (New York: Doubleday, 1984).
9. Martin Walker, *The Waking Giant: Gorbachev's Russia* (New York: Pantheon, 1986), 46–47.
10. See the discussion and citations, ibid., 47–49; Martin Walker, *The Cold War: A History* (New York: Holt, 1994), 281; and Martin Malia, *The Soviet Tragedy: A History of Socialism in Russia, 1917–1991* (New York: Free Press, 1994), 408.
11. Roderick MacFarquhar, "The Succession to Mao and the End of Maoism," in MacFarquhar, ed., *The Politics of China, 1949–1989* (Cambridge: Cambridge University Press, 1993), 275–278. The following account is based largely on MacFarquhar's analysis.
12. Cited in Richard Baum, "The Road to Tiananmen: Chinese Politics in the 1980s," in MacFarquhar, *Politics of China*, 345. On the economic reforms more broadly, see Dwight Perkins, "China's Economic Policy and Performance," in Roderick MacFarquhar and John K. Fairbank, eds., *Cambridge History of China*, vol. 15, *The People's Republic*, Part 2, *Revolutions within the Chinese*

*Revolution, 1966–1982* (Cambridge: Cambridge University Press, 1991),
475–539; Jack Gray, *Rebellions and Revolutions: China from the 1800s to the
1980s* (Oxford: Oxford University Press, 1990), 382–391; Elizabeth Perry and
Christine Wong, eds., *The Political Economy of Reform in Post-Mao China*
(Cambridge: Council on East Asian Studies, Harvard University, 1985); and Stuart Schram, "Economics in Command? Ideology and Policy since the Third
Plenum," *China Quarterly*, 99 (September 1984), 417–461.

13. Joseph Fewsmith, "The Dengist Reforms in Historical Perspective," in Brantly
Womack, ed., *Contemporary Chinese Politics in Historical Perspective* (Cam-
bridge: Cambridge University Press, 1991), 24. See also Tang Tsou, "Political
Change and Reform: The Middle Course," in *The Cultural Revolution and Post-
Mao Reforms: A Historical Perspective* (Chicago: University of Chicago Press,
1986), 219–258.

14. See Baum, "Road to Tiananmen," 341; and Tsou, "Political Change and
Reform."

15. Terry Sicular, "Rural Marketing and Exchange in the Wake of Recent Reforms,"
in Perry and Wong, *Political Economy of Reform*, 83–109.

16. Richard Smith, "The Chinese Road to Capitalism," *New Left Review*, no. 199
(May–June 1993), 61.

17. Vivienne Shue, *The Reach of the State: Sketches of the Chinese Body Politic*
(Stanford: Stanford University Press, 1988), 3; Shue, "State Power and Social
Organization in China," in Joel S. Migdal, Atul Kohli, and Shue, eds., *State
Power and Social Forces: Domination and Transformation in the Third World*
(Cambridge: Cambridge University Press, 1994), 65–88. Shue's analysis builds
upon the earlier work by G. William Skinner on Chinese economic geography,
cited above in chapter 5, note 51.

18. Susan Shirk, "The Politics of Industrial Reform," in Perry and Wong, *Political
Economy of Reform*, 210–216. On the compatibility between Maoism and certain aspects of recent economic reforms, see Gray, *Rebellions and Revolutions*,
382–391.

19. Zhao's second "whatever" was merely the reverse: "whatever is detrimental to
this growth goes against scientific socialism and is therefore not allowed to
exist." See Baum, "Road to Tiananmen," 410–411. Zhao's statement was made
at the Thirteenth Congress of the CCP, held October 25–November 1, 1987.

20. Indeed, since taking over from Zhao, Jiang Zemin has distinguished himself by
nothing other than continuing the campaign against corruption. See Joseph Fewsmith, "Jockeying for Position in the Post-Deng Era," *Current History* (September 1995), 252–258.

21. Nicholas Lardy, "Is China Different? The Fate of Its Economic Reform," in
Daniel Chirot, ed., *The Crisis of Leninism and the Decline of the Left: The Revolutions of 1989* (Seattle: University of Washington Press, 1991), 155–159.

22. On the implication for China's politics, see Gordon White, *Riding the Tiger: The
Politics of Economic Reform in Post-Mao China* (Stanford: Stanford University
Press, 1993).

23. See Leszek Kolakowski, *Main Currents of Marxism: Its Origins, Growth and
Dissolution*, vol. 3, *The Breakdown* (Oxford: Oxford University Press, 1978),
450–478.

24. Leszek Kolakowski, "Hope and Hopelessness," *Survey* 17/3 (Summer 1971), cited in Gale Stokes, *The Walls Came Tumbling Down: The Collapse of Communism in Eastern Europe* (New York: Oxford University Press, 1993), 20–21. Such views produced visible consternation among Western Marxists. See, for example, Edward Thompson, "An Open Letter to Leszek Kolakowski," in Ralph Miliband and John Saville, eds., *Socialist Register* 1973 (London: Merlin Press, 1973); and Kolakowski's devastating reply: "My Correct Views on Everything," in Miliband and Saville, *Socialist Register* 1974 (London: Merlin, 1974).

25. Civil society may be provisionally defined by Ernest Gellner as "that set of diverse non-governmental institutions which is strong enough to counterbalance the state and, while not preventing the state from fulfilling its role of keeper of the peace and arbitrator between major interests, can nevertheless prevent it from dominating and atomizing the rest of society." See Gellner, *Conditions of Liberty: Civil Society and Its Rivals* (New York: Viking Penguin, 1994), 5. Gellner goes on to insist that civil society be further distinguished from states and societies in which communities are independent of the state but are themselves self-contained and all-encompassing. On the connection between civil society and the prevailing political psychology of communist political systems, see Ken Jowitt, "The Leninist Legacy," in Ivo Banac, ed., *Eastern Europe in Revolution* (Ithaca: Cornell University Press, 1992), 206–224, and his more extended treatment, *New World Disorder: The Leninist Extinction* (Berkeley: University of California Press, 1992), esp. chapter 2.

26. Charles Maier, "Democracy since the French Revolution," in John Dunn, ed., *Democracy: The Unfinished Journey* (Oxford: Oxford University Press, 1992), 148. See also Ferenc Fehér, Agnes Heller, and György Márkus, *Dictatorship over Needs: An Analysis of Soviet Soviet Societies* (Oxford: Basil Blackwell, 1983); and Jeno Szucs, "Three Historical Regions of Europe," in John Keane, ed., *Civil Society and the State* (London: Verso, 1988), 291–332.

27. Patrick Seriot, "Officialese and Straight Talk in Socialist Europe of the 1980s," in Urban, ed., *Ideology and System Change*, 202–212. Parody and allegory could be very powerful, of course, as Polish writers and filmmakers in particular would prove. Among the former, see esp. Ryszard Kapuscinski, *The Emperor: Downfall of an Autocrat* (New York: Harcourt, Brace, 1983; originally published in 1978).

28. Joseph Rothschild, *Return to Diversity: A Political History of East Central Europe since World War II*, 2nd ed. (New York: Oxford University Press, 1993), 209–211.

29. See Stokes, *The Walls Came Tumbling Down*, 26–28.

30. Karol Wojtyla, speaking in 1977, and quoted in Joel Kovel, "The Theocracy of John Paul II," in Ralph Miliband, Leo Panitch, and John Saville, eds., *Socialist Register 1987* (London: Merlin Press, 1987), 465.

31. Stokes, *Walls Came Tumbling Down*, 34.

32. The rise of Solidarity has been well chronicled. See, in particular, Timothy Garton Ash, *The Polish Revolution: Solidarity* (New York: Vintage, 1985); Neal Ascherson, *The Polish August: The Self-Limiting Revolution* (New York: Viking, 1982); David Ost, *Solidarity and the Politics of Anti-Politics: Opposition and Reform in Poland since 1968* (Philadelphia: Temple University Press, 1990); and

Roman Laba, *The Roots of Solidarity* (Princeton: Princeton University Press, 1991).

33. Rothschild, *Return to Diversity*, 199–200.

34. Cited in Stokes, *Walls Came Tumbling Down*, 39.

35. Whether Soviet troops would have intervened if Jaruzelski had failed to act or if, in acting to suppress Solidarity, he had failed to do so effectively, remains an open question. Some members of the Politburo, like Andropov, were strongly opposed; others were more willing to contemplate intervention. The issue is discussed extensively in Mark Kramer, "Poland, 1980–81: Soviet Policy during the Polish Crisis," *Cold War International History Project Bulletin*, no. 5 (Spring 1995).

36. On the growth record of the Eastern European economies over the postwar era, see Charles Maier, "The Collapse of Communism: Approaches for a Future History," *History Workshop*, #31 (Spring 1991), 34–59.

37. For a series of quite useful interpretations and analyses, see Ivo Banac, ed., *Eastern Europe in Revolution* (Ithaca: Cornell University Press, 1992); and Stephen Graubard, ed., *Eastern Europe...Central Europe...Europe* (Boulder: Westview, 1991). The narrative with the most "immediacy" is probably William Echikson, *Lighting the Night: Revolution in Eastern Europe* (New York: Morrow, 1990).

38. The dimensions of the problem are discussed thoughtfully in Albert O. Hirschman, "Exit, Voice and the Fate of the German Democratic Republic: An Essay in Conceptual History," *World Politics*, XLV (January 1993), 173–202; and in Norman Naimark, "'Ich will hier raus': Emigration and the Collapse of the German Democratic Republic," in Banac, *Eastern Europe in Revolution*, 72–95.

39. Stokes, *Walls Came Tumbling Down*, 138.

40. Konrad Jarausch, *The Rush to German Unity* (New York: Oxford University Press, 1954).

41. Tony Judt, "Metamorphosis: The Democratic Revolution in Czechoslovakia," in Banac, *Eastern Europe in Revolution*, 96–116; and Stokes, *Walls Came Tumbling Down*, 148–157.

42. Ken Jowitt, "The Leninist Extinction," in Chirot, *Crisis of Leninism*, 74–99, esp. 79–81.

43. Alice Amsden, Jacek Kochanowicz, and Lance Taylor, *The Market Meets Its Match: Restructuring the Economies of Eastern Europe* (Cambridge: Harvard University Press, 1994).

44. Curiously, the collapse of communism has led to a revival of interest in functionalism and its derivative, modernization theory, presumably because of its message about the tendency for diverse societies to converge over time. One would have thought that the lesson of 1989 and 1991 would be bleaker and more Darwinian. See Jeffrey Alexander, "Modern, Anti, Post and Neo," *New Left Review*, no. 210 (March/April, 1995) 63–101.

45. Boriev, *Staliniad* (1990), quoted in Ryszard Kapuscinski, *Imperium* (New York: Knopf, 1994), 307–308.

46. These statements come from minutes of the Politburo meeting of July 12, 1984, printed in the *Cold War International History Project Bulletin*, no. 4 (Fall 1994), 81.

47. Malia, *Soviet Tragedy*, 424.

48. On the responsiveness of different sectors of the bureaucracy, and on the deeply entrenched character of those attached to the ministries dealing with economic matters, see David Lane and Cameron Ross, "The CPSU Ruling Elite, 1981–1991: Commonalities and Divisions," *Communist and Post-Communist Studies*, XXVIII, 3 (September 1995), 339–360.

49. Another, less attractive parallel was perhaps the Nazi-Soviet pact of August 1939, by which fittingly the Soviet Union recovered most of the territory lost at Brest-Litovsk. For still earlier parallels, see Valerie Bunce, "Domestic Reform and International Change: The Gorbachev Reforms in Historical Perspective," *International Organization*, XLVII, 1 (Winter 1993), 107–138. On Brest-Litovsk, see Malia, *Soviet Tragedy*, 413–414.

50. Tatyana Zaslavskaya, *The Second Socialist Revolution: An Alternative Soviet Strategy* (Bloomington: Indiana University Press, 1990).

51. Quoted in Anders Åslund, *Gorbachev's Struggle for Economic Reform*, 2nd ed. (Ithaca: Cornell University Press, 1991), 15.

52. Alec Nove, "Soviet Agriculture: The Brezhnev Legacy and Gorbachev's Cure," in Ferenc Fehér and Andrew Arato, eds., *Gorbachev—The Debate* (Atlantic Highlands, N.J.: Humanities Press, 1989), 169–220, esp. 205–220.

53. See, for example, David Remnick, *Lenin's Tomb: The Last Days of the Soviet Empire* (New York: Vintage, 1994), 180–197.

54. Arkady Vaksberg, *The Soviet Mafia* (New York: St. Martin's, 1991), 232–234.

55. See Stephen Handelman, "Crime and Corruption in Russia," Briefing of the Commission on Security and Cooperation in Europe, Washington, D.C. (June, 1994); and Handelman, *Comrade Criminal: The Theft of the Second Russian Revolution* (London: Michael Joseph, 1994). For a deliberately contrary but not uncommon view, see Edward Luttwak, "Does the Russian Mafia Deserve the Nobel Prize for Economics?" *London Review of Books*, August 3, 1995.

56. Westwood, *Endurance and Endeavour*, 519–526; and Stephen White, *Gorbachev and After* (Cambridge: Cambridge University Press, 1991), chapter 4.

57. Anders Åslund, *How Russia Became a Market Economy* (Washington, D.C.: Brookings Institution, 1995), 152.

58. Ibid., 48.

59. White, *Gorbachev and After*, 129.

60. See Nicolai Petro, *The Rebirth of Russian Democracy: An Interpretation of Political Culture* (Cambridge: Harvard University Press, 1995); and, for a somewhat more pessimistic view, James Scanlon, "Reforms and Civil Society in the USSR," *Problems of Communism* (March–April 1988), 41–46.

61. See, for example, Jerry Hough and Merle Fainsod, *How the Soviet Union Is Governed* (Cambridge: Harvard University Press, 1979); and, more recently, S. Frederick Starr, "Soviet Union: A Civil Society," *Foreign Policy*, no. 70 (Spring 1988), 26–41.

62. M. Steven Fish, *Democracy from Scratch: Opposition and Regime in the New Russian Revolution* (Princeton: Princeton University Press, 1995), 10–15.

63. Moshe Lewin, *Russia/USSR/Russia* (New York: New Press, 1995), 311; and Lewin, *The Gorbachev Phenomenon* (Berkeley: University of California Press, 1991).

64. Seweryn Bialer, "Gorbachev's Program of Change: Sources, Significance, Prospects," in Bialer and Michael Mandelbaum, eds., *Gorbachev's Russia and American Foreign Policy* (Boulder: Westview, 1988).

65. Zaslavskaya, *Second Socialist Revolution*, 10.

66. Cited in Hélène Carrère d'Encausse, *The End of the Soviet Empire: The Triumph of the Nations* (New York: Basic Books, 1993), 4.

67. The ambivalence went back to the days of Lenin. See Lewin, *Russia/USSR/Russia*, 245–275.

68. Ronald Suny, *The Revenge of the Past: Nationalism, Revolution and the Collapse of the Soviet Union* (Stanford: Stanford University Press, 1993).

69. Mikhail Gorbachev, *Perestroika: New Thinking for Our Country and the World* (New York: Harper and Row, 1988), 11.

70. Andrei Amalrik, *Will the Soviet Union Survive until 1984?* (New York: Harcourt, Brace, 1970), 27–28.

71. The "return of history" in this usage follows Remnick, *Lenin's Tomb*, chapter 4.

## Chapter 8    *The World after the Cold War*

1. As Adam Przeworski has argued, what died in Eastern Europe in 1989 was not some distorted version of socialism but the entire tradition: "The socialist project—the project that was forged in Western Europe between 1848 and 1891 and that had animated social movements all over the world since then—failed, in the East and in the West." See Przeworski, *Democracy and the Market: Political and Economic Reforms in Eastern Europe and Latin America* (Cambridge: Cambridge University Press, 1991), 7. Others have seen the impact of 1989 in even more decisive terms. As Arrighi, Hopkins, and Wallerstein argue, "In 1989, not only Leninism, but national liberation movements, social-democracy, and all the other heirs of post-1789 revolutionary 'liberalism' collapsed ideologically, that is, as strategies for efficacious action in the transformation of the world." See Giovanni Arrighi, Terence Hopkins, and Immanuel Wallerstein, "1989, The Continuation of 1968," *Review*, XV, 2 (Spring 1992), 221–242, esp. 239.

2. See G. O' Tuathail, "The Bush Administration and the End of the Cold War," *Geoforum*, XXIII (1992), 437–452; and Paul Dukes, *The Last Great Game: USA versus USSR* (New York: St. Martin's, 1989).

3. See Arno Mayer, "Internal Crisis and War since 1870," in Charles Bertrand, ed., *Revolutionary Situations in Europe, 1917–1922* (Montreal: Interuniversity Centre for European Studies, 1977), 201–232; Mayer, *Why Did the Heavens Not Darken? The 'Final Solution' in History* (New York: Pantheon, 1988); and Gabriel Kolko, *Century of War: Politics, Conflicts and Society since 1914* (New York: New Press, 1994).

4  Bruce Cumings, "The End of the Seventy-Years' Crisis," in Meredith Woo-Cumings and Michael Loriaux, eds., *Past As Prelude: History in the Making of a New World Order* (Boulder: Westview, 1993), 9–32.

5. This is the central argument made by Fukuyama and, stripped of its rhetorical excesses, it is difficult to refute. See Francis Fukuyama, "The End of History?" *National Interest*, no. 16 (Summer 1989), 3–18; Fukuyama, *The End of His-*

*tory and the Last Man* (New York: Free Press, 1992).

6. Charles S. Maier, "Empire or Nations? 1918, 1945, 1989..." paper presented to the Center for European Studies, Harvard University, April, 1995.

7. Anders Stephanson, "The United States," in David Reynolds, ed., *The Origins of the Cold War in Europe: International Perspectives* (New Haven: Yale University Press, 1994), 23–52, refers to this appropriately as "the systemic aspect, for the cold war was at once a socio-economic, ideological-cultural and military-political conflict" (50).

8. On the relative ease and peacefulness with which the transition was accomplished, see John Mueller, "Quiet Cataclysm: Some Afterthoughts on World War III," in Michael Hogan, ed., *The End of the Cold War: Its Meaning and Implications* (Cambridge: Cambridge University Press, 1992), 39–52; Michael Howard, "Impressions from a Journey in Central Europe," *London Review of Books*, October 25, 1990; and Ralf Dahrendorf, *Reflections on the Revolution in Europe* (London: Chatto Counterblast, 1990).

9. See Fritz Scharpf, *Crisis and Choice in European Social Democracy* (Ithaca: Cornell University Press, 1991); Perry Anderson and Patrick Camiller, eds., *Mapping the West European Left* (London: Verso, 1994); and Martin Ball and Paul Heywood, eds., *West European Communist Parties after the Revolutions of 1989* (London: Macmillan, 1994).

10. These outcomes should have come as no surprise to those familiar with the lineaments of power in both states. See, among others, Karel van Wolferen, *The Enigma of Japanese Power* (New York: Knopf, 1989); David Williams, *Japan: Beyond the End of History* (London: Routledge, 1994): Matt Frei, *Getting the Boot: Italy's Unfinished Revolution* (New York: Times Books, 1995); and Patrick McCarthy, *The Crisis of the Italian State: From the Origins of the Cold War to the Fall of Berlusconi* (New York: St. Martin's, 1995).

11. The conservative party that did not stumble but instead moved decisively to put its stamp on the emerging post–Cold War world was the German CDU/CSU led by Helmut Kohl, which staked its future on rapid reunification. The returns on that gamble have been on the whole very favorable. See Timothy Garton Ash, "Kohl's Germany: The Beginning of the End?" *New York Review of Books* (December 1, 1994), 20–26.

12. This is not to suggest, however, that there is no force whatever to the moral and legal pressures that the world community, organized largely through the UN, can bring to bear. See, for example, Robert Jackson, "The Weight of Ideas in Decolonization: Normative Change in International Relations," 111–138, and Kathryn Sikkink, "The Power of Principled Ideas: Human Rights Policies in the United States and Western Europe," 139–170, in Judith Goldstein and Robert Keohane, eds., *Ideas and Foreign Policy: Beliefs, Institutions and Political Change* (Ithaca: Cornell University Press, 1993).

13. Western acquiescence in the dismemberment of Bosnia has undoubtedly been demoralizing, as Edward Luttwak has argued in his essay "Toward Post-Heroic Warfare," *Foreign Affairs*, LXXIV, 3 (May/June 1995), 109–122. It is nevertheless easy enough to characterize Western policy as "appeasement" and its makers as "accomplices to genocide" (see *New Republic*, August 7, 1995), but far more difficult to formulate a workable alternative policy.

14. Ali Mazrui, *Cultural Forces in World Politics* (Portsmouth, N.H.: Heinemann, 1990), esp. 239–243. For a rather different perspective, see Adda Bozeman, "The International Order in a Multicultural World," 387–406, and Ronald Dore, "Unity and Diversity in Contemporary World Culture," 407–424, in Hedley Bull and Adam Watson, eds., *The Expansion of International Society* (Oxford: Clarendon, 1985).

15. This continuity makes it possible to speak of the end of the Cold War as "the end of the modern age." See John Lukacs, *The End of the Twentieth Century and the End of the Modern Age* (New York: Ticknor and Fields, 1993).

16. Geoffrey Barraclough, *An Introduction to Contemporary History* (Harmondsworth: Penguin, 1968), 221–227; Robert Skidelsky, *The Road from Serfdom* (New York: Viking Penguin, 1996), 195.

17. Felipe Fernández-Armesto, *Millennium: A History of Our Last Thousand Years* (New York: Simon and Schuster, 1995).

18. Alfred Chandler, *Scale and Scope: The Dynamics of Industrial Capitalism* (Cambridge: Harvard University Press, 1990); and Michael Best, *The New Competition: Institutions of Industrial Restructuring* (Cambridge: Harvard University Press, 1990).

19. The first thorough argument about Fordism was M. Aglietta, *A Theory of Capitalist Regulation: The US Experience* (London: New Left Books, 1979); the most persuasive was Michael Piore and Charles Sabel, *The Second Industrial Divide: Possibilities for Prosperity* (New York: Basic Books, 1984). For a useful discussion of the argument about Fordism and of the theoretical framework of the so-called regulation school from which the notion came, see Robert Brenner and Mark Glick, "The Regulation Approach: Theory and History," *New Left Review*, no. 188 (July/August 1991), 45–119.

20. Robert Brenner, "Uneven Development and the Long Downturn: The Advanced Capitalist Economies from Boom to Stagnation," *New Left Review* (forthcoming); Herman van der Wee, *Prosperity and Upheaval: The World Economy, 1945–1980* (Berkeley: University of California Press, 1986), 258–269; and Philip Armstrong, Andrew Glyn, and John Harrison, *Capitalism since 1945* (Oxford: Basil Blackwell, 1991), 151–158.

21. An indicator of this increased competition was the slight decrease registered in the share of industrial assets held by the two hundred largest firms in the United States over the course of the 1970s. See David Gordon, "Chickens Home to Roost: From Prosperity to Stagnation in the Postwar U.S. Economy," in Michael Bernstein and David Adler, eds., *Understanding American Economic Decline* (Cambridge: Cambridge University Press, 1994), 65–68. During the 1980s, it may be suggested, competitive pressure continued to mount from rival firms and was joined by pressure from stockholders encouraged by the wave of hostile takeovers to demand higher returns on their investments. See Edward Luttwak, *The Endangered American Dream* (New York: Simon and Schuster, 1993), 165, on the trend away from so-called "satisficing" and toward profit maximization; and, more generally, Jeff Madrick, "The End of Affluence," *New York Review of Books*, September 21, 1995, 13–17.

22. They would deteriorate still further from the 1970s through the early 1990s. See

Paul Bairoch, *Economics and World History* (Chicago: University of Chicago Press, 1993), 115–117.

23. Nigel Harris, *The End of the Third World: Newly Industrializing Countries and the Decline of an Ideology* (London: I. B. Tauris, 1987), 12–18. The strategy was accompanied by attempts to remake the political context within which development occurred. On this effort, see Robert Mortimer, *The Third World Coalition in International Politics* (New York: Praeger, 1980).

24. Peter Smith, "The State and Development in Historical Perspective," in Alfred Stepan, ed., *Americas: New Interpretive Essays* (New York: Oxford University Press, 1992), 30–56.

25. Harris, *End of the Third World*, 71–72.

26. Jyotirindra Das Gupta, "India: Democratic Becoming and Combined Development," in Larry Diamond, Juan Linz, and Seymour Martin Lipset, eds., *Democracy in Developing Countries*, vol. III, *Asia* (Boulder: Lynne Rienner, 1989), 53–104, esp. 84–86; and Lloyd Rudolph and Susanne Rudolph, *In Pursuit of Lakshmi: The Political Economy of the Indian State* (Chicago: University of Chicago Press, 1987).

27. Van der Wee, *Prosperity and Upheaval*, 265.

28. The literature on these issues is now enormous. For a useful summary and overview, see Jeffrey Hart, "A Comparative Analysis of the Sources of America's Relative Decline," in Bernstein and Adler, *Understanding American Economic Decline*, 199–239; and Hart, *Rival Capitalists: International Competitiveness in the United States, Japan, and Western Europe* (Ithaca: Cornell University Press, 1992).

29. For a review of this literature, see Peter Hall, "The Political Economy of Europe in an Era of Interdependence," paper presented at the Center for European Studies, Harvard University, February 1995. For an impressive example, see William Lazonick, *Business Organization and the Myth of the Market Economy* (Cambridge: Cambridge University Press, 1991). Many of the themes struck by these various critics of the fetishism of the free market have been taken up in Francis Fukuyama, *Trust: Social Virtues and the Creation of Prosperity* (New York: Free Press, 1995). For a more skeptical view, see Paul Krugman, *Peddling Prosperity: Sense and Nonsense in the Age of Diminished Expectations* (New York: Norton, 1994).

30. Armstrong, et al., *Capitalism since 1945*, 328–332; Andrew Graham and Anthony Seldon, eds., *Government and Economies in the Postwar World: Economic Policies and Comparative Performance, 1945–85* (London: Routledge, 1990); Peter Hall, *Governing the Economy: The Politics of State Intervention in Britain and France* (New York: Oxford University Press, 1986).

31. John Vickers and Vincent Wright, eds., *The Politics of Privatization in Western Europe* (London: Frank Cass, 1989).

32. Van der Wee, *Prosperity and Upheaval*, 386–390; Richard Gibb, "Regionalism in the World Economy," in Gibb and W. Michalak, eds., *Continental Trading Blocs: The Growth of Regionalism in the World Economy* (New York: Wiley, 1994), 18–22.

33. Hall, "Political Economy of Europe," 18; Angus Maddison, *Dynamic Forces in*

*Capitalist Development: A Long-Run Comparative View* (Oxford: Oxford University Press, 1991), 74–76.

34. See George Ross, *Jacques Delors and European Integration* (New York: Oxford University Press, 1995), 26–39; and Andrew Moravcsik, "Negotiating the Single Act: National Interests and Conventional Statecraft in the European Community," *International Organization*, XLV (Winter 1991), 19–56.

35. Robert Gwynne, "Regional Integration in Latin America: The Revival of a Concept?" in Gibb and Michalak, *Continental Trading Blocs*, 189–207.

36. See Richard Blackhurst and David Henderson, "Regional Integration Agreements, World Integration and the GATT," in Kym Anderson and Blackhurst, eds., *Regional Integration and the Global Trading System* (New York: St. Martin's, 1993), 408–435; and Mark Wise, "The European Community," in Gibb and Michalak, *Continental Trading Blocs*, 82–86.

37. See Peter Gowan, "Neo-Liberal Theory and Practice for Eastern Europe," *New Left Review*, no. 213 (September/October 1995), 3–60; and Ivan Berend, *Central and Eastern Europe, 1944–1993: Detour from the Periphery to the Periphery* (Cambridge: Cambridge University Press, 1996).

38. Anne Appelbaum, "The Fall and Rise of the Communists: Guess Who's Running Central Europe?" *Foreign Affairs*, LXXIII, 6 (November–December 1994), 7–13.

39. Karen Dawisha and Bruce Parrott, *Russia and the New States of Eurasia* (Cambridge: Cambridge University Press, 1994), 161–194.

40. Ivo Bicanic, "The Economic Causes of New State Formation during Transition," *East European Politics and Societies*, IX, 1 (Winter 1995), 2–21.

41. James Fallows, *Looking at the Sun: The Rise of the New East Asian Economic and Political System* (New York: Pantheon, 1994), 401–406.

42. The classic statement is Immanuel Wallerstein, *The Modern World System* (New York: Academic Press, 1974).

43. See Susan George, *A Fate Worse than Debt* (New York: Grove Press, 1987); and Jeff Frieden, *Banking on the World* (New York: Harper and Row, 1987) and *Debt, Development and Democracy: Modern Political Economy and Latin America, 1965–1985* (Princeton: Princeton University Press, 1991).

44. Ajit Singh, "The Lost Decade: The Economic Crisis of the Third World in the 1980s," *Contention*, I, 3 (Spring 1992), 139. The relationship between debt, or "debt overhang," and growth has been much debated. See, for example, Jeffrey Sachs, "A Strategy for Efficient Debt Reduction," *Journal of Economic Perspectives*, IV, 1 (Winter 1990), 19–29; and Jeremy Bulow and Kenneth Rogoff, "Cleaning Up Third World Debt without Getting Taken to the Cleaners," *Journal of Economic Perspectives*, IV, 1 (Winter 1990), 31–42.

45. Chris Carvounis and Brinda Carvounis, *United States Trade and Investment in Latin America* (Westport, Conn.: Quorum Books, 1992), 48–50.

46. "Whatever Happened to Third World Debt?" *Left Business Observer*, no. 62 (March 1994), 4–5, citing the October 1993 issue of the IMF's journal, *World Economic Outlook*.

47. See John Coatsworth, "Pax (Norte) Americana: Latin America after the Cold War," in Woo-Cumings and Loriaux, *Past As Prelude*, 159–177; Smith, "State and Development"; and Jorge Castañeda, *Utopia Unarmed: The Latin American*

*Left after the Cold War* (New York: Knopf, 1993), on the diminished support for such strategies even on the left.

48. Harris, *End of the Third World*, 30.

49. Soogil Young, "East Asia As a Regional Force for Globalism," in Anderson and Blackhurst, eds., *Regional Integration and the Global Trading System*, 126–143.

50. Piore and Sabel, *Second Industrial Divide*, 226–229.

51. Organization for Economic Co-operation and Development, *The OECD Jobs Study: Evidence and Explanation*, Part I, *Labour Market Trends and Underlying Forces of Change* (Paris: OECD, 1994), 53–55. The OECD report saw fit, it should be noted, to qualify the claim implicit in the phrase.

52. See *OECD Jobs Study*, Table 1.1; and also Gosta Esping-Andersen, *Three Worlds of Welfare Capitalism* (Cambridge: Polity, 1990).

53. Bruce Western, "Union Decline in Eighteen Advanced Capitalist Countries," *American Sociological Review*, LX, 2 (April 1995).

54. The ratio of female to male wage rates is roughly 50 percent in Third World countries, much lower than in more advanced economies; and the male wage is low enough. See Kathryn Ward, "Introduction and Overview," in Ward, ed., *Women Workers and Global Restructuring* (Ithaca: ILR Press, 1990), 13; and Valentine M. Moghadam, "Bringing the Third World In: A Comparative Analysis of Gender and Restructuring," in Moghadam, ed., *Democratic Reform and the Position of Women in Transitional Economies* (Oxford: Clarendon, 1993), 327–352.

55. The judgment is that of a Mexican scholar quoted anonymously in Peter Winn, *Americas: The Changing Face of Latin America and the Caribbean* (New York: Pantheon, 1992), 229.

56. John Goldthorpe, "The End of Convergence: Corporatist and Dualist Tendencies in Modern Western Societies," in Goldthorpe, ed., *Order and Conflict in Contemporary Capitalism* (Oxford: Clarendon, 1984), 315–343.

57. See, for example, Michael Hammer and James Champy, *Reengineering the Corporation: A Manifesto for Business Revolution* (New York: Harper, 1993). For a penetrating critique, see Simon Head, "The New, Ruthless Economy," *New York Review of Books*, February 29, 1996, 47–52.

58. For a review of technological developments in the leading firms and their rapid emulation elsewhere, see Mary J. Cronin, *Doing More Business on the Internet* (New York: Van Nostrand Reinhold, 1995).

59. See Heinz-Herbert Noll and Simon Langlois, "Employment and Labour-Market Change," in Langlois et al., eds., *Convergence or Divergence? Comparing Recent Social Trends in Industrial Societies* (Montreal: McGill-Queen's University Press, 1994), 89–113.

60. The most judicious assessment is in Bennett Harrison, *Lean and Mean: The Changing Landscape of Corporate Power in the Age of Flexibility* (New York: Basic Books, 1994), though its compass is less than global. See also Charles Tilly, "Globalization Threatens Labor's Rights," *International Labor and Working-Class History*, no. 47 (Spring 1995), 1–23, and the responses by Immanuel Wallerstein, Aristide Zolberg, Eric Hobsbawm, and Lourdes Beneria in the same issue; and, for an earlier, perhaps therefore slightly premature and hence a bit overly schematic, effort see Alain Lipietz, *Mirages and Miracles: The Crises of Global Fordism* (London: Verso, 1987), 69–111.

61. The phrase "dirty Taylorism" and its less pithy variation, "primitive Taylorization," come from Lipietz, *Mirages and Miracles*. For a useful critique, see Alice Amsden, "Third World Industrialization: 'Global' Fordism or a New Model?" *New Left Review*, no. 182 (July/August 1990), 5–31. Amsden's alternative formulation is given more extended treatment in *Asia's Next Giant: South Korea and Late Industrialization* (New York: Oxford University Press, 1989).

62. Alice Amsden et al., *The Market Meets Its Match: Restructuring the Economies of Eastern Europe* (Cambridge: Harvard University Press, 1994).

63. Anders Åslund, *How Russia Became a Market Economy* (Washington, D.C: Brookings Institution, 1995); and Daniel Yergin and Thane Gustafson, *Russia 2010: And What It Means for the World* (New York: Random House, 1993), provide very useful overviews on the transition from a command to a market economy, its progress and pitfalls.

64. See James R. Millar and Sharon Wolchik, eds., *The Social Legacy of Communism* (Cambridge: Cambridge University Press, 1994); and Boris Kagarlitsky, *Restoration in Russia: Why Capitalism Failed* (London: Verso, 1995), 75–92.

65. Åslund, *How Russia Became a Market Economy*, 224.

66. Ibid., 185. Linda Cook, "Workers in the Russian Federation: Response to the Post-communist Transition, 1989–1993," *Communist and Post-Communist Studies*, XXVIII, 1 (March 1995), 13–42, provides rather lower estimates, but Åslund's data are based on more recent calculations.

67. See M. Steven Fish, *Democracy from Scratch: Opposition and Regime in the New Russian Revolution* (Princeton: Princeton University Press, 1995); and Michael McFaul, "Russian Politics: The Calm before the Storm?" *Current History* (October 1994), 313–319.

68. See Barbara Einhorn, *Cinderella Goes to Market: Citizenship, Gender and Women's Movements in East Central Europe* (London: Verso, 1993); and also Moghadam, *Democratic Reform and the Position of Women*.

69. On the distinctiveness of "late industrializing" development, especially the role of the state, see Amsden, "Third World Industrialization." The framework represents an updating of the classic treatment by Alexander Gerschenkron, *Economic Backwardness in Historical Perspective* (Cambridge: Harvard University Press, 1962) On labor in the "four tigers," see Frederick Deyo, *Beneath the Miracle: Labor Subordination in the New Asian Industrialism* (Berkeley: University of California Press, 1989).

70. The term *semi-periphery* has been given most explicit definition by Wallerstein, *Modern World System*.

71. The spread of highly advanced agriculture in non-Western countries has been considerable. See Paul Kennedy, *Preparing for the Twenty-First Century* (New York: Vintage, 1993), chapter 4.

72. Feroz Ahmad, *The Making of Modern Turkey* (London: Routledge, 1993), 177–178, 204–205.

73. Paul R. Brass, *The New Cambridge History of India*, IV.1: *The Politics of India since Independence*, 2nd ed. (Cambridge: Cambridge University Press, 1994), 354–357.

74. Amsden, "Third World Industrialization," 30.

75. See Basil Davidson, *The Black Man's Burden: Africa and the Curse of the Nation-State* (New York: Random House, 1992); Jacques Attali, *Millennium: Winners and Losers in the Coming World Order* (New York: Times Books, 1991), 73; and Colin Leys, "Confronting the African Tragedy," *New Left Review*, no. 204 (March/April 1994), 33–47.

76. *OECD Jobs Study*, Table 1.1.

77. Gosta Esping-Andersen, "The Equality-Employment Trade-Off: Europe's Welfare States at the End of the Century," paper presented to the Center for European Studies, Harvard University, March, 1996.

78. Wolfgang Streek, "German Capitalism: Does It Exist? Can It Survive?" in Colin Crouch and Streek, eds., *Modern Capitalism or Modern Capitalisms?* (London: Francis Pinter, 1995).

79. Eric Hobsbawm, *The Age of Extremes: A History of the World, 1914–1991* (New York: Pantheon, 1994), chapter 10. See also Harold Perkin, *The Third Social Revolution: Professional Society in International Perspective* (London: Routledge, 1996); and Göran Therborn, *European Modernity and Beyond: The Trajectory of European Societies, 1945–2000* (London: Sage, 1995).

80. The same mismatch between the needs of unskilled entrants to industry and the stage of industrial development appears to account for the persistence of poverty among African-Americans in the United States. See, for example, William Julius Wilson, *The Declining Significance of Race*, 2nd ed. (Chicago: University of Chicago Press, 1980); and Wilson, *The Truly Disadvantaged: The Inner City, the Underclass, and Public Policy* (Chicago: University of Chicago Press, 1990).

81. See John Esposito, *The Islamic Threat: Myth or Reality?* (New York: Oxford University Press, 1992); and Emmanuel Sivan, *Radical Islam: Medieval Theology and Modern Politics* (New Haven: Yale University Press, 1985).

82. Kennedy, *Preparing for the Twenty-First Century*, 62–64.

83. Charles Tilly, *Coercion, Capital, and European States, AD 990–1990* (Cambridge, Mass.: Basil Blackwell, 1990), 192–225.

84. See David Rieff, *Slaughterhouse: Bosnia and the Failure of the West* (New York: Simon and Schuster, 1995).

85. Robert Jackson refers to this phenomenon as the spread of a kind of "negative sovereignty," which the international system of states confers primarily upon postcolonial states that lack the capacity ordinarily associated with effective statehood, and dates its spread from roughly 1960. The ending of the Cold War seems to mark a further stage in the spread of this practice and thus further redefines, in a downward direction, the prerequisites of sovereignty. See Jackson, *Quasi-States: Sovereignty, International Relations, and the Third World* (Cambridge: Cambridge University Press, 1990).

86. See J. Eatwell, "A Global World Demands Economic Coordination," *New Economy*, 1 (1994), 146–150; Philip Cerny, "The Infrastructure of the Infrastructure? Toward 'Embedded Financial Orthodoxy' in the International Political Economy," in R. P. Palan and B. Gills, eds., *Transcending the State-Global Divide: A Neostructuralist Agenda in International Relations* (Boulder: Lynne Rienner, 1994), 223–249; and Vincent Cable, "The Diminished Nation-State: A Study in the Loss of Economic Power," *Daedalus*, CXXIV (Spring, 1995), 23–53.

87. James Rosenau, *Turbulence in World Politics* (Princeton: Princeton University Press, 1990).

88. See Douglas Kellner, *Television and the Crisis of Democracy* (Boulder: Westview, 1990); Herbert Schiller, *Culture, Inc.* (New York: Oxford University Press, 1989); and Robert Putnam, "Bowling Alone: America's Declining Social Capital," *Journal of Democracy*, VI, 1 (January 1995), 65–78.

89. See, for example, Michael Ignatieff, *Blood and Belonging: Journeys into the New Nationalism* (New York: Farrar, Straus and Giroux, 1993); and Paul Hockenos, *Free to Hate: The Rise of the Right in Post-Communist Eastern Europe* (New York: Routledge, 1994).

90. Eric Hobsbawm, *Nations and Nationalism since 1870*, 2nd ed. (Cambridge: Cambridge University Press, 1992), 165. See also Benedict Anderson, "The New World Disorder," *New Left Review*, no. 192 (May/June 1992), 3–13.

91. Ryszard Kapuscinski, *Imperium* (New York: Knopf, 1994), 309–310. See also Bogumil Jewsiewicki and V. Y. Mudimbe, "Meeting the Challenge of Legitimacy: Post-Independence Black Africa and Post-Soviet European States," *Daedalus*, CXXIV, (Spring, 1995), 191–207.

92. Robert Jackson, "The Weight of Ideas in Decolonization: Normative change in International Relations," in Judith Goldstein and Robert Keohane, eds., *Ideas and Foreign Policy: Beliefs, Institutions and Political Change* (Ithaca: Cornell University Press, 1993), 111–138.

93. In this regard Edward Said's *Orientalism* (New York: Pantheon, 1978) must be read in part as the response of a member of a colonial or postcolonial elite to slights and misrepresentations committed by metropolitan elites. Rather more poignant are the questions raised by those who seek to understand what the masses of colonized peoples thought and felt about their conditions. On this, see Gayatri Spivak, "Can the Subaltern Speak?" in Spivak, *In Other Worlds: Essays in Cultural Politics* (New York: Methuen, 1987), who clearly asks the right question, even if her answer remains depressingly opaque and frustratingly ambivalent.

94. The phrase "imagined community" comes from Benedict Anderson's *Imagined Communities: Reflections on the Origins and Spread of Nationalism*, rev. ed. (London: Verso, 1991). The concept, however, has a longer pedigree. Compare, for example, the much older formulation of Edmund Burke: "Commonwealths are not physical, but moral essences. They are artificial combinations and...arbitrary products of the human mind." The statement comes from Burke's "First Letter on a Regicide Peace," and is cited in Robert Jackson, *Quasi-States*, 4.

95. Ignatieff, *Blood and Belonging*: and Daniel Chirot, *Modern Tyrants: The Power and Presence of Evil in Our Age* (New York: Free Press, 1994), 410–421.

96. Contrast, in this regard, Benjamin Barber, *Jihad vs. McWorld: How the Planet Is Both Falling Apart and Coming Together—And What This Means for Democracy* (New York: Times Books, 1995), and Tom Nairn, "All Bosnians Now," *Dissent* (Fall 1993), 403–410.

97. The literature on these cases is enormous, but one might start with Ian Lustick, *Unsettled States, Disputed Lands: Britain and Ireland, France and Algeria, Israel and West Bank-Gaza* (Ithaca: Cornell University Press, 1993).

98. Dilip Hiro, *Holy Wars: The Rise of Islamic Fundamentalism* (London: Routledge, 1989), 68–69; Kanan Makiya, *Cruelty and Silence: War, Tyranny, Upris-*

*ing and the Arab World* (New York: Norton, 1993), 312–314.

99. Inevitably, the precise timing of the turn from secular to sacred politics varied from country to country. In Algeria, for example, a typically "Nasserite" regime held power until the death of Boumedienne in 1978, although the sequel was even less attractive. See, for a short but useful review, John Howe, "The Crisis of Algerian Nationalism and the Rise of Islamic Integralism," *New Left Review*, no. 196 (November/December 1992), 85–100. More generally, see Mark Juergensmayer, *The New Cold War? Religious Nationalism Confronts the Secular State* (Berkeley: University of California Press, 1993).

100. On the relation between nationalism and Islam, see Ira Lapidus, *A History of Islamic Societies* (Cambridge: Cambridge University Press, 1988), 884–890.

101. Roger Owen, *State, Power and Politics in the Making of the Modern Middle East* (London: Routledge, 1992), 179.

102. Quoted, *ibid.*, 185.

103. On Islam and the law, see Ann Elizabeth Mayer, *Islam and Human Rights* (Boulder: Westview, 1991).

104. There has been considerable effort, both scholarly and political, to locate the existence of autonomous institutions of "civil society" in the Middle East. The effort has turned up rather little, but enough for some writers to maintain an optimistic stance. See, for example, Saad Eddin Ibrahim, "Civil Society and the Prospects for Democratization in the Arab World," in Augustus Richard Norton, ed., *Civil Society in the Middle East* (Leiden: E. J. Brill, 1995), vol. I, 27–54; and Jillian Schwedler, "Civil Society and the Study of Middle East Politics," in Schwedler, ed., *Toward Civil Society in the Middle East? A Primer* (Boulder: Lynne Rienner, 1995), 1–30. For a more pessimistic view, see Ernest Gellner, "Civil Society in Historical Context," *International Social Science Journal*, no. 129 (August 1991); and Fred Halliday, "Relativism and Universalism in Human Rights: The Case of the Islamic Middle East," *Political Studies*, XLIII (1995), 152–167. See also Juan Goytisolo, "Out of Stagnation: Parallels between Old Spain and Islam Today," *TLS* (February 2, 1996) 14–16, who maintains his optimism by adopting a very long-term view.

105. The fate is poignantly described in Makiya, *Cruelty and Silence*; and in Darius Shayegan, *Cultural Schizophrenia* (London: Saqi, 1992).

106. See Catherine Boone, "States and Ruling Classes in Postcolonial Africa," Michael Bratton, "Peasant-State Relations in Postcolonial Africa," and Naomi Chazan, "Engaging the State: Associational Life in Sub-Saharan Africa," in Joel Migdal, Atul Kohli, and Vivienne Shue, eds., *State Power and Social Forces: Domination and Transformation in the Third World* (Cambridge: Cambridge University Press, 1994), 108–140, 231–254, 255–289; and Colin Leys, "Confronting the African Tragedy"; Davidson, *Black Man's Burden;* and Ali Mazrui, "Africa Entrapped: Between the Protestant Ethic and the Legacy of Westphalia," in Bull and Watson, *Expansion of International Society*, 289–308.

107. See Atul Kohli, *Democracy and Discontent: India's Growing Crisis of Governability* (Cambridge: Cambridge University Press, 1990); and Amartya Sen, "The Threats to Secular India," *New York Review of Books* (April 8, 1993), 26–32.

108. Brass, *Politics of India since Independence*, 231 and passim.

109. Robert Eric Frykenberg, "Constructions of Hinduism at the Nexus of History

and Religion," *Journal of Interdisciplinary History*, XXIII, 3 (Winter 1993), 523–550. See also Frykenberg, "Hindu Fundamentalism and the Structural Stability of India," in Martin Marty and Scott Appleby, eds., *Fundamentalisms and the State* (Chicago: University of Chicago Press, 1993), vol. 2, 233–255; and Ramila Thapar, "Imagined Religious Communities? Ancient History and the Modern Search for a Hindu Identity," *Modern Asian Studies*, XXIII (1989), 209–232.

110. The literature on democracy and political modernization is extensive, though much of what was written in the early postwar era was deeply implicated in the ideological conflicts of the Cold War and is thus of more polemical than analytical value. The more recent literature is much more sophisticated and provides the basis for what follows. See, among others, Guillermo O'Donnell, Philippe Schmitter, and Laurence Whitehead, eds., *Transitions from Authoritarian Rule: Prospects for Democracy* (Baltimore: Johns Hopkins University Press, 1986), whose four parts constitute, in effect, four separate volumes devoted respectively to Southern Europe, Latin America, Comparisons, and Conclusions; Larry Diamond, Juan Linz, and Seymour Martin Lipset, eds., *Democracy in Developing Countries*, 4 vols. (Boulder: Lynne Rienner, 1988); and Dietrich Rueschemeyer, Evelyne Huber Stephens, and John Stephens, *Capitalist Development and Democracy* (Chicago: University of Chicago Press, 1992).

111. The centrality of issues of land reform to democracy is illustrated by the examples of Korea and Taiwan. In both nations land reform was undertaken by occupation forces who thereby eliminated the social class most resistant to democracy *and* to modern society more generally. The absence of a landlord class was undoubtedly a major factor allowing relatively peaceful democratization to occur in these states at a later period. It has also arguably been a important precondition for their rapid economic growth. See Harris, *End of the Third World*, chapter 2.

112. See Albert O. Hirschman, "The Turn to Authoritarianism in Latin America and the Search for Its Economic Determinants," in David Collier, ed., *The New Authoritarianism in Latin America* (Princeton: Princeton University Press, 1979), 61–98; and also Juan Linz and Alfred Stepan, *The Breakdown of Democratic Regimes* (Baltimore: Johns Hopkins University Press, 1978).

113. Kathryn Sikkink locates the origins of the new concern for human rights in the revulsion against the Vietnam War. See Sikkink, "The Power of Principled Ideas: Human Rights Policies in the United States and Western Europe," in Goldstein and Keohane, *Ideas and Foreign Policy*, 139–170; and David Forsythe, "Human Rights and U.S. Foreign Policy," *Political Studies*, XLIII (1995), 111–130.

114. John Vincent, *Human Rights and International Relations* (Cambridge: Cambridge University Press, 1986), 66–69; and Martin Walker, *The Cold War: A History* (New York: Holt, 1993), 228–230.

115. Raymond L. Garthoff, *The Great Transition: American Soviet Relations and the End of the Cold War* (Washington, D.C.: Brookings Institution, 1994), 695n.

116. See Samuel P. Huntington, *The Third Wave: Democratization in the Late Twentieth Century* (Norman: Oklahoma University Press, 1991); and Francisco Panizza, "Human Rights in the Process of Transition and Consolidation of Democracy in Latin America," *Political Studies*, XLIII (1995), 168–188.

117. Thus the Pope's visit to Africa in September 1995 was accompanied by a formal denunciation of the continent's undemocratic regimes.
118. See Penny Lernoux, *People of God: The Struggle for World Catholicism* (New York: Penguin, 1989).
119. Derrida is, of course, correct in criticizing Fukuyama for "manic triumphalism" and "evangelism" when the latter anounces that "liberal democracy remains the only coherent political aspiration that spans different regions and cultures around the globe." One need think only of Islam. Nevertheless, Fukuyama's fundamental point about the trend toward political democracy is empirically irrefutable. See Fukuyama, *The End of History and the Last Man*; and Jacques Derrida, "Spectres of Marx," *New Left Review*, no. 205 (May/June 1994), 38–44.
120. On the unraveling, or at least slowing down, of the movement toward European political union, see Ross, *Jacques Delors and European Integration*.
121. See Susan Strange, "The Defective State," *Daedalus*, CXXIV (Spring, 1995), 55–74; David Held and Anthony McGrew, "Globalization and the Democratic State," *Government and Opposition*, XXVIII, 2 (1993), 261–285; Philip Cerny, ed., *Finance and World Politics: Markets, Regimes and States in the Post-Hegemonic Era* (Aldershot: E. Elgar, 1993); and Herman Schwartz, *States versus Markets* (New York: St. Martin's, 1994). For a mild dissent, see Michael Mann, "As the Twentieth Century Ages," *New Left Review*, no. 214 (November–December, 1995), 114–120.

# Index